# The Christian and the "Old" Testament

**Other books by the same author:**

*Classical Evangelical Essays in Old Testament Interpretation*
(editor) (1972)
*The Old Testament in Contemporary Preaching* (1973)
*Toward an Old Testament Theology* (1978)
*Ecclesiastes: Total Life* (1979)
*Toward an Exegetical Theology: Biblical Exegesis for Preaching and
Teaching* (1981)
*A Biblical Approach to Personal Suffering: On Lamentations* (1982)
*Toward Old Testament Ethics* (1983)
*Malachi: God's Unchanging Love* (1984)
*The Uses of the Old Testament in the New* (1985)
*Quest for Renewal: Personal Revival in the Old Testament* (1986)
*Quality Living: Bible Studies in Ecclesiastes* (1986)
*A Tribute to Gleason Archer; Essays in Old Testament Studies* (co-
editor with Ronald Youngblood) (1986)
*Have You Seen the Power of God Lately? Studies in the Life of
Elijah* (1987)
*Toward Rediscovering the Old Testament* (1987)
*Hard Sayings of the Old Testament* (1988)
*Back toward the Future: Hints for Interpreting Biblical Prophecy*
(1989)
*"Exodus" Commentary in The Expositor's Bible Commentary*
(1990)
*Mastering the Old Testament: Micah, Nahum, Habakkuk, Zephaniah,
Haggai, Zechariah, Malachi* (1992)
*More Hard Sayings of the Old Testament* (1992)
*The Journey Isn't Over: The Pilgrim Psalms (120–134) for Life's
Challenges and Joys* (1993)
*An Introduction to Biblical Hermeneutics: The Search for Meaning*
(co-author with Moises Silva) (1994)
*"The Book of Leviticus: Introduction, Commentary and
Reflections" in The New Interpreter's Bible* (1994)
*The Messiah in the Old Testament* (1995)
*Proverbs: Wisdom for Everyday Life* (1995)
*Psalms: Heart to Heart with God* (1995)
*Hard Sayings of the Bible* (1996)
*A History of Israel: From the Bronze Age through the Jewish Wars*
(1998)
*An Urgent Call for Revival and Renewal in Our Day* (1999)

# The Christian and the "Old" Testament

Walter C. Kaiser, Jr.

*William Carey Library*
Pasadena, California

Unless otherwise noted, the author has used his own translation from the original languages of the Bible.

Published by
**William Carey Library**
P.O. Box 40129
Pasadena, California 91114
(626) 798-0819
inquiries@wclbooks.com
www.wclbooks.com


**Library of Congress Cataloging-in-Publication Data**

Kaiser, Walter C.
　　The Christian and the "Old" Testament

　　Includes bibliographical references and indexes.
　　1. Bible.　O.T.—Theology.
I. Title.
BS1192.6.K29　1998　　　　230.0411—dc21　　　　98-33174
ISBN 0-87808-292-1


*Printed in the United States of America*

*For George and Helen Bennett,*
*gracious friends and wise counsellors*
*in the cause of the Gospel of our Lord Jesus Christ*

# Contents

# Foreword

Ralph D. Winter

No single question about the Bible is more crucial, more basic, more troublesome, more significant, more complex, more profound, more weighty, or more urgent than the question of the true nature of the connection between the religion/faith of the Old Testament and that of the New Testament. Indeed, as you will see in the leaves of this book, in the answering of this question even the name "Old Testament" will be seriously and rightly questioned. This question affects our understanding of the Jewish people, the Jewish phenomenon. It gives us vital insight into the mysterious and momentous presence of the huge number of Jewish synagogues throughout the Roman Empire and beyond. It cuts to the heart of the often misunderstood dynamics of the global mission movement. It sheds light on practically every page of the Bible.

No single person I know of has been more central and important and influential in giving a satisfying, substantial, both striking and meaningful answer to this question than Walter Kaiser, Jr., for many years the inspiring theological and biblical anchorman at Trinity Evangelical Divinity School, and now President of Gordon-Conwell Theological Seminary.

No single book of this significant man more simply and informally shares his superb insight into this question than the lectures in this book. Here Kaiser is at his best, warmly down to earth, personable, exuberantly encouraging, making profound insights plain, working vitally without belaboring the massive scholarship upon which his every word actually rests. Probably no other book can more effectively tune your senses to all other books you will ever read about the Bible. It does not replace all these other excellent books. It introduces them—in a new light, in an impelling and crucial new perspective. We are not talking now about common knowledge, widely accepted perspective; in these talks you will find unusual insights that are not common, although they ought to be and must be.

Underlying the extravagant language of these few words is the simple fact that, understood rightly (even though rarely), the Bible does in fact record a single story of truly cosmic significance. And only with this single story in mind is it possible for a book composed by many authors over many centuries, in more than one language and geographical locus, to come into being as a single book. No wonder this single book—the Bible—is without comparison the prime mover of everything on our planet today that moves with anything like the incredible redemptive impact it has sustained over the last two millennia. It is truly an international, planetary book, undergirding and inspiring and explaining, for example, the thousands who have gone out across the earth in the name of God to work an utterly unprecedented transformation: the schools, the hospitals, the governmental structures of the non-western world owe more to the direct and indirect disturbance of this book than any other, even remotely.

What a joy, then, what a privilege, to give this word of recommendation for this truly remarkable book about *the* book. It is vigorous, exciting, awesomely important. It is a prize.

RALPH D. WINTER
General Director
Frontier Mission Fellowship

# Preface

For all too many believers, the first thirty-nine books of the Bible remain a dark and closed enigma. This is all the more a shame since it represents over three-fourths of what God has to communicate to us in our generation.

Yes, the Old Testament is reliable and relevant for all who will enter into its pages with a searching and believing heart. Repeatedly in the New Testament, both our Lord and his disciples demonstrated their confidence and trust in this older word. For them the Old Testament supplied the grounds of what had been expected and now was happening in their midst. It also was the joy of their lives, for it gave them sustenance and guidance for their daily lives.

In a similar way, that same Old Testament is still our guide as we seek to live not merely by bread alone, but by every word that proceeds from the mouth of God. Moreover, as we live in the corridor between the two comings of our Lord, we too look toward that same Old Testament in order to verify the proofs of Jesus' first coming and the signs of his second coming.

There is more, however. This set of studies will fill what almost certainly is one of the largest vacuums in modern day believers' handling and understanding of the Bible: an overall plan for the total 66 books of the Bible. The Bible wants us to see that despite all the variety and variegated forms of literature, subjects, and personalities, God has been at work in carrying out a single plan that embraces loads more than just the plan of salvation, the promise of the coming of the Messiah, or any other single theme. This set of studies, first given as lectures nearly a decade ago, will argue that there is an all-embracing promise-plan of God that includes scores of other topics (such as the kingdom of God, the rest of God, the work of the Holy Spirit, the salvation of the Gentiles, the resurrection, and on and on) all in the one plan called the "Promise."

The Old Testament never got around to focusing on a single name for this on-going plan of God, but referred to it under a constellation of terms: the covenant, the blessing, the rest, the oath, the word, and more. Only when we arrived at the New Testament did the Spirit of God finally reveal that the name for this plan was the "Promise" of God.

It is my prayer that as you study and prayerfully and thoughtfully reflect on these materials you will be led to a whole new appreciation for what our Lord has provided for us in such a dramatic and orderly way. God bless each one to the honor and glory of his name, for great will be that day when we shall see him and worship him for all ages, world without end.

WALTER C. KAISER, JR.
President
Colman M. Mockler Distinguished
Professor of Old Testament
Gordon-Conwell Theological Seminary

# Acknowledgments

The lectures on which this book is based date back to 1988. It was the late Dr. Harold Van Broekhoven of the Institute of Theological Studies who suggested that they be recorded for a broader audience. It is a joy to acknowledge his work and that of the audio engineer from Amway, Inc.

The course utilizing my taped lectures continues to be offered for independent study through ITS (3140 3 Mile Road, N.E., Grand Rapids, Michigan 49505). ITS's pioneering work in providing theological education through distance education methods has been of great service to thousands of students literally around the world.

To be able at last to put this discussion of issues central to the unity of Scripture—and crucial for understanding the Bible's message—in the hands of an even wider audience is gratifying.

A number of friends at the U.S. Center for World Mission—especially Joyce Renick, Lois Baker, Beth Snodderly, Corinne Armstrong, Jeff Borowiecki, Ron Shaw, David Sherbrooke, Lisa Sells, and Dwight Baker—have played a midwife's role in bringing the printed version of this material to publication. Alex Pak designed the cover.

Thanks to each.

# Chapter One

# The Christian and the Old Testament

## The Old Testament as the Master Problem

What is the significance of the Old Testament for us today? Why should the Christian even concern himself with the Old Testament? Some years ago, in 1955, Emil Kraeling said, "The Old Testament is not just one problem among many, but it is *the* master problem of theology." Indeed, as we attempt to determine how the Christian is to use the Old Testament, we situate ourselves at the heart of current theological discussion.

This issue is, I think, the most important question for the contemporary Church. It affects almost everything else we do. Some have pointed out that our answer to this problem will determine how we understand Jesus Christ in his historical character, for our Lord said, "These are the Scriptures that testify about me" (John 5:39, NIV). The Old Testament texts help us understand his Jewish context and his divine validation from heaven above. The Christian's view of the Old Testament determines how the Church views itself, as an aspect of the mystery of God. It determines our interpretation of the salvation which is offered in Jesus Christ. It decides our view of earthly, temporal life: how we are to live here and now. It decides the relationship between God's chosen people, Israel, and the Church. And it determines our view of where history is going and how the kingdom of God is unfolding. The answer to this Old Testament issue, i.e., the relationship between the Old Testament and the New Testament—or between the Old Testament and the contemporary Christian—is not an unimportant one at all!

A. H. J. Gunneweg echoed the same sentiment when he said, "It would be no exaggeration to understand the hermeneutical problem of the Old Testament as *the* problem of Christian theology. It is not just one problem among others. It is *the* problem because all other questions of theology are affected in one way or another by the solution to this problem." We can see its influence on the great Christological arguments and trinitarian arguments, as well as on those regarding soteriology and even the atonement.

1

Practically every contemporary theological argument has its roots in some aspect of Old Testament interpretation.

No less adamant was Bernhard Anderson. He said, "No problem more urgently needs to be brought into focus. It is a question which confronts every Christian in the church, whether that Christian be a professional theologian, a pastor of a congregation, or a layperson. It is no exaggeration to say that on this question hangs the full meaning of the Christian faith."

That's quite a claim. Yet I would support this assertion as well as the other two. Whether we are reading Kraeling or Gunneweg or Anderson or doing our own personal study, we must realize that in the Old Testament we have over three-fourths of God's Word; actually it is 77.2 percent of the Bible. Some people speak of it as the first half of our Bible. Come on! It's the first three-fourths of what God had to say! And, by the way, it *is* what *God* had to say. It is *his* revelation, and that is tremendously significant.

So much for the statement of Emil Kraeling, by way of introduction, that the Christian and the Old Testament is *the* master problem of theology. It truly is! All we have to do is check out the great theologians of our day to find out where they have tripped up. We'll find it is usually in their understanding and their mastering of the Old Testament problem.

## New Testament Appraisals of the Old Testament

Let's go to the New Testament and see how well the disciples understood the Old Testament. We must keep in mind that, for the disciples, the book of Malachi was the most recently written revelation. We can best see how well the disciples understood the Old Testament in Luke 24:13-25, where the Lord is taking that famous Emmaus Road Walk alongside the disciples. The Bible doesn't say, but I have an idea they are so downhearted that they are looking down at the road, kicking stones in front of them, and scuffing up their sandals. They are really depressed. And of course, there had been those events of the past weekend: there had been a crucifixion on Friday. What a despicable thing to see a human form stretched out on a cross up there on the hill! And the one between the two thieves was the leader of their movement whom the disciples had hoped was the one the Scriptures pointed to.

And now, our Lord himself, who had been on that cross, is walking along beside the men, but they don't even realize it. I don't believe the Lord gave those two disciples a passing grade for their understanding of the Old Testament. For he says to them, "O fools, and slow of heart to believe all that the prophets have spoken" (AV). Or as other translations say, "How foolish you are!"

Then he says, "Wasn't it necessary? Didn't it need to happen?"

He uses a little Greek particle here, *dei*, it *ought* to happen. It *had* to take place! There was divine necessity and urgency in the very flow of things. Christ had to suffer these things and then enter into his glory. Wasn't that necessary? Wasn't that the order of things?

As they continue on their walk, Jesus explains to them what he had said in all the Scriptures concerning himself, beginning with Moses and all the prophets. He says, in effect, "It had to take place. Come on, men! Where did you go to seminary? Who taught you? Didn't you know anything about this? Didn't they say anything about me in the Pentateuch? Didn't they teach you anything about me in the Psalms? How about your course on the Prophets? Did your teachers say anything about me? And didn't you know that I had to suffer and that I was going to be glorified? Didn't you know that this was going to take place at all? Come on, men, you guys are dummies!"—I think that's the modern translation for fools. "O fools, and slow of heart—flunkies—you really have failed the course!"

Let's go back to the phrase, "And beginning with Moses and the Prophets … and all the writings." This, as you know, is the famous three-part division of the Old Testament Torah. The first part of the Torah is the Law. Sometimes it is spoken of as the books of Moses, since he was the writer of the first five books. The second section, the Prophets, is sometimes called by its technical name, the *nebi'im*, and includes what has been categorized as the four major prophets and the twelve minor prophets. It includes the earlier prophets, too: Joshua, Judges, Samuel, Kings. So we have the six earlier books and these sixteen latter prophets in this Jewish grouping. By the way, these books are not historical books—they are not just sheer history—for in them God is fulfilling his word, even in the earlier prophets. The third part of the Torah is called the Writings, or the *ketubim*, which is the Hebrew word for 'writings'. These include Psalms, Job, Proverbs, Ecclesiastes, and the smaller books as well. The Writings conclude with Ezra, Nehemiah, and Chronicles. So, we have this threefold division. And our Lord "walked through" the entirety of what we now call the Old Testament as he traveled alongside his disciples.

By the way, the designation 'Old Testament' is a comparatively recent one. It began with the Church Father, Origen, in Alexandria, Egypt, in the second and third centuries. Basically, he used the vocabulary of Jeremiah 31:31-34, the New Covenant. And he referred to what came before as the Old Covenant. So in a sense, we are following tradition—continuing what the Church Father, Origen, began—when we use the terms, the "Old Testament" and the "New Testament." There is no biblical precedent that says, "This is the end of the Old Testament and now begins the New."

Now, what was the appraisal of the Old Testament by our Lord himself? He says that those writings spoke of himself. People could—if they would—see him and understand him from those Old Testament texts. Our Emmaus Road narrative goes on to say, "Then their eyes were opened and they recognized him, and he disappeared from their sight. They asked one another, 'Did not our hearts burn within us while he talked with us on the road and opened the Scriptures to us?'" (Luke 24:31-32). In verse 44, Jesus says, "This is what I told you while I was still with you: Everything must be fulfilled that is written about me in the Law of Moses and the Prophets ...." This time, instead of calling the third division of the Scriptures the Writings, he says, "... in the law of Moses, and in the Prophets, and in the Psalms, concerning me." (The Psalms is the largest book in the collection of Writings.) Luke then says in verse 45, "He opened their minds so they could understand the Scriptures," which he previously had said included the three divisions we have talked about. This passage is the first and, I think, one of the great endorsements of the Old Testament.

Turn to Matthew 5:17-18 for a second appraisal of the Old Testament. Jesus begins with, "Do not think ...." Apparently some opponents of our Lord were thinking thoughts that they shouldn't think. (This needs to be said today, too.) "Don't think .... Don't think .... Don't think I've come to destroy the Law." Now, if you thought that Jesus came to destroy the Law, you're in trouble with our Lord, not with me! He says, "Don't think that I've come to abolish the Law or the Prophets; I've come not to abolish them, but to fulfill them. I tell you the truth, until heaven and earth disappear, not one jot or one tittle shall pass from the Law, till all be fulfilled." Here he uses a hyperbole: he consciously exaggerates. Jesus says that not even the smallest letter of the Hebrew alphabet, the *yod*, will disappear from God's law. Nor will the little crenelation—the little flurry—that's on the end of the Hebrew letter, the *tab*. God says not even the *yod* or the flourish on the letter "t" will disappear, by any means, until heaven and earth disappear. In Matthew 5:19-20 he says, "Anyone who breaks one of the least of these commandments and teaches others to do the same will be called least in the kingdom of heaven, but whoever practices and teaches these commandments will be called great in the kingdom of heaven. For I tell you that unless your righteousness surpasses that of the Pharisees and the teachers of the law"—the Scribes—"you will certainly not enter the kingdom of heaven."

We could say a lot more about that verse, but certainly we can hear our Lord saying, "Don't think that my mission is to cut loose, to abolish the law [probably the most difficult part of the Old Testament for most believers]. I've come here to see the purpose accomplished; to get to the goal post; to reach the teleological conclusion toward which this law is headed." Remember, Christ announces through Paul, in Romans 10:4, that he himself is the goal—"the end"—of the law. One way to understand that phrase, "Christ is the end of the law," is to understand the Greek word *telos*. Christ is the *teleo*logical purpose, the goal post where games are won. Here is another victory as the Old Testament reaches its intended goal.

We don't want to belabor the point, but another verse can be brought up here. In John 5:39 we have another instance where our Lord teaches on this same point. He says, "You diligently study the Scriptures"—the *graphe*. What *graphe* did they have? To them, the Scriptures were exactly the thirty-nine books of the Old Testament. "You diligently study them because you think that by them you possess eternal life. These are the Scriptures that testify about me," says Jesus. "That's the whole point! If you don't understand *me* from the Old Testament, you've missed it. And apparently you have missed the point, for you refuse to come to me and have life." He emphasizes this same point again, in John 5:45-46: "Do not think that I accuse you before the Father. Your accuser is Moses, on whom your hopes are set. If you had believed Moses, you would believe me. If you had listened to Moses, it would have led to me, for he wrote about me. But since you do not believe what he wrote, how are you going to believe what I say?" That question is a very modern question, too. That is, if you don't believe what the Pentateuch says, how are you going to believe Matthew, Mark, Luke, and John?

There are other places where it comes to the fore: let's see what Paul does in Romans 15. He strings together a whole set of verses on this issue, determined to make the point. Romans 15:4 says, "For everything that was written in the past"—that refers to the Old Testament—"was written to teach"—them? *Them* is the pronoun we would expect. But, no! He says instead, "It was written to teach *us*." We can't say, "That was written for someone else," for that is not biblical. Paul teaches, under inspiration, that the Old Testament was written to teach *us*, "so that through endurance and the encouragement of the Scriptures we might have hope." I've gone through the New Testament to check this out. So often when I would have expected the third person pronoun, I find instead the first person plural: us, we, our. Those words were written for *our* encouragement; they were written for *us*.

Just as a parenthesis in our discussion of Romans 15, notice this same pattern in Hosea 12, where Hosea is preaching on the life of Jacob. When Jacob was in the womb, he grasped the heel of his brother; he wrestled with God; he wrestled with the angel. (Hosea says both "the angel" and "God.") He then says, "There God spoke with—*us!*" Hosea says this about Jacob near the beginning of the eighth century—in the high 700s BC. Jacob lived in 1700 BC. In other words, there's a millennium—1000 years—between the two events. But Hosea said, "God is still speaking to *us*."

Now back in Romans 15:8, Paul goes on to speak of the promises made to the patriarchs. And what were those promises? They were promises concerning Gentiles. Again Paul strings together a whole series of verses from the Old Testament which refer to Gentiles, beginning in 2 Samuel 22:50: "Therefore I will praise you among the Gentiles." Deuteronomy 32:43 says again, "Rejoice, O Gentiles"—or "all nations"—"with his people."

Then he quotes from Psalm 117, which says, "Praise the LORD, all ye peoples, all you Gentiles, and sing praises to him, all you lands." In Romans 15:12, he continues citing Old Testament passages, quoting from Isaiah 11:10: "The Root of Jesse will spring up, the one who will arise to rule over the nations, and in him the Gentiles will hope." So Paul constantly underlines that it was written for *us* and for *our* encouragement.

We could use other passages to make this point. Then we should move on. In 1 Corinthians 10, Paul recounts the history of the Exodus and the crossing of the Red Sea. He recalls when Moses struck the rock and water came out. Then in verse 11 Paul says, "These things happened as examples and were written down as warnings for us." For *us*! So 1 Corinthians 10:11 says the Old Testament gives *us* examples and gives *us* warnings. Notice the 'us' and the 'we'. Similarly, this same little pronoun, first person plural, comes up in Hebrews 6:18. The writer of Hebrews says that God made a promise to Abraham and gave him his word. God also swore on his life and took an oath. The "word" was used in Genesis 12; the oath was used in Genesis 22, at the sacrifice of Isaac. So the writer says that by these two unshakable, unchangeable, unrustable, unbreakable things—or however we want to translate Hebrews 6:17-18—God cannot lie. It's impossible for God to lie. This knowledge gives *us* great consolation; it gives *us* strong courage. Are we saying that Genesis 12 and Genesis 22 are for *us*, that *we* might have encouragement? Yes, that's the point! That's the whole point here, that *we* might have a strong consolation. So clearly the New Testament's appraisal of the Old Testament is very, very strong.

## Master Questions the Old Testament Poses

What questions does the Old Testament pose as part of that master problem of theology?

### First Question

I think the first and greatest problem is this: Is the God of the Old Testament a different one from the God of the New? You remember that, somewhere around AD 114–124, a shipping magnate named Marcion was very influential in the early Christian church. Marcion was one of the first who really took major exception to the Old Testament, and so today, within the church, we speak of all those who have a fear of or objections to the Old Testament as having Marcionite tendencies. Marcion spoke of the God of the Old Testament as being a demiurge—a lesser god—a god who created the world, but certainly one who was different and separate from the God and Father of our Lord Jesus Christ. He felt that this strange-acting god of the Old Testament couldn't possibly be linked with the God of the New Testament. There could be no connection between the two.

Marcion's teaching forces us to come to terms with this problem of the Old Testament as *the* master problem of theology.

My response to Marcion is to turn to Scripture itself. In Hebrews 1:1, we learn that God spoke to our forefathers by the prophets many times and in many and various ways. "But in these last days he has spoken to us by his Son, whom he has appointed as heir of all things" (1:2). As far as the writer of Hebrews is concerned, it is the same Lord, the same God, who is speaking in both epochs. The God who spoke by the prophets to our forefathers and to those in the Jewish community is the same Lord who has spoken to us through his Son.

So I see Hebrews 1:1-2 as the basic response to Marcion's challenge. But I think there is also another way to respond to this charge: We can listen to the words of those in the early church. Listen to the testimonies of those who were there. They saw it first; they have the right to be heard. They were not separated by time and distance as we are. In John's Gospel (12:20 ff.) the Lord is talking before a crowd. He predicts his approaching death. Then John quotes from Isaiah 6:10: "And he blinded their eyes and deadened their hearts so that they could neither see with their eyes nor understand with their hearts nor turn, so that I would heal them." Isaiah said this because he had seen Jesus' glory in a vision. Who was it that Isaiah had seen, dressed in royal attire, high and lifted up in the temple in heaven? He had seen Jehovah (or YHWH, which is the tetragrammaton), the living God himself!

Now, the testimony of John is that when Isaiah, in a vision, saw the Lord in the temple and the seraphim cried, "Holy, Holy, Holy," he and the seraphim were seeing the glory of none other than Jesus (John 12:41). I am afraid that we tend to theologize this word *glory* and make it into a sentimental concept. In any case, this word seems to be a problem for us. For help, we can look to etymological studies, doing so with care because they can lead us to incorrect roots. But here I think the etymology is legitimate: It seems to me that in the phrase "the glory of the LORD," we can understand the meaning from the Hebrew root, "to be heavy," *kabed*. "To be heavy" gives us a concept of the sheer gravity of God's presence. Whenever the Scriptures speak of the basic concept of the glory of the Lord, our first impression should not be of the effect. True, there is an "out-splashing" of his glory; there are rays. But more importantly, our understanding should be that he is there! *The God who is there* from glory …. The whole idea of God's glory is found in his "thereness." That's what the word *Jehovah*—more accurately, Yahweh—means. Yahweh is from the verb *hawah*, meaning "to be." The *yah* form is just a prefix, "he will be." He will be what? He will be [there]. It is God: he will be [there]. (We put 'there' in brackets because it is understood; it is not here in the Hebrew.) The whole point in our John 12 passage is that John claims that when Isaiah wrote that he saw God's glory, Isaiah was speaking concerning Jesus.

Let's review before going on to a second question which the master problem of theology poses. Is the God of the Old Testament different from the God of the New? The answer is, "No! He is the same!" as Hebrews 1:1 tells us. He is the one who is revealed in our Lord Jesus Christ. The one whom Isaiah saw was the very one whom John depicted as being our Lord Jesus.

### Second Question

Now for the second question: Is there a Christian canon within the canon of the Bible? The answer here, I think, can be found in 2 Timothy 3:14-17, where we find Paul teaching Tim. I call him Tim because I think I know him well enough; I have read these passages frequently. Paul is talking to this young pastor-friend. He says, "Tim, preach the Word. Keep your finger right there on the text. Don't depart from the Writings. You know what Writings we have. You know our B-I-B-L-E." (In their little Sunday schools, when they sang "The B-I-B-L-E, Yes, that's the Book for me," what would they have held up as their Bible? It would have been the thirty-nine books from Genesis to Malachi.) Paul continues, saying in effect, "But as for you, continue in what you have learned and what you have been convinced of, because you know from whom you have learned it. Don't forget, Timothy, what I have taught you. Don't forget what your grandmother taught you. Don't forget that faith that is also in your mother, and then how from infancy you have known the holy Scriptures, which are able to make you wise unto salvation through faith in Christ Jesus." What are the holy Scriptures here? The holy *graphe*? What are the Writings? In this case, they are Genesis, Exodus, Leviticus, Numbers, Deuteronomy; indeed, the whole Old Testament! Paul says, "You have known these Writings from a little tot on up. These are able to make you wise unto salvation."

Fancy that! Paul says we can be saved by reading the Old Testament. I didn't say that. I wouldn't have the nerve! But the Bible says the Old Testament can make us wise for salvation through faith! How do you think that the early church came to know the Lord? Well, we could say, there was the preaching of the apostles. Yes, but the Bereans were not satisfied just to be told something; they checked out the apostles' messages (Acts 17:11). They searched the text. They felt they had to validate the apostles' words, so they went back to the Prophets; they went back to the Writings; they went back to the Law.

Paul, in 2 Timothy 3:16, goes on to say, "All Scripture is inspired of God, and it is profitable, it is useful." Then he gives us four purpose clauses. It is profitable and useful in what ways? What do we get out of the Old Testament? We get teaching—doctrine. We also get rebuked. One purpose of the Bible is to reprove. Sometimes the saints need that. In ministry we don't like to touch the "weeds," the heresy. However, without appropriate rebuke, a particular group might say that God has raised it up in the latter days to emphasize a neglected truth. This is the way heresy is born: such a group takes one truth out of the context of all the rest of truth.

Therefore, the Old Testament is for teaching and for doctrine. We get—we *must* get—doctrine from the Old Testament. Where are we going to get the doctrine of creation if it is not from Genesis 1–2? Where are we going to get a finer statement on the Fall than in Genesis 3? Where are we going to get a better statement on the nature of the atonement than from Isaiah 53? Where are we going to get a higher statement on the incomparability of God than from Isaiah 40:18: "To whom, then, will you liken God?"

So since the Old Testament is for doctrine, for rebuking, for correcting, and for training in righteousness, what will be the result of our study of the Old Testament? It will result in the person of God—the "man" of God—being thoroughly equipped for every good work. Without an understanding of the whole corpus of the Word of God, there cannot be total preparation for the work of the ministry. People will not be thoroughly equipped if they can't handle 77.2 percent of the Bible—over three-fourths of God's Word.

### Third Question

A third question is posed here: Isn't Christianity a brand new thing since it is based on a new covenant? This brings up the use of the word *new* in Jeremiah 31:31. Jeremiah said, "Behold, God is going to give to us a new covenant." He refers here to a new covenant with the house of Israel and with the house of Judah. In Hebrew, only one word is used to express both 'new' and 'renew'. In the New Testament where Greek is used, however, and in most Indo-European languages, we have two words. We can distinguish between 'new' and 'renew'. There is one situation in English where we do interchange the two words: we refer to the new moon. But I'm sure you understand it is actually the same moon which we call a new moon each month. The word for 'new' and the word for 'moon' in Hebrew are related to each other. Thus, just as the new moon is actually the same moon that appears each month, so is the "new" covenant the same covenant made with Abraham, Isaac, Jacob, and David, but with some new additions. It has the same basic root. But in Greek you can make the same distinction as we make in English by using 'new' and 'renew'.

My point is this: The new covenant in Jeremiah 31 is a renewal of the ancient promise given to Abraham, Isaac, Jacob, and David—with an addition. What makes it new is that God renews what he has said and then goes on to add some brand new things. There is a "brand-newness." Of course, as we analyze the elements of the New Covenant (as we will in this course), we will find that over 50 percent of the items mentioned are citations from the promise given to Eve; the promise given to Abraham; the promise given to Isaac; the promise given to Jacob; the promise given to David. These promises are repeated over and over: "I will be your God ... You shall be my people ... I will dwell in the midst of you ... I will forgive you of your sins." But in addition, he goes on to speak of things which the Israelites have never heard of before. He speaks of universal peace and universal blessing; a time will come when there will be no need to teach on these subjects anymore, for everyone will know the Lord. Now, that doesn't sound like anything the patriarchs have heard before! So we find some brand new promises as well as some renewed promises.

### Fourth Question

We come to the fourth question: Are not the objects of faith, the methods of salvation, and the doctrines of repentance, of sin, and of hope beyond the grave different in the two Testaments? Are not the Old Testament and the New Testament so different that they signal two different faiths? My brief answer to that is found in Romans 4:1-17. Here, Paul refers to two great examples when he talks about justification. He says, "Listen, Abraham was justified by faith. David was justified by faith. We are justified the same way as were these men."

What was the object of Abraham's faith? It was the man of promise who was to come. Abraham did not put his faith in the *name* of Jesus—he didn't know the name of Jesus yet—but rather he put his faith in the one coming through the seed of the woman, through his own family. He had only the word of God, and that was enough for him. The object of his faith was the one who was coming. That is the point of Paul's argument in Romans 4:1-17. The gospel is the same, too, Paul argues in Galatians 3:8. He says, "This same gospel is identical to the one we have now."

As we conclude this chapter, I want you to see that this faith in the one who is to come is indeed exactly what Paul is talking about. Paul tells us in Galatians 3:8 that "the Scripture foresaw that God would justify the Gentiles by faith"—that he had announced the gospel in advance to Abraham, saying, "In your seed, all the nations of the earth shall be blessed." Paul says, "Did you hear that? That's the good news! That is the gospel! 'In your seed shall all the nations of the earth be blessed.' That's *euangelion*" (Paul uses this Greek term for the evangel to identify the gospel). Let's hear that again! What was the gospel? The gospel was Genesis 12:3 and 22:18: "In your seed shall all the nations of the earth be blessed." The same gospel was pre-announced by the prophets, as Romans 1:1-4 says. Hebrews 4:2 states that we are saved just as the people of Israel were saved. The writer of Hebrews questions why those carcasses fell in the wilderness. What was wrong with them? Why weren't they saved? He says that they had the same good news which has come to us, but they did not believe!

So we think that it is relevant for the contemporary Christian to study the Old Testament. In the Old Testament there is salvation; there is teaching; there is reproof; there is correction; there is training in righteousness. And the reason for our study of the Old Testament is so that we, as men and women, might be thoroughly prepared by God for every good work.

# Chapter Two

# The New Testament Problem:
# God's Central Plan

In this chapter, it will be my thesis that the theme of the promise-plan of God runs throughout the Bible and is used by the biblical writers to unify and integrate the message and the deeds of the Old and the New Testaments. However, as we talk about systematic theology and biblical theology, we will also see that there are other themes that can bind the two Testaments together. But how do we isolate these unifying themes? This brings up the question: What do we mean by biblical theology? And how does biblical theology differ from systematic theology?

## Definition of Biblical Theology

In systematic theology, we go through the Bible and pick out verses on a certain subject. We could compare these verses to flowers picked and made into a bouquet: It would be our bouquet, but it would be made out of "biblical flowers." The way we put together these verses would be ours. This arrangement is an "analogy of faith." The analogy of faith says that since the whole Bible is the product of God, we can, with one grand sweeping motion, go through the Bible and pick out all the verses on justification by faith or all the verses that deal with sanctification. From these verses, we can form a statement: a doctrine of justification by faith; a doctrine of sanctification. This is systematic theology. The organization of systematic theology is external to the biblical text.

Then there's biblical theology. By biblical theology, however, we do not mean a theology that is just biblical. As a discipline, biblical theology attempts to go through the Bible diachronically: *dia* means *through*, and *chronos* means *time*. We go through time, attempting to sort out the various epochs and eras and to determine the major emphases of each. We could compare these epochs to a staircase built on a solid base. Each period is like a step added to the base made out of the same substance or material, usually with much spilling over from the previous period. The process of biblical theology is one in which we go through the Bible and sort out the major teachings of each epoch or era.

## The Eleven Epochs of Old Testament Biblical Theology

Deciding on these epochs is admittedly arbitrary, and my division of time is no exception. For example, I have chosen as the first period or step on the staircase, the pre-patriarchal time of Genesis 1–11. The next step represents the era of the patriarchs, as found in Genesis 12–50. These patriarchs, or fathers of their country, include Abraham, Isaac, Jacob, and some would include Joseph. Then follows the Mosaic epoch: this would be everything from Exodus through Numbers. Following that, we have the time before the monarchy—the premonarchical times—which include Deuteronomy up through the time of Saul. This would take us up to Saul, God's elect, in 1 Samuel 10. Then the period of the monarchy covers Saul, David, and Solomon, up to the division of the kingdom. This is found from the middle of 1 Samuel through 1 Kings 11.

From the period of the monarchy, we move on into the wisdom period. During the time of Solomon, the Spirit of God gave us a large section of the Old Testament which not only includes the royal psalms of David and other psalms he wrote before becoming king, but also the books of Ecclesiastes, the Song of Solomon, and Proverbs. This is the great wisdom literature of the biblical text. Then comes the period of the prophets, as we move on through each of the centuries. The first prophets would probably be found in the ninth century BC, where Joel and Obadiah are almost contemporaries of Elijah and Elisha. In the eighth century BC we find the great group of Isaiah prophets, along with Amos and Micah, Jonah, and Hosea. Seventh century BC prophets include the Jeremiah group, which includes Zephaniah, Habakkuk, and Nahum. Then come the sixth century BC prophets during the exile. Here we would place Daniel and Ezekiel. Following that, in the fifth century BC, the postexilic period finds Haggai, Zechariah, and Malachi at work. Probably 1 and 2 Chronicles come at this particular time as well.

## An Organizing Center to Biblical Theology

In going through this exercise, we have basically walked through each epoch. We have added each roughly-delineated time period as a step to our base to form a stairway of Old Testament biblical theology. Yet no discipline has struggled more valiantly to fulfill its basic mission with more disappointing results than Old Testament biblical theology. Inherent in the very name of the discipline itself is some kind of inner unity—*an* Old Testament theology. We don't say Old Testament theologies, as if it were plural. It is assumed that some kind of unity binds the collection together. However, we also talk of the biblical theology of both the Old and the New Testaments. How are we to do this?

It is very disappointing to look for an answer in what has been written on the subject, for the main mood of contemporary literature, both within and without our circles, is to stress pluralism. Contemporary literature says that there is no way to get such a mass of materials together and to be able to find any central motif—a sense of unity about an ongoing plan of God. If this is so, I find that very disappointing! Indeed, that is where most scholars are at the present time.

Simply stated, the problem is this: Does the Bible, and the Old Testament in particular, provide a key for an orderly and progressive, but inner arrangement of subjects and themes and teachings of the Old Testament? And here is the most crucial question of all: Were the Old Testament writers consciously aware of such a key as they continued to add to the historical stream of revelation? The answer to these two questions is critical.

### The Writers' Awareness of This Center

I would like to answer the first question by saying, Yes, there is a key! The key is to be found in the promise theme of the Old Testament. So as not to confuse what we are talking about with the "promise-fulfillment" terminology, maybe we should use a hyphenated word: the promise-plan of God. Then when we ask the question, Were the Old Testament writers conscious of this promise-plan? we can answer very positively, Yes, they were!

First Peter 1:3-12 is a great text which really backs up this answer. Peter is discussing the "so great salvation" that we have. He cannot believe it! So amazing is this gift of new life that Christ has given to all who believe. He goes on to describe it, and he says this salvation is unbreakable. It is unrustable—he doesn't really use that word, but he says that it won't corrupt at all. Then he says, "concerning which salvation the prophets searched and inquired diligently. ..." The prophets were saying, "*Oy vey!* What is this all about?" We might say, "Ah ha! The prophets were not very clear on things." And it is true they were probably scratching their heads about a certain detail, but they were knowledgeable about the promise of God.

So before we jump to conclusions too quickly, let's see what they were confused about. The prophets knew about the salvation which was to come, but there were two elements they didn't know. Look at what the text says: "For they were searching and inquiring diligently concerning what or what manner of time." The Greek phrase here is very, very critical: εἰς τίνα ἤ ποῖον καιρόν. Ποῖον καιρόν is generally translated as "what was the manner of time" or "the circumstances" or "what were the circumstances."

The words εἰς τίνα mean "until what." We would say the phrase today as "what or what manner of time." In other words, we have a tautological statement here.

The biblical writers said they did not know the time, nor did they know the circumstances. But the text goes on to state five things the prophets did know. It says they wrote concerning the Messiah, the Christ. The word *Christ* is the Greek word for Messiah, as you know. Secondly, the text says that they wrote about his sufferings: they knew that he would come to suffer. Thirdly, they wrote about his glory. The biblical writers knew that he would come triumphantly. Fourthly, they knew the order: the glory would follow his suffering. Fifthly, the text says that they were prophesying these things not just for their own benefit. To some extent, it would involve the believing church. Peter says to the first century church in 1 Peter 1:12, "They were also given for us." It was revealed to the Old Testament prophets that they were not serving themselves, but us, the church. The prophets "spoke of the things that have now been told *you* by those who have preached the gospel to you by the Holy Spirit sent from heaven" (NIV).

The prophets knew these five things, but one thing they did not know. What was it that they did not understand? They did not know the time or the circumstances. Or we can say that the prophets did not know two things: the time *and* the circumstances. That, I think, is what needs to be seen here with regard to the answer to our second question.

Were these men aware of what they were doing, and did they see some unity to the whole thing? Yes, they did. They saw a unity focusing on the person of Christ. It was not Christo-exclusive. It centered on him; however, that does not mean that Christology is all that the Old Testament was about, or that when we have preached the Messiah, we have preached the Old Testament. Oh, no! There are loads of areas which the Old Testament text touches on. It gives us reproof and instruction and correction and wants to make us wise unto salvation.

It seems to me that locating a unifying structure is extremely important. I don't think we should impose a grid over the Bible; i.e., overlay, as it were, a particular plan of organization on the text. It is much better if a structure springs from the text itself. That is why I find that biblical theology is preferable, if at all possible. I think that by inductively studying the various epochs as we have outlined them—thinking of them as stair steps—we can see a biblical content develop. Beginning back in Genesis 3:15 with the promise of the seed of the woman, the promise-plan theme takes form and keeps enlarging and is repeated and repeated and repeated. The sheer repetition should help us to determine that this is central; this is the *mitte*; that is, the "center" or focal point for the whole of theology. I think that biblical theology is a better method than systematic theology. Otherwise our system would be like a modern divining rod which we could hold out over the text to see if the stick bends on a certain verse:

if it bends, we could say, "Ah, here we have a theological point." As you know, this is not the way to do it.

Scholars have suggested all sorts of central themes, such as the holiness of God, his lordship, the knowledge of God, communion with God, the rule of God, the kingdom of God. All these are good. But I would suggest we look for an all-embracing theme that begins early in the Scriptures. It is the burden of this chapter to show you that the central concept of Scripture is one that begins where the text begins. The theme of the promise-plan begins right away in Genesis 3:15.

## Definition of the Promise

How then shall we define this word *promise*? Our English word *promise* comes directly from the Latin form *promissa*, meaning a declaration or an assurance made to another person with respect to the future. The promise of God begins with a declaration. It is a word of assurance concerning what someone will be or what someone will do. It stresses both *being*, which is ontology, and *doing*, which concerns deeds. It has an activist side to it: what that person will be or do or will refrain from being or doing, so as to bring advantage or pleasure to the persons concerned. The promise usually stresses the positive side, the pleasure side. It does not stress, generally, the judgment aspect. I will come back to that when we distinguish promise from prophecy, for example. That is why I think we should stay away from the use of promise-fulfillment themes. Promise fulfillment is not what I am talking about here at all. The promise begins with a declaration; in this case, it begins with a declaration by God. The promise is God's word or assurance first given to Eve in Genesis 3; then given to Shem or the Shemites (or Semites as we call them now) in Genesis 9; and then given to the patriarchs, Abraham, Isaac, and Jacob. This famous statement is going to be repeated over and over again in a tripartite formula. It is repeated over fifty times in the Old and the New Testaments.

### The Tripartite Formula of the Promise

The first part is the assurance or declaration of the living God, "I will be your God." The second part is "And you shall be my people." This phrase "my people" is going to be tremendously significant. The third part contains the extremely important word *dwell*. "And I will 'pup-tent,' I will dwell, in the midst of you." I will *shakan*; I will tabernacle; I will dwell. Watch that word *dwell*. "I will dwell"—not far off, but "in the midst of you." There is an imminent theology here. The promise begins in Genesis, with God's word to Abraham: "I will be your God." But God adds to it in Exodus 4: "You shall be my people." As a matter of fact, God says in Exodus 4:22-24, "You are my son; Israel is my son; Israel is my firstborn." This is technical terminology. In Exodus 19:5-6, God tells Moses that Israel is to be a kingdom of priests, a royal priesthood. This is a statement about what it means to be "my people." Then, in Exodus 25, God again adds something to the promise: Here comes the tabernacle theology; the concept of God dwelling—God tabernacling—in the midst of them with the *shekina* glory. *Shakan* means *to dwell*. So we have the whole concept of shekina glory, the dwelling glory. God dwells in the midst of men and takes up his residence there, while at the same time he remains the high and lofty God, a transcendent God.

That tripartite word of assurance begins with a declaration of what someone will be. But the promise also includes the deeds of God: his great action in history. He delivered the people out of bondage—the Exodus. He instituted the Day of the Atonement and the Passover, where the great act of substitution illustrates what God himself will provide through his Son. These events illustrate—tell in pictographic form—what God is going to do in the final day. Here we have deeds backing up the words and the assurance of this promise. That is how the promise-plan begins to build and develop. As a more complete definition of the promise, we would say that it is the divine declaration or assurance made to Eve, to Shem, to the patriarchs, and to the whole nation of Israel that God would be their God and that they would be his people and that he would dwell in the midst of them. This is the divine assurance; this is the divine declaration!

### The Importance of the Collective Singular "Seed"

Now there is an even more surprising development in this promise. The text goes on to say that through Israel's seed, God will send a man of promise. This is an interesting development! By the way, we must retain the awkwardness of the word *seed* or the word *offspring* rather than the word *descendants*. Why? Because we must meet the demands of the text, and here we need a collective singular word which exists in Greek, Hebrew, and English. We need a word like our word *deer*. We say one deer or five deer, but we don't say five deers. We need a word here that will refer to one, the representative person, "offspring." We can use the word *offspring* for one or for many. We can use the word *seed* for one or for many. But we cannot use the word *descendants* to refer to one; it can refer only to many. The translation "descendants" is inaccurate; as a matter of fact, it is false. If we speak of children or descendants, I think we miss the point. That is Paul's argument, too, in Galatians 3:16, where he doesn't say "seeds," which are many, but he says "seed," which is one. Furthermore, he says before he finishes that chapter, "If we believe, we are Abraham's seed."

The promise-plan underlines the uniqueness of this word. Through this seed, God would send the man of promise; and through this seed, blessing would come to all peoples on the face of the earth. That point has to be included here. The promise-plan is not only Christological—about the Messiah—but it is also missiological. The mission is as Genesis 12:3

says: "In your seed shall all the peoples of the earth be blessed." The phrase "all the peoples" refers to the seventy nations that have just been listed in Genesis 10. They are all the families of the earth! So God tells Abraham, "What I am doing here for you is not a chauvinistic, special deal in which I have picked you out as my pet project or people. I am doing this for you so that, through you, all the nations on the face of the earth might be blessed." Yes, it is missions, as well!

If I were to choose a verse to summarize God's great promise-plan, it would be Genesis 12:3: "In your seed all the nations of the earth shall be blessed." I think that is the gospel; I think that central theme is the organizing plan of the Bible. Albrektson writes in *History and the Gods*, his book on revelation in history: "If I could accept Genesis 12:3 as being passive in form, I would see this as the whole plan of God." As a matter of fact, it does happen to be passive in form: the Greek renders it as "be blessed." It is not, as the RSV or some others render it, "bless themselves." It is not as if the nations look around and say, "Hmmm, not a bad deal; I think we will bless ourselves." That would be a reflexive concept. There is a way to say that in Hebrew, but this is the *niphal* form. Therefore, the passive form is the very best—and I think the only—way we can translate it. That phrase epitomizes for me the whole plan of God: He would form a nation, and out of that nation, he would bring the one by whom salvation would come to all nations. This would be a great blessing to all mankind. The central theme of the Bible, it seems to me, is right here.

### Old Testament Words for "Promise"

In the Old Testament itself, ordinary words encapsulate the pivotal promise of God around which everything else revolves. For example, the words *to speak* or *to say* could just as well be rendered as *to promise*. This happens some thirty times in the Old Testament. The promise concept in the Old Testament is actually a constellation of words. We can refer to the promise as God's *oath*, as his *word*. We can refer to the promise as the *rest*, the *inheritance* that God has given. We can refer to the promise as the *kingdom* that God has given to David; the *throne*, the *dynasty*, the *house*. In other words, the promise-plan does not remain static and unchanged from the time it was given in the Old Testament until it is fulfilled in the New Testament. Rather, the promise-plan grows and expands. True, it is basically a plan by which God is going to send the Messiah and, through the Messiah, is going to bless all the nations upon the earth. But those are only the bare bones of the plan. The plan grows and takes on a body. It includes missions. It talks about inheriting the land. It talks about fearing God so that we might know how to conduct life as good fathers, how to be wise. In the book of Ecclesiastes, it talks about how to fear God in order to know how to go to school, and then how to use leisure time—how to eat and drink and enjoy our paychecks—for this is the gift of God. Part of the great promise-plan of God includes mundane things like the marriage relationship and marital love, as found in the book of Song of Solomon. That, too, is a part of the plan of God. So the promise-plan embraces much more than what we have just seen as being Christological or as being the doctrine of salvation and how we could come to know the Savior.

### The New Testament Formulation of the Promise

It is true that the word *promise* is used for the first time in the New Testament, but it reflects the Old Testament. I really got the idea to call this the promise-plan theme from my reading of the New Testament, where 'promise' is used fifty-one times as a noun and eleven times as a verb. Only six books of the New Testament do not have a reference using the word *promise*: Matthew, Mark, John (two Synoptic Gospels and the Johannine Gospel), and then James, Jude, and Revelation. The promise in these fifty-one plus eleven references may denote the form, the content of the words, or the things promised themselves; that is, the promise may refer to the substance that is pointed to or it may refer to the verbal assurance before the substance is seen. Hebrews later makes the distinction that some received the promises, but had not yet received the substance, the reality: "That they without us should not be made perfect" (AV). We who receive the substance are the fulfillment of what they received in words by faith. The writer of Hebrews makes the very distinction I am making here.

## The Elements in the Promise

Although God's promise-plan is one plan, it has many specific aspects. Eleven times the word is used in a plural sense. What can we see in this promise-plan? The list is too long to name completely.

### The Resurrection of Jesus Christ

For example, the resurrection of Jesus is part of the promise as seen in Acts 13:32. From the offspring—from the seed of this man—God has brought to Israel a Savior, Jesus, whom he raised from the dead. There the theme of the resurrection is tied to the promise. In Paul's speech in Antioch of Pisidia he says, "We preach to you the good news about the promise made to the fathers, that God has fulfilled this promise to our children in that he raised Jesus from the dead" (Acts 13:32-33). Again the resurrection is linked to the promise.

### The Coming of the Holy Spirit and Jesus Christ

The promise includes other things, also. It includes the theme of faith. For example, in Romans 4:13-14, 16-17, we see the promise to Abraham and to his seed "that he would be heir of the world." And Paul goes on with this discussion to say that he speaks for this reason: it is by faith, that it might be in accordance with grace, in order that the promise may be certain to all the descendants, to all the seed. Again, we see the theme of faith. I understand this to mean that there is more to the promise than just the seed himself. Jesus is the center of this promise in order that Galatians 3:14 be fulfilled: that the blessing of Abraham might come to the Gentiles so that we might receive the promise of the Spirit and the promise, too, of Jesus Christ. Here we can see that the promise involves the coming of the Holy Spirit as well as the coming of Jesus Christ.

### The Rest or Inheritance from God

Another theme is found in Galatians 3:14-29, where there are six references to the promise—to the inheritance and its rest. The inheritance that is spoken of in the Old Testament is both spiritual and physical. There was the land of Canaan: that was the physical inheritance. Some of the Israelites didn't get into the land, as the writer of Hebrews says in Hebrews 3:11. Hebrews 4:1 says, "Therefore, let us fear, lest while a promise remains of entering his rest ...." There is a spiritual inheritance, too, which we enter into by faith. Some of the people of Israel got into the land—the physical inheritance—but did not enjoy the spiritual inheritance: rest as part of the promise of God.

### Summary of the Promise Elements

So we can see that the promise theme encompasses many ideas. If we were to break down the sixty-two references to the promise in the New Testament, we would find that about 20 percent of the promise references are to the nation of Israel; about 6 percent concern the promise of Christ's second coming; about 16 percent deal with the promise of the resurrection from the dead; 11 percent concern the promise of Jesus as Messiah; 20 percent refer to the promise of redemption from sin; 16 percent concern the promise of the gospel for the Gentiles; and another 5 percent refer to the promise relating to the Gentiles as such.

### The Promise as a Single Plan of God

The New Testament writers then, I think, use this promise as a way of emphasizing all that was found in the biblical text. I first thought of the promise in this way when reading Willis J. Beecher's book, *The Prophets and the Promise*, the content of which was given as the 1904 Stone Lectures for Princeton Seminary. There he analyzed it very beautifully and argued that it was a single promise. Paul said to Agrippa in Acts 26:6-7, "Now I stand to be judged for the hope of the promise." The promise was the basis for his stand for the Lord, which brought him to trial. We can paraphrase what Paul is saying in these two verses. He says, "I am on trial for the hope of the promise made by God to our fathers whereunto our twelve-tribe nation hopes to attain. We hope to come to receive all that was spoken back there to Abraham, Isaac, and Jacob. That is what this trial is about." In substance, that is what he stood for.

### The Single Promise Has Many Specifications

But remember, the promise has multiple aspects. So in Hebrews 11:13, 17 the writer speaks of receiving the "promises," because there are so many aspects to that one promise. It is eternally operative and irrevocable, as Hebrews 6:13 says: "For when God made the promise to Abraham, since he could swear by none greater, he swore by himself." He goes on to say in Hebrews 6:17-18, "Wherein God, being minded to show more abundantly unto the heirs of the promise the immutability of his counsel, interposed with an oath: that by two immutable things, in which it is impossible for God to lie, we may have a strong encouragement." Galatians 3:16-18 tells us: "Now to Abraham, to whom the promise is spoken, and to his seed, the law does not disannul so as to make the promise of none effect, but God granted the inheritance to Abraham by promise."

The theme of the promise, it seems to me, is very, very clear.

## Four Unique Moments in the Promise-Plan of God

What, then, are the four great unique points in the promise? I would like to suggest that there are four great moments—four great mountain peaks—to aid our understanding of the promise in the Old Testament.

### Genesis 3:15

Genesis 3:15 has got to be one of the great moments in the Old Testament, where in the midst of curses—judgment upon Eve, upon Adam, upon the serpent, upon the ground, and upon the soil—suddenly from behind all those dark clouds there breaks through a ray of sunshine. God suddenly intervenes, saying, "I, God, will put enmity between the serpent's seed and her seed." But then—surprise! The surprise is that the woman will have a male descendant, and that male descendant will crush the head of the serpent. The promise from the very beginning is to be a two-sided victory. The victory is to be seen here in the male descendant. I think that was pre-Christian, and was understood that way. As a matter of fact, even the Greek translators of that phrase broke the rules of agreement, thereby showing that three centuries before Christ they understood this to be a male descendant who would indeed deal a lethal blow to the head of Satan himself. A nip on the heel can be healed; a crushed head is somewhat difficult to put back together again. And that is what is promised here.

### Genesis 12:2-3

The second mountain peak of understanding the promise is found in Genesis 12:2-3. This is another great statement! The promise here culminates in the finest statement of the gospel, the finest statement of missions, the finest statement of the whole purpose-plan of God. Genesis 12:2-3 says, "In your seed shall all the nations of the earth be blessed." It is the finest statement anywhere, and Paul enthuses when he quotes it in Galatians 3:8. He says, "Did you hear that?" He says that the gospel—the Good News— was pre-announced; he says that Abraham was pre-evangelized. Paul uses the prefix 'before', *pro*, and then the word 'to evangelize': *proeuangelizomai*. Abraham was pre-evangelized when he received this word—the gospel— which announced, "In your seed shall all the nations of the earth be blessed." It is, in effect, as if God is stating a basic truth here; he says to Abraham, "God loves you and offers a wonderful plan for your life."

### 2 Samuel 7

A third great moment in understanding the promise occurs in God's promise to David in 2 Samuel 7. We see this especially in verses 16-19, where God is basically saying, "I will give to you a throne, a kingdom, and a dynasty. It will never, never collapse." A lot of kings stay up late at night wondering what's going to happen to their kingdom. Neb did. Nebuchadnezzar couldn't get to sleep; he had bad dreams. But God says to David, "I am going to give the kingdom to you, David. Now, David, about building that house ...." Remember Nate—Nathan—had said when asked about building a house for God, "Yes, I think it is a good idea." But God goes on, "Well, I have talked to Nate about that, and thus saith the LORD, you shall not build the house. There is too much blood on your hands. But rather, I will make a house *out of you*." How about that? "Instead of you building a house for me, I will make a dynasty—a House of David—out of you, and it will be forever. And your kid will be mine. I will adopt your son as my son; I will be daddy to him; I will be father to him."

And then God goes on to quote in such a way that David understands that he is using the John 3:16 passages from Genesis, Exodus, Leviticus, Numbers: he is quoting the great promise statements of Genesis 3:15, Genesis 12, Genesis 18, and Genesis 22. This blows his mind! David goes in and sits down before the Lord and says, "I can't believe the whole thing! I just can't believe it! LORD, who am I, and what is my family that you have done this for me? And as if this were too small a thing, you have spoken for generations to come and this should be the Torah for all of mankind!" He can't believe it. By the way, neither can the translators. None of them gets it right. The text simply says, *we-zo't*, 'that this' should be the *Torah*, or in the construct *Torat*, 'Law' or 'charter,' of man: that this should be the *torat ha-'adam*. *Adam* is Adam or man or mankind. David is saying here that this should be the charter, the law, governing all of mankind.

### *Jeremiah 31:31-34*

Then, of course, there comes the fourth passage which helps us understand the promise-plan in the Old Testament. This last mountain peak is in the great New Covenant passage found in Jeremiah 31:31-34.

These are the four peak moments: Genesis 3:15; Genesis 12; 2 Samuel 7; and Jeremiah 31. Understand those great moments and you will understand the heart of the promise-plan of God. You will be at the center of the great plan of God.

# Chapter Three

# Three Foundational Blessings

## Genesis 1-11

In this third chapter we want to talk about the opening portion of the Bible, that magnificent text in Genesis 1–11 which covers the whole of biblical history from creation all the way down to Abraham.

## Introduction: The Creation

If you were to ask me, "Where can we put the creation in time?" I would say that the only place I can locate it with authority is "in the beginning." On that date, I can be very firm. The important thing, it seems to me, is the great theme of creation by the word of God. From a theological stand-point, the text constantly stresses that the mechanism of creation was by his word.

### Creation by the Word

It's a cop-out—and an over-concession to a curious age—for the contemporary church to say that the Bible *only* discusses *that* God created. The text does very clearly say, "God created." That's what Genesis 1 and 2 are all about. But the text also wants us to know, at least to some extent, *how* the world was created: "And God said ... And God said ... And God said ... And God said ...." Ten times this is repeated. The Psalmist will pick up on that: Psalm 33:6, 9 states that "by the word of the LORD were the heavens created."

This emphasis on God's creative capabilities is found also in the New Testament. In Matthew 8, we see an example of the emphasis put upon that word: Jesus was told by the centurion, you remember, who had a sick person at home, "Lord, don't bother coming to my house. Only speak the *word*." We believe that he spoke the word and in that moment the sick individual was healed. Then why is it that we have such great difficulty —if we believe it in the gospel account—seeing also the creative ability of the word as that declaration of God by which each of the basic forms came about?

Going from creation, we will move up to Abraham in this chapter; however far this may be, it is a large chunk of time. It is at least as large a chunk of time from "in the beginning" to Abraham as it is from Abraham up to Christ. It is *at least* that amount of time! During this time period, we will find three great moments of tragedy and three moments of blessing. There are three crises. First of all, there is the fall of man (Gen 3). The flood comes as a second great crisis (Gen 6–8). Then there is the tower (Gen 11). The fall; the flood; then the tower of Babel, which was a flop, as you know.

### *The Promise as the "Blessing" of God*

These crises did not just result in failures; things did not stay that way. Genesis 1–11 not only talks about the great moments of judgment—crises, as we have called them here—but also talks about three great moments of blessing. The word *blessing* is used advisedly, for this is the form of the promise in Genesis 1–11. The promise-plan of God is depicted through this word *blessing*. It is the word by which God brings relief from the failure of individuals.

Out of the first failure of the fall comes the great verse in Genesis 3:15. Out of the flood comes the great verse in Genesis 9:27. And out of the flop of the tower experience comes the great plan which becomes normative for the rest of Scripture, Genesis 12:1-3. The call of Abraham and the Good News—the gospel—is found in the third verse. So we have three great moments of catastrophe and three great moments of blessing and of promise which give unity to this section.

As an introduction to our unit we will look at the blessing of creation. Indeed, it is a blessing; it is the gift of God for all mankind. Then comes the blessing of the seed which will be the main theme of Genesis 3:15. And then the blessing of God who comes and dwells with man: the God— here's that great theology of dwelling—who *dwells* with Shem, the Shemitic or Semitic peoples. Finally, the third blessing is the blessing of the gospel for all nations, which becomes salvation and also suggests missions, which speaks of the universal application and understanding of this word. That is the outline which we wish to follow in this chapter.

## The Blessing of Creation

Let's look more particularly at the first blessing: the blessing of creation in Genesis 1–2. An awful lot can be said here about the theology of this passage. Certainly, there is an argument for an absolute beginning, for what the scientists call the Big Bang. The Big Bang theory says that creation started from a single point, and that's the emphasis of Genesis 1:1: "In the beginning God ...."

God was the one who created the universe. Since there is no Hebrew word for universe, the easiest way to express it is "the heavens and the earth," which means the entirety, the whole thing. This kind of dual expression is used to say that he created everything.

The text goes on to say, "In the beginning God created ...." The word *create* is used in a unique way in the Bible: it is used 45 times, always with God as the subject, and never with the material of agency. It happens to be a clear statistical fact that, out of all 45 times, there is no instance where he uses matter or any material. 'Create' is a word reserved for God. There are other kinds of creation by men, but this word *bara'*, which is the Hebrew word for 'to create', is not used in those instances.

The Genesis 1 text goes on to show the stages of creation, as it were, for the writer now says, "The earth was formless and empty." The Hebrew expression is *tohu bohu*, which is what I call the hurdy-gurdy or zuit-zuit construction; these are simply words that sound alike. I wouldn't make any special deal out of what we translate as "formless and empty." He is saying that it was still undefined matter; as God began, the "stuff" came first. "Darkness was over the surface of the deep, and the Spirit of God was hovering over the waters. And God said, 'Let there be light.'"

And so we have the creative word of God that, after initially bringing matter into being, begins to purposefully set order in each category. He starts with light: "God called the light 'day', and the darkness he called 'night'." Then the text goes on to speak of other things that he creates. He creates them; he names them; he looks at them; he pronounces them good.

By the way, this brings up the idea of a theology of material things. In and of itself—apart from the discussion of human sinfulness—matter is not the problem. In itself—as it represents the creation of God—matter is good. Therefore, all attempts to play down the *physical* or *matter* or the *material* as opposed to the *spiritual* lead us to the Gnostic system of thinking. We've seen this over and over again in the history of human thought: the "downstairs" and the "upstairs" worlds.

"Downstairs" was always said to be evil, whereas "upstairs"—in the realm of God and the realm of the universal—was always said to be good. The world of the phenomenal and the realm of the material was always considered evil. This is wrong; this teaching is incorrect and gets very close to gnosticism. The biblical text says that God created the world and called it good. He called it *good*. And he gave names to things, too, which means that he is the Father of matter: we name things that really belong to us. How did he bring these things into existence? By his word! So from the very start, the promise theology has to do with the declaration—with the word—from God.

The word is extremely important. Modern man desperately wants to hear a word; he wants to know if there is anyone at home in the universe. Is anyone at home or are we alone? *Are we alone?* We've got big astro-radios to listen to other planets, to those little green men—the Martians—with horns and all. We would just like a signal from someone: *"Please* say something if you're there!" I think, under the guise of listening for people on other planets, modern man is really expressing his hunger for a word from God. Will he say something? The biblical text says, "In the beginning God … And he said … He said … He said …." That theme is repeated throughout.

Then at the pinnacle of the whole process of creation, what does God do? He makes a man and he makes a woman. So we have God creating Adam and Eve in his image: "Male and female created he them in his image." We don't have more of the image of God in maleness than we have in femaleness. That is why Genesis 1:27-28 says, "So God created man in his own image, in the image of God created he him; male and female created he them. And God blessed them" (AV).

Some people divide this blessing, making the blessing one thing and the command another: "So he blessed them; and he said …." Notice the punctuation here. It's critical. If it is "God blessed them; and he said, Be fruitful and multiply," we have two distinct things. If it is, "God blessed them: Be fruitful and multiply," then we have one thing. My suggestion is that, based on the way this phrase is used throughout the rest of Genesis by the same writer, it is the latter. "God blessed them: [colon]." Now notice the content of what he said: "Be fruitful and multiply." In other words, he's talking about multiplication, or population explosion. I'll even be more critical. That which is meant by population explosion at this point would not permit us to brag, to put our thumbs to our chests and say, "Now there's one commandment we've kept. We've filled this world jolly well full! The world is overflowing now, see. We did that one, didn't we?"

The biblical text says, "Wrong again!" The point here is that "Be fruitful and multiply" is the blessing of God. "Be fruitful and increase in number; fill the earth and subdue it. Rule over the fish of the sea and the birds of the air and over every living creature."

We can paraphrase Lynn White, who wrote, in effect, in *Science* magazine in 1967: "Ah hah, so indeed—we can now give you credit. You biblical people, you were right. You sponsored the technological revolution, and Western science is possible because of the church and because of what you taught about man ruling over, and having dominion over, the whole created realm. That was the great impetus for the natural and physical sciences and the technological revolution that came.

"However, we take back some points from you," says Lynn White, making the point which so many have wanted to make for so long, and so few have grudgingly acknowledged. He goes on to say (again, I'm paraphrasing): "Ah hah—but you too are responsible for polluting the whole universe, since you are the ones who said, 'We're ruling over it.' Some of you live as if ruling over it means that if you can make more bucks by dumping waste products off into the Grand River, then let her go! What does it matter if you pollute the environment, pollute the air, as long as you get rich as fast as you can!"

He is saying that the ecological mess is the fault of the evangelical Christian. And he makes quite a case! But I think he is wrong, because 'rule and subdue' doesn't mean we can trample all over everything. I think we could profit here from word studies on 'subdue' and 'have dominion' or 'rule over'. The whole point is that we hold the position of a vice-regency under God in which we report to the ultimate supervisor of the creation even for the way in which the world is run at the present time.

The New Testament bears this out, by the way, with a text that isn't often quoted in connection with this: 2 Corinthians 5:10. "For we must all"— did I say *all*? Yes!—"We must all appear before the judgment seat of Christ" to give an account for the deeds done in the body. (See also Romans 14:12.) Would that include industrialists? It would! Would that include researchers? It would! Would that include experimenters—biomedical, biochemical experimenters? It would! "Give an account for the deeds done in the body."

## The Blessing of a Male 'Seed'

Before we move on from the blessing of creation to the blessing of the seed, let's look at the first world crisis. This crisis comes in chapter 3 where the text says, "Now the Serpent ...." The word *Serpent* always has the article, *ha-naḥash*. I think the word should be capitalized here, because it is not being used of an animal form, but rather it is being used as a title: that old Serpent, the Dragon, the Devil. I'll tell you why I think this is true: The Serpent has personal knowledge of what God has said. He is more than just a reporter, for he acts on his own in conversation with the woman. She is not surprised that a reptile is speaking with her. Whenever surprise is expressed in the biblical text, there is the acknowledgement of surprise. But here the woman doesn't say, "*Oy vey*! When did *you* start talking?" There is no word like that at all, nor does she jump and say, "Ah! I was frightened by that talking reptile."

More than that, by the time we get down to verse 15, it is clear that the biblical text is not using this word to place the Serpent in the class of animals, as some translations do in 3:1: "Now the Serpent was more subtle than any of the wild beasts of the field." The words *any of* come from the Hebrew *mik-kol*. It literally means *from all*. The *mik* is 'from', representing the word *min*, 'from', and then with the word *kol*, 'from all'. This can be taken in either a comparative sense or in a partitive sense.

In the comparative, we would translate it: "Now the Serpent was more subtle *than* the animals of the field." In the partitive, it would be translated as "any *of* the animals of the field." Do you see what the translators have done? They must have had a debate, for it seems that they divided up their vote. In 3:1, it says, "any *of* the beasts," and in 3:14, it says, "*than* the beasts of the field." My suggestion is that it is not partitive in either of the verses, but rather it is to be seen in both instances as being comparative: "*than* the beasts of the field."

So what was the point? The whole point of the Evil One was to tempt the woman and to trick her, because she had not walked and talked with God in the garden as long as had Adam. When a person is not taught sufficiently, he can be tricked. That's the point of 1 Timothy 2. Eve was thoroughly tricked; she was really roped in; she was duped because she wasn't sufficiently taught. Notice that Paul's point is not that one sinned and the other did not. Both Adam and Eve sinned, but one was thoroughly deceived. To deceive is to trick. We can trick kids; we can trick people whose eyes are not fast enough to see things; we can trick people who have not been taught. But when a person is taught, the trick doesn't work. Maybe when we try the trick again, that person will say, "Ah, I know what's up your sleeve. You can't trick me anymore." Please remember that Eve was thoroughly tricked. (The lesson here should be helpful to the church.)

At any rate, here the text says that she was deceived. How did she get deceived? Well, there was gross exaggeration on the part of the enemy, whom I take to be a supernatural being, Satan himself. What form he appeared in I have no idea; I don't think that we can know. But he is called by his title: that old Dragon; the Serpent. And he says in exaggeration, "I understand you people are real narrow. You can't eat from any of the trees in the garden."

Eve says, "What do you think we are? We're not *that* narrow! There are only two trees we can't eat from. And furthermore—" Now she becomes evangelistic; I think she even adds to God's commandment—and she says, "Yea, God says, 'You shouldn't even touch it.'" This is the clincher. To come up with that kind of statement, she must have felt she needed to defend God's honor.

At any rate, we know what happened: she ate and then the man ate. What is the point? Were there sin enzymes in that tree? No, I don't think there were sin enzymes that were communicable through certain kinds of fruit. Rather, this was a symbol. It was symbolic just as is the Lord's Supper, the Eucharist. We warn people, "Look, if you're not a believer, help us pass the elements but don't partake of them. You mustn't say, 'Oh, what am I supposed to do? I'm in church and I don't want to look foolish—so I'll just take some of the bread and some of the wine and I'll partake.'"

The biblical text says, "Don't do it! It will hurt you. You'll get sick from it and it will kill you." So what was Eve doing here? By partaking of this fruit, she symbolically went against the command of God, much as some do in disobeying the instructions for the Lord's Supper. This is an argument developed in Geerhardus Vos's *Biblical Theology*. I think Geerhardus Vos is very, very good on this point and should be checked out for further discussion.

So both Adam and Eve sin, and as a result, you remember, the curse comes upon the woman. God says, "I will greatly increase your pains in childbearing." This statement needs to be understood. A book published by InterVarsity Press, *Hard Sayings of the Old Testament*, really explains that passage, I think.

Then God goes on to say, "And your desire shall be to your husband." I don't think that word *desire* is properly translated. This mistaken translation began with a monk in the 1500s who thought that it had something to do with sexual desire. It has nothing to do with sexual desire. *Teshuqa* means "your *turning* shall be to your husband, and as a result of this turning he will take advantage of you." It is a prophecy, a prophecy of judgment. It has nothing to do with normativeness. The word *yimshal* is 'he will rule'. It doesn't mean that he shall, or he must, or he's got to, or it's imperative. It's a plain statement of judgment: he will rule. Some men will take advantage of you. He *will* rule over you.

And then to Adam, God says, "The ground is cursed before you, and it will produce thorns." It's not that it *shall* produce thorns. By the way, it's the same form as we just saw. If the text in the previous verse is saying that the man *must* rule the woman, then it would follow logically that farmers should not use weed killer, because the ground *must* produce thorns and thistles. Same argument. If farmers can use weed killer, then it seems to me we must go back and take a look at verse 16.

In the middle of all this, the great thing is that God intervenes with a word in Genesis 3:15. Here's what he says: "I will put enmity (1) between the Serpent"—that old Dragon, the Devil, and notice again I capitalize his name—"and (2) the woman," Eve. Then God says, "I will continue that enmity"—here's the surprise—"between (3) the Serpent's seed and (4) the woman's seed," Eve's seed. She is to have offspring and this enmity will continue. Isn't that surprising? Why should God continue this hostility?

But then the clincher. There is to be (4a) a *male* descendant: *he*, not *she* as in some translations, and not *it* as in other translations. The pronoun is clearly in the third person masculine singular. The Serpent will nip 4a's heel. The 4a, the male descendant, will stamp on the head of the Serpent and crush its head, dealing a lethal wound. This is the first announcement of the Good News.

There are in history, then, the good guys and the bad guys. The bad guys are the Serpent and his kids. The good guys are Eve and her kids. But more particularly, from Eve's seed and from her offspring there will come a male descendant. That male descendant is the one who shall have victory over (1) the Serpent himself.

Now that we've seen the first announcement of the gospel, let's go on to the flood in chapter 6. Here, particularly in 6:4-5, we are told that men and women are continuing to do evil. Time has gone on—a millennium or more has rolled by—and people have had plenty of time to start doing their own thing. And they are! Here we have the question of the "sons of God." I don't think these sons of God represent the godly line, the good fellows; nor do I think that they represent angels, as in the book of Job. Here, it would seem to me, it's a title for aristocracy, for rulers: the Son of Re; the Son of Amun; the son of any kind of god. Ancient rulers usually can claim fifty or more gods as being part of their basis for their work, feeling they are sons of all these gods.

These rulers, the sons of God, see that the daughters of men are beautiful. By the way, if these sons of God are actually angels who have sinned, then the flood is misdirected; the flood should be in heaven, not on earth. I just mention that as a side point. It is on earth that the problems come, so we must be dealing with earthlings of some sort. And what are they doing? They are choosing daughters, as many and whomever they wish. Verse 4 says they are heroes, men of a name, or men of renown. That word here means 'a quest for a name'. The word for 'name' is *shem* (the *e* is pronounced as the *a* sound in 'shame'). Shem is also the name of the second son of Noah, so the Semites go back to Shem whose name literally means *name*. 'Semites' is the Greek form of the Hebrew word *Shemites*, so we speak of the Semitic peoples.

Therefore we see that we have here people who are searching for a name. This is going to come up in the tower of Babel, too; they also want to make a name for themselves. In Genesis 11:4, we're going to see the parallel; we can compare Genesis 6:4 and Genesis 11:4. They want to make a name for themselves. Everyone yearns after a reputation; everyone wants to be remembered. But God will turn to one man in particular to give him a name! God will give Abraham a name. "I will make your name great."

So, you understand, we have here man's quest for a reputation, for achievement, for pride, for some kind of honor. But man wants all this for himself, on his own terms rather than on God's terms. God, on the other hand, wants to give a name as a blessing, and so he gives it to Abraham as a freebie. Abraham definitely won!

## The Blessing of the Dwelling of God among Mortals

Going back to Noah: in Genesis 9:27 we have another promise of God. He spells it out in verses 25, 26, and 27 with each of the three sons of Noah: Shem, Ham, and Japheth. But first, before we get to the promise, there is a problem with Ham, and the story concentrates on Canaan, his son (Gen 9:20-25). Because of this problem, Canaan is the one who is cursed. And what is this problem? When Noah awoke—he being drunk from the wine—he remembered that the other two sons, Shem and Japheth, refused to enter into Ham's sporting of their father's nakedness. Now the text doesn't say, but it looks as if Ham is into sexual mischief here, apparently some form of homosexuality. The other two boys refuse to take part. Instead, they walk backward to their father and cover his nakedness. Noah, when he awakens, knows what Ham has done, and he says, "Cursed be Canaan" (v. 25). Why does he say, "Cursed be Canaan" instead of "Cursed be Ham"? Because he sees—prophetically or realistically—in Ham's son, Canaan, the same perversion as in the father. Therefore he says, "Cursed be Canaan."

Look in Genesis 10:6 to see where the text gives the names of Ham's four sons. Who are the sons of Ham? They are Cush, Mizraim, Put, and Canaan. So here is a man, Ham, who has four sons who settle over a wide area and who become eponymous, i.e., they give their names to different territories. The Cushite territory becomes Ethiopia. Mizraim settles in Egypt. The Libyans and North Africans are descendants of Put. And then there is Canaan. Canaan is basically Syria and Palestine. Well, so much for the story of Ham and Canaan.

Let's go back to Genesis 9:26 where Noah blesses Shem. "Blessed be the LORD, the God of Shem!" (NIV). Verse 27 names all three together, Japheth, Shem, and Canaan. About Japheth, Noah says, "May God extend the territory of Japheth." (This is the Japhetic peoples: the Indo-Europeans. Most of us would trace our roots back to them.) Then he says, "May God dwell in the tents of Shem." Since the Hebrew says, "May he dwell," some assume it means that Japheth shall dwell in the tents of Shem. But I think it's really a promise. The second blessing is that *God*, not the descendants of Japheth, will come and dwell with the Shemites. Here God is choosing the Semitic people. (In grammar, the subject of the first clause is the antecedent for the pronoun used as the subject of the second clause.) So we have the promise of God coming and dwelling with men. This is the second great promise.

## The Blessing of the Gospel

Now finally, as we conclude this chapter, we have the third world crisis: the flop of the tower. We then have the third great moment in the unfolding of the blessing-plan. This begins with Genesis 3:15 and continues with Genesis 9:27. After the failure of the tower, what does God say? He calls a name, Abram (chap. 12). He says, "Leave your country down there in Babylonia and Mesopotamia, Ur of the Chaldees, and I'll make you a great nation. I'll bless you and I'll make your name great."

Three blessings are given here: (1) "I will make you a great nation," (2) "I will bless you," and (3) "I will make your name great." That is God's answer to the quest for a name in Genesis 6:4 and in Genesis 11:4. God gives a name. But along with these three blessings, he gives a purpose clause:

"So that you will be a blessing." God says, "I will do this so that you will be a blessing." Interesting!

God is not playing favorites here. The 'while' or the 'and' shows there's a purpose: that is, "in order that you may be a blessing." Then he goes on to say, fourthly and fifthly, "I will bless those that bless you, and whoever curses you I will curse." Why? "So that in your seed"—now the final purpose—"all the nations of the earth might be blessed."

The final purpose of God's blessing on Abraham is to give him the Good News. I am using the word here that comes out of Galatians 3:8: "So that in your seed all the nations of the earth might be blessed." And that 'seed' is one, namely, Jesus Christ (Gal 3:16).

So in these opening chapters of Genesis we have three of four foundational blessings. We can put the fourth one—which really belongs to creation—separately, and then keep together the other three of the seed, the dwelling, and the gospel. And there we have the whole thrust.

We have the word of creation which begins "in the beginning." God brings a blessing—a material blessing—for all the people upon the face of the earth. Then he brings a spiritual blessing, the blessing of the seed. From the woman one will come who will be the answer to the historic polarization of the Serpent's seed and the woman's seed. God becomes even more specific. That seed will be Shemitic, from the Shemitic peoples, the Shemites, Shem: "God will dwell with Shem."

God then chooses one Shemite named Abraham, and God will make him great; God will bless him and will give him a great name. God will make him into a great nation. Why? So that he may be a blessing. But how? And to whom? He will be a great blessing through the Good News which will be for all the nations upon the face of the earth. And there comes the final answer.

Genesis 1–11 begins to build the groundwork for our own understanding of the gospel. It is so foundational to see the messianic concept, the immanency concept, the choice concept of a nation. And then we must also see the means here: "So that through your seed, this may be a blessing for all the nations."

The key word that pulls this all together is 'blessing'. *Blessing*. Notice how the word *to bless*, or *blessing*, occurs five times in Genesis 12:1-3. As if to summarize the whole thing so that we might understand it, he repeats the word over and over again. He says, "I will bless you … so that you may be a blessing…. I will bless those that bless you," and this is "so that all the families on the earth might be blessed." These are the foundational blessings of Genesis 1–11.

# Chapter Four

# Three Foundational Promises

## Genesis 12–50

Our fourth chapter takes us to Genesis 12–50, which covers what is generally called the patriarchal period. Beginning with Genesis 12, we find a new departure in divine revelation. We turn from the universal history which has occupied us for the first eleven chapters—a universal history that treats all men—and we suddenly narrow down to one man, Abraham. We started with all of the human race having its fountainhead in Adam. From there it branched out into seventy different nations. But out of all those nations, interestingly enough, only one has been selected: the nation of Shem, the Semites—and one Semite in particular, Abraham. The interesting thing is that, while Genesis 1–11 is universal in its scope, now the text suddenly narrows down to one person who, indeed, is to have a ministry to all the nations. So it's somewhat of a reversal, and in that sense it is a new start. We went from one to the many; now we're going from the many back to one.

### Introduction: The Patriarchs as Prophets of the Word

The material in Genesis 12–50 focuses on three great fathers of their country. Just as we call George Washington, Thomas Jefferson, and James Madison fathers of our country, we consider Abraham, Isaac, and Jacob—or Israel, which, of course, will become his new name—as the three great fathers of their country. Simply calling them great fathers of their country, however, is not enough; we are going to give them an even fancier name: patriarchs. Had these men known they were to become patriarchs, I am sure they would have been impressed!

Now, the distinctive feature of this age is the increased prominence given to the word of God. The word springs forth! For this reason, these three men are also called prophets. It is surprising to find the title of prophet used so early in biblical history. For example, Genesis 20:7 refers to Abimelech, a Philistine king, who is told with regard to Abraham, "Now return the man's wife, for he is a prophet." That also is reflected in the Psalms. If you like to mark up your text, and if you think that it is appropriate, here is a Psalm you can mark. Psalm 105:15 makes an allusion to the reference about Abimelech which we just read in Genesis 20:7. It says, "Do not touch my anointed ones"—here *messiahs* is used, or 'the ones who are anointed'—and "do my prophets no harm." In this context he is talking about Abraham, Isaac, and Jacob.

So these men are called prophets. Why are they called prophets? Because they are men of the word. The use of the word *prophet* surprises us, because it is generally not thought of in connection with this part of Genesis. I am afraid that most look at Genesis 12–50 only for moralistic teaching. But these are men who deal in the word. For example, the word of the Lord comes to Abraham eight times in at least three or four different ways. The clearest way heads this section on the patriarchal period with the simple phrase in Genesis 12:1, "The LORD ... said to Abram." Then, in Genesis 13:14, "The LORD said to Abram." Or again, in 21:12, "God said." Or, in Genesis 22:1: the word of the LORD came to Abraham when he was sent up to Mount Moriah for the sacrifice of his son in that great testing chapter.

But there is a second way in which the word comes: through visions. We think of visions as having different scenes and different settings; the person can see events roll before him like a movie. Genesis 15:1 (which we will look at in more detail in the fifth chapter) says, "The word of the LORD came to [him] in a vision." So here we have one of the early patriarchs, at 2000 BC, receiving the word of the Lord in a vision. This is very similar to Ezekiel's visions or Daniel's visions.

In four or five other instances the Lord himself appears to Abraham. For example, Genesis 12:7 says, "The LORD appeared to [him]." Also note Genesis 17:1. With these appearances, we now have the new phenomenon of the Angel of the LORD. The Angel of the LORD, I think in these instances, is what we technically call a *Christophany*: an appearance of Christ in his pre-incarnate form. This is not his permanent flesh which he took on at Bethlehem when he came as a baby. But definitely there seems to be a real individual who is accorded worship and is treated as divine. There is some discussion of it, back and forth, but I am surprised how frequently the Angel of the LORD makes an appearance in these texts. Note Genesis 16:7; 21:17; 22:11. The Angel of the LORD intervenes just as Abraham is about ready to plunge a knife into his son, Isaac. We also see the Angel of the LORD in Genesis 24:7, 40; Genesis 31:11, 13; Genesis 32:24, 30. And then, in the Joseph story in Genesis 48:15-16, we again see a visible manifestation of the second person of the Godhead.

Note that the Hebrew and the Greek do not use the article here; he is called "an angel of the LORD." Of course, we must be careful, because

Hebrew does not make the fine distinction we can make in English between *a* and *the*—between the articular form and the non-articular form. But do please notice here that we have the patriarchs as recipients of revelation from God. Recipients of revelation from God! And the plan of God is being carried out. Strong emphasis is put on his word. So any teaching or preaching in this section of Scripture will have to put a heavy accent on the whole matter of the word of God.

Now, since we've titled this fourth chapter "Three Foundational Promises," let's look at those promises.

## The Promise of an Heir

The first foundational promise concerns an heir. The promise of an heir was given centuries—millennia—ago. We can watch the development of this promise as it was given by revelation to Abraham, Isaac, and Jacob. At the very beginning, in Genesis 3:15, there had been the promise of the seed to the woman.

### 'Seed' as a Collective Singular

We noted in the previous chapter that this word *seed* was singular, but it was a collective singular. It was not the plural *seeds*, and therefore it would be improper to translate it in English as 'descendants'. So that, without giving duality to its meaning, 'seed' can simultaneously indicate the one who is representative of the group and yet signal the many who are embodied in that whole group. It is deliberately done this way. That is why Paul, in writing Galatians 3:16, will also insist that Scripture does not say *seeds*, which means many, but *seed*, which is one. And that one is Christ, he says. Paul then goes on to say that if we believe, we are Abraham's seed (Gal 3:29).

And so, in the scope of Galatians 3:16-29, the one and the many are embodied in his single idea. It is too bad that many think that Paul is reading back into the Old Testament text something that happens in New Testament times, saying in effect, "Look, I can put a Christological inter-pretation on this." Paul is not forcing an eisegesis or a new interpretation or a rabbinic Midrash on the text. *Nein! Nix! Ne pas! Nyet!* He is simply arguing from the text itself.

What about this heir who is mentioned here? The first place it occurs is in Genesis 12:7, where God talks to Abraham: "The LORD appeared to Abram and said ...." If you like to note the "first references" in the Bible, here is one: this is the first reference to "the LORD appeared to him." We would expect something significant to be said on this first appearance of God to man. And yes, there is! He says, "To your offspring I will give this land. To your seed I will give this land." And we are introduced to this concept of the seed.

### Obstacles to God's Promise of an Heir

As we progress through the patriarchal story in Genesis 12–50, we will notice a number of obstacles. It is amazing how the many obstacles thrown up would seem to take us in opposing directions.

**1. The threat to Sarah and Abraham.** First of all, there is going to be Sarah's entrance into Pharaoh's harem. In the last part of chapter 12, you remember, there comes a discussion as a result of famine in the land. So Abram goes down into Egypt and he says, "Sarah, I know you're a beautiful woman, and, frankly, my life's going to be in jeopardy. I think Pharaoh is going to make a pass at you, and if it becomes a problem, I know what Pharaoh is going to do: off will go my head so that he can marry you! So let's agree. Why don't you help me a little bit; tell him you're my sister." And so he forms this lie. On the other hand, of course, it is a half-truth: Sarah was his half-sister, as you know. However, I still think it falls under the category of lie.

But the point is, the lies of a patriarch were not going to help bring about the plan of God. God's plan was going to come about without any human agency. It had nothing to do with merit. There are big letters over this whole section: G-r-a-c-e. Grace! It's the "giftiness" of God. Everything in this whole section of Genesis 12–50 is grace. It is a gift of God.

**2. The threat to Isaac and Rebekah.** As we continue with Genesis 20:1-18, it happens again! But please notice that the grace of God is prevailing; in each of these instances, God's plan has nothing to do with the conniving, with the lying, with the trickery, and with the deceit that is practiced by Abraham and Isaac. Sarah must have been a ravishingly beautiful woman! With Isaac's wife, Becky (I call her Becky; it was Rebekah, but I feel I know her since I have worked through this text so much), the same trick is pulled again (Gen 26). So strike one for Abraham and Isaac. As a matter of fact, strike two for Abraham; he does it twice. But please notice that the grace of God is prevailing!

**3. Sarah's old age.** Also, look at other obstacles. How about Sarah's old age in chapter 18? What a chapter that is, where the Lord appeared to Abram! You remember, three men came, and Abraham offered them hospitality. Now, hospitality is a wonderful thing in the Near East. The host is responsible for his guest; he must give his life to protect him. It would be a blot on his family if anything happened to his guest while under his protection. Even today, this is true in the Near East.

During World War II, one of my teachers was getting information out in the desert, being far away from modern communication systems. He helped the American cause by listening at water holes, where Americans were getting more information than they were getting through secret codes, wireless, and all kinds of radar. What my teacher would do is to go to the strongest tribe and make a covenant of salt. When they had shared salt, nothing could happen to him. If any other hostile group attacked him and he lost his life, it would be the responsibility of the group with which he had made the covenant of salt. Hospitality is taken very seriously in the Near East.

So here in Genesis 18, these three men come to Abram, and it's quite clear that one of them must be the Angel of the LORD—a Christophany, an appearance of Christ—because of the way in which he is treated. Also, the text alternates between LORD and *Angel of the LORD*. For, whereas it had been the angel speaking previously, we see in verse 10: "Then the LORD said to him, 'I will surely return about this time next year, and your wife Sarah will have a son.'"

When Sarah heard that, her reaction was typical. Like many women, she was curious about what was going on, so she listened through the tent flap to the conversation of the men outside. When she heard the angel say, "Your wife, Sarah, will have a son," she snorted and said, "That's a joke!" She said, "There are basic laws of biology that apparently this gentleman doesn't know. I am ninety; Abraham is one hundred."

God said, "The joke is on you!" In verse 13, the Lord said to Abraham, "Why did Sarah laugh and say, 'Will I really have a child, now that I am old?'"

Verse 14 gives a very beautiful theological principle: "Is anything too hard for the LORD? Is anything too *pela'* for the LORD?" This word *pela'* is the same word that occurs in the great name given to the Savior in Isaiah 9:6: "His name shall be called *Pela'* Counselor, Wonderful Counselor." The word in the verbal form means to do difficult things, to do marvelous things, to do wonderful things, to do the miraculous. So the name of our Lord Jesus is The One Who Does Miracles, The One Who Does Wonderful Things. And the question asked here is interesting because it ties in to the Messianic line, to the one who is to be born at this time, Isaac. "Is anything too wonderful? Is anything too miraculous?" We could translate it: "Is anything too difficult, too hard, for me?" It's a beautiful theological statement.

The word study is worth checking out in other texts. Jeremiah must be reminded of the same thing in Jeremiah 32 when he is told to purchase land. Twice the Lord tells him to do this. And Jeremiah says, "I feel crazy! Here's the conqueror coming in; the whole city has gone up in smoke. Real estate has bottomed out—and I'm out buying!" He says, "Everyone else is selling, and I'm buying! This is a crazy time to be buying!"

And the Lord says, "Is anything too *pela'* for me?"

**4. The threat of barrenness.** Well, we see the obstacles. Not only do we have the possibility of a monarch like Abimelech or Pharaoh stealing Sarah or Becky, but we have Sarah's old age. We also have the barrenness theme. Rebekah, Isaac's wife, is barren; Jacob's wife, Rachel, is barren. Those stories are found in Genesis 25:21 and Genesis 30:1. And we have the threat to Jacob's own life, too, by Esau, his brother. It looks as if they're going to polish each other off.

With all these threats and obstacles, we must hold our breath. Uh-oh! Are Christmas and Easter going to be cancelled? Could the whole thing be over before it even gets started?

**5. The threat of famine.** There's famine, too, in the opening verses of this section (Gen 12:10). What sent Abraham down into Egypt in the first place? It was famine. And it will be famine once again that God will use to preserve the nation when we get into the Joseph story, starting with Genesis 37.

**6. The threat of adultery.** Then there comes a digression in the narrative. Here is Tamar—Tammy—and she is given to each of Judah's three sons in turn. The first son is killed because he was wicked and did an abomination; so wicked that the Bible won't even tell us what he did. As for the second son, he was into inheritance control—that's what we would have to call it—and he wouldn't raise up children to his brother; so therefore we have the sin of Onan. When it comes to the third son, Judah says, "I won't give any more sons! I can't risk this; this girl's gone through two of my boys already. This is my last chance!"

Remember, everything's wrong in this story. Judah commits incest with Tamar, his own daughter-in-law. He thinks of her as a harlot and he suggests hush money. "What would you like? What's the price?"

She says, "What about a goat, a young goat, a kid?"

He says, "Fine."

She then says, "Well, give me some identification."

He says, "How about my driver's license?" He takes the signet seal off his neck. (The signet seal was a little thing, not as big as a piece of chalk, about an inch long and maybe about a half inch thick, which had a hole through the center and was worn as a necklace. In business transactions, it was rolled across wet clay so it would leave its mark.) Like a driver's license, it is Judah's personal identification. He also gives his shepherd's staff. When he goes to redeem them, she is gone.

Three months later she turns up at a party, pregnant, and he is angry! He says, "My daughter-in-law, what in the world is wrong with you?"

And she says, "Well, I'll tell you *who* it was. Here's his driver's license."

He looks at it, gulps, and says, "You're more righteous than I am."

Twins are born. And of the twins, Zerah is the one through whom comes the line of the Messiah.

We can say, "*Oy vey!* All this is happening here? How can the plan of God be working out? There is a mess all the way: obstacle, obstacle, obstacle, obstacle, obstacle, *obstacle!*" And yet, through the whole thing, the grace of God is triumphing. That's how this passage is to be understood. For an heir is coming! There is a series of sons: to Abraham is born a son, Isaac; and to Isaac is born a son, Jacob. Their God is maintaining his pledge that he will give the seed to the woman, through whom ultimately *the one* who represents all of mankind will come! An heir will be born. So we have this theme.

### The Pledge of God's Divine Presence

The promise of divine presence, along with the promise of an heir, is also to be seen throughout the whole patriarchal narrative. This theme, "I will be with you. Fear not, for I will be with you," occurs 104 times. Phobias go way back; they're not just a modern invention. Over and over again, the Bible has to tell us, "Fear not ... Fear not ... Don't be afraid ... Fear not!" We in ministry must understand: people are afraid. People do silly things, crazy things, to overcompensate for their fears. God's basic answer is, "I will be with you."

Two little prepositions are used in connection with this: *'et*, which occurs over and over again, and *'im*. These two little particles are used in connection with God 104 times in the Old Testament: "I will be *with* you." Often today when we use the word *with* we ruin its full meaning. We say, "Yeah, I'm with you. I'm behind you." We never say how far behind, but we're behind the person in general. That is not what God means when he says, "I'll be with you." He means *he will be there.* As we will see in another chapter, his name is Yahweh, the God who will be there. But in this short section of Genesis 12–50, he says 14 times, "I will be with you. I will go with you." With this word God guarantees his personal presence. If you wish to see the stress put on this great theme, see the *Theological Dictionary of the Old Testament*, volume 1, pages 450-463.

One of the places where the promise of divine presence occurs in Abraham's life is Genesis 21:22: "At that time Abimelech and Phicol the commander of his forces said to Abraham, 'God is with you in everything you do'" (NIV). Here is the testimony of a Philistine who says that "God is with you in everything that you do." Again, in Genesis 26, we see it in the life of Isaac. Verse 3 says, "Stay in the land for a while. I will be with you and I will bless you." Or again in Genesis 26:24 which says, "That night the LORD appeared to him and said, 'I am the God of your father Abraham. Do not be afraid, for I am with you.'" There's the classical form: "Do not be afraid—fear not, for I am with you." And again in verse 28: "They answered, 'We saw clearly that the LORD was with you.'" So again, in the life of Isaac, it is proving to be true that God is with him.

We can see it later on in other passages. I notice in passing that Genesis 28:15 says, "I am with you and will watch over you wherever you go." This occurs in Jacob's dream at Bethel, when he also is at a crossroads in his life. In Genesis 31:3, Jacob is fleeing from Laban, when the Lord says,

"Go back to Canaan, to the land of your fathers, for I will be with you."
We will find it when the narrative continues. In Genesis 35:2-3, there is a
great revival when Jacob returns to Bethel, and God says there, "Get rid of
your foreign gods, and get rid of all that stuff you've gotten into, for I have
been with you wherever you've gone."

Mention a key transition in a patriarch's life—mention some great,
dramatic thing—and we will see that with it comes the great promise,
Emmanuel, God with us. *God with us*. He will stamp his name upon the
men. God will be with us!

And then, in the life of Joseph, God's presence is stressed four times in
one chapter, Genesis 39. When Joseph was taken advantage of by Potiphar's
lusting wife, "The LORD was with Joseph .... And his master saw that the
LORD was with him ..." (Gen 39:2-3, AV). Then again we see it in Genesis
39:21, where Joseph was thrown into prison: "The LORD was with him,
and showed him kindness and granted him favor." And then there is a
cumulative effect of God's presence as Genesis 39:23 shows us: "The warden
paid no attention to anything under Joseph's care, because the LORD was
with Joseph." So this great theme of the presence of God is to be seen along
with the promise of the heir.

The patriarchs, then, were promised a seed, a posterity, an heir, a
descendant. From this descendant would come an innumerable host that
could not even be numbered. His posterity would be like the sands on the
seashore or like the stars in the heavens above. It's a hyperbole, to be sure;
but on the other hand, it is a promise of a *large* group of people. This promise
occurs in several different passages, including Genesis 13:16, 22:17, 28:3,
32:12, 35:11, and 48:4. Not only would they be an assembly of nations, but
they themselves would be a great nation (Gen 18:18). This heir would be
the one from whom would come a great nation. Kings would spring from
them; we have the promise that this seed would produce royalty—a whole
line of royalty. This is given as early as Genesis 17:6, 16, and again in Genesis
35:11.

So there's an awful lot in the Bible about this seed. We are not told that
he is the Messiah; we are not told that his name is Jesus. We are not given
that information, but we certainly are given a lot of other information. It
is recorded that people born to Abraham will be as countless as the stars;
that an assembly of nations will come from him; that kings will spring
from him; that, indeed, there will come a great nation.

## The Promise of an Inheritance

The second foundational promise of the patriarchs is the promise of an
inheritance. This is the whole theme of the land which plays an extremely
significant part in the theology of that day—and of today, as well. It continues to be one of the great sources of division in our midst.

On this matter of the land, there are varying theological estimates. There is, for example, Albrecht Alt who says that the land theme was added to the original promise of the heir. He sees the land as secondary.

We might say, "Yes, but it's in the text."

"Well," he would answer, "you must edit those out."

We might say, "What's your manuscript evidence for that?"

He would say, "Trust me." Basically, I think this is subjective reasoning.

Secondly, there's Gerhard von Rad, who says that this whole matter of the land came from an earlier religion that was transferred to the patriarchs and then was made part of the twelve-league nation. Again, I could ask von Rad, "Where did you get that?" He would say, in effect, "Trust me." This is the work of scholarship.

Martin Noth, however, says both the land and the seed promises were part of patriarchal faith. And I say, "Bully for Martin!" because that's the way I read the text. I have no other evidence that says anything different.

So we have several theological estimates. If you wish to study this more, look it up in the *Theological Dictionary of the Old Testament*, volume 1, pages 401-405. You can follow up what I have just given you in very rapid detail.

What is the extent of this land? We are told that it would go from the River Egypt all the way to the Grand River, or to the Pahrat. Now, this can be politically sensitive so we must be very careful. But I will try to give you an idea of the boundaries.

Some have thought that the River Egypt is the Nile. For example, if you look in the *Zondervan Pictorial Dictionary*, you will find that my good friend, Bruce Waltke, has an article in which he identifies the River Egypt with the Nile River. My complaint about that, however, is that if this is true, then Goshen qualified as part of the Promised Land. Goshen is where the people of Israel were staying, up in the northeast corner of that sector of the Nile delta—and they should not have moved on. If the boundary is the Nile, they were already within the Promised Land.

However, at the spot where the treaty after the Six Day War was drawn, at El Arish or Wadi Arish, there is also a *mitsor* which is found in Assyrian documents and other places. This is just south of the Gaza Strip and is the site of a present-day city. And there's a wadi that goes off in a south-easterly direction, moving down to Elat, at the head of the gulf.

It is not without significance that the peace treaty set after the Six-Day War established the boundary precisely, I think, where Genesis 15:18 says: the River Egypt. This is the Wadi Nahal Mitsur. In Hebrew, the word *nahal* is used for a smaller stream, as opposed to *nahar* which is used for a river. I note the distinction here. The Nile, by the way, would be called a *nahar*. Also, the Nile, in the Bible, always has the distinctive word which is a cognate of 'Egyptian', *yi'or*. That would be another reason for ruling out the Nile River.

So the boundary would be south of the Gaza Strip. As for the northern boundary, some texts talk about the Euphrates River, the Great River which is the Euphrates. There's no doubt about that. But other texts also mention a Great River. Here's where it becomes politically sensitive. Go north up the coastline of the Mediterranean Sea, above Mount Carmel, above Tyre and Sidon and Beirut, and continue north to the present boundary between Lebanon and Syria. (If we go up Lebanon to Beirut, where all the civil war fighting took place, we are halfway up the coast.) The northern boundary of Lebanon is, I think, where we have the definition of the Great River. I say this is sensitive—very, very politically sensitive. On the other hand, it appears that the boundaries come down here. Now we can trace through Lake Huleh, the eastern boundary, then down to the Sea of Galilee, a little heart-shaped lake, and on down the Jordan River, through the Dead Sea, and finally to the port of Elat. Notice, everything on the West Bank, except for a corridor reaching through Damascus, going up through the Golan Heights, and extending over to the Euphrates River. This would seem to be the Promised Land.

Never was the Promised Land occupied as such during the time of the patriarchs nor during the time of Solomon. (We'll argue about that later.) Some think that the promise of the land inheritance was fulfilled in 1 Kings 8:65. But we argue that even in Zechariah 10, in the postexilic period, the Jews are still being promised this section of land. So there is the theme of the land which is called "Jehovah's heritage" in 1 Samuel 26:19. In other passages it is called "the land of the LORD," or "the land of Yahweh," or "my land."

## The Promise of the Heritage of the Gospel

The third and final foundational promise to the patriarchs is the promise of the heritage of the gospel. This third promise is always found in a prominent, climactic position in the text. In Genesis 12:3, it's the last thing in a series: "In your seed shall all the nations of the earth be blessed." This we call the gospel, the heritage. It occurs again in Genesis 18:18. Also we find it in Genesis 22:18, in 26:4, and finally in 28:14.

Five times this prophecy is given to Abraham, to Isaac, and, yes, to Jacob. Always it occurs in the climactic position. How shall we translate it? Will it be active, or reflexive, or passive? Is this something each will do for himself? The answer is, No. It is to be translated in the passive. It is distinctly in what we call the passive or the *niphal* stem. Note Genesis 12:3, 18:18, and 28:14. In two cases, the reflexive stem is used: "They will bless themselves" (Gen 22:18; 26:4). But note how frequently the New Testament picks that up and makes it into a passive. Notice, too, that even the so-called reflexive *hitpa'el* stem is itself translated in the passive.

So we believe that it's a work that God does. Human beings cannot say, "I think we'll bless ourselves," or "I think we'll do what Israel has done." It is a work of God! It is *his* work by which *he* will give an heir as the object of faith. God will provide the one through whom the work of salvation will come.

So while he gives the inheritance of the land to Israel, he is also doing it to benefit all nations. This is a blessing that will be to the advantage of all who will believe. This includes the universal list of nations in Genesis 10. The phrase "all the families of the earth" is picked up from Genesis 10. Therefore we have the concept of missions. The everlasting plan of God is his promise. This word, I think, helps us to understand Genesis.

So we have three foundational promises. We have the heir, who is the Messiah, to be born through Abraham, Isaac, and Jacob; and we have the promise: nothing is too difficult for God, and he will be with them. Then we have the inheritance of the land; this promise is not just spiritual. It is also the promise of God working physically and materially in this world down here. And then we have the means, the mechanism, by which the promise is to come. That is to be the heritage of the gospel through belief in the one, the Messiah, who is to come. This great section of biblical text, Genesis 12–50, gives us these three foundational promises.

# Chapter Five

# The Theology of Saving Faith in the Old Testament

I find the topic of this chapter to be an intriguing one: the theology of saving faith in the Old Testament. Contrary to popular opinion, it was not an earned salvation or a do-it-yourself job in olden times as compared to salvation by grace for us today. It wasn't the self-made man type of salvation. It wasn't that way at all!

It is true that the New Testament goes beyond the Old Testament, both in its description of saving faith and in the revelation of what is actually happening. But the New Testament does not change the ground rules, nor does it change the basic results. Nor does it change the object of faith. (In saying this, I do think that I exceed what is generally taught on this subject.)

## The Delay in Mentioning Abraham's Faith: Genesis 12–13

In this discussion, let's start where there is agreement. All agree that Abraham came to know the Savior by means of grace through faith plus nothing. That's the old Reformed definition. Salvation is by grace alone because it's a gift, and it is by faith because it is simply a forsaking of all. F-a-i-t-h is a helpful acrostic here: Forsaking all, I take him. So we have the means of faith and the means for establishing it. Mankind is converted by grace through faith plus nothing. This is the way men and women receive eternal life; this is the way they are said to be made right with God.

The key question on which we have disagreement, however, is this: Who or what was the *object* of their faith? Was it God in the Old Testament and Christ in the New Testament, or was there some other object?

The key verse, of course, for our discussion is going to be Genesis 15:6. There it simply says, "Abraham believed the LORD, and it was credited to him"—or God credited it to him—"as righteousness." God added it up; he reckoned it; and God said Abraham was righteous. Paul will appeal to this verse in Romans 4. James will also argue from it. It is one of those great statements of justification: God *declares*—not *makes*—Abraham righteous. It is like when a judge taps his gavel and says, "Case dismissed!" God says, on the merit and the work of God, "The case against Abraham is dismissed." We're talking mathematical terms here: God adds it up; he reckons it; he credits it to him. And in his reckoning God says, "You don't owe any more."

The great problem, it seems to me, is why we do not find a statement about Abraham's faith until Genesis 15. After all, we meet him several chapters earlier. Isn't it true that Abraham responds obediently when God says to him, "Leave your country, your people, and your father's household, and go to the land that I will show you"? I mean, for that day and age to pick up and move across the country was quite a feat! He is moving about 1,500 to 1,800 miles, which is not your basic short haul. He couldn't call up Allied or United and say, "Would you give me some suggestions on how I can ship my herds and how I can pack up all of my goods?" This man has to go from way down in Mesopotamia. (Remember, the Tigris River goes like an arrow right down to the Persian Gulf.) Mesopotamia—present-day Iraq—is between the two rivers, the Tigris and the Euphrates: *mesos* meaning 'between' and *potamos* meaning 'river'. It is down in the area almost to the Gulf where Abraham lives in the little city of Ur of the Chaldees—a thriving city, by the way.

Sir Leonard Wooley, a Britisher, excavated the city many years ago, finding two-story homes with indoor plumbing. Some of the most magnificent pieces of artwork we have ever seen were found in the royal tombs of Ur. These tombs were like pieces of history, frozen in time. When a king or queen died, everyone in the royal palace would be drugged. Then, holding onto the manes of horses or onto carts, they would accompany the casket down into graves in underground vaults. The tombs were then sealed off, leaving those who were in the cortege to die as the oxygen was used up. We have found bodies with animals fallen on top of them. This frozen bit of history—room after room—was loaded with the most magnificent gold and silver! It was an extremely luxurious time, and we have not seen work like that until the modern era. Some of their jewelry in gold leaf and silver, using gemstones of lapis lazuli, is an inspiration for jewelry being produced now.

So Ur is not a deadbeat town; actually, when Abraham lives there it is posh. I mean, it is a five-star town! But Abraham leaves that behind and goes up along the east side of the Euphrates River to little Mesopotamia, where we have the city of Haran. As is true also of Ur of the Chaldees, Haran is a center for the worship of the moon god. Abraham camps here for a while, and then God directs him to go north and then swing southward around American archeologist James Breasted's famous Fertile Crescent, all the way over into Canaan. This is a long way to drive sheep and herds, to get them and one's family all over there safely.

### The Focus of Genesis 12

Why do the Scriptures delay discussing Abraham's faith until Genesis 15 when his story really begins in Genesis 12? I think that there are some good reasons. First of all, the focus of Genesis 12 is on the land. In Genesis 12:7, the Lord says, "To your offspring I will give this land." So Abraham built an altar there to God who had appeared to him. The land promise takes precedence in this part of Abraham's story. Notice that this focus is interrupted by famine which becomes a threat to the land. In order to sustain life, he and his family must leave and go down into Egypt.

### The Focus of Genesis 13

When we come to Genesis 13, the focus is still on the land. Abraham and Lot are disputing over where their flocks and herds can graze because they have so many animals. Abraham makes a magnanimous gesture. He says to Lot, "You choose."

Lot says, "Well, I'll go down there; I'll take that posh, luxurious section down by the Dead Sea. I'll go over there by Sodom and Gomorrah, Admah, Zeboiim, and Zoar, the five cities of the plain. That has the best grass around here."

So Abraham is left with the hills. But Abraham trusts God. And, of course, Lot is caught in the snare of city life, being too close to the world.

By the time we get to Genesis 14, we find that four kings from Mesopotamia come to fight for this luxurious spot, too. Critics say this is impossible: people just did not travel that far. Even Abraham could not have made that kind of trip, they say.

But scholars have found indications that people did travel great distances. East of the Tigris River in what today is Iran, there is a little site called Nuzi or Nuzu. (Most scholars say Nuzi, but some call it Nuzu.) A group of tablets was found at this site which came from the period right after the patriarchal times. One of the tablets was like a Hertz or Avis rental contract—I don't know which agency was "trying harder"—stating that a rented wagon must not be taken all the way to the Mediterranean Sea. Now, if a contract for renting wagons had a warning not to take the wagons as far as the Mediterranean Sea, it means some were doing just that!

Also, up on the Euphrates River is a site named Mari, which dates from approximately the time of the patriarchs. I think that is where the tablet with the rental wagon contract actually originated. That ought to answer the question whether people could travel that far or not.

So these four kings come over to this place along the Dead Sea, probably right where there is a little extension of land on the Jordanian eastern side which we call the *lashon*, meaning the 'tongue'. To get down there, the kings would have traveled the distance of the heart-shaped Sea of Galilee, the distance of the squiggly Jordan River—about 65 miles as the crow flies,

200 miles by rowboat—down to the Dead Sea. We used to think they went down to the lower end of the sea, which is about 53 miles in length. But now we have identified five sites with the five cities of the plain. It was probably to the area of these five cities that Lot went with his herds.

Well, these kings knew about the luxuriousness of these cities, which, as we've seen, were not just wide spots in the road. At Bab ed Dra, Jordan, located just up the hill a little bit from the five cities of the plain, excavators have uncovered a site dated 2000 to 1800 BC, from the time of the patriarchs. And we have found there—hold on to your hats!—500,000 graves! A half million people over a period of 200 years!

There is wickedness in these five cities. God sees that and wants to destroy them. But Abraham, over at Hebron up in the highlands, bargains with God and says, "Lord, if there are 50 people there who believe in you, will you save the place?" (Some who are unfamiliar with the population might think: Boy, that would be everyone there, if they all believed!) Abraham continues bargaining with God, "Would you make it 35?" Then, "Lord, sorry to bring up the question again, but what about 20?" And soon Abraham is saying, "Look, Lord, how about 10? If there are 10 righteous people there, will you save the city?"

This brings up the whole principle of the moral minority, the remnant theme. Listen to me carefully: it's very interesting to note how God deals with this moral minority group. If we divide the population into generations, I figure we're talking about 75,000 to 100,000 people living there at one time. So actually Abraham is saying to God, "For 10 righteous people, will you let 75,000 go?" Those are the proportions. The Lord says, "Yes, I will save the city if there are only 10 righteous out of 75,000." Very interesting!

In any case, we remember how this episode ends. Punishment in the form of fire and brimstone comes in Genesis 18–19. But previous to the destruction of Sodom and Gomorrah, the four kings go to war against the five kings of the plain. The four kings take everything from Sodom and Gomorrah, including Lot and his family. By the time Abraham finds out about this and catches up to Lot, they have gone all the way north of Dan. Abraham outmaneuvers the group and the four kings and catches up to Lot at night with 318 trained servants. Now, we're not talking about 318 simple shepherd boys. These fellows are Abraham's CIA, or the equivalent of Brink's officers! Abraham has his capital with him—capital meaning in that day head of stock. And this man has an enormous bankroll. So we can understand why Abraham has these men with him; he has a vested interest in the matter. He leaves all of his flocks and goes overnight and overtakes them, and whips the four kings! And then he brings Lot and his goods back.

That is when Melchizedek, apparently a Canaanite—a non-Israelite—comes out of Jerusalem, the city of peace, and says, "Hallelujah! Praise the Lord! This is wonderful!" Melchizedek seems to come from nowhere.

He blesses Abraham, and in turn Abraham gives Melchizedek tithes, one-tenth of what he brought back in spoils. The king of Sodom offers to allow Abraham to keep all the spoils of the raid except the people captured. But Abraham says, "I don't want anybody saying that I made myself rich. If anything's going to happen, God's going to make me rich; so take the loot."

## The Expression of Abraham's Faith: Genesis 15

Those are the concerns of Genesis 12, 13, and 14. In these chapters, something is being put into place; then finally in Genesis 15 the text does more than just mention Abraham's faith. Here is the first real expression of it.

### Its Preparation

What important things needed to surface before Abraham's faith is talked about? First, there is the problem of the heir. The text says in Genesis 15:1-2, "After this, the word of the LORD came to Abram in a vision: 'Do not be afraid, Abram. I am your shield, your very great reward.'" And Abram says, "O Sovereign LORD, O LORD of Hosts, what can you give me since I remain childless? I mean, I've had this promise now for many years." Abraham is now 100 and the promise was made to him when he was 75 years old, several chapters back in Genesis. Twenty-five years have gone by. He's not getting any younger, and all there is to the promise is words! Words, words, words!

So Abraham decides to make a move, perhaps thinking to himself, "Isn't there a verse that says, 'God helps those that help themselves'?" So he says, "Look, God, I've got this Arab, Eliezer from Damascus, working for me as the steward of my house." (Can you imagine that? Those were different days, weren't they!) He says, "I can arrange this legally; I'll just adopt this fellow as my son." I've seen references to this type of "legal fiction" in the tablets uncovered at Mari. Real estate could not be sold; it had to be kept within the family. But by legally adopting a son, people could pass land back and forth. So Abraham figures he can arrange it this way. He says, "There, Lord, I helped you. You gave me an heir, right?"

The Lord says, "Wrong! Don't try to help me. I'll do it myself." The Lord says to him, "This man will not be your heir." That's clear. According to Genesis 15:4, God says, "A son coming from your own body will be your heir."

Why does the Genesis text wait this long to tell us about justification and to tell us about Abraham's belief in God? Because the topic of the heir —the son—needed to be brought up, that's why. There is a theological pause in Abraham's story: chapters 12–14 talk about the land and the rescue and establishment of Lot. Finally in Genesis 15 it is time to move from a discussion about the inheritance to a discussion about the heir.

## Its Substance

So moving on to the heir, God says, "A son coming from your own body will be your heir." He takes Abraham outside and says, "Look up at the heavens and count the stars—if indeed you can count them. So shall your offspring be. What do you think, Abraham?"

Abraham says, "Amen! If you say it, God, I believe it. It's good enough for me."

The Lord says, "Good. You know what I figure that to be?" God adds and adds and adds and gets the grand total, tax and all. He says, "Justified!"

Abraham believed God! In what way did he believe God? He believed the word of God about the promise of the seed. We must give this its full theological weight. We cannot just quote Genesis 15:6 as a Bible verse of systematic theology on believing: "Abraham believed the LORD." No, it is much more than that! Abraham believed *on Yahweh*; he believed *to Yahweh*; and he believed *for Yahweh*! It isn't enough to say that it is *Elohim*—that it is God in general—in whom he believed. In that case, Abraham would be a theist, you see. Now, would God reckon *that* to him as righteousness? With this kind of interpretation, it is no wonder we get into problems.

I told you that the Old Testament is *the* master problem of theology. Indeed, this point is important because it has implications for missions: *Are the heathen lost who have not heard?* Would we say that it counts to the heathen for righteousness if the Hottentots or the Aborigines believe generally—as a theist—in God? We call that 'essential faith'. Why would this idea even occur to us? We could incorrectly think, Well, as in the Old Testament, Abraham just believed that there was a God and he was saved. Was that all there was to it? The answer to this master problem of theology will affect missions.

Many people have used such reasoning with me, and they worry me because they don't understand the text. In searching to understand a passage, they forget the basic context. Context! When you do biblical studies, you need to focus on "Context! Context!" just as on a football field after a goal is scored, the crowd wants the team to focus on "Defense! Defense!" So what is the context?

Let's look at it. The context says, "Look, this man won't be your heir, but a son coming from your own body will be the heir. And not only will you have a son, but your seed will be as numerous as the stars in the sky, so many that you can't count them. Do you believe that?" And Abraham believed God. He believed *God*. God what? The God who said that there would be an heir coming from Abraham's body and that, indeed, his seed would be as numerous as the stars. We've got to understand the context! Context! Context!

So then, what was the object of faith? On what did faith terminate, i.e., what was its object? Who was the object? Is it right to say that in the

Old Testament people believed in God in a general way? *Nein! Nicht! Non! Nyet!* Rather, they believed in the man of promise who was to come. I don't think we can put it any other way. They believed in the heir; they believed in the seed of the woman that had been promised ever since Genesis. That is the great theme and the passion of my heart in this section.

Something new appears in Genesis 15:1: "Fear not; do not be afraid." That's the cue: Fear not. Then the text talks about human means once again; works are contrasted with faith. And the works here are an obstacle. Abraham's trying to solve the problem by himself is not a good move. God reacts to the human means Abraham concocts to establish Eliezer, an Arab from Damascus, Syria, as his heir. God says, "No, no, that's wrong." In Genesis 15:5, God repeats his promise and enlarges on it. So we have the progress of revelation going on here. The substance of that promise, then, is quite clear.

But several texts are used incorrectly with regard to faith in the Old Testament. In my textbook, *Toward Rediscovering the Old Testament,* I have cited certain texts like Acts 17:30, where Paul is on Mars Hill. This text is used by some to say that the people in the Old Testament did not know about Christ. But understanding the context makes all the difference! Look at what Paul says: "In the past God overlooked such ignorance." Some understand this to mean the ignorance of the people in the Old Testament. Well, I want to tell you that using this Scripture passage that way is improper. This interpretation is incorrect. The 'ignorance' spoken of here is the ignorance of the Athenians, not that of people in the Old Testament.

In the same book I also cite Romans 3:25, which says that God presented Jesus "as a sacrifice of atonement, through faith in his blood. He did this to demonstrate his justice, because in his forbearance he had left the sins committed beforehand unpunished." The question here is of the forbearance of God: Did he leave sins committed beforehand unpunished? It is certainly a difficult passage. But on the other hand, I think that the suggestion that I have attempted to make in this same textbook, *Toward Rediscovering the Old Testament* (p. 126) is at least somewhat helpful. The tolerance shown by the forbearance of God for the sins committed beforehand, as Romans 3:25 says, was only with regard to the final work of satisfaction of the justice of God in the death of Christ, and not with regard to a special deal on sinning without any culpability or record of the sins during Old Testament days, since they were done in ignorance.

As we have seen, the "times of ignorance" in Acts 17:30 involved the Athenian Gentiles, not Israel. But appropriate for Israel was the rebuke made to the two disciples on the road to Emmaus in Luke 24:25: "O fools, and slow of heart to believe all that the prophets have spoken" (AV).

That some in Israel were just as ignorant as the Athenians of the Messiah and his work, we cannot argue with that. John 1:21 and John 7:40

make it obvious that some did not know. Even the two disciples on the road to Emmaus were ignorant. But that does not detract one iota from what they could and what they should have known. In fact, 1 Peter 1:10-11 specifically affirms that the only item on which those who had the Scriptures could plead ignorance was the matter of time. To not know other facts was to be culpable.

So we must ask the question: Does Genesis 15:6 mean that it was at that point that Abraham first believed? And we answer, No! It was not at that time that he first believed, but it is the first time in the text that we see a statement of his justification. Indeed, it would appear that his belief was expressed quite early through his actions. In the New Testament, Jesus says, "If you love me, then do the things I say." So it would seem that Abraham loved God and really knew him, because when the Lord said, "Leave Ur of the Chaldees," he obeyed. Ur of the Chaldees was where his wealth was, where his friends were, where he could find entertainment. It was where the good life was for him, where his kids were established in their high schools with their friends. He had all the things which attract and draw us in our lives today, and yet he left. So way back at this time, we could make a case for the idea that Abraham believed God.

But the discussion of it in Genesis does not come up in chronological order; rather, it appears in topical order. It is in this order because we needed to wait for the crisis concerning the heir, so that we might see that faith is grounded in evidence. And that is what is taking place here. Abraham believed God, and what he believed God about was the seed that was to come. This is a very key chapter in relating to us the expression of Abraham's faith.

### The Dream

A very important scene takes place here in which God comes to Abraham in a dream (Gen 15:12ff.). Toward the end of the day, as the sun is setting, Abraham falls into a deep sleep. A thick, dreadful darkness comes over him. Then the Lord says to him, "Know for certain that your descendants"— or, better translated, your seed—"will be strangers in a country not their own, and they will be enslaved and mistreated four hundred years. But I will punish the nation they serve as slaves, and afterward they will come out with great possessions. You, however, will go to your fathers in peace and be buried at a good old age. In the fourth generation your descendants will come back here, for the sin of the Amorites has not yet reached its full measure." (By the way, from these verses we have the basis for arguing that a generation was 100 years at that time in history. God says 400 years and in the fourth generation: 400 divided by four equals 100 years. Another indication as to the length of a generation is the Syriac word for generation: 80 years. So let's be careful about saying that a generation is only 40 years.)

Genesis 15:17 says, "When the sun had set and darkness had fallen, a smoking firepot with a blazing torch appeared and passed between the pieces …" (NIV). We see this dividing into two halves of the heifer, the she goat, and the ram in Genesis 15:9-10, which sets the stage for the covenant. What is a covenant? A covenant is an agreement made between two parties; it can be bilateral or unilateral. In a bilateral covenant, the two sides participate equally—obligate themselves equally—to maintain the agreement. In a unilateral agreement, only one side obligates itself to the benefit of the other side. Here we have the word *covenant*, with the more complete expression being 'to cut a covenant'; *karat berit* means 'to *cut* a covenant'; however, we translate it 'to *make* a covenant'. To cut a covenant in the Near East meant to literally take animals and divide them in half, putting one-half of the animal on one side of an aisle and the other half of the animal on the other side. Birds which were too small to be divided were put on one side, but all other animals were divided. Then the two persons entering into the agreement would ceremonially walk between the pieces, saying in effect, "If I fail to keep the parts of this agreement, may it happen to me what has happened to these animals. May I die!"

So the sun has gone down. Abraham has laid out the pieces on the two sides of an aisle. He falls asleep and sees God in a vision, moving as a smoking torch—a burning furnace—passing between the pieces of animals. (One of God's manifestations is fire. For example, Hebrews will say: "Our God is a consuming fire.") God moves through these things and obligates only himself, saying a horrendous thing: "May it happen to me what has happened to these pieces—may I, God, die—if I don't fulfill what I told you about an heir, about an inheritance, and about the heritage of the gospel. May I pass off the scene." May God drop dead!

Remember the God Is Dead movement? Here is the one circumstance in which that could possibly happen. God is saying, "May God drop dead!" We could say, "What about Abraham? Let's have him walk through as well, in essence saying, 'If I don't keep up my side of the bargain, then God is off the hook.'" That is the way some people do read this, but the text explicitly says that Abraham does not walk through the pieces. So forget that idea; the agreement was not bilateral. What we have here is an unconditional agreement. I don't see how we can argue it any other way. The agreement that God makes—with regard to salvation, with regard to Abraham's son, with regard to the land, and with regard to the gospel itself—is not based upon *if* we keep up or *if* we do or *if* we maintain our side of the bargain. That would not be grace; that would be merit.

Now, some will agree that this is a unilateral covenant with regard to the gospel and with regard to the Messiah, but would say that it is not true as it concerns the land. As you know, at this point in history there is a debate about the land boundaries. The Reformed element is less interested in this question than the Dispensationalists. But at the turn of the century, this question was not a problem for at least five leading theologians in the Reformed group. And had there not been the Six Day War in 1967, Hendrikus Berkhof, a neo-orthodox writer (not to be confused with Louis Berkhof), would have made a proposal to the World Council of Churches that we stop our spiritualizing, our dichotomizing, and that we make a statement that the gospel given to Abraham was also connected with the material promise that God gave to the land of Israel in an everlasting covenant.

However, one month before that proposal was to be introduced and voted upon, the Six Day War broke out; it then became politically inadvisable to bring it up. The substance of the proposal and the history behind it appeared in *Encounter* magazine, which is the organ of the World Council of Churches or at least represents the ecumenical point of view. That is not my own point of view, but it is an interesting thing that such a resolution almost passed in our time. And so, we see a difference of opinion as to the covenant, whether it is unilateral *in all its elements*.

As our narrative continues, God passes between the pieces in an *unconditional* agreement. Had both God and Abraham passed between them, then it would have been conditional. Then it would have been merely a social contract; that is, if one side faulted, then both sides would have been relieved of responsibility. But that is not what we have here. We have an unconditional agreement. I'm sorry, I can't read it any other way.

## The Similarities of Abraham's Faith to Our Believing in Christ

The last thing that needs to be brought up here is the similarities between Abraham's faith and our own believing in Christ.

### In Its Exclusion of Merit

In both cases, merit is excluded. God does the accounting; God does the reckoning; God does the crediting; God does the justifying—the declaring of this man to be just. Abraham does nothing. God gave the promise which Abraham had only to receive. Sometimes the question is asked, Is believing a work in itself? Do we have "faith in faith"? Can we pull ourselves up by our own bootstraps? The answer, of course, is that faith is passive. It is a passive act. It is like receiving a Christmas present: we put out our hands to take, to accept, to receive. There is nothing more than a passive act here. We don't earn our Christmas presents. The same is true with faith.

Any time Abraham attempted to earn his faith, he dug himself deeper into a hole. This was true with regard to Sarah, with regard to the famine, with regard to the legal fiction of an heir. Later on, even in the case of Jacob's trying to patch things up with his own brother, Esau, it got them into trouble. So faith is exclusive of merit. The text communicates that over and over again. Without using the word *grace*, it has all the earmarks of grace. It really does.

### In Its Employment of Terms

We need to look at several other terms used here. What does it mean here to 'believe'? It means to accept, to trust. We might answer that it is a mental, an emotional, a volitional act. Perhaps. None of that is fully stated here, except that Abraham does agree with God when God says that he will do the impossible. And we must agree that it does look impossible, with Abraham being 100 years old and Sarah being 90 years old. And God says, "Look, there's still coming a child out of your own loins. I want you to understand that." "Okay," Abraham responds, "that's your problem." And he believes God. He trusts God. His faith is not just faith in faith, but faith in God who can do what he says with regard to this heir.

So it is like John 3:16. It is believing that God gave his son, his heir. "There is no other name given under heaven"—*none*—"whereby we must be saved" (Acts 4:12). The object of faith is the same for us as it was for Abraham. It can only come from belief in that one who is to come, our Lord Jesus. It is not of works, lest any man—including Adam, Eve, or Noah—should boast and say, I did it myself.

The Scriptures in Ephesians are clear: "Not of works lest any should boast." *Any!* And I take that to mean *any ever*, *any any*where, *any any*time. No one in heaven will say, "I earned my way here." No group of self-made men will sit in one corner of heaven, saying, "I did it myself!"

What does it mean to be declared just? I think that this is the root, *tsadaq*, *ts-d-q*—three letters (*ts* represents one letter, *tsade*, in Hebrew): *ts-d-q*. It's *tsadaq*, which means to justify, to *declare* just. It does not mean to *make* just. It is a declaration of God.

And what does the phrase "of grace and not of works" mean? The illustration from Abraham's own life can help us here. Abraham suggests helping God: "Well, now that I see we're not able to have children and that Sarah is in menopause, I'll help you. I will take this man—I will take Eliezer—and I will adopt him." But God says no to that, too.

I think that is the heart of the Christian theology of saving faith. God's answer is: "You will have a son, and your children will be as numerous as the stars in the sky. Do you believe that?"

Abraham, looking up at the stars, says, "Yes."

God says, "It's done! *Declare that man just.*" To me that's a beautiful, simple, yet complex picture of what saving faith is all about. It is God's work for individuals.

# Chapter Six

# The Theology of the People of God

## Exodus 1–19

Between chapter 5 and this chapter, 400 years have passed. No one disputes the 400 years of silence between Malachi and the New Testament, but not everyone realizes there was another approximately 400-year period of silence between the end of Genesis and the beginning of Exodus. In our last chapter we learned in Genesis 15 that the people of Israel would go to Egypt for four generations and be there for 400 years. Now that time has expired. However, these 400 years did see the fulfillment of the word given in Genesis 15:12ff.

As we begin the book of Exodus, remember God's word in Genesis 1:28 which says, "Be fruitful, and multiply, and fill the earth." Look at what we have now. The Israelites have multiplied greatly. They have become so exceedingly numerous that the land is filled with them. Exodus 1:7 uses seven Hebrew words to speak of the fulfillment of the word that God gave to Abraham that his seed would become numerous and that he would increase and multiply. In the English language we do not have all of the seven Hebrew words for 'increase'—this would be too tautological and overextended—but this verse certainly underlines the fulfillment of Genesis 1:28. Here, then, is the formation of a nation. It is an amazing thing to see the plan of God develop: a nation is formed and, more than that, a people of God is formed. So now we come to the concept of a 'people'.

## Introduction

Already in the patriarchal age God promised, "I will personally be your God." In the book of Exodus two other elements are added to that formula. First God states, "You will be a people." What does it mean to be a people of God? Second, God promises to come and personally dwell in the midst of us. The theme "I will be your God, you shall be my people, and I will dwell in the midst of you" stretches from Genesis—or at least here in the book of Exodus—all the way through Revelation. As a matter of fact, as we conclude the last book of the New Testament, which talks about the new heaven and the new earth, God is saying, "Now I am your God, you are my people, and I am dwelling in the midst of you" (Rev 21:3). The last word that we hear in the Bible's closing scene is that God puts his final mark and stamp on history: God stamps it "Finished!"

As a matter of fact, there are three times in history when God said or will say, "It is done. *Finis*." The first one was when God marked the end of his work in creation and the beginning of his work in providence. That moment in history is called the 'stop day,' *shabbat*. God stopped; God ceased his work on the Sabbath. The Hebrew word *shabbat* means to stop or cease. It is done!

So his work in creation was done and he began his work in providence and history, which he continues even now. During this period of time in history, the phrase, "It is finished," occurred a second time. Traditionally we speak of the Seven Last Words or last cries of Jesus on the cross. Two of these are quotations from Psalm 22, which indicates that this entire psalm was on the mind of our Lord. The fourth cry from the cross was "My God, my God, why hast thou forsaken me?" (AV) which is found in Psalm 22:1. By the way, we pronounce that *Eli* as "*my* God, *my* God." I hear so many read that Scripture improperly and make it into an oath, but to put the emphasis on God reverses the meaning. Only those who claim God as *their* God can cry out to him in distress and expect relief, which does come in this psalm. Psalm 22:31 concludes this passage with "It is done—he has done it." The sixth cry of Jesus on the cross was "*Tetelestai*—it is done!"

The third instance in which God will say "*Finis*" will mark the boundary between history and eternity, when God will have completed his work and will have finished his promises in time and in space, and then will go on into eternity. God will say one more time, "It is done" (Rev 21:6).

So we've got three *tetelestai*'s, in effect: three times when God says, "It is done." We could actually map out the works of God in three great segments with the three times he said, "It is finished": creation ending with *shabbat*; providence and history; eternity.

Peppered throughout the second great segment of providence we find this tripartite formula of promise: "I will be your God, you shall be my people, and I will dwell in the midst of you." It is the 'peopleness'—the peoplehood—that we want to talk about in this sixth chapter. What is God's motivation for this peoplehood concept? The motivation is shown in Exodus 2:24, where God heard the groaning of the people in Egypt and remembered his covenant; "he remembered his covenant with Abraham, with Isaac and with Jacob." So God *remembered*.

This theology of remembering is extremely important. What the Bible means by remembering is a lot different from our definition. (The Hebrew word *zakar*, 'to remember', is the root of the name Zachariah, for instance.) Remembering does not mean merely to call to mind. When 1 Samuel 1:19 says the Lord "remembered" Hannah, it does not mean God slapped his forehead and said, "Hannah, now what was your request?" because he suddenly remembered her. That's not what it means. To remember is not only to call to mind; it is also to act. When the Lord remembered Hannah, she became pregnant. He did something on her behalf.

Therefore, in our communion service when we say, "Do this in remembrance of me," it does not simply mean to squint our eyes and think about a hill roughly in the shape of a skull with three crosses on it, the one in the middle traditionally taller than the other two. No! To remember the Lord is to bring to mind what he did and to act appropriately. To remember calls for a corresponding response-action, because of the one who gave so much for us. That is what it means to remember the death and the resurrection of our Lord.

So we must keep in mind biblical terminology; we must get used to the Bible's way of using words. When the Lord says he remembers Israel, it does not mean that, all of a sudden after 400 years, he is saying, "Oh, no! I forgot! There's Isaac, Jacob, Israel. I had forgotten them." No, it means that he is now ready to act and he will act on their behalf. That is the motivation for peoplehood. And because he has acted on his words before, he will do it again. We can depend on it.

The basis for this also becomes the revelation of a new name for God. Even though way back in Genesis 4, during the days of Cain and Abel, people began to call on the name of Jehovah, or *Yahweh*, we will argue that the nature or the personality or the characteristics of the name were not known by the people. These had not yet been revealed. Yet there are over 150 references to Jehovah in Genesis prior to the revelation of all the name meant in Exodus.

It is a fact that the name *Yahweh* does appear in Genesis, and yet there is a verse in Exodus which says, "I appeared to Abraham, to Isaac and Jacob as *El Shaddai*, God Almighty, but by my name *Yahweh* I was not known [or, I did not make myself known] to them." This causes a problem for some as to the authorship of Genesis. Critics say, See that! (By the way, there are several verses which critics believe very, very literally. For instance, there is the one in John 17, "That they may all be one.") But the verse we are talking about here is Exodus 6:3, which non-evangelicals have traditionally used as the basis for attributing authorship. Since Exodus says God was not known to them by that name, and since the name *Yahweh* does appear in Genesis, non-evangelicals tell us that this indicates the 'J' document. Therefore, according to these people, it was a later document.

This idea really captured a lot of unsuspecting, woolly-headed, fuzzy-minded thinkers who were former conservatives. You understand, today's conservatives are tomorrow's liberals. Tomorrow's liberals are in conservative seminaries today. Never forget that! The liberal camp is not being bolstered by liberals witnessing in downtown Detroit, or Chicago, or Los Angeles. No, that's not happening. What is happening is that those who are coming to the Savior through the witness of fundamentalists and evangelicals later change their views. A devolution of views comes about. So we must understand that when we're dealing with a liberal, we're usually dealing with someone who used to travel with us and went out from among us.

But now, as we begin to look at the Mosaic period of revelation, it seems to me that God is going to do something brand new. God calls a man by the name of Moses.

Let's look at the life of Moses rather briefly by way of introduction. I think the best way to look at his life is to note the backdrop of servitude. Exodus 1 uses seven words in the second paragraph to stress servitude, rigor, and affliction. Just as there were seven words for increase in the first paragraph ending with verse 7, so in the second paragraph, verses 8-14, seven words stress hard bondage. Exodus 1:14 says the lives of the people of Israel are being made bitter with the hard labor of working with brick and mortar. Then, from verse 15 through the rest of the chapter, we have seven words for midwives. So if you happen to like the number seven, this is a great chapter: seven words for increase, seven words for servitude, and now seven words for midwives. However, I am not sure this number seven here has any significance.

The Hebrew midwives, Shiphrah and Puah, cannot possibly serve a whole nation of 2,000,000 people. We can assume that there are 2,000,000 people because the text says that there are 600,000 fighting men. We can also assume there is a wife and at least one child for each man: 3 x 600,000 = 1,800,000. So 2,000,000 is not too far off. We might ask if statistically, mathematically, this can really take place. Oh, yes, and the population could be much higher. Actually we could get almost double that number using the Malthus Population Growth Theory of doubling every 25 years. We start with Abraham in the year 2000 BC. The people of Israel spent 200 to 215 years in Canaan and 400 years in Egypt. This brings us up to 1400 BC. Yes, a population of 2,000,000 could very easily have been reached.

So we are at a very serious moment in the Israelites' history. These two women, Shiphrah and Puah, are called in by Pharaoh and are told that in his next pogrom he plans to rid the land of every Hebrew male child. Pharaoh, just as Hitler would, has all kinds of pogroms for getting rid of the Jewish population. For this latest one, he says, "Hey, kill every male child! I don't want any competitors."

But God has a wonderful sense of humor: Pharaoh, who wants to get rid of all the kids, makes one exception for his daughter who finds a Hebrew baby boy. He brings the boy up on a special scholarship and sends him to the best schools, which, of course, will be needed if he—unknown to Pharaoh—is going to lead the people of Israel. He will need to speak

Egyptian; he will need basic leadership training; he will need to master geography; he will need the camping experience of an Outward Bound program. And he gets all of this training.

By the way, we have many textbooks from Egypt devoted to this period. We even know what the geography lessons were like. The lessons progress in the Socratic method: When you come to such and such pond, what will you see? The answer is that when you come to pond such and such, you will see the following. The lessons proceed all the way through Palestine and Syria, so Moses apparently was given a Rand McNally mapping course, special courtesy of the man who hoped a leader would never appear for the Jews! What irony that Pharaoh was the very one responsible for the training of this leader!

When Pharaoh asks, "Have you had any male deliveries recently?" the midwives, Shiphrah and Puah, lie: "No, babies are being born all over the place, but we haven't made any male deliveries recently. Or the boy babies are born before we get there." One of my good friends, a faculty colleague from the past, argued in one of his books on ethics that this lie was for the greater good. Lying to protect life is not a problem, because God would say to choose the greater good. Saving lives would be more important than telling the truth.

Of course, this is similar to the Reformed position: Choose the lesser evil. According to this position, after leaving Pharaoh's presence, the midwives could just get down on their knees and confess their sins and say, "Dear Lord, I'm sorry I lied. Forgive me my sins." That's called choosing the lesser evil.

Now, I would take the position of non-conflicting absolutes. I think there is a way through the pass where dangers lurk on both sides. There is a way of escape: 1 Corinthians 10:13 says that God is faithful. "There has no temptation taken you but such as is common to man: but God is faithful and will provide with the temptation a way to escape." I think there is a way to escape here.

But these women choose the lesser of two evils and are lying through their teeth. "Who, us? No, we haven't made any male deliveries recently. Every time the baby is either a female or we miss the birth." The biblical text says that they feared God, though, and the Bible does approve of them! But we cannot say that endorsement in one area is an endorsement in all areas. This is another ethical principle the Bible teaches: God's approval of one thing in a person's life does not mean that he approves of all. For instance, David was a man after God's own heart, but I can think of some things that God didn't like. And Solomon is called Jedediah, "loved of the LORD." Here when this text says that God "built the midwives into houses," it means that he gave them families and perpetuated their families in Israel because they feared God more than they feared the king of Egypt, Pharaoh. But that was not an endorsement of everything they did.

We could say the same thing for Rahab. In the story of Rahab and the spies, we might say, Well, what choice does she have? She hides the spies. Then when the king of Jericho comes and says, "Hey, have you seen any Jews here recently?" she says, "Yeah, they went that-a-way." Now, the Bible doesn't stop and explicitly point out, "Uh-oh! Look at that! Look at what she just did!" Rather, it expects us to read it in context. We might say, What could she have done? I think she should have hidden the spies; yes, that was right. But she had no right to tell a lie. I think she should have said, "You think there are spies here? Come in and search for yourself."

Corrie ten Boom and her sister faced an identical situation in Holland during World War II. Corrie told the truth. I think she did the right thing; she hid the Jews well from the Nazi soldiers, and she answered the soldiers without giving a yes or no answer. There comes a point when some people forfeit their right to know *all* of the facts.

It is the same way in 1 Samuel 16 when Saul is in a stormy mood. The Lord tells Samuel, "Go up and anoint David."

Samuel says, "I should go and anoint David? Saul will have my head! That man is a maniac! How can I go?" "'*eyk 'elek?*" he asks in Hebrew, "How can I go?"

And the Lord says, "Take a sacrifice."

So when Saul meets Samuel, he says, "Hi, Samuel! What are you doing up here? This is not your circuit for today."

Samuel replies, "That's true, but I came up here."

"Why?"

"The Lord told me to come."

"What did he say?"

"Well, he said to offer a sacrifice."

"Oh, okay!"

If Saul had said, "And what else did he say?" then I think Samuel would have been stuck. Saul didn't ask for further information, so a partial truth was not an untruth. I think Saul had forfeited his right to know everything.

The same thing can happen to a pastor when visiting someone who is really sick. The doctor has even confided to the pastor how deathly sick the person is: "To tell you the truth, I've never seen a worse case. I don't even know if it's worth going to see him; he's way beyond anything I've ever seen. It's hopeless." Would the pastor repeat to the patient what the doctor said in private about his condition? We would say that would be cruel to put it that way to the patient. If we can accept not blatantly stating the whole truth in this situation, then why not accept it also in biblical terms?

At any rate, the family hides this child, Moses, but soon he is old enough that they can no longer contain his crying. So the mother has an ingenious plan. She says, "Miriam, you're older." She was about eight or so. "You go with him. Take him down to the river; you know, where Pharaoh's daughter comes down to bathe. Now, I don't think any woman can resist a baby when she hears him crying. I think there's an instinct put there by God, so I'll be praying that the princess will take our baby. You watch, Miriam, and when the princess says, 'What are we going to do for Similac?' that's when you say, 'I know where you can get a wet nurse.' And then bring him back home again." This is an ingenious plan, well-devised, and that's exactly what happens. For the Lord works in the heart of the princess, who goes to her daddy and says, "Oh, Daddy, can't I have just one little Jewish boy?" He says, "Fine, yeah, it's okay." So, Moses was that one Jewish boy, raised in the royal court.

One day when this young man has grown, you remember, he sees an Egyptian pummeling a Hebrew. And he says, "This is not fair!" Boom! Pow! Wham! Bam! And he kills the guy. This is murder! Augustine rationalizes it by saying that he did it by the Spirit of God, but I don't see that. I just think he broke. Look at his conscience: he looks this way and he looks that way, and then he digs a grave and gets rid of the *corpus delicti*. He does not want any evidence left out in the open. That shows a guilty conscience.

The next day he sees two Hebrews fighting. This fellow just can't stand injustice! There he comes again. He may not come out of a phone booth with his cape on like Superman, but there he comes charging in. And then, like a slap in the face, one of his fellow countrymen says, "Are you going to kill me the way you killed the Egyptian yesterday?"

He straightens up fast and says, "How did you know that?"

The other man says, "It's known all over."

And Moses decides, It's time to make that trip to Midian I've been thinking about.

As a matter of fact, when he comes over into Midian, he is still wearing Egyptian clothes. The seven daughters of Reuel are trying to draw water at the well, but shepherds chase them off. So Moses says, "That's not right! Those women were there first!" He holds the shepherds at bay. Wham! Pow! He's not at all sheepish about it. He tells them, "Stand aside! These women were here first." And he even helps the women draw water.

There is a beautiful story here about Moses and Zipporah, one of the seven daughters of Reuel. (Zipporah comes from *tsippor*, meaning bird, and *ah*, which is the feminine ending.) She goes home and says to her father, "Daddy, we're home early today because an Egyptian helped us! I can't believe it! This guy is macho! He's a real brute."

So Reuel says, "Bring that man home! Don't you know Emily Post etiquette?"

Moses comes to live with them; Moses and Zipporah fall in love; and Moses continues to live with them for forty years in the desert.

So, having gone to Thebes Tech for forty years, now he goes to the Midianite school for forty years. That early morning episode shows that he really needs God's training. He has blown it because he is so impetuous. Because of his sense of fairness and justice, he has taken things into his own hands. He still needs more time in God's school.

Moses settles down on a ranch in Midian, and then after forty years God shows him a burning bush. As Exodus 3 tells us, God is going to call him through this burning bush. If it had been up to us Americans, we would have done it in a more grandiose way, setting the whole desert on fire or putting up a big sign: "Moses, go to Egypt now!" But here's just another tumbleweed on fire. If you have ever kicked those things around or gotten them in your foot or tried to pull them out of the feet of sheep and goats, you would say, "Burning? Praise the Lord! I hope they all burn!" But there is just this one burning bush. And God looks to see if this man is too big to take notice.

Moses does look to see why it won't burn up. God calls to him, "Moses! Moses!" (*Moshe! Moshe!*).

Moses answers, "*Hinneni.* Here am I."

God commands, "Take off your sandals."

"What do you mean, take off my sandals? These sandals are a part of me. I feel authentic in these things. I've been trucking around in them for forty years."

God says, "Take them off."

"What do you mean, God? This is the Now Generation! This is mod! What do you mean, take them off?"

God says, "Take them off because this is holy ground."

"Holy ground? No offense, Lord, but sheep and goats went across it yesterday, you know. How can this be holy ground?"

"Take them off. Take them off, Moses."

"Why? I don't understand."

"Because I am present."

There is a lesson in worship here. In the 1960s, people had three-piece suits sitting at home in their closets, but they decided they were just fine in cloroxed jeans. Theologically speaking, what's so important about the sandals Moses is wearing? Or for that matter, the tattered jeans of the 1960s? Nothing, except that taking his sandals off is a way of wholistically acknowledging the presence of God. We can extend this wholistic attitude about our bodies and our clothing to our preparation for meeting with God, just as Moses was commanded to do. This is the theology of worship.

There at the burning bush God tells Moses to go back to Egypt. Exodus 4:22-23 tells us that Moses is commanded to go see Pharaoh and to say to him, "This is what the LORD God says: Israel is my son, even my firstborn." This is one of the first great developments in the theology of the people of God. God invests this theology of his people with more meaning as he calls them his son, his possession, his kingly priest. We shall look into these for the remainder of this chapter.

## Israel as God's Son

First, Israel is God's son. Here "my son" and "my firstborn" take on the significance of corporate solidarity. These two terms are used for the one who represents the group and also for the many who will be "my son, my firstborn." Deuteronomy 1:31 and 32:6 give us this concept of 'my son'. In the New Testament, Matthew 2:15 says, "This happened to bring about what the Lord had said through the prophet: 'I have called my son out of Egypt.'" The prophet quoted here is Hosea, who says, "When Israel was a child, I loved him, and out of Egypt I called my son" (Hos 11:1). Hosea is not giving this a spiritual meaning, but is referring to the exodus of the children of Israel from Egypt. The emphasis should fall on "*My son* I called out of Egypt" rather than put the emphasis on "*Out of* Egypt I called my son." The important thing here is *my son*. The point is that in the exodus, God preserved Christmas. God preserved Christmas—*my son*—for there is collective solidarity here. He protected the Messiah's coming as a baby at Christmastime when he led Israel across the Red Sea.

Notice that the prophet Hosea is quoted in Matthew 2:15 as Mary, Joseph, and the baby Jesus leave Nazareth to go down *into* Egypt; the passage is not quoted at the time when they *leave* Egypt. Had it been quoted at the time of their exodus from Egypt, the passage would be found around Matthew 2:20-22. So, just as God has preserved his nation in Egypt, he also preserves his son in that land! The point of this passage is preservation and the corporate identity of the group, rather than a reference to exodus, the fulfillment of exiting. This I argue in fuller detail in my book, *The Uses of the Old Testament in the New* (Moody Press, 1985).

Not only is Israel God's son, but Israel is God's *firstborn*. In this sense, the firstborn does not mean first in chronology, but rather first in rank, first in preeminence. In the case of Esau and Jacob, who is called the firstborn? It is Jacob, or Israel as he is later called. Is he the older twin? No, Esau was born before Jacob, and yet Jacob is called firstborn.

The same thing is true in the life of Joseph. He, also, has two sons, Ephraim and Manasseh. Who is the firstborn? Ephraim is called the first-born. Jeremiah 31:9 says, "Ephraim is my firstborn." But who came first chronologically? Manasseh was first in chronology. Who was first in rank? Who was first in preeminence? It was Ephraim.

When we come to the New Testament, we find many texts which call Christ the "firstborn." Romans 8:29 says that Christ is the firstborn among many brothers; Colossians 1:15 and 1:18 say that Christ is the firstborn over all creation and the firstborn from among the dead (also Rev 1:5); Hebrews 1:6 says that our Lord Jesus is God's firstborn. Some would argue from these texts that God came first, then he created Jesus, and then he created the world. This is the Arian heresy. This is the JW—Jehovah's Witnesses—heresy, for they teach that God made Jesus first, and therefore he is firstborn. This heresy results from a failure to understand biblical terminology. Firstborn doesn't mean first in order of appearance, but first in rank, first in preeminence. In each case in the Bible—at least in the cases that I've given you here—firstborn refers to rank.

Added to this meaning of preeminence is the idea of corporate, collective solidarity: the one and the many. What does Hebrews 12:23 say? "And to the church of the firstborn, ones whose names are written in heaven." So he refers to all believers as the firstborn, the firstborn ones. We have the firstborn who is Christ and then all who believe who are called the first-born, just as we have 'seed' which refers to the one and 'seed' which refers to all who believe. Or just as we have 'my son' which is one and 'my son' which is the whole nation of Israel. Again, we've got to come to terms with biblical terminology, with the collective solidarity of terms.

The significance is clear, then, in terms of Christ being God's firstborn, and believers, whether Jewish or Gentile, being firstborn ones. By the way, this verse was written in a Jewish book: Hebrews.

## Israel as God's Possession

But there is more. Israel is not only God's son and God's firstborn, but, secondly, Israel is God's *possession*. To the text in Exodus 4:22-23, add a second great text, Exodus 19:5-6. It's extremely important. God sends Moses back to Egypt, after he graduates from the Midianite school, to rescue his firstborn. The Israelites travel out of Egypt. In the third month they come down to the desert of Sinai. There we have the famous Eagle's Wing speech of Moses, which describes how God carries them just as a mother eagle takes her eaglets way up high and lets them go and then swoops down underneath them to catch them on her wings so they get the idea of how to flutter and fly. Just so, God has borne us up. This figure of speech, by the way, is also used in Genesis, where the Spirit of God is hovering, bearing up, sustaining the whole created order.

What is being said in Exodus 19:5-6? "Now if you obey me fully and keep my covenant, then out of all of nations you will be my *treasured possession*" (NIV). The word here, which used to be rendered 'peculiar people', comes from the word *pecunium*, which means money. It doesn't mean peculiar in the sense that Christians are oddities, that they have tics and odd mannerisms and idiosyncrasies. We do have those naturally; we don't need to ask for those by grace. But this is something other than our peculiarities. This is God saying, "You are my *segullah*." The word here in the original means 'movable treasure'. There is real estate which is fixed and presumably cannot be moved. Then there are things like jewelry and money that are movable. God puts us in the second category. He has real estate which cannot be moved, and he also has "un-real estate" which is movable treasure. That is the word used here.

So when God thinks about his portfolio and what he is really worth, he is worth us! That's an amazing statement. His worth is the believing community. So we have the concept of "You are my treasured possession," a very beautiful statement. Also, other names are given in this text, but we'll come back to that.

Let's go to an earlier statement during the Passover in Exodus 12:3. Here, according to the law of first reference, we find that the community is called a congregation for the first time: "Tell the whole community of Israel that on the tenth day of this month each man is to take a lamb" (NIV). The expression here is the whole *'edah*, meaning the whole congregation. Rather than translating it 'whole community', as some do, I think there is a better word. It is a congregation; it is an assembly of people which meets for purposes of carrying out the divine word.

As God's possession, they also become a *people*. Over and over again, Moses says to Pharaoh, "Let my people go ... let my people go." A nation, my people, a congregation, a treasured possession: we are establishing concepts for "You shall be my people."

In the midst of this narrative about Moses leading Israel out of Egypt, there comes in Exodus 6:2-8 one of the most significant passages on the revelation of God's name as Jehovah. The whole concept of "the God who is there" has not been revealed as fully up to this time as it is now to be revealed. God is going to show, now that he has formed a people, what it means for him to dwell in the midst of them. "I appeared to Abraham, to Isaac, and to Jacob by the name of God Almighty, but by my name Jehovah was I not known to them." The preposition here, known as a *beth essentiae*, is to be translated 'as' and means that God showed himself to Abraham, to Isaac, and to Jacob in the character of *El Shaddai*; but "in the character of my name *Yahweh* I did not make myself known to them." The *beth essentiae* (*beth* here being the second letter of the Hebrew alphabet—aleph, beth— and *essentiae* taken from the Latin) should be translated 'in the character of' or 'in the nature of'. The Gesenius-Kautzsch translation of the Hebrew grammar attests that it means 'in the character of'.

Such an analysis of Exodus 6:3 may be borne out by Exodus 3:13, where Moses protests that he does not actually want to lead the children of Israel. He counters, "They will say to me, '*What* is his name?'" It is not that Moses is afraid that he doesn't know God's name. That question would be asked with the interrogative *mi*—like the first part of Michael or Michelle or Micah. *Mi* means *who*. Michael means "Who is as God? Who can compare with God?" But here the Israelites ask not just, "What is his name?" but they ask a question with the interrogative *mah*, which goes far beyond that. *Mah* in the Hebrew asks, "What is his nature? What is his character?

What can he do in this kind of situation? What stuff is he made out of?" This is a very different question from simply asking, Who is this God? So the revelation of God's name is very important.

## Israel as God's Kingly Priests, a Holy Nation

Let's come back to a third name for Israel in Exodus 19:5-6. Israel is God's "kingly priest," a "holy nation." The text says that "Out of all the nations you will be my treasured possession. Although the whole earth is mine, you will be for me a kingdom of priests and a holy nation." Here, God shows his intention of making a priesthood of believers out of the whole nation.

Now, it's interesting that the Israelites will shrink back from this. When they hear the voice of God from heaven, they respond, "This is too awesome. We cannot stand in the presence of God. Moses, you be our representative and go up." God therefore delays until the New Testament times the full demonstration of the priesthood of believers. First Peter and Revelation show that we as Christians are a royal priesthood, a holy nation. What was announced in the Old Testament will be implemented in the New.

But at this point, God does invite the nation of Israel to be ruling mediators with direct access to God—the holy nation—on behalf of all the other nations of the world, that they should become leaders. Israel thus becomes a nation set apart, as God says through Moses in Exodus 20:20: "Do not be afraid, fear not, for indeed God has come to test you so that the fear of the LORD will be with you to keep you from sinning." Israel is a nation set apart. And so I take it that here God is going to ask them for holiness: "If you have come to believe in me, now therefore, how then should you walk?"

We need to ask one last question: Is the 'if' of Exodus 19:5 conditional, and does this change the unconditional promise of God into a conditional promise? "If you will obey my voice and keep my covenant ...." We must take this up in succeeding chapters. But we answer provisionally, No. The 'if' here is no more conditional than in John 15: "If you love me, keep my commandments," or the 'ifs' in the book of Hebrews. It is a call or election for service and, therefore, a holiness of life that ought to be an outcome and evidence of real faith and trust in the coming man of promise. We will develop this in subsequent chapters.

# Chapter Seven

# The Theology of the Law of God

## Introduction

The theology of the law of God is one of the most debated topics in the Christian world today. It is debated mainly because of the question of relevance. The authority of the text is not questioned, for that is the formal principle. Everyone says that, according to the formal principle, all parts of the Old Testament have equal authority over us. The material question, however, is the one where we have debate.

On this, Christians generally have two views. The first one says that everything the New Testament specifically *repeats* is normative. We could also express the first view in the negative: everything that the New Testament does not repeat from the Old Testament is now passé. The second view basically says that everything the New Testament *does not change* is normative. Two of the reformers, Luther and Calvin, illustrate these different approaches and this dichotomy of thinking on the relevance of the law.

Luther dismissed all attempts to base the current practice of Christians on the Old Testament. In arguing monastic vows, Luther said, "There is one answer that can be made to all attempts to cite passages from the Old Testament to support [monastic vows]. 'Do you Christians want to be Jews?' Prove your case from the New Testament. The Old Testament has been set aside through Christ and is no longer binding" ("An Answer to Several Questions on Monastic Vows," in *Luther's Works*, ed. Helmut T. Lehman [Philadelphia: Muhlenberg, 1960], 46:146). Well, that was pretty clear. Luther was saying, in effect, since the New Testament did not repeat what the Old Testament said, we're finished with the Old Testament. It is passé.

"To be sure," I say in *Toward Rediscovering the Old Testament* (Grand Rapids: Zondervan, 1987, p. 148), "Luther was not always consistent with this hermeneutic, for he could, on occasion, rest his whole case on the

68

Mosaic Law and Israelite practice." See his tract, for example, "That Parents Should Neither Compel Nor Hinder the Marriage of Their Children and That Children Should Not Become Engaged Without Their Parents' Consent." That was the title of one of the tracts found in *Luther's Works*, in which he based the whole point of what he was saying on the Mosaic Law. So there was ambivalence in Luther's thinking.

But his general policy was made famous in his essay on the topic of the law, "How Christians Should Regard Moses." Luther intoned in that essay (*Luther's Works*, 35:164-65):

> The Law is no longer binding on us because it was given only to the people of Israel. ... Exodus 20[:2] ... makes it clear that even the ten commandments do not apply to us. ... The sectarian spirits want to saddle us with Moses and all the commandments. We will skip that. We will regard Moses as a teacher, but we will not regard him as our lawgiver—unless he agrees with both the New Testament and natural law.

Luther was saying, "We cannot accept it." And his clear teaching has set a pattern for today. Many who are not within the Lutheran stream would say that teaching basically expresses their attitude.

Calvin, on the other hand, refused to relegate the Mosaic Law to the past. Instead, he pointed to Deuteronomy 32:46-47 and warned, "We are not to refer solely to one age David's statement that the life of a righteous person is a continual meditation upon the law ..., for it is just as applicable to every age, even to the end of the world" (*Institutes of the Christian Religion*, ed. John T. McNeill, trans. Ford Lewis Battles [Philadelphia: Westminster, 1960], 2.7.13). He was referring to Psalm 1:2, and he was saying that it's unfair to assume that, since that is part of the Old Testament, it refers only to that time. Therefore, we will say the same thing about Moses. This was his reasoning on Deuteronomy 32:46-47.

So what, we would ask Calvin, has been abrogated in the law? Did not Paul write that we are free from the law? Calvin's response was clear:

> What Paul says, as to the abrogation of the Law [Gal 3:10] evidently applies not to the Law itself, but merely to its power of constraining the conscience. For the Law not only teaches, but also imperiously demands.... We must be freed from the fetters of the law, ... those of rigid and austere exaction.... Meanwhile, ... the law has lost none of its authority, but must always receive from us the same respect and obedience [*Institutes*, 2.7.13].

Now we've got a dilemma. We have two of the heroes of the Reformation battling it out. Of course, both of these men are now in glory and probably have been to seminars on the subject, and I assume that they have straightened it out. So I would like to help you see their revised heavenly views.

## The Relationship of Promise to Old Testament Law

Actually, up to the present moment the issue is unresolved. But we are going to tackle it. We must ask, first of all: What is the relationship of promise to Old Testament law? So far in our study we have tried to establish that the plan of God through the Old Testament was basically the substance of the covenant. We have found that the New Testament writers, in reflecting on this, called the covenants the promise of God, the *epangelia*, or to coin an English word from the Greek term, the "epangel."

### The Distinction between the Unconditional and Conditional Covenants

This promise or covenant of God gets us into one of the most serious theological problems of our day. Are the covenants conditional or unconditional? As I've said, this discussion is still unfinished business left over from the Reformation. It is amazing how much difficulty we get into when we just theologize. What is needed in our day is a biblical theology that will take us back into exegesis of some of these problems.

We must simply ask two questions. First, is the Abrahamic-Davidic promise or covenant beyond cancellation? This is the promise first given to Eve, then to Shem, then to Abraham, then to Isaac, then to Jacob, then to David in the great passages of Genesis 3:15, Genesis 12, and 2 Samuel 7, as we've seen in earlier chapters. Is that particular promise or covenant beyond cancellation? Is it unconditional in the sense that, no matter what anyone does, it will still remain in force?

Secondly, we need to ask the question: Is the covenant given to Moses at Sinai—the Sinaitic covenant—dependent solely upon human response and on human obligation? Since we know how humans respond and that they are fickle, does this mean that man's failure results in immediate dismissal and cancellation? Is the Sinaitic covenant dependent upon human obligation and compliance, on penalty of retribution, whereas the other covenant—the Abrahamic-Davidic covenant—is not subject to human compliance and is not subject to any kind of penalty of retribution if men do fail?

Amazing answers have been given to these two questions! For example, take the German scholar, Antonius H. J. Gunneweg, who in his book, *Understanding the Old Testament*, says both answers are true. He does not want to make any enemies and so decides to split the baby both ways—as Solomon did—and give both sides the answer they want. He says, rather despondently (p. 139), "If we keep within the bounds of the Old Testament, either description is possible, since both are given. There is no possibility of drawing a line [i.e., of connecting] from law to covenant or from covenant to law." (He means from law to promise or from promise to law.) He says you cannot draw a line, and so he throws up his hands and says the case is lost. There is no way out of the dilemma.

"To be sure, Gunneweg does note," as I wrote in *Toward Rediscovering the Old Testament* (p. 151), "that this issue is bound up with another: is the rule of God with his people brought into being in *this* world and in our history," and is it also bound up with the rule of God which extends *outside* of our world and history? To appreciate his somewhat oblique and irrelevant answer, one must recall that the Sinaitic covenant called for the dissolution of the nation with the imposition of all the horrible curses that are found in Leviticus 26 and Deuteronomy 28, two chapters we will be discussing when we come to the Prophets.

Few chapters in the Bible are more important for understanding prophetic material than these two chapters, which give the alternative prospect: "If you obey me and if you walk in my way, then I will bless you and I'll do this." This is repeated fifteen times over, stating all the good things God is going to do. This is not to be understood as the health-wealth-prosperity gospel that is sometimes preached today: name it and claim it. Rather, there is, on a national level, promised blessing to that particular people and nation.

By the way, it is "principle-ized," too. In Jeremiah 18:6-10 we will find Jeremiah down at the potter's house principle-izing and quoting God as saying, "At whatever time, whatever nation, whatever people, if I've ever said to them, 'I'll bless you and I'll make you great', if indeed that people and that nation"—it's already principle-ized—"if they turn away from me, then I'll repent of the good that I said I would do to them. If, on the other hand, I pronounce against a nation"—judgment then, pulling and tearing them down and demolishing them—"if they repent of their evil, then I too will repent of the evil that I had said I would bring upon that people, that nation."

So this is not just a message sent from God to Israel. It is mail, a message, that is relevant for Canada. It is mail that is relevant for Mexico. It is mail that is relevant for Russia. It is mail that is relevant for the People's Republic of China. And it is a message that is relevant for the U.S.A. Remember the remark in 2 Samuel 1:20: "Tell it not in Gath ..."—i.e., don't let our enemies hear of our coming judgment or they will dance for joy!

So God says, "If you do not serve me, then I'll bring judgments upon you. I'll send lack of rain on the land. If you still don't hear me, then I will bring other disasters upon your nation. And if your nation still doesn't listen to me, I'll increase it more!" He keeps upping the ante—up! up! up! —and increasing the severity of the judgment. Why? Because of his love! He is trying to capture the attention of the people, although they have become tone deaf. Their response has been, "Oh, words! Words, words, words! That's all we hear." It's true that in our society we are bombarded with words. We turn on our radios and get a message from the sponsor. We turn on our TVs and get another message. We go to church, where we get a word from our pastors. A constant barrage of words. And we can't handle all these words. Now, what are we to do with these words that seem to threaten to cancel all the good things that God said he would do? This is actually what Gunneweg has in mind.

A second response is to say that both the Sinaitic and the Abrahamic-Davidic covenants are conditional. This response is given by both Oswald T. Allis, a distinguished Old Testament professor—now in glory—who was at Westminster Seminary for a number of years, and Ron Youngblood, at Bethel West Seminary in San Diego. They say that both covenants are conditional. Youngblood goes through every text he can think of, finding 20 to 25 texts where he can say, "Look, these verses show the covenants are conditional."

For example, he says to look at the conditions in Genesis 12:1. I looked, and was I surprised! I said, What is he talking about? Youngblood quotes the Lord saying to Abraham: "Leave your country, your people and your father's household and go to the land I will show you" (NIV). A commandment precedes the promise. He says that there is an implicit condition here.

This passage is not one of the clearest used by Youngblood. There are others, which I myself have treated in one text or another, but we can't treat all of them here. I have seen at least five alleged conditions. For example, Genesis 22:18 says, "Because you've obeyed me, Abraham ...." It seems to imply—and I must stress that it *seems* to imply—the condition of obedience for Abraham's receiving the promise. And he did obey. Later on, Isaac will be told, "Because your father Abraham obeyed me ...."

Using the strength of these texts, O. T. Allis and Ron Youngblood say that both the Sinaitic and the Abrahamic-Davidic covenants are conditional and that there is no such thing as an unconditional covenant. But for the time being, I must remind you of Genesis 15. Who passed through the pieces? In that symbolic vision, only God—as the smoking torch, the burning furnace—went through the pieces, down the aisle with animals split in half and placed on both sides. Abraham did not. So it was not a bilateral covenant; it was a unilateral covenant. There was obligation on one side only. For that reason, I still think we should stress that the Abrahamic-Davidic covenant was unconditional. I do not agree with O. T. Allis's solution, nor with Ron Youngblood's.

There is a third answer to the question of conditional and unconditional covenants. A former colleague, Tom McComiskey, wrote that the people of God are under two covenants simultaneously. One is unconditional—and he agreed that the arguments for the Abrahamic-Davidic covenant were unconditional, as I've just rehearsed for you. But then he added that there is another covenant that is conditional; that is an administrative covenant. So he said there are simultaneously a promissory covenant and an administrative one. And he said both are operative.

They are not worked out in exactly the same way, but on the other hand, you must understand this is how he analyzed these problems. In this case, it's as if the covenants are two different flavors. Dr. McComiskey's work puts the new covenant under the second flavor, under the heading of administrative covenant. So we would have this Sinaitic, new covenant being in the conditional as an administrative type, and the Abrahamic-Davidic being in the unconditional.

Why did Dr. McComiskey do that? Because in the new covenant, God said he would take his *Torah*, his law, and write it on people's hearts. Since Dr. McComiskey knew that Sinai would, somehow or other, be connected with the new covenant, it forced him, I think unnaturally, to put the new covenant in the conditional category. But this all goes to show that we have not understood the problem yet.

There is a fourth view, and this one sounds to me as if we are getting closer to what I think Luther and Calvin's revised views from heaven would be. Willis J. Beecher presents a view which I think is the most helpful and has solved the most difficulties. Beecher says that the promise to Abraham and to David cannot be cancelled—it is not conditional; even though some in that messianic line do not personally participate in it, they still transmit it. And so the way in which he tries to solve part of the problem is this: Here we have a continuing seed of representative individuals who have transmitted the promise, the seed. Abraham has Isaac, who has Jacob; David has Solomon, who has Rehoboam, who has Ahaz, who has Hezekiah. These people were all under the obligation to transmit the promise because of its divine unconditionality.

But does that mean that they are "shoo-ins" to participate in the benefits of faith? No! We can draw a dotted line, and put above the line the names of those linking the promised seed, who *must* bring it down through history. Below the line we can put those who do not personally participate. They do not participate in the promise because of 1) the lack of faith and 2) the lack of evidence of obedience which is a corollary of genuine faith. As the book of James says, "If you really believe, then show me the stuff and show it to me by the evidence of your life."

Willis J. Beecher commented on this in his book, *The Prophets and the Promise* (1905; reprint, Grand Rapids: Baker, 1963, pp. 219-220). He says:

> Ordinarily Yahweh's promises to men are conditioned on obedience. Even the promises of eternal blessing to Israel are thus conditioned (e.g. Deut iv:40, xii:28). In some passages it is perhaps fairly implied that the promise to Abraham and Israel for the nations is conditioned on Israel's obedience. However this may be, there are a few remarkable passages in which the promise is expressly declared to be unconditional—not forfeited even by disobedience. In Leviticus, for example ... [after] a series of terrible ... punishments ... in retribution for sin ... [it says] ... "I will not reject them, neither will I abhor them, to destroy them completely, and to break my covenant with them" (Lev xxvi:44-45).

So, continues Beecher,

> It is not difficult to solve the verbal paradox involved in thus declaring this promise to be both conditional and unconditional. So far as its benefits accrue to any particular person or generation in Israel, it is conditioned on their obedience. But in its character as expressing God's purpose of blessing for the human race, we should not expect it to depend on the obedience or disobedience of a few. ... Israel may sin, and may suffer grievous punishment; but Israel shall not become extinct, like other sinning peoples. The promise is for eternity, and Israel shall be maintained in existence, that the promise may not fail.

That's a long quote from Beecher, but it does seem to me to be an important contribution to our discussion.

Well, how does the promise relate to the law? Can we make a distinction between the conditional and the unconditional? The answer is, Yes. There is a distinction between the two. However, it is not such an enormous distinction that the Abrahamic-Davidic covenant is sharply separated from the Sinaitic. It will be our purpose in the rest of the chapter to show strains of continuity between the two.

We would say that, indeed, faith is the very basis for the reception of all of the blessings of the promise that was given to Abraham, to Isaac, to Jacob, and to David. And the covenant at Sinai was given to those who truly believed. It was the answer to the question, How, then, shall we live? It was given to them as a method of expressing the reality of their faith.

So I see the relationship between Abraham and Sinai to be the same as the relationship between Romans and James. If we can solve the problem between Romans and James, then we can solve the problem between these two, Abraham and Sinai. As a matter of fact, I have written of this in the final chapter of *Uses of the Old Testament in the New*. Surprisingly, the book of James is probably a series of sermons based upon an exposition of Leviticus 19:12-18. Throughout the book of James are at least eight quotes from that particular chapter in Leviticus. It has long been noted that the "royal law" of love, as James calls it in James 2:8—that you should treat your neighbor with love—is from that particular section. But what we failed to notice was that the rest of the book of James was a commentary, either by direct citation or by allusion, on the rest of the teaching of this pericope, or selection, from Leviticus. This is a most amazing find!

So we ask not only the distinction between the conditional and the unconditional in this whole matter of the relationship of the promise to law, but we ask, secondly, what does the New Testament say about the matter, faith and obedience, and the Christian's response to the law? We will answer in terms of three basic texts.

### The New Testament Relationship of Faith and Obedience

First of all, we want to look at that famous text in Matthew 5, in the Sermon on the Mount. The first thing the New Testament teaches us—by no less authority than our Lord himself—is not to teach others to disregard the law. Our Lord Jesus gives a warning in Matthew 5:17-20: If you do teach others to disregard the law, it will not go lightly with you. For he says in verse 19: "Anyone who breaks one of the least of these commandments and teaches others to do the same ..." (NIV). Now, some would say that the commandments referred to here are the ones Jesus has just been talking about. But that won't actually wash, because the citations in this passage are too obviously from the Old Testament law. Others would say that the commandments mentioned in this verse have already been fulfilled and, therefore, there is no more need for them. But that doesn't seem to be fair exegesis either, because Jesus says that these will not pass away until heaven and earth pass away. Now, I checked very recently, and I can assure you that heaven and earth are still around. So, unless some change has occurred in the last few minutes, these commandments are still in vogue. When we see the heaven and the earth disappear, we can count on the law going out as well. I didn't say it—don't get angry with me! Get angry with our Lord. He is the one who made that connection.

He goes on, "As a matter of fact, if you think the Pharisees are rigid"— and they really are persnickety about keeping the minutiae of the law, though Jesus thinks their attitudes and motivations are wrong—"I tell you that your righteousness must exceed theirs." Must *exceed* theirs! So he ends in this passage with the same teaching on the Christian's response to law, faith and obedience.

The second thing the New Testament seems to teach is that some things in the law take priority over others. Yes, I think that is true. But don't forget that I say that on the authority of the founder of our religion, who taught that some things are weightier. Matthew 23:23 teaches us that while there is one law, some things in it are heavier. But we must always keep in mind that the law is one.

The scribes and Pharisees come to Jesus asking, "Since we're still under the Old Testament law, should we be tithing mints and anise?" Jesus answers surprisingly, "Yes. These ought you to have done, and not to have left undone the weightier matters"—the heavier, the more important things—"of the law."

So our Lord is saying that there is some kind of ranking, some kind of priority, within the law. We may not like the distinction which has been in vogue since the early church, but I think Jesus is saying that the moral law—as a ground and a base—is the weightier matter as compared the civil and the ceremonial law. Our Lord gives an illustration of this. He's quoting from Micah 6:6-8, "... the weightier matters of the law, like justice and mercy and walking humbly with your God." There he penetrates to the heart of the argument and begins to show that there are abstract principles that govern the particular, and that these principles, as I think we're going to see, refer back to his character.

The third thing we need to say here is from Romans 3:31. Paul asks our question for us: Are the promises then related to the law of God? Or have the promises made null and void the law of God? *Katargeo* is the Greek word there: have they rendered the law inoperative. And Paul says, *Negative! Nein! Non! Nyet!* He answers, No! He stamps his foot and says, "No, God forbid!" This oath in the King James translation is a very strong negative. Rather, Paul says, by faith we establish the law.

We can argue all we want, for there is a mass of texts. And I must confess that I don't understand all of them. But at least Paul does ask my question one time. And he answers quite clearly that faith establishes rather than contravenes the law. Faith does not render the law null and inoperative, but rather it establishes the law of God. That, I think, must be a factor in our working on a solution.

## The Relationship of Moral Principle to Particular Specificity

We come now to the second main point of this chapter, moving from the relationship of promise to Old Testament law, to the question of the relationship of the moral principle to particular specificity. What is the relationship between moral principle, or the abstract in the law, to the particular, to the specific, to the individual examples that are given in the law?

### The Moral Law

We would suggest, based upon the fact that our Lord said some things are weightier, that, although we call it the Law of Moses, it actually was given by God. As such, it was a reflection of God himself. We may call the law—and this is terribly arbitrary—the moral law of God. What makes this weightier, or more important, is that it is based on the character of God. The character of God remains the norm for all decisions on right and wrong. Here we have God's Bureau of Weights and Measurements. Here is the standard; here is the norm. And that norm is nothing less than the nature and the character of God. That norm determines what is true, what is false, what is right, what is wrong, what is just, what is unjust, what is good, and what is evil.

We desperately need this standard. During the 1960s, society said, "Men, love is the fulfillment of the law." That's true. Paul says that in Romans 13:10. Love is indeed the essence of it, for love gets down to the heart of how we are going to do whatever it is that we're going to do. But I must warn you, love is a *how* word. Love is not a *what* word. Love will never tell us what to do.

Joe Fletcher came along in the 1960s with situational ethics. The whole church was caught in an embarrassing situation, and is still paying for this problem. We lost the sixties generation, and we're still losing them. The present sexual revolution is in part due to the church! Because we said, "Whatever you do, do it in love." That's what Joe Fletcher said, but it didn't sound quite right. "If you love each other, fine, go ahead! You're consenting adults." There's something wrong about that. We must understand, then, that love tells us *how*, but love will not tell us *what*. We have therefore reaped a whirlwind—a tremendous backlash—in our present day.

Where can we go to understand *what* to do? Here, it seems to me, we must go back to the character of God. He sets the norms. Where can we find a discussion of his character, and where does it become principles based on his character?

We suggest that it becomes principles mainly in the Decalogue, the Ten Commandments. In Exodus 20 and in Deuteronomy 5 we find statements about the character of God. Now it is true that they are mixed, giving both the general and the particular, especially in the commandment concerning the Sabbath day. That commandment is mixed, in that it specifies a particular time; namely, the seventh day. There's no question about it: God is the Lord of time, for he made all time. Therefore, he has a right to ask for a portion of our time in worship and service and rest. He who made us knows best, for he himself instituted the day of rest prior to the law. He did that in creation, so it is a "pre-law" law. As a matter of fact, prior to the formal dictation of the Law of Moses in Exodus 20, all of the Ten Commandments can be observed already in force in Genesis.

The point here is that the Ten Commandments express God's character. Take the sanctity of truth, for example, for he is "the way, the truth, and the life." That's the norm. And if we want to express the moral law in its simplest form, it is he in the law of holiness found in Leviticus 18–20. Simply stated there (in Lev 19:2), it is the "Be holy *as* I, the LORD your God, am holy." How holy, how righteous, how just, how good should a person be? "Holy as I, the LORD your God, am holy." Let's put aside trying to understand what 'perfect' means in Matthew 5:48b, which comes up in discussions on this subject. Let's work on *as*, first of all. It's the *as*ness here that is the point of this chapter. That is the goal to be held up here. "Be holy *as* I, the LORD your God, am holy."

We would argue, then, that the moral law as found in the Decalogue is based on the character of God. And it is found dozens of times in the law of holiness in Leviticus 18–20.

### The Ceremonial Law

The ceremonial law is that which is found mainly from Exodus 25 through Leviticus, and has a built-in obsolescence. That is, there's a built-in time factor. There was a warning in the text: Look out, this is going to go out of style when the real comes. Where do we find that warning? For one example, in Exodus 25:40 the Lord took Moses up the mountain and showed him a pattern, modeled after the real thing in heaven. This gives us a clue that we are dealing with typological things which are only a shadow of the final reality. Not in a platonic sense, but in a biblical sense in which we know that, when the real comes, these which are only symbolic pictures are going to be outdated. And so we find repeated here the word for *pattern*—a model, a sample, an illustration—something that is not the final reality. And this provision of the ceremonial law, interestingly enough, is for those who fail to keep the law. That is the interesting thing: it is for those who *fail* to keep the law.

### The Civil Law

Then there is the civil law. The third part is also illustrative of the moral law. The civil law is like the practical part of the epistles of Paul: first Paul writes a doctrinal section and then he gets to the practical things. "I urge Euodias and Syntyche to be of one mind" (Phil 4:2). We can say, Well, I'm not Euodias and I'm not Syntyche, so we can skip that verse! Oh no, we can't do that, because there's a principle behind it. The principle is love one another; be kind to one another; be tender-hearted; be forgiving. Why do we know that? Because Paul has said that elsewhere. When we read these words about Euodias and Syntyche, we see the principle being applied. Why don't we do that when we come to the civil law? Indeed, that's exactly what needs to be done.

For example, in Deuteronomy 25, we read: "Don't put a muzzle on the ox." Why? Give the oxen some corn. Why? Because this is Be Kind to Animals Week? No, not because it's Be Kind to Animals Week but rather because something happens to us—or to me—as the farmers. When we obey this law, a sense of generosity and of sensitivity is being cultivated in us. This cultivation of some part of God's character is Paul's basis for saying, "Take up an offering for me when I come to preach." He is saying in effect, "I want something to happen to you. I don't need money. I don't need it at all. But I want something to happen to you, the givers. I refuse to beg for God's work. I never will." That was Paul's principle and the specific application.

The civil law is an illustration of the principles of the moral law which is found mainly in the covenant code in Exodus 21–23. It's found also in Deuteronomy 5–26, which is actually an explication of the Ten Commandments, proceeding in order through them.

### The Problem of Particularity and Specificity

We conclude, then, with the problem of particularity and specificity. Why does the Bible have so many particulars here? They were not meant to make it difficult for us, but rather were meant to help us and to reduce our frustration in applying the law. The civil law wants to help us to understand how, indeed, we can apply the moral law.

This problem of particularity and specificity is shared with narrative text and historical text. We deal with the same problem when we come to narrative texts. The texts are very particular, very specific, but they give us illustrations of how to apply the general principle. And so the principle will be there with its conclusion of a single meaning to the text, yet with the idea of multiple equity or multiple application. We have a single meaning of the text, but that single meaning has thousands of applications.

This leads us to develop the principle which we will take up in the following chapter, the Method of Middle Axioms. To illustrate, we will use the method of inference and the method of the ladder of abstraction. With the ladder of abstraction, we will use a diagram of two ladders. (You may want to look at the diagram on page 166 of my *Toward Rediscovering the Old Testament*.) On one ladder, we move from the Old Testament specific situation at the bottom, up to the Old Testament institution, and then on up to the top of the ladder to the general principle. This general, abstract principle at the top, illustrating the character of God, is common to both the ascending ladder of the Old Testament and the descending ladder of the New Testament. We move down the second ladder to the theological and moral principle, to the New Testament institution and situation, on down to the practical illustration and application in our culture.

So we're moving up and back down these two ladders, from specific to general, the general principle coming from the same Writer who taught us in his book the principles which are now being very specifically applied. That will help us as teachers and preachers of that Word to assimilate, to apply, and to teach God's principles based on his character.

# Chapter Eight

# Aspects of the One Law of God

## Exodus 20 through Deuteronomy

## Introduction

The point is often made that there is one Law which comes from one lawgiver, our living God. Who can argue with that principle? And yet, we saw in chapter 7 that some parts of that one Law are "weightier" than others. The Bible does not wish to give the impression that the whole Law is given with the same force, with the same kind of obligation in our day. The Bible is, however, anxious that we speak to such questions as, What ought I to do? or, How should I act so as to do what is good and right? or, How shall we define the good? These are all biblical questions, it seems to me. If the Bible does not tell us how to behave, where are we to find it? Should another book have been written to tell us how we should live? The answers to these questions are found in this section of the Old Testament.

The interesting thing is that here we have a major source of theology—some refer to it as a major religion of the world—and yet the Old Testament has no term for ethics. There is no term for theology. The closest we will come in the Old Testament Hebrew to a term for theology is 'the knowledge of God.' And the closest we come to a word for ethics or virtue or ideals is the Old Testament word *musar*, which means discipline or teaching, or perhaps the Hebrew word *derek*, the way, the path.

So from the Hebrew perspective, we're not talking about an abstract ideal, but rather about something concrete. It's the way we walk; it's the path on which one goes. Just so Proverbs speaks over and over again of the way, the path, in which we should walk. It speaks of the discipline, the teaching, of the Lord. Even in the New Testament, we have this Semitic concept in the Greek with a word referring to one's *walk*. That's about as close as we're going to get to an abstract term for ethics.

## The Possibility of a Biblical Ethic

But even though we do not have an abstract term for ethics, we still need to take up, first of all, the question of a biblical ethic. What can we say about the possibility of a biblical ethic?

### It Rests on Three Assumptions

First of all, the possibility of a biblical ethic rests on three assumptions. The first assumption is that *the particular commands of the Old Testament can be universalized.* The particular, very specific commands given in the civil law—the covenant code of Exodus 21–23—can be universalized. How would we argue this? Well, the Old Testament moral statements were meant to be applied to a universal class of peoples, tribes, and conditions. The moral statements of the Old Testament were not, as it were, chauvinistic. God was not playing favorites; he was not concerned only with the children of Israel. We must understand that there was an international, a global, consciousness and consideration. Remember that the promise doctrine is a continuous happening, so that all the peoples upon the face of the earth might be blessed. The blessing was to come through the Messiah, but the blessing was also to come through the revelation of the word of God.

Paul will ask in Romans 3:1: "What advantage hath the Jew?" Much, he will say, "because to them came the oracles of God." So what's the big deal about that? They got the revelation of God. But they were not to keep it to themselves; it was to be shared.

I think this demonstrates that the particular was meant to be universalized. Hidden behind almost every specific injunction in some particular situation is a reference to the universal. I say *almost* every specific, because as a scholar I should never say *always*—or *never*! Someone might challenge the *always* statement, saying, Prove it! So the safest thing to do is pull back a bit and say that behind almost every specific injunction is a reference to the universal.

I gave you in the preceding chapter an illustration from the New Testament where, in one of his letters to the churches, Paul has to tell two ladies, Euodias and Syntyche, to be of one mind. Hidden behind that particular illustration is an abstract, but universal, principle: believers are to be tenderhearted; they are to be kind; they are to be forgiving of one another. To announce the particular application is not to exclude the principle.

We find that over and over again in the New Testament. This will be true in almost all of the conclusions to Paul's epistles. So why do we not apply the same process in the Old Testament, especially when we see the writers themselves doing this to their own material?

Another argument bearing out that particular commands can be universalized is that biblical ethics are possible because some of the Bible's commands contain references to universals. This is very plain. This helps us to understand that some of those particular injunctions deliberately refer to universals. God will say, for example, "When you see your enemy's donkey in the ditch weighted down and it can't get up, you're to take the burden off and help the donkey up, because"—and he gives us the reason and motivation—"you should love your enemy." The specific command to help the donkey up is given, while the universal, love your enemy, is also given. Actually we don't live in a culture in which our enemies have overloaded donkeys which risk being stuck at the side of the road. We don't use donkeys as shipping vehicles; we now have tractor trailers. But we do have trouble with the universal: loving our enemies. So this is an illustration of the particular and the universal.

The second assumption in formulating a biblical ethic is that *the commands of the Old Testament exhibit consistency*. How would we argue this point? We would say that a biblical writer has, in another part of his writings, given us a pattern of thought that shows us what universal lies behind a particular injunction. We would refer to the same writer because this is a principle of exegesis. If we are to extract the meaning from the text, we ought to give the first consideration to the sphere of intent of the author himself, the true intention of the author. So we look for a text where the pattern of his thought is given which could lead to this particular injunction.

We also argue that the commands of the Old Testament have a consistency by virtue of the fact that the writer of Scripture does not change his mind from one moment to the next, but maintains his same thought and same attitudes. In this case, his principle will stand for similar situations, regardless of times or cultures. This is a transtemporal and transcultural phenomenon. If what the writer says in one particular instance exhibits the universal and if he doesn't change his mind later in his ministry— say, in a month, or in two years, or in fifty years—doesn't that show that the same principle would hold true for other times and other cultures? That is, unless other conditions are present that mitigate the principle.

The third and final assumption which gives us the possibility for an Old Testament biblical ethic, I think, is that *the commands of the Old Testament are prescriptive and make demands or claims upon us*. We have argued that the commands can be universalized; we have argued that there is a consistency between cultures and times and within the thought of the writer. Now we are arguing that the commands are prescriptive and that they can make— and do make—a claim on us. Why is this?

It is because all mortals are made in the same image of God. We argue, first of all, that we are dealing with people who are not diverse, but rather are the same in that they are made by God. Stamped on the life of every person are the words, *Built by God*. And I don't mean just in terms of shape or form, but also in terms of that image of God, the *imago Dei*. This is explained in Scripture in various ways. We are renewed in knowledge after the image of him who created us, so I think knowledge is part of it. We are renewed in righteousness after the image of him who created us. The ability to communicate seems to be another indication of the image of God. The ability to love and to express love is another indication of the image of God.

These are points of contact with the image of God—distorted by sin, to be sure, but they're still there. It's like a tuba that has been beaten up and put into a violin case. Now, you have to work pretty hard on a tuba to smash it down to the size of a violin. But that doesn't change the fact that it's a tuba. Yes, it's contorted, distorted, crumpled up, but there still exists the faintest impression of the original point of contact. And in that regard, then, all nations, whether in Israel's day or in our day, are made in the image of God. All mortals are made in the same image of God.

Therefore, whether the Old Testament ethical material is in the imperative or indicative mood makes no difference, for they both purport to direct behavior. Whether by description or through commands, what the Bible says requires certain responses of us.

At this point, we do need to make a distinction between what the Bible *describes* and what the Bible *prescribes*. We could say this another way: there is a difference between what the Bible *records* and what the Bible *teaches*. The Bible records: "The fool has said in his heart that there is no God." At least in this case, the fool is smart enough to say it internally, unlike some today who just blurt it out. This man says in his heart, "There is no God." Now, the Bible is not teaching that there is no God; the Bible simply records what the fool says to himself. The Bible records but doesn't condone in this case. So we must make the distinction.

This is always a problem for the exegete as he goes through narrative material in the indicative mood. In these descriptive passages, only certain matters have been selected to be included in the story. This is not a stenographic report of everything that took place. For example, in the Samson story, certain items in his life were selected; they were arranged in a certain way. The arrangement is also significant.

And then, what were the key speeches? Usually a speech put in the mouth of one of the key speakers becomes exceedingly important, especially if the writer, as he may on occasion, comes in and gives us his own values or morals. He may put a moral to his story. But almost always he will refrain from doing so and will allow the story to tell itself. In the book of Judges, for example, there are only three times, as I recall, when the writer gives us his own moral to the story. When this happens, there are clues which say, Reader beware! Here in Judges it is recorded: "Every man did that which was right in his own eyes. ... And there was no king in Israel in those days." These are clues. The author is saying, This material you are about to read may not be fit for normative usage in the life of the believer. Nevertheless, there are still principles behind the negative and the positive material, and the text does want to command us. It does want to prescribe; it does want to direct our behavior. In that sense, the Old Testament is prescriptive, and it can make demands of us.

So just to review, there are three assumptions that we make as we discuss the possibility of a biblical ethic. We assume that the text can be universalized; we assume that it has a consistency within itself; and we assume that the commands are prescriptive. Of course, these need to be demonstrated, too. But if we are to form any kind of direction for the believing community today on how we ought to behave, these three assumptions must be part of our thinking.

I must tell you that in my day and age, it is not so chic to look for any kind of consistency or for a unifying factor. As a matter of fact, the search for diversity in answers is more condoned and seems to be more scholarly than the search for unity. I don't know why, but the scholar gets more points in the eyes of his contemporaries, both believers and unbelievers, if he searches for and exhibits diversity than if he searches for any kind of unity. The search for diversity and pluralism in ethical standards is as much the result of a prior methodological decision as is the search for unity and harmony of standards. So one may not say that the search for diversity is more scientific or that it is more objective than the search for harmony. Unity or diversity must be decided on the basis of an internal examination of the material, not on the basis of an external decision foisted over the text, which has been dropped as a grid on top of the text.

So the possibility of an Old Testament biblical ethic, we say, rests on three assumptions. It also exhibits five noteworthy characteristics.

### A Biblical Ethic Exhibits Five Characteristics

In contrast to philosophical ethics, which tends to be more abstract and man-centered, biblical morality is directly connected with religious faith. Hence, immoral men and women are irreligious men and women. By the same token, irreligious persons are also immoral persons. The biblical text does not have a middle category. Psalm 14:1 says, "The fool said in his heart, There is no God." The biblical text goes on to say that this individual is corrupt and then makes the statement that, indeed, "there is none that does good."

What are the five characteristics? The first is that Old Testament biblical ethics is *personal*. It is not an abstraction. The point here is that it is God's character that really preserves the norm. Consequently, we are urged in Leviticus 19:2 to "Be holy because I, the LORD your God, am holy" (NIV). The word *holy* here supplies the root concept: If there were a way to express the promise doctrine in ethics, I think it would be *holiness*. It is too bad this has become such a specialized religious word. Previously in English the word *whole* stood for wholeness both in the secular and in the sacred contexts. But then came a time when we kept the word *whole* as a secular word and made *holy* the sacred word (dropping 'w' off and adding 'y'). But basically the two words mean the same thing: wholly set apart or given over to something.

We've done this with another word, *fan*. If we go to the ballpark and support a team, we are fans. But when we are wholly given over to religious things, we add 'atic' onto the word, and we become 'fanatics'.

Now, the word *holiness* in the biblical sense of *q-d-sh* (*qadosh*) means that a person is set apart entirely to God. The positive aspect of the word is the more important part of its meaning: set apart *to*. Oh, yes, it does have a negative aspect; since a person is set apart to God, there is also separation *from*. I don't think we should be afraid of a biblical doctrine of separation from all that is evil, all that is sin, and consequently that which represents the opposite of God. But this separation can be seen as being so totally set apart *to* him that it is not necessary to express what we are set apart *from*. Some people are known primarily by their 'from-ness'. The biblical text would like us to be known by our 'to-ness', even though it does not disassociate itself from the necessity of being set apart from.

Biblical ethics is, thus, first of all *personal*. The moral and ethical demands of the Bible are very personal. Thus, "If you follow my decrees," says Leviticus 26:3, "and are careful to obey my commands ...." God calls them *my* decrees, *my* commands. We should stop talking about the Law of Moses. Who said Moses invented this thing? We are dealing with God; we are dealing with God's Law.

Or we can put it in personal terms of the New Testament: "Whatever is true, whatever is noble, whatever is right, whatever is pure, whatever is lovely, whatever is admirable" (NIV). Here we have spiritual and moral criteria; but notice the list begins with truth criteria: "Whatever is true" (Phil 4:8-9). Our generation hates that. But the list starts off with truth; then, if anything is excellent or praiseworthy, think about these things. Think about lovely things in the natural world, in the artistic world, in the intellectual world, in the spiritual world, in the emotional world. "Whatever is true, whatever is noble, whatever is right, whatever is pure, whatever is lovely, whatever is admirable—think about such things" (NIV).

And "whatever you have learned or received or heard or seen in me, *do*." Uh-oh, that's legalism! Then Paul adds, "Put these into practice. And the God of peace will be with you." "I will be with you." God stamps *Emmanuel* all over it! He doesn't say, "Go to it, tiger! I'll be back to check on you later to see how you're doing." No! He says, "I will stand alongside. I will be *Emmanuel*." That's Philippians 4:8-9. Who or what then is the standard? The standard becomes the living God.

The second characteristic is that Old Testament biblical ethics is *theistic*. For this is what it means to know God: it is to *do* what he says. Jeremiah 22:15-16 teaches that when the king did what was right and just, all went well with him; when he defended the cause of the poor and the needy, all went well. "Is this not what it means to know me?" says the Lord. It's like two children who say to one another, when one is trying to get a taste of the other's ice cream cone, "I know you; we know each other." When we have experiential fellowship with someone we know, we express it by sharing. We say, "Here, have some!" So this is an interesting question in Jeremiah 22:15-16: "Is this not what it means to know me?" Proverbs 3:5-6 reinforces the same message: "Trust in the LORD with all your heart ...." Then it says in conclusion: "And he will make your paths straight." 'Path' is the word here for ethics: "And he will direct your *paths.*" So, significantly, the biblical text is ethical.

Biblical ethics is personal; it is theistic; and it certainly is *internal.* Biblical ethics is internal rather than external. This is a difficult concept to get across. Most people contrast the New Testament and Old Testament, saying the Old Testament was external: there were so many things to do. That's not true at all! First Samuel 16:7 says, "The LORD looks at the heart." In my book, *Toward Old Testament Ethics,* a long section deals with the internality of the Law. God constantly judged a person, not primarily by what he did, but primarily by the motivation in his heart.

This is the constant cry of the prophets: "What is the meaning of all this—these new moons and these feasts and the keeping of Sabbath and assemblies?" Isaiah 1 has a most graphic description of God's disgust with religiosity. God says, "I'm fed up with the whole thing! When you come before me and spread forth your hands, you say, 'Now let us pray.'" God is saying, "How nice! You go ahead and do your thing, because I'm not even going to look. It is formal; it is dull; it is boring. It doesn't mean anything to you and it doesn't mean anything to me." God says, "Come now, and let us reason together, ... though your sins be as scarlet, they shall be as white as snow" (Isa 1:18, AV).

What change is God asking of his people? He is not saying, Why don't you redo your services? Why don't you bring me some more sacrifices? No, none of this! But he is saying, Change it, and change it in your heart right away. That's the great theme here: The LORD looks on the heart.

Jeremiah 7:21-23 exhibits the same thing, as well as Hosea 6:6 and Micah 6:6-8. As a matter of fact, Jesus teaches in the New Testament in Matthew 9 and Matthew 12: "You want to learn the Old Testament? Go home and think about these things. Think about Hosea 6:6, think about Micah 6:6-8. That's where it begins." So biblical ethics is internal.

The fourth characteristic of Old Testament biblical ethics is that it is *future-oriented.* Over and over again, we are taught the concept that all of life is inspectable at the final judgment. This is true even in a book like Ecclesiastes, where Solomon comes to the conclusion (in Eccl 12:13-14): "Fear God and keep his commandments, because ...." God says, This is all reviewable. God will be able to bring everything out into the open. And so it is not that deeds in the Old Testament are to be done out of sheer rote, but rather good deeds should have another motivation, just as the New Testament states in 2 Peter 3:11-12: "You ought to live holy and godly lives as you look forward to the day of God and speed up his coming" (NIV). Here we see future orientation.

Finally, the fifth characteristic is that Old Testament biblical ethics is *universal*. It embraces the same standard for righteousness for all nations on earth as the standard God required of Israel. Old Testament biblical ethics is universal in that sense. What God requires of Israel, he requires of the nations.

Is that not the point of Abraham's discussion with God about the fate of Sodom in Genesis 18:25? Abraham addresses God, saying, "Will not the Judge of the whole earth do what is right?" God is not the judge of Israel; he is the judge of the whole earth. I understand this verse in that sense. The five Gentile cities of the plain are wicked and are sinning greatly. And whom do they sin against? Genesis 13 answers that they sin against the Lord. Does the text say that the five cities of the plain, the five Gentile cities, are wicked and that they are sinning against each other? No! They are sinning against the Lord.

Even Joseph knows this when Potiphar's wife tries to seduce him day after day: "Come, let's go to bed." He refuses to do so. Then he says, "Listen, my master trusts me and has given to me the whole house, everything under his domain, except you. How can I do this great sin against my master and against God?" He understood even before the Ten Commandments were given that committing adultery was a sin against God. That occurs in Genesis 39.

Large sections of the biblical text are specifically addressed to the *nations*: Isaiah 13–23; Jeremiah 45–51; Ezekiel 25–32; Daniel 2, 7; Amos 1–2; the book of Obadiah; the book of Jonah; the book of Nahum; part of the book of Ruth. It seems to me that they are all externally directed.

## The Moral Law of God

We have argued that biblical ethics has five characteristics. We want to talk now not only about the possibility of a biblical ethic, but about the moral law of God, how it demonstrates this great principle.

### Its Basis

The basis of the moral law of God, we argued, is the character of God. This comes through in several dozen references, beginning in Leviticus 18:5-6. Notice the famous verse, Leviticus 18:5: "Do this and you shall live." This is a verse which is quoted at least three times in the New Testament: "Do this and you shall live." In this particular text, we need to note the beginning and end of the chapter: "I am the LORD your God." Only those who have the Lord as their God can be addressed as this chapter is going to address us. In other words, these are insider instructions for believers. The warning at the beginning of the chapter and the almost signature-like statement at the end puts it into a frame of context.

When God says, "Do this," he is condemning the Canaanites, who were into idolatry, for he has said, "You should love the LORD your God only." This becomes an explication of the first commandment, "Thou shalt have no other gods before me." The result of obedience is, "Do this and you shall live." Does he mean eternally, and is that the point of his text here?

I don't think so. He is not talking about eternal life. If you wish to put it in New Testament terms, "I've come that you might have life, and that you might have it more abundantly." He is talking about exhibiting the sphere of blessing of being in the Lord even in the New Testament. In Galatians 3 and in Romans 10 he speaks of the whole matter of living not by means of doing these things, but living in the sphere of them. I don't think it is an instrumental use of the Greek preposition *en* here. It is rather a locative use of the preposition, to live "in the sphere of" these things.

So the basis of the moral law continues to be the character of God or, as in Philippians 2:5, the character of Christ: "Let this mindset be in you, which was also in Christ Jesus: who, while existing in the form of God and continuing to exist in that form, didn't think it beneath himself that he should come and suffer on the cross. But he divested himself of the outward kind of regalia of all his glory," just as the high priest takes off his robe and puts on the linen robe as he goes into the Holy of Holies on *Yom Kippur*, the Day of Atonement. So our Lord temporarily divested himself of what was—and continues to be—eternally his.

By the way, I don't like the third verse of the Wesley hymn, "And Can It Be." Can it be that he "emptied himself of all but love"? That's what I say: Can this be! I can't believe that, so I don't sing that little phrase in the third verse. I just let it go by: La-la-la! Of course, now that I've made this point a number of times, people keep watching me when we come to that part. It's a great hymn, but I don't like that part. That's poetry gone awry. There was more than love on the cross. Otherwise it would be *kenosis*, i.e., 'an emptying', with a vengeance. But sometimes hymnology teaches bad theology, and people believe it. Well, enough said. Selah!

We must distinguish *moral* law from *positive* law. Positive law is true because someone said it to a particular person and had the authority to command. For example, in the New Testament we have commands—positive laws—like "Get in the boat!" "Loose the colt!" Have you ever kept these commands? They are New Testament commands. Why have you never done them? Have you ever decided, Okay, my verse for today is "Get in the boat!" So you find a lake and get into a boat. Or you're driving along and you see a little horse tied up. You say to yourself, Hmm, today my verse is Matthew 21:2, "Loose the colt!" I wonder if I shouldn't do that. It's an imperative and it is a part of God's message to us.

This is what we call positive law. Now, it's true that behind it lies the universal: the Lord who has the right to command his disciples to do such and such. Yes, we need to recognize that. But we don't understand Mark 6:45 to mean for us to get in a boat. People who get in the boat and say, "Ah ha! I've obeyed another verse today on my vacation!" are somewhat deficient in their understanding of biblical truths. We see the same deficiency in the Old Testament when people who "get in boats" think they are doing what the text says. A distinction needs to be made here; there is a difference between moral law and positive law.

### Principles for Interpreting the Moral Law

What are principles for interpreting the moral law? The first principle is its prologue. The moral law, such as the Ten Commandments starting in Exodus 20:2, has the environment of grace. "I am the LORD your God who brought you up out of the land of Egypt, out of the land of slavery." That was g-r-a-c-e. No one there earned it; everybody there was in trouble. Moses himself will be disobedient, and many a time we hear the murmuring of the Israelites.

They murmur about the dining hall food. They say, "This is just an attempt to gag Israelites. That's what this is. It's the same stuff all the time. Manna, manna, manna! What's for lunch today? Manna! What was for lunch yesterday? Manna! That's all we get here—manna!"

When they don't have water, you remember, it is the same grumbling. This happens in the fortieth year, and Moses has had it with these people! All of them are saying, "We want a drink! We want a drink!" I doubt that you can imagine 2,000,000 people standing in front of you and saying, "I want a drink!" What does Moses do? He gets up there and the Lord tells him, "Speak to the rock."

"Speak to the rock, Lord? They already doubt that I have the marbles to lead them. They're out there saying that this man is 120 years old. 'Old gray Moses ain't what he used to be! He should have retired at 100. But no, this man is still leading us! What we should have is people out digging wells, searching for water. But what's he doing up there? Talking to a rock! Yoo-hoo, rock!' This does not make sense at all, Lord. What is the point?"

And the point God wants to demonstrate is that the only connection between their needs and his supply is his word! He wants to help these people understand. "Speak the word," he is saying. That very morning, God sent bread. Couldn't he just as easily have sent a shower, too? It is as easy to send a shower as it is to send manna. But he says, "Speak to the rock."

Instead of speaking to the rock, however, Moses takes his staff and says to the people, "You rebels, you want me to bring you water? Okay,

I'll give you water!" And he slugs the rock! He slugs it twice. Some say he broke the type (a type of Christ, who, once crucified, does not need to be crucified again), but it wasn't that he broke the type. It was rather that he spoke inadvisedly; that's the biblical commentary. I know that some footnotes in our Bibles tell us differently, but the inspired part of the text says that he spoke inadvisedly with his lips (Ps 106:33). He stole glory from God.

Why did God bless them? It's the environment of grace. The prologue has grace as the basis for any of its requirements.

Secondly, all moral law is double-sided. This means we can express it either positively or negatively. Since our freedom is the much larger part, the easier way is to express it negatively: when we say what we can't do, we imply all that part that we must do.

Another way to put that is the third principle of interpretation: The mere omitting or refraining from doing a forbidden act is not a moral response. By mere omission, I mean, for example, that I never killed anyone and I'm certainly not going to take up a knife or get a gun and shoot someone. However, that is not observing the commandment, "Thou shalt not kill." That is not a moral response. It is death. To do nothing is death in the moral realm.

The fourth principle in interpreting moral law is that the opposite good of a forbidden evil must be practiced if we are to be obedient. I must actively seek to protect the life and to encourage the life of others if I am indeed carrying out "Thou shalt not kill."

### The Three Areas of the Decalogue

To help us in our understanding of the moral law, we can divide the Ten Commandments into three categories. These are: 1) right relations to God, 2) right relations in the use of time, and 3) right relations with society. Under the first heading, right relations to God, we can list the first three commandments:

Commandment 1:  In internal worship.
Commandment 2:  In external worship.
Commandment 3:  In verbal worship.

Under the second heading we have:

Commandment 4:  Right relations in the use of time.

Under the third heading, right relations with society, we list commandments five through ten:

Commandment 5:  The sanctity of family and superiors. "Honor your father and mother."
Commandment 6:  The sanctity of life.

Commandment 7:   The sanctity of marriage and sex.
Commandment 8:   The sanctity of property.
Commandment 9:   The sanctity of truth.
Commandment 10: The sanctity of motive.

By the way, commandment five does not say "obey"; it says "honor." The Bible only says "obey" when it qualifies it with "in the Lord." Our parents are always to have due reverence and respect, but they are not necessarily to be obeyed in every circumstance. There is a teaching abroad that misses that fine point.

### The Moral Law Is Illustrated

We argue, then, that the moral law is illustrated in the Book of the Covenant, Exodus 20:22 through chapter 23, which is civil law; in the law of Deuteronomy 5–26, which is civil law; and in the law of holiness, Leviticus 18–20. These are the aspects of the one Law of God.

The next chapter will show how another aspect of the Law—the ceremonial law of God—is carried out.

## Chapter Nine

# The Theology of the 'Tabernacling' God
## Exodus 25 through Leviticus

We come now to Exodus 25, where we begin the last section in our work together on the Law: This is the ceremonial law. At the heart of the ceremonial law was the establishment of the tabernacle and all of the institutions that came with it. Here, the third part of the tripartite formula was fulfilled: "I will dwell in the midst of you." The first part was "I will be your God"; the second part, "You shall be my people." We have discussed what it means to be God's firstborn, his son, his possession, a royal priesthood. Now we come to the third part: "I will dwell in the midst of you."

That theology of dwelling is pointed out in Exodus 29:42-45, where God says, "For the generations to come, I will meet you and speak to you at the tent of meeting. There also will be the place consecrated by my glory. So I will consecrate the tent of meeting and the altar, and I will consecrate Aaron and his sons to serve me as priests. Then I will dwell among all the Israelites and I will be their God." This passage expresses two parts of that tripartite formula. Exodus 29:46 continues, "Then they will know that I am the LORD their God, who brought them up out of Egypt so that I might dwell among them." So twice in these verses we have a reference to dwelling in the midst of them. At the end, almost like a signature, God says, "I am the LORD their God." I am Jehovah. Signed: *Yahweh*.

## Introduction

Bernard Ramm in his popular commentary on Exodus, entitled *His Way Out* (Glendale, Calif.: Regal Books, 1974) points out that the first part of Exodus is on redemption, the middle section on morality, and the last part on worship. The Exodus text moves from redemption to living to worshipping. Ramm says (p. 148), "Redeemed man is called to morality," and hence the Ten Commandments are the center of the book. "Moral man is called to worship"; hence the tabernacle comes at the end. "The redeemed man shows his repentance in the quality of his moral life; he shows his gratitude in his worship."

One of the most divisive issues appearing in the church these days is the theology and practice of worship, with tension between liturgical and nonliturgical modes of worship. Should we sing our songs out of five-pound hymnals or from words projected by overheads on the wall? This is dividing the church. We have the "new lights" and the "old lights." I do declare that before we are finished, we will have the "off-the-wall people" and the "out-of-the-book people." And this is just one issue.

This is only a small expression of the question of the *theology of worship*; the problem continues to grow. In the more liturgical expressions, should we allow more lay involvement in the prayers of the people, in the testimony time, or in greeting other worshippers during the service? This last practice is what I call the seventh-inning stretch—greet the brethren time. I have never quite become accustomed to this. The church service, through the liturgy or song service, is building—building—building up to the sermon—and then suddenly the leader says, "Let's all stand and shake hands." So everyone goes wandering around the sanctuary, greeting the brethren. I have even been abandoned on the platform by those who are off down the aisle greeting others. I call this a theological seventh-inning stretch. The worship service has a natural progression and—whoom! The bottom drops out of it. Then for the speaker to come on the program and try to speak defies all the laws of gravity!

On the other end of the spectrum are those who have been brought up in a strict fundamental church and who have reacted against this. They go on the "Canterbury Trail" in search of a high liturgical expression in worship.

I am not making value judgments here, even though I have fun talking about "off-the-wall singing" or about the "Canterbury Trail." Some people hunger for a more candid, a more involved, kind of expression of their worship, while others long for an expression of the majesty of God and the *mysterium*, the mystery, of God. The search for these two modes of worship is going on simultaneously.

All the while, what is lacking is a theology of worship and some discussion on the practice of worship. We need this desperately, for it represents another vacuum where the times have moved beyond us. People are asking better questions than anyone is prepared exegetically to discuss. We need to prepare ourselves to discuss the problem soon, before the whole thing is polarized with people positioning themselves as the "new lights" and the "old lights," in both the liturgical groups and the nonliturgical groups. It will split both traditions.

## The Tabernacle: The Dwelling of God

It is in this context that I introduce the tabernacle. The tabernacle is the dwelling of God, and it seems to me that as the tent of meeting, it stresses both God's transcendence and his immanence.

### The Tent of Meeting Stresses God's Transcendence

In the tabernacle we can see the transcendence and *mysterium*—the mystery—and the majesty of God: God is totally other. This is stressed by the fact that this is the only place where he comes to dwell, to *shakan*. One of the names for the tabernacle is the *mishkan*, coming from the verb *shakan*, to dwell. Most scholars, though some think the point is overdrawn, feel that this is a temporary tenting—pup tenting, if you please: tabernacle-dwelling with men. It is temporary because heaven is really the permanent dwelling place of this transcendent God.

Reflecting this particular concept, to 'dwell' or to 'tent' or 'to tabernacle' with man, is the word *shakan*. As a matter of fact, from that verb we get the expression, the *shekinah* glory of God, the indwelling glory of God.

In Exodus 25:8, God tells Moses to speak to the children of Israel, saying, "Have them make a sanctuary"—a tabernacle—"for me, and I will dwell among them" (NIV). The concept of God coming to dwell among men, dwelling in their midst, is definitely connected with the tabernacle and is connected with worship. Our word *worship*, of course, comes from an old root which we have shortened in English. It is 'worthship', which has been shortened by dropping the 'th'; the 'ship' on the end makes it abstract. It is basically an expression of God's worth, his value, his significance in our lives. Worship is an attempt to address back to God what he means to us and to hear God state who he is. Hence, we come with the purpose of collective or gathered worship: corporate worship.

Exodus 25:8 brings together sanctuary and dwelling. In the next verse we find, "Make this tabernacle and all its furnishings exactly like the pattern" (NIV). The word for pattern is a signal that this is only a model; it is our clue that these instructions, which will concern not only the tabernacle and its furnishings but also the services that are to be accomplished there, have a built-in obsolescence. They are to be valuable only for a period of time. When the *real* comes, then these will be outdated. It is a built-in warning which says, Be careful! What is here has only pictorial value. It is only a blueprint. The real exists somewhere else.

In the Old Testament, the services and the sacrifices and the priests and the whole liturgy were only a shadow of things to come. It is out of this same theology that the book of Hebrews talks about the shadow of those things to come. They were representations of what was coming, the actual or the real in the death and burial and resurrection of our Lord Jesus on the first Good Friday and Easter. The last verse of Exodus 25 says,

"See that you make them according to the pattern that I showed you on the mount." This is not the only time when the idea of a pattern is stressed; it is a primary concept in this important series of discussions on the tabernacle. Things are to be done according to the pattern that God shows to Moses on the mount. The tent is there only as a copy; the real is to come later. The tabernacle is God's temporary abode.

But this did communicate a new sense of God's closeness and, therefore, of his actual presence. God begins to be featured not only as a remote God who is way up there, but also as immanent. He is right here in the work with us. If we spell the word *immanent* with an *emi-*, that is a different theology: God is eminent and exalted. If we spell it with an *immi-*, it means something that is threatening to come, such as the imminent appearing of Christ. These are two very different words. We mean the word that is the opposite of transcendent: 'immanent' stresses his nearness.

### The Ark of the Covenant Stresses God's Immanence

Part of the theology of God's immanence is found in the central feature of the tabernacle, to which the text turns in Exodus 25:10: the ark of the covenant. This is the most important piece of furniture. So the instruction on the tabernacle begins with the ark of the covenant, for it is significant both in position and in theology. What is stressed here with regard to the ark of the covenant?

We have already talked about the verb *shakan*, which means to 'dwell'. Here another verb is important: *yashab*. Rather than dwelling, *shakan*, now we have *yashab* (the 'b' pronounced as a 'v' here under certain conditions), which means to 'sit' or to 'be seated'. This would seem to stress a permanent dwelling of God, that he is in the midst of his people.

Where is the ark of the covenant to be found? As we know, the tabernacle was divided roughly into two main sections. There was a larger portion known as the Holy Place, where most of the furniture for the tabernacle was kept. And then there was a cubicle called the Holy of Holies, the more remote of the two sections, which was reserved for the ark of the covenant in the center, with two cherubim—those winged creatures covered with gold—extending to the walls of that particular room. The room was separated from the Holy Place by a curtain and entered only once a year on Yom Kippur, the Day of Atonement, the day of "at-one-ment" between God and man. We will look at this theology of atonement and the at-one-ment, the state of being at one with God, in the next chapter.

The priest would go in past the incense altar, which signified the prayers of the saints going up before God. Hence incense went up; God loves to hear both the praise and the requests and intercession of his saints. Not that God is hungry for praise. He is not saying, "Praise me! Praise me! Praise me!" As if by praising God, we could add something to him! But as C. S. Lewis said, it's like a picture that is praiseworthy. The picture sits there on the wall and it is not saying, "Praise me and my painting will become different. My colors will take on different shapes." Nothing happens to the picture, but something happens to us when we praise the picture.

Did you ever climb a mountain on a clear day and get to the top of the mountain all by yourself with no one to talk to and share with: "Wow, isn't that beautiful!" So you say it out loud anyway, "Wow, look at that!" Your enjoyment is not complete until you find someone to share it with. And when you get down that mountain, if you have breath left, you will tell the first person you see, "It was the most sensational experience I've ever had!" You've got to get that out! You've got to share it! That's what it's like to praise God, and that partly takes place in prayer.

God is enthroned, seated, in the Holy of Holies. He sits between the cherubim and over the ark of the covenant. He is seated, *yashab*, between the cherubim. Not that God is squashed in between these creatures, as it were; rather, he is seated. "Court is in session," we could say. God is in session, and he is in the midst of his people.

As a symbol of this, over top of the tabernacle is a cloud by day and a pillar of fire by night. Can you imagine what a camp for 2,000,000 people would be like with this giant mercury light that lights up all those acres at night? That is the symbol that *God is there*. In the day it looks like a nuclear plant with a huge head of steam on a cold day, extending like a thunderhead over the whole camp. That is a symbol of the presence of God. We will talk about those a little later.

So, God sits on the throne above the ark, between the cherubim. This is indicated in 1 Samuel 4:4, in 2 Samuel 6:2, and in Psalm 99:1. Those are only some of the places where it occurs. God says in Exodus 25:22, "I will meet with you and give you all my commands for the Israelites" (NIV). Where does it say that he will meet them? Over the cover of the ark, between the two cherubim that are over the ark of the covenant. That was the meeting place between God and man. And that meeting place is the place where God and man can become at one. So the state of becoming at one, we call at-one-ment: *atonement*. We created this word in English to represent this root, k-p-r in Hebrew: *kippur—Yom Kippur* or the Day of Atonement. It is the state of being at one.

So here we have the tabernacle, God's *mishkan*, God's temporary dwelling. There is not only the emphasis that he is dwelling temporarily, for he is permanently in the heaven of heavens, but there is simultaneously a stress on immanency in this theology of the tabernacle and the ark.

## Four Other Forms of the Divine Presence

Four other forms of the divine presence are found in this section. The first of the four forms is the *face* of God as a representation of his presence or of his appearance.

*The "Face" Appearance, or Presence, of the Lord*

The face, of course, is that part of the body which expresses the greatest variety of feelings and attitudes. Our faces really tell others what is on the inside. Someone has said that you can't do much about your face when you're born, but you certainly are responsible for what you look like at forty or fifty. Our faces reflect our history; they reflect our lives. The biblical text, I think, uses the word *face* as a statement for the variety of God's feelings, his attitudes, his expressions to us, and, therefore, his presence.

Just so, Deuteronomy 4:37 says, "He brought you out of Egypt by his face." "By his face," literally. It was the face of God that brought them up. In other words, 'face' means his presence which expressed his feelings; his presence which expressed his attitude toward them; his presence which expressed his grace for them. For he was putting up with an awful lot! The whole time there was murmur, murmur, murmur! Complain, complain, complain! I think if I had been God, I would have been tempted numerous times to say, "Forget the whole deal! These people don't deserve it. Moses doesn't deserve it; Aaron doesn't deserve it; the elders don't deserve it; the leaders in the tribes don't deserve it. No one deserves it!" In fact, the children of Israel deserved to be deserted.

At any rate, the attitude of God toward his people is expressed by the face of God. In an interesting text, Exodus 33 speaks of the face of God. The passage is an interlude in all those instructions to Moses about the tabernacle. Moses was on the mount getting the Ten Commandments, which were written with the finger of God. As a matter of fact, God has no finger any more than he has a face, but this must be a way of stating how the commandments were written on stone tablets. Cecil B. DeMille had his own ideas about this and used the image of lightning bolts to engrave the rock. Of course, there is no evidence for that, either.

To be sure, the commandments were written in some direct way, much like a hand that comes on the wall and writes the words that so frighten Belshazzar: *"Mene, mene, tekel, upharsin."* You remember, Belshazzar has been drinking, but what he sees is enough to sober him up. He says, "I see something!" And so do all the rest of the guests. So we do have this concept of the finger of God here while Moses is on the mountain.

As our narrative continues, God suddenly says, "Go down, because the people have fallen into idolatry." Moses goes down and there he sees that the people have "risen up to play" (Ex 32:6). Now, obviously, that's a euphemism: the people are into religious prostitution and sexual immorality. While Moses was up on the mountain, they have cast off their clothes. They have made the icon of which they have said, "This now is our God"— or "our gods"—"that brought us up from the land of Egypt." And they begged Aaron to make a god for them.

Moses says, "Aaron, brother, how could you have done this?"

And with the weakest excuse ever given in the history of mankind, Aaron says, "Well, I threw this gold into the fire and out came this calf." That's exactly what he says here!

Moses says, "You've committed a great sin!" And he says, "This is terrible!" Exodus 32:25 says he "saw that the people were running wild" (NIV). They had cast off all restraint and were out of control, so that they had become the laughingstock of their enemies.

By the way, that verse is picked up again in Proverbs 29:18. There is an informing theology and allusion to this text. "Where there is no vision" —where there is no *revelation*—"the people perish." This verse is not saying that you should have a five-year plan, although I do believe in that. Or a ten-year plan. That's good too. Or a fifteen-year plan. Bless you! But that is not what the verse is saying. Proverbs 29 says that where there is no input of the divine Word—when there is absence of the Word of God— the people will "bust loose." The word is just that: they will break loose. That is what happens here in Exodus: the children of Israel are running wild. It is the same verb. Proverbs is the only other place where it occurs with this meaning. Solomon is saying, "Fail to preach the Word and you will find that the people will run wild." We saw some of that, I think, from 1963 to 1969. There was a famine of the teaching of the Word of God.

There's a difference between talking *about* the Bible and "putting your finger on the verse." I tell my students, When you preach, keep one finger on the verse and gesture with the other hand. Then when that arm gets tired, put that finger on the verse and gesture with the opposite hand. That way, you're constantly bringing your attention back to the text. If you do not have a verse or paragraph or series of paragraphs in mind to support what you say, then don't say it. Or at least be honest with the people and say, "This week I prepared a message, but I don't know where the passage is to support it. However, I really would like to talk to you about this. If any of you can think where this passage is by the time we conclude, would you please mention it to me? As a prize, there will be a free book put out by one of our Christian publishers, of course." I think that would be fair. I have never heard of this being done, but it would be one way to do it.

As I said, we talk too much *about* the Bible. As a matter of fact, I am in such reaction that I have advised my students to preach topically once every five years and then go back to preaching exposition. I do not have a Bible verse to support that; it is just a reaction, and my students understand that I have swung way over to the other side. I just think that there is a famine of the Word of God today. "Where there is no vision"—where there is no input, no *ḥazon*, no revelation from God—"the people break loose." This might be the reason some in the ministry say, "I can't keep the church together. What can be wrong?" The difficulty could be in part a lack of teaching. Perhaps there has been a vacuum, and problem weeds have had a chance to spring up.

Now, in the context of this disobedience and this "breaking loose," it looks as if God is going to be forgetful of his promise. For the moment, it looks as if Moses may be more merciful than God. But don't forget that it was God who prepared Moses to stand in the gap. For Moses says, "Lord, what will the enemy say? No, Lord, don't do that! Take me instead of them. Let me be an atonement, a substitute for the people."

God says, "No, there's no need for that." Then, "All right, I will forgive them for your sake—for your praying and standing in the gap." Moses was a man who stood in the gap, prepared by God.

Because of his confession and his offer as a *substitute* here—it uses the word—God said, "All right, I will continue to bless them." This is a difficult thing to understand, but I sense that is what the text is saying.

Moses says, in Exodus 33, "Lord, let me see your face. Give me some guarantee."

The Lord answers, "No one can see me and live. You can't look on me and live."

Moses continues, "Well, Lord, I need some kind of assurance."

"All right," says the Lord. "Get in the cleft of the rock and I will cause all my goodness to pass by." In other words, God has his nature, his characteristics, his glory, his presence pass by in front of Moses.

Notice the mixed figure of speech here in Exodus 33:22-23: "With my hand ...." With his hand, God protects Moses in the cave as he passes by and Moses is able to see God's 'aḥar, says the Hebrew. This is often poorly translated as 'his back', but God does not have a back. "God is spirit: and they that worship him must worship him in spirit and truth." I realize that verse is from the New Testament in John 4:24, but Isaiah 31:3 also says that God is not like the Egyptians or like their horses: they are made out of flesh. Both the Old Testament and the New Testament teach that God does not have flesh. So what is this? I think it means that God causes his glory to pass by and Moses sees the 'after', that which follows. The word 'aḥar is 'the back' or 'that which follows' or 'the end'. I think we would translate it today as 'the afterburn'. The glory of God goes by and Moses sees the afterburn. He cannot look on the glory of God: the effulgence, the brilliance of the reality of his presence. But what he can look on is the effect, and he sees the afterburn—the afterglow—of the glory of God that has gone by.

"Let me see your face," Moses says. Notice how the face, then, stands for the presence of God.

By the way, this concept of the goodness of God passing in front of someone occurs one other time. This is in Elijah's case after Mount Carmel; he runs away from Jezebel. Remember, Jezzie has threatened him. (I call her Jezzie because I think I know her.) She's a real rascal of a gal. How did Ahab ever come to marry her? She really has him tied up in stitches.

I mean, she says to him, "What! are you a man or are you a mouse? Daddy wouldn't have done this! When my father rules up in Lebanon, I tell you he knows how to rule. There's a man for you! What are you doing here? You've got problems with Naboth and his vineyard? Come here and let me settle the thing." I mean, that's the kind of take-charge woman she is.

Her husband comes home one day and says, "Honey, we did not have a very good day today. I think you lost all 850 prophets of Baal and Asherah. The prophet Elijah polished them off. I tell you, there's no seminary left. The whole thing is gone!"

She really gets furious. But does she go out and get Elijah? Oh no! Smart woman that she is, she intimidates him. She says to Elijah, "I'll give you twenty-four hours to get out of town. Stay around here and make my day! Stay around here and see if I don't do the same to you as you did to those 850 prophets. Or else I'm not Jezebel!"

So what does Elijah do? He runs! After having gone ninety miles, down near Beersheba he sits down under a broom tree and says, "Oh, Lord, take my life! It's not worth it. Let me go eat worms. Nobody loves me and everybody hates me. I was pent up for three years, part of the time with the birds bringing me food. Ravens. You know they're unclean. And they'd bring me this stuff to eat. Actually, I should have thought I'd have heavenly waiters, but what did I get? Birds! This thing is for the birds!"

He goes on, "Then I was with this woman—a Gentile woman and this kid—pent up all the time. I tell you, it really bugs me! Here I am a great prophet of the Lord and could have been out among thousands of people. What did I have? The kid. Three years of my life! And I thought one great revival would do it." But he continues, "What is it? And she's going to kill me for this. No revival." So he says, "Take my life."

We know he's kidding, because if he wanted someone to take his life, all he had to do was stay around. Jezzie would have done it free of charge. But, no, he runs away, and is sitting down there moaning, "Take my life! Take my life!"

Then he goes down "to the cave" as 1 Kings 19 says. The English says "a cave," but the Hebrew says "the cave." We say, What cave? No cave has been immediately mentioned. But remember, he is at Sinai and he comes to "the cave," and God says, "Come out and stand in the presence of the LORD, and I will cause all my goodness"—i.e., I will cause my name—"to pass by." This is right out of the same context of informing theology from Exodus 33:19. This man, Elijah, needs a whole new view of God; exactly what Moses had as well.

So to see the presence of God is to see the character of God. It is to see the person of God. That is the theology of worship here: a new view of the presence of God. This brings life into proportion and brings life's problems into proportion. Great worship occurs when there is a great view of God!

God must be exalted in the speaking; he must be exalted in the praying; he must be exalted in the singing.

And great theology centers around great doxology! We can't have great preaching without great singing—without a great praising of God. They go together. Most of our worship services are deficient in doxology. Rote singing of the Doxology, "Praise God from whom all blessings flow," won't do. Praise-singing springs from a heart that just came in from the past week and says, "We narrowly missed a terrible accident and God spared us. The car's gone but we're here. Praise God from whom all blessings flow!" If you can sing that on Sunday, you know you've been there. That is where the people in the Old Testament came from, too.

Well, that was one of the principles, the face of God.

### The Angel of the Lord

A second form of divine presence is the "angel of the LORD." Exodus 23:20-21 is a most amazing passage with regard to the angel of the Lord: "See, I am sending an angel ahead of you to guard you along the way and to bring you to the place I have prepared. Pay attention to him and listen to what he says. Do not rebel against him; he will not forgive your rebellion, since my Name is in him" (NIV). That angel of the Lord had the very name of God. The character, the being of God was in that angel, which I think is a way of saying the angel was synonymous with the second person of the Trinity. So we have here the angel that went ahead of them, the presence of God indicated by an angel.

It is interesting that we see divine causation along with human responsibility. As symbols of God's presence there were the pillar of cloud, the angel of the Lord, the face of God, the glory of God. There is also the ark of the covenant going before the Israelites through the wilderness. Moses also hired his son-in-law to give them direction. In addition, all that Moses knew from his years of studying in Pharaoh's court and in Midian was used as he led these people. Isn't that interesting? So we see human responsibility side by side with divine sovereignty.

This is the same angel of the Lord that appeared to the patriarchs: it is the angel who manifests his *person*. If the face of God shows his attitude and his feelings, then the angel of the Lord demonstrates his person—the very person of God.

### The Glory of the Lord

Then there is the glory of God. It is the uncovered holiness of God; that is, the totality of all his qualities. Holiness stands for God, what he is wholly. The wholeness of God is that which shows his divine power; it is his visible extension in order to manifest himself to man.

This wholeness of God is manifested in the cloud in the tabernacle. At night the cloud became a pillar of fire which, as I understand it, gave iridescent light and illuminated the entire group of tents surrounding it. Remember the burning bush in Exodus 3, where again the glory of God is connected with luminosity. But more than luminosity or radiance or effulgence and outshining, there is the basic root of the word for 'glory', which means 'to be heavy'. It speaks of the sheer gravity, the sheer weight of his presence. Wherever we have this concept of the glory of God in the Bible, it is not just a theological term. Sometimes we limit our recognition of the power of this word because it is just a part of our religious vocabulary: "the glory of the LORD." We may stretch out our arms and say "the g-l-o-r-y of the LORD!" But what the word really means is the fact of his presence: he would be there. The effects of his presence are the rays, the light, the outshining.

That is what we have when God calls Ezekiel and gives him a vision of his glory. Ezekiel saw this heavenly dune buggy-like vehicle: there was a platform with a throne supported by a living creature at each corner. Each had four wings. Two were stretched out—sort of like oriental furniture around the corners—supporting the throne; the other two wings of each creature covered the legs. The creatures "were associated with wheels that apparently were much like modern desk furniture wheels; they were able to turn in any direction without the need of a steering mechanism," as I wrote in *Toward an Old Testament Theology* (Grand Rapids: Zondervan, 1978). The whole point of this vision was to give a picture of the glory of God. He was telling Ezekiel—and us: "Don't be afraid. This thing doesn't have a steering wheel. You can go east, west, north, or south. You can go off in any angle—a 45 degree angle, a 68 degree angle, any angle—and God will be there. *He will be there!*" The "there-ness" of God—the glory of the Lord—is being stressed.

Look at the text in Acts 7. It is an amazing passage which tells us of the presence of God all the way back in Mesopotamia at Ur of the Chaldees. You remember Stephen, in his defense, reviews the history of the children of Israel and the concept of the glory of God. In Acts 7:2 he says, "Brothers and fathers, listen to me! The God of glory"—here's the concept of glory— "appeared to our father Abraham while he was still in Mesopotamia." Then the amazing text in Acts 7:55, where Luke writes, "But Stephen, full of the Holy Spirit, looked up to heaven and saw the glory of God" (NIV). He saw the glory of God!

Now comes the Greek *kai* clause, and how shall we translate this *kai*? He saw the glory of God. I think it is ep-exegetical; it is in apposition. I would translate it: He "saw the glory of God, *even* Jesus standing at the right hand." *Even* Jesus standing at the right hand: the presence of God. The presence of God, in this case, looks like a Christophany. It looks as if the second person of the Trinity was moving along with them. In other words, the real presence of Jesus accompanied the children of Israel as they went through the wilderness. This is a rather exciting and a very important concept. I think that the *and* should be understood as *even*: He "saw the glory of God, *even* Jesus standing at the right hand of God" the Father. As Isaiah 40:5 says, this is "the glory of the LORD" that "shall be revealed, and all flesh shall see it together."

### The Name of God

The fourth and final form of divine presence in the worship theology of the Old Testament is God's name. In Exodus 33:19, it is Yahweh himself who is mentioned, for he says, "I will cause all my goodness to pass in front of you, and I will proclaim *my name*" (NIV). The name of God is that which will accompany his people. Deuteronomy 12:5 says he will form a place—the tabernacle and later the temple—where he will put his name, his presence. The name of God safeguards the unity of God, because the name and the person are identical.

We can look at several other passages where *name* is used. Revelation 3:4 uses the word *names* to indicate persons: "You have a few names in Sardis"—a few *persons* in Sardis. The word *name* stands also for Jesus' *doctrine.* He says in John 17, "I have taught these men your name." He does not say "your name, Elohim"; here he means that he taught them the doctrine. Psalm 22 says: "They taught them the name." 'Name' also stands for the *ethic*: "They walk in the name of the LORD." It doesn't mean they step on Elohim, El Shaddai—and say, "Hi, there!"—and then go on stepping across. No, the name of God is a path of morality or ethics in which they walk. And the name of God is his very character. That is why we should not take the name of the Lord God in vain.

And so we conclude this chapter on the theology of worship, especially as it centers in the tabernacle in the Old Testament.

# Chapter Ten

# The Theology of the Atonement

## Leviticus 16 and Isaiah 52:13–53:12

### Introduction

The theology of the atonement is basically found in the great teaching passage of Leviticus 16. But before we turn to Leviticus 16, we want to say something about the third aspect of the Law, which embraces the Day of Atonement, *Yom Kippur*. That is the ceremonial aspect. It is the ceremonial segment of the Law which provides men and women in the Old Testament with a way of being reconciled to God.

The great problem is that the standard of the Law is set so high. That standard is the very character of God. Of course, the immediate reaction of all sinning mortals since Adam is that the standard is set too high. Who can attain unto it? This is why we have the ceremonial aspect of the Law. While the Law does set a high standard, it also provides a way of being reconciled, of getting right with God, in the event, which is inevitable, of failure.

There is something arbitrary about our taking the Law apart and talking about the moral aspect, the civil aspect, and the ceremonial aspect. Please understand that these are not hard and fast categories that we find in the biblical text; these are categories of convenience. And just as we speak of three aspects of the one Law, we will speak of this ceremonial aspect of the Law as having at least three strands. We have already talked about one strand in the previous chapter: the tabernacle. The tabernacle provides both the setting and the context for worship.

But we want to consider two other strands. The second strand is the clean and the unclean, and the third strand is sacrifices. All together these three strands make up the one ceremonial law, just as the ceremonial law along with the moral law and the civil law are parts of the one Law given by God.

104

Though that Law is one and is, in itself, inseparable, yet we have learned that our Lord said some things are "weightier." We talked about how we thought the "weight" belonged to the moral law of God, for that reflects his character. Then we talked about how the civil law was nothing more than illustrations of the moral law in everyday life, as it was worked out mainly in the political and family and personal institutions in the life of Israel.

Now we will see the ceremonial law as a further explication of the moral law, particularly with regard to the command, "Be holy as I, the LORD your God, am holy." It has to do with holiness or wholeness, being totally separate and distinct and set apart to God—the call for believers to be *different*.

So we will talk about the ceremonial law as having three strands. The first is the tabernacle, which stresses the dwelling of God: God who will dwell in the midst of men. Second, there is the clean and the unclean. Leviticus 10–11 will speak particularly of this matter. Third, we will talk about sacrifices. We cannot take these up in detail, but we can see that there is a connection here.

## The Strand of Clean/Unclean

First of all, let's take the strand of the *clean* and the *unclean*. Note that *this is not to be equated with what is forbidden or dirty*. This does not mean that "cleanliness is next to godliness." That is not exactly the point of this particular teaching. Rather, the point here, it seems to me, is that life has many unavoidable, legitimate aspects which make a person temporarily unclean: for example, preparing a body for the grave; giving birth; the menstrual cycle; sexual relations. There is nothing wrong with these things. As a matter of fact, they are necessary. They are God-given in many instances. So the laws were not primarily to teach hygiene or to teach sanitary standards, though one of the effects of these teachings would be standards of hygiene and sanitation. Instead, many of these rules just show that the Lord is still sovereign; he is Lord over all aspects of life.

For example, there is the very unusual requirement here to abstain from the marital act during menstruation for women, and during menopause. I think that this is a way of saying that no individual is sovereign over his/her marriage partner. This is simply another area where God is demonstrating himself to be Lord. So this is a symbol of the special work of God.

What do we mean by *clean/unclean*? It seems to me that it was simply *the qualification for meeting with God*. As the Israelites came to the dwelling place of God, there was a wholistic approach which involved more than the heart. Yes, it always began in the heart, for without preparation in the heart, there was no use in going ahead with a sacrifice. The text will say over and over again, What is the purpose of all these sacrifices? What is the purpose of the new moon meeting, the feast, the calling of assemblies, the bringing of your tithes? Why do you bring them if you don't bring yourselves?

The injunction in the biblical text is that before we put anything else in the offering plate, we should "jump in ourselves." We are to give ourselves! God always looks at us before he looks at our sacrifices. God always looks at us before he listens to the prayers that we bring. God looks at us before he listens to the songs, the solos that we sing to him. This is part of the biblical teaching, that goes from the beginning of the text to the end.

Meeting with God in worship is so serious that one needs to prepare wholistically. Though preparation begins in the heart, it has an effect on the entire person. I wish we had taught this during the 1960s when some said, "What difference does it make? I feel authentic when I show up at church in cut-off jeans. I've even bleached them, you know. And I've got these sandals which I made out of a tire. This is the way that I want to come to church. After all, God looks at the heart. Isn't that right?"

I remember a fellow asking me during those days, "What difference does it make if I take up an offering in a tee shirt?" I said, "None, frankly, if that's all you have. But if you get married in a tux and you take up an offering in a tee shirt, I think that you show partiality, and therefore, you shout loud and clear what you think about God. For the Bible does say something about where you put value and what gets your priorities and your respect." I said, "If you had an appointment with the President of the United States or with another head of state, wouldn't you ask, 'What is the proper decorum? What is expected of me?'"

Some years ago, the president at one of the institutions I attended had a very important engagement with Emperor Haile Selassie. The president was instructed by our State Department on how to treat a king of another country. One of the instructions was not to turn his back. He was to walk in and back out, so that his back was never turned to the sovereign. That may sound ridiculous, but it was the cultural way of showing deference, not to the man, but to the requirements of the state and to the other person's culture.

I think that in the biblical text God tries to help his people realize that some things temporarily disqualify individuals from meeting with God. Not that these, in and of themselves, have any negative value, for there is an arbitrariness to them. But in the arbitrariness, there is a boundary that separates the spheres of the common and the sacred. For indeed there is a need to pay attention to the boundary between the secular (i.e., the common or the ordinary) and the sacred.

It is too bad that some erect such an enormous barrier between culture and Christ that they completely divorce the two. So we must warn: do not divorce Christ from culture! That is a terrible methodological mistake, according to biblical instruction. On the other hand, do distinguish between the two. To fail here is also a mistake. Bishop Robinson in his book, *Honest to God*, could not distinguish between the two. (In my judgment, he should have called his book *Honest to Robinson*, because his idea of God was wrong.) He said that the marital act was like taking communion or the Lord's Supper, that it was sacramental. Now, surely he was confused. He needed to know the difference between culture and Christ, but he could not distinguish them. He had so blended the two that he lost the correct perspective. Others so divide the two spheres that they see no relationship one to the other, and have built them into two separate worlds.

The biblical text wants us to fall in the middle, keeping a balance by not divorcing the two, but properly distinguishing between them. Thus it is that at the burning bush, Moses is told to take off his sandals. I can imagine this scenario. Moses complains, "Lord, why? Why take off these sandals? I feel authentic in them. I've been trucking around in them for forty years. Why take these things off?"

The Lord says, "Because you're standing on holy ground."

Then I can imagine Moses saying—and you realize, this is all strictly imagination—"But Lord, no offense! Sheep and goats went across this just yesterday. How can this be holy ground?"

"Because I am present."

So there was a line of demarcation between the secular and the sacred, between the common or the profane and the holy. The word *profane* is taken from *pro*, meaning 'before' or 'outside of', and *fanum*, meaning 'temple'. It is that which was separate from the temple, you see. We call that profane because it is common; it is the ordinary; it is the secular. Then there is the holy. Thus it was that when Moses went up on the mount, a boundary was set between the holy and the common. "Do not let your flocks, do not let any of your people come over this boundary, for God has come down on the mountain and it is holy. It is set apart for him."

Sometimes in our evangelical tradition we enter into the act of worship in a nonchalant and even flippant way, as if there were no line of demarcation between the common—the ordinary—and God. While we want to stress God's approachableness and his immanency, we must not forget his transcendence.

As theology teaches us, there is a gap between God and man; there is the subject of God and there is the subject of man. And a gap exists between these two circles: God, the top circle, and man, the bottom circle. The gap between the two is a gap of *ontology*, which simply means 'being'. God is separate in being from who we are. Secondly, a moral gap exists here. God is perfect, God is sinless; and we ourselves are sinners. So there is a gap between God who is creator and us who are creatures; between God who is sinless and us who are sinners. This gap, which is so extremely important, marks the boundary line between that which is holy and that which is common and belongs to the profane, the ordinary, the secular world.

So with two words, we see mortal conflict between the whole concept of *Christ and culture*. Incidentally, even in the word *holy* these two cultures are brought into direct conflict, for the word 'to be holy', *qadash*, means 'set apart'. Yet it also is the word used in the biblical text for a male prostitute, one who is set aside to the cult god in religious prostitution. Usually translated in the Authorized Version as 'dogs', it was a term of disgust; Jewish homes generally did not have dogs. It is also a word for a female prostitute, who is also set apart. So in one word we have two opposite applications: wholly set apart to God or the holiness of God, and wholly set apart to a deity or wholly set apart to a goddess. It is the same word. So the word *holy* in itself became a battle ground between two cultures.

God told Moses to remove his sandals so that he could demonstrate, in his body as well as in his heart, that he was in the presence of God. We must give serious consideration to the principle found in this text: There is a curtain pulled down between the ordinary, or common, and the presence of God that must in some way be preserved. That is partly what we learn from clean and unclean. This teaching on clean, therefore, is closely aligned with the teaching on holiness: "Be holy as I, the LORD your God, am holy."

Let me back up and stress the importance of the priority of the heart before we leave this section on clean and unclean. I'd like to illustrate this with the Cain and Abel story. In Genesis 4 we find a real contrast between the two boys and their worship, and there is an emphasis upon the heart. The words in Genesis 4:3 slow down the pace of the narrative. "In the course of time." We can almost yawn when we read that: "In—the—course—of—time—." Cain says, "I'd better go pick some stuff out of the garden." So he picks some stuff up and brings some fruits of the soil as an offering to the Lord. But Abel brings the *fat pieces* from some of the *firstborn* of his flock.

Here is a contrast in the two men shown by the contrast of two types of offering. From the beginning, even before there was a written ceremonial law, and without God having said that it should be done, the human family is shown in an act of worship by bringing sacrifice.

We do not know the origins of sacrifice. This is the first time it is recorded, and there is no word from God: "Bring me a sacrifice." At least, we have no knowledge of such a command at this point. So, what is the difference between these two sacrifices? You and I were probably taught that the difference was that one was a bloody sacrifice and the other was a bloodless sacrifice. Therefore, one truly pointed to the substitutionary atonement of our Lord and the other did not. However, that is tradition; it is not from the biblical text. For all of us who love the text and love to "keep our finger on the text," it is hard to demonstrate that teaching. Let me read the text. It says, "He brought fat portions." He did not get rid of all of the fat, as we are so concerned to do at home in our cooking or in our ordering when we go to a restaurant. Oh no! Those were the choice pieces in the ancient Near East.

On top of that, to bring the firstborn, that was like putting our first $50 in the offering plate. We might be tempted to say today, "Look, Lord, I've been out of work for a long time. I just made $50. Tell you what: I'll invest it and after ten years, we'll share. Okay? You'll be getting a whole lot more that way, and I will too, of course. I'll make you a deal." So we might want to hold on to the firstborn and not give it to the Lord. I was raised on a farm and I know that when you have a heifer, you wait for two or three years before the heifer has a calf. Then in ten years, you could have seven, eight calves. You might be tempted to say, "Lord, why give that heifer away? I'll tell you what: I'll split eight of the calves. I'll give you four during the ten years. You can have four and I'll have five, the original heifer plus four calves. Now don't you think that's a good deal, God?"

Contrary to this attitude, Abel brought the first fruits, the firstborn, to the Lord. The text says, "The LORD looked with favor on Abel and his offering, but on Cain and his offering he did not look with favor" (NIV). Notice where the emphasis is in this text. The Hebrew text says *Abel*, the personal name, then the pronoun *he*, then the adverb *he also*, then *he brought*. The emphasis here is obviously on the individual. It is Abel, he, he also. He ... he ... he .... It is difficult not to understand what is the most important thing in that sentence. This is emphasis with a vengeance!

Then the text says, *Cain, he, he also, he brought*. Once again an emphatic position, coming first in the Hebrew text: the man's name, the personal pronoun, the adverb, and then the suffix on the end of the verb, *he brought*. So where is the focus of God? It is on the man.

Notice the verb about God, too: "He had respect." The verb there means to show respect, or as it is translated in some Bibles, "He looked with favor." "To show respect" is an even better translation, for that verb shows us that it has to do with people, not with things. Again, the focus is upon people.

What is the point? The point is that God looks at me before he looks at what I bring. God looks at my heart before he looks at the way I'm dressed. The emphasis is on the priority of the heart. There is no reference to smoke, no reference to a knife, no reference to an altar, no reference to blood, no reference to any of those things that I would expect to be in the text. The emphasis of the text is God looking at the *man*: Abel; he; he also; he brought.

One last remark about this strand of the ceremonial law: the clean and the unclean. There is a good text in Leviticus which talks about the life of the flesh being in the blood (17:14). Go ahead and preach it! But don't apply it to the situation of Cain and Abel. That is what we call eisegesis: reading into the text and bringing in a later portion of Scripture to apply to an earlier time.

# The Strand of Sacrifices

Let's talk about the third strand of the ceremonial law, sacrifices. What we have seen here by way of illustration of the priority of the individual and the heart will also help us in thinking about the sacrifices in the ceremonial law.

## The Old Testament Concept of Sin

First of all, let's look at the Old Testament concept of sin. Most of the Hebrew vocabulary for sin falls under three categories. Sin has that three-fold picture vocabulary: sin as a *digression* or falling short; sin as a *transgression* or a shooting over; and sin as a *direct affront*, running right through.

In both Old Testament and New Testament terminology, we have the idea of a mark which is set up. The mark in this case is not as in archery. Of course, in the New Testament we also have the concept of an archer's arrow falling short of the mark. But the mark here is the Law—or if that sounds too Reformed and gives you problems, then let's say the mark is the Law or the will of God. Either way it is the same thing: sin is a falling short of the mark. The second word picture for sin is a shooting over the will of God. Some think they have a better idea than God—which is really something we cannot afford to do—and they go shooting over the will of God. The third word picture is running right through the will of God: direct confrontation. So we have these three ideas: sin as a *deviation* from or a falling short of the Law or will of God; sin as a *transgression* or a going over the will of God; and sin as *wickedness* or a direct affront. Of course, all three result in guilt before the Law or will of God. In that sense, we can define sin as a deliberate deviation or defection, an overriding or affront to the person, character, or Word of God, which results in a state of alienation. We are not talking about *guilt feelings*, but *real guilt* and alienation from God.

Sin, therefore, is a calculated act and is a state of real guilt. David confesses in Psalm 51:5 that, already before his act of sin, there was a nature—a drift, a propensity—toward opposing God which existed in him even from his mother's womb. He says, "In sin did my mother conceive me." He's giving expression to the fact that sin is the great problem. It is this part of the Law that, therefore, tries to help us with the wholeness and healing which are possible.

## The Source of Sin

What is the source of sin? The source of sin is the corrupted heart. Genesis 6:5 has already taught: "Every inclination of the thoughts of the heart was only evil all the time." The writer was talking about that culture and generation which God finally destroyed with the Flood. But where was the problem? It was in the inclination (*yetser*) of the heart and the thoughts of the heart. Jeremiah will say later on: "The heart is deceitful above all things and beyond cure. Who can understand it?" (Jer 17:9, NIV).

So the Old Testament teaching does focus on the heart and inner thought. Notice the thirty times 1 and 2 Chronicles focus on the heart, teaching that from the heart issues the life of a man. But even without taking into consideration 1 and 2 Chronicles, we can go through the Law itself and see the references to the heart. Notice, too, the emphasis upon the thought and the intention. I have gathered together these passages in my book, *Toward Old Testament Ethics*, where I have tried to show how many times the thought and the intention of the heart is the source of the problem; and that is what God really speaks to.

For example, in David's sin with Bathsheba, it is not merely the act that is sin; it is also the desiring and the looking. The narrative portrays in graphic detail how, as he is walking in the cool summer evening and looking down upon one of the roofs, he sees Bathsheba. Bathsheba is taking her ritual bath on the roof of her dwelling, for it is the time that is required for her to take the bath according to the Law.

Another clue that inner thoughts are at the heart of ethical teaching is found in the tenth commandment about desire and coveting. Paul says, "That's what did me in. I could keep the first nine commandments, but when I got to the tenth one, it did me in. But now I realize that it wasn't the mere act, but I needed to go back and review all the commandments, because they talk about the things that lead up to the act as well as to the actual deed itself."

Some misunderstand the Sermon on the Mount, where Jesus says, "You have heard it said ...." He is not contrasting what he says with what the Old Testament said. He does not say, "You have seen it *written*," but rather he says, "You have *heard it said*." He is talking about those "fiddlers on the roof." Tradition! Tradition! And what is the scribal tradition saying there? It repeats what was in the Old Testament: "Thou shalt not commit adultery." Jesus says, "Well, I tell you, whoever looks on a woman and lusts after her ...." Some say this is a new addition. Not so. Long before, Job said, "I made a covenant with my eyes ...." Talk about a covenant! There's one: "I made a covenant with my eyes not to look upon a maiden to lust after her" (Job 31:1). I can show you other passages like that where the same phenomenon was already in the Old Testament. So this whole idea of coveting and desiring shows us that the source of sin is in the heart and is in the intention; it is in the thought.

### The Division between Unconscious and Deliberate Sins Is Unbiblical

Is there not a distinction in the Old Testament between deliberate acts of sin and those which are sins of ignorance, unwitting sins? What about that distinction? It has been taught for years in our circles that there are deliberate sins and for these, apparently, according to the teaching of our tradition, there is no sacrifice. This seems to be taught in Numbers 15. On the other hand, sacrifice is possible for those unconscious, unwitting sins of ignorance in which we did not know what we were doing.

Well now, think of the logic behind that! If this were true, then it would seem that the best thing would be not to tell people what is sinful. This would give them a larger scope for sacrifice and for forgiveness. The meanest thing we could do is teach people about the Law of God, so that they would know more, and in that case, more of their sins would be deliberate and thus there would be no sacrifice for them.

But that does not seem to ring true either. How can David find forgiveness if this system is in operation? David with his complicity and murder; David with his sin of adultery. How can he pray the way he does in Psalm 32 and Psalm 51? How can he find forgiveness?

At first, David decides to tough it out. During the nine months of Bathsheba's pregnancy he says, "I'm cool. I'm not going to say anything about it. I'm just going to tough it out, stonewall it." But later he says, "Oh, my, it felt as if my bones were coming apart! I felt as if I was drying up inside" (Ps 32:3). And he says to himself, "Look here, dummy, why don't you confess it?" (I'm giving you the *Living Kaiser* translation here; that's not exactly what Psalm 32 says.) He says, "I finally said, 'Confess the thing.' Oh, the happiness! What a release it was!"

This is how to spell 'relief' in the Old Testament: c-o-n-f-e-s-s-i-o-n. This is how to spell relief in the New Testament, too: we confess to God. David says, "Let me make a recommendation to all of you. I'm going to give you my professional opinion. If you have sinned, out with it before God!" He was very conscious of sin and of the *relief* found in confession.

So how are our categories working out? They are not operating at all! This makes me think that the division is wrongly placed. How then shall we divide between the sins here, for definitely Numbers 15 does talk about something that seems to be very serious. It looks as if there is a sin for which there is no forgiveness. I would like to suggest that it is the so-called "sin with a high hand." And that is exactly what it is. It is bending the arm in a menacing fashion, clenching the fist hard, and shaking it against heaven. That is a sin with a high hand. I think we ought to put a sign in churches: a big circle with a clenched fist and a red slash through it, like our traffic signs. People in church would understand. No Defiance Against Each Other or Against God! No rebellion. You just can't do that here!

It was even more serious in the biblical text, for in Numbers 15:17 ff. we notice that the Lord says to Moses, "Speak to the Israelites and say to them ...." What does verse 30 say? "Anyone who sins defiantly ...." That is sin with a high hand. That is the clenched fist. That is literally the expression here. It says "sin with a high hand." It's a clenched-fist, in-your-face defiance.

Moses says, "If a person sins defiantly with a high hand, he blasphemes the Lord." I think what we are seeing here is what Matthew 12:31 calls blasphemy against the Holy Spirit, which is described in Hebrews 10:26-31. This is the same thing that is called the unpardonable sin in the New Testament—the only sin which is unpardonable. This is the decision to take God on. It is blaspheming him and his Word.

That is why there is no forgiveness; for the person committing this sin despises the Lord's Word, breaks his commands, and must surely be cut off (Heb 10:26-31, 39). His guilt remains on him. I understand this to be a person who, out of the goodness and kindness of God, has had continual chastening, just as Psalm 23 says: "Surely goodness and mercy shall follow me all the days of my life." *Yirdephuni.* Literally, goodness and mercy shall *chase* me all the days of my life.

I can picture these things graphically in Old Testament concrete terms. Here goes an individual down the road and along comes Goodness running after him like the roadrunner in the American cartoon. Beep! Beep! The person keeps saying, "Get off my back, God! I'll do it myself. Leave me alone." But God keeps sending Goodness, and God keeps sending Mercy. Beep! Beep! "Wait up! Wait up! We want to bless you; we want to help you."

This continues. Surely Goodness and surely Mercy continue to run after the ungodly. We might say, "Why is God so good to the ungodly? Why do the wicked seem to be prospering? I can think of some people who had just a camper last year at vacation time. This year on the back of the camper is a dirt bike and also a big motor boat. It's a parade! I can't believe it!" Remember Psalm 23: there goes Goodness and there goes Mercy chasing after them, all the days of their life.

So here we have one division: (1) There are sins of inadvertence where not all the facts were known; the person sins unintentionally. (2) There is forgiveness for every sin, except the sin of blasphemy against the Holy Spirit. So there we have that division.

## The Provision of Old Testament Sacrifices

We want to conclude by talking about the provision of Old Testament sacrifices as God's answer to the sin problem. How effective were these sacrifices? Here I am thinking particularly of the sin offering and the guilt offering which really dealt with this problem. The answer is that, subjectively, the sacrifices were totally effective. Psalm 103:12 tells us, "As far as the east is removed from the west, so far has he removed our transgressions from us." That's pretty good! The writer does not say "as far as the north is from the south"—these are two poles fixed geographically. Instead he says "as far as the east is from the west," where there are no fixed poles. "Gone! Gone! Gone! Gone! Yes, my sins are gone!"

The sins are not just forgiven, but they are also forgotten. That is the point Leviticus 16 is teaching in the Day of Atonement, where two goats are used for one sin offering. *All* the sins of *all* Israel are confessed over the head of one goat; therefore it becomes the substitute. It is killed and the blood is taken into the Holy of Holies once a year and put on the seat of atonement. It speaks of an atonement, a *k-p-r*.

There are four Hebrew roots from *k-p-r*. One means a lion. The second one means a village. For example, take the name Capernaum: *kippur*, village, becomes *Caper-*, and the village is Naum, so we have Capernaum. A third root for *k-p-r*, meaning to caulk a boat, is found one time in Genesis 6–8 where Noah's boat is sealed inside and out.

But there is a final one found over 100 times. It means to ransom or to deliver by a substitute. Here the substitute is a goat. How many sins were confessed on the head of this goat? Leviticus 16:20-21 says the sins of all who genuinely afflicted their souls, *all* sins of *all* Israel. Subjectively then, the sacrifice was totally effective.

But the sacrifice is not finished. Obviously they cannot resurrect the first goat, so they need a second goat to take out into the wilderness and lose as an illustration of sins being forgotten. By the way, it is one sin offering with a two-part illustration of sins forgiven and sins forgotten. So subjectively, the sacrifice was totally effective.

Objectively, were the sacrifices effective? No! The people had to wait for Christ to come, so this had to be done every year. It was an animal; it was not a person. Many things were not true of the Old Testament sacrifice. Hebrews 10 says, "The blood of bulls and goats could not take away sin." But frankly, never did the Old Testament say that animal sacrifices *could* take away sin. Nowhere does the Old Testament say that the blood of bulls and goats took away sin. We must understand, therefore, the animal sacrifices were not effective objectively.

Authoritatively, the sacrifices rested for their effectiveness on the word of God. All sins were forgiven, except the sin with a high hand.

We conclude by saying that Leviticus 16 is the great chapter of atonement and the Day of Atonement. It speaks to the fact that all sins could be forgiven of those who genuinely afflicted their heart and soul on the basis of a divinely authorized substitute, God himself, who would come one day and be that substitute for us.

# Chapter Eleven

# The Relationship between
# the Promise and Wisdom

We have now seen three major steps in time: The Prologue of the Promise, Genesis 1–11; The Provisions of the Promise, Genesis 12–50; and The People of the Promise, Exodus, Leviticus, and Numbers. Let's briefly review these, using the outline in my book, *Toward an Old Testament Theology*, pages 43-54.

First of all, in the Prolegomena to the Promise we saw three crises and three promises of God. There were the Fall, the Flood, and the flop of the Tower. But God sent the blessing of the heir; he sent the blessing of dwelling in the midst of his people; and he sent the blessing of the gospel. Then we talked about the patriarchal period found in Genesis 12–50 with the Provisions of the Promise, in which there were three great provisions: an heir who was the seed, an inheritance of the land, and a heritage of the gospel. It was impossible for God to lie, both in his word and in his oath. Thirdly, we looked at the People of the Promise. Here we took up five concepts in particular: the people were called my son, my firstborn, my treasured possession, my kingly priests, my holy nation.

I have called the fourth step in time the Place of the Promise, the place being where God would cause his name to dwell. It is the promise of Jerusalem and the building of the temple. There were three major developments here. First, there was the doctrine of the inheritance or the rest in the land, where God gave the people rest, and that becomes one of the great transitional themes. There was also the theology of the ark of the covenant, found in 1 Samuel 4–7. The ark of the covenant was the central piece of furniture in the tabernacle. And there was the provision of a perpetual priesthood, which was spoken of during the days of Eli.

Let's move ahead to the sixth major step in time to deal with Life in the Promise. For the moment, we are by-passing the King of the Promise, for I am going to discuss the monarchy and David's kingship and the idea

115

of the Messiah when we take up the prophets in a later chapter. But now we come to this matter of Life in the Promise, and wisdom literature.

## The Theme and Roots of Wisdom

What is the connection between wisdom and the promise? There is no more difficult transitional move in biblical theology of the Old Testament. It is a difficult transition because none of the wisdom books mentions or even alludes to Israel's covenants or promises. Some theologians would strongly suggest that this marks the end of the promise as an integrating theme for Old Testament theology. There is no reference in wisdom literature to the covenant made with the patriarchs; there is no reference to the nation or people of Israel. On the surface, it looks almost impossible to find a connection.

Yet, I think that it is there. On this point, I've received negative reviews from critics, as does anyone who writes an Old Testament theology, especially of the wisdom books. We, as preachers and teachers, are put in a vulnerable position when we take on books like Proverbs, Ecclesiastes, Song of Songs (or Song of Solomon), or portions of the Psalms, particularly those wisdom psalms.

Nevertheless, I'd like to tackle this theme of wisdom and the roots of wisdom.

### The Theme: The Fear of God/the Lord

First of all, what would be the major theme for all of the wisdom books? Almost everyone concedes that one major theme occurs repeatedly: the fear of God or the fear of the Lord. We will try to demonstrate in this chapter that there was, as early as Abraham, this connection of wisdom to the promise eventuating or being worked out in the concept of the fear of God. "Fear of God," *Elohim*, and "fear of the LORD," *Yahweh*, are used interchangeably.

As for the book of Proverbs, I have yet to see a commentary on this book which does not say that this is a major theme. Proverbs 1:7 suggests the motto: "The fear of the LORD is the beginning of knowledge, but fools despise wisdom and discipline" (NIV).

Solomon is saying the same thing in his book of Ecclesiastes. He says, in effect, "Did you understand? In my book, I am talking about fearing God and keeping his commandments, for this is the *ha-kol*"—this is the 'entirety'. The word *duty* is not used here. Rather the Hebrew says: This is the entirety of a man; this is the wholeness of a woman. So if we want to know what maleness is about—if we want to know what femaleness is about—here is the answer: Fear God and keep his Word. That's what it is all about (Eccl 12:13-14).

This is true for all of Ecclesiastes. Look at the last chapter, verses 13-14: "Let us hear the conclusion of the whole matter ...." By the way, these last two verses are so suspect by non-evangelicals that it is almost part of liberal orthodoxy to say that they were added later. Of course, there is a problem here: What is the evidence for that? Who added them? Do we have a manuscript in which the two verses are absent? The truth is, we have no manuscript where these two verses are missing. The text says, "Let us hear the conclusion of the whole matter ...." What is the conclusion? "Fear God." Fear God!

Solomon says, "That's what my book, Ecclesiastes, is about." Some might say, "Is it? I didn't get that. I went through the book and it seemed to me that the book was about zero, about 'vanity of vanities, all is vanity.'" I will come back to that.

When the writer of Ecclesiastes says, "Let us hear the conclusion of the whole matter," it is a similar formula to the one John uses in John 20:30-31: "These are written that you might believe that Jesus is the Christ." He says, "That's why I wrote the book." Just so, the writer of Ecclesiastes, whom I think to be Solomon, says, "Here's the conclusion to my book. Here's what I was trying to prove. I want you to fear God; I want you to keep his commandments; I want you to be a whole person. So fear God; that's the only way you can be a whole person."

Now we look in the book of Job, where the theme is also the fear of the Lord. I think Job comes from an earlier period—from the time of Abraham, Isaac, and Jacob—for the culture, the words, and the vocabulary seem to be patriarchal in setting. Yet, the book itself is wisdom-like. For example, over and over again the central character is referred to as a man who "feared God, and eschewed evil." As this old English word *eschew* indicates, he steered clear of evil. It doesn't mean he "chewed" on it. It means he stayed away from it in spite of all the stormy debate surrounding this man who suffered so much misery from all sides.

Can you imagine being really sick and having three friends come and sit on your bed for seven days, saying nothing? That's what happened to Job. These three just sat there, moaning and groaning and looking at him. And Job could tell what they were thinking: "Oh, brother, what on earth did you do this time!"

After seven days of silence with these three friends keeping him company—just pouring dust on their heads and looking at him in an accusing way—Job answered them. The text says, "Then Job answered them and said ..." (Job 3:1-2). He finally opened his mouth. The English doesn't translate it that fully, because it doesn't make sense. How could he answer friends who hadn't said anything? But he answered their looks, their accusations. And they did have a very single view of evil: suffering is the result of sin. Period! Their logic said that since Job was suffering, he must have sinned. No way around it! And Job said, "Oh, no! I didn't sin at all!" But Eliphaz, Zophar, and Bildad persisted in presenting their arguments—and not doing such a good job at that! After each discourse by one of his friends, Job protested.

Well, a battle goes on back and forth. In the middle of that comes Job 28:28, like the eye of a hurricane in which there is a moment of relief and the sun breaks out. Here we find relief in the verbal storm surrounding Job, just as it happens when the sun breaks out, and wisdom shines through. In this chapter is a poem almost like: "Dear Reader, Where can you go to find wisdom? Shall you dig down in the earth for this? Shall you go into the depths of the seas? Shall you climb up into heaven? No, I'll tell you where it is. It's in the fear of the Lord." That's the whole point of this poem on wisdom in Job 28. So a generic statement of wisdom would be that it is found in the fear of the Lord. That's wisdom. And to shun evil, that's understanding. It's a very smart person who stays away from evil, and it's a very wise person who fears God.

We could also argue that in the book of Proverbs the noun, the *fear* of the Lord, occurs fourteen times in fourteen separate passages. This does not take into account the word in its verbal form.

The fear of the Lord is featured in many of the wisdom Psalms, too. For example, in Psalm 111 we find this theme: "The fear of the LORD is the beginning of wisdom; all who follow his precepts have good understanding. To him belongs eternal praise" (v. 10, NIV).

How shall we define the fear of the Lord? Now there is a gigantic task, for the concept encompasses so much. I have yet to read a concise, practical definition of the fear of God. It is, of course, the attitude of belief. It is, indeed, that! But it goes beyond the fact of belief to encompass everything that accompanies it: the fear of God is a result of hearing, learning, responding to God's word. It is a position which begins in belief and trust and issues in awe and deep regard and worship and love and service for God.

So the link between the promise and wisdom is extremely important.

### The Source of This Theme in Antecedent Scripture

We have looked at the theme of wisdom, which is the fear of the Lord, so now let's take up the source of this theme in antecedent Scripture. Can we find it in the time of The Prologue to the Promise and The Provision of the Promise and The People of the Promise and The Place of the Promise? As we've said before, these are somewhat arbitrary, but generally agreed upon, major movements through the earlier portions of the Old Testament text. Can we find any reference to the fear of God back in these antecedent Scriptures? The answer is, Yes.

For example, we find it in that very famous incident in Genesis 22 where God tests Abraham. Wouldn't it have been wonderful for Abraham to know: "This is a test! This is only a test!" as we hear on the airwaves frequently. "The following is only a test. In the event of an emergency, you will be instructed to …."

Unfortunately, Abraham, like Job, was not told this. If only these two men had known "The following is a test," they could have better endured their testing, realizing that God was in charge. It was only somewhat later that the text says, "God tested Abraham." At the time, God said, "Abraham?" And Abraham said, "Here am I." God said, "Take your son, your only son, your wonderful son who came in such a miraculous way when you were a hundred and Sarah was ninety. Now take that son and sacrifice him."

What a test for Abraham! As a father he certainly did not want to lose his son. And what about the theological implications of the promise? Abraham had waited twenty-five years for this boy, who must by now have been in his late teens. This was somewhere near forty-five years after the promises were given, and it looked as if the whole thing was going to come crumbling down. A person would instinctively say, "I'll take care of getting a sacrifice for you, God. Let me help you." But God says, "No!" God doesn't want any help.

What was going through Abraham's mind on this three-day journey from Hebron all the way up to the future site of the temple in Jerusalem? We can only imagine. Abraham and Isaac took along enough wood for a burnt offering. They took ropes; they took a knife; they took fire. But what about the sacrifice?

Isaac must have noticed this and spoke up: "Dad, aren't we missing something? We have fire; we have wood; we have a knife. Isn't there something else we should be taking?"

"Son, don't worry. The Lord will provide."

"Dad, why are you tying me up? Dad, is everything okay? Dad, I don't want to be up here on this altar. Get me off!"

At least, that is a possible conversation that could have taken place!

There was no hint yet from God about the sacrifice.

Isaac did not prevent Abraham from going ahead; he is not even a foil, for he seemed to be, by faith, trusting his dad. The knife was in the air; Abraham was just about ready to plunge it into the heart of his son, when there came a voice from heaven: "Don't do it! Don't do it!" The Lord said, "Do not lay a hand on the boy. Do not do anything to him. Now I know that you fear God" (Gen 22:12, NIV). This is the first instance where the concept of *the fear of God* is used. This is the law of first reference.

Interestingly enough, Abraham had told the servants at the foot of Mount Moriah: "Stay here. I and the boy will go up and we will worship and we will return." The Hebrew text tells us with certainty that Abraham thought the son was going to come back with him. Abraham had confidence in God: "I believe God can raise my son from the dead." No wonder

Jesus said, "Abraham saw my hour, he saw my day, and he rejoiced" (John 8:56).

This statement by Jesus shows that Abraham in some way penetrated the meaning of his own experience with Isaac and could see the resurrection. For if God could give a son to him who was as good as dead and then give the same son back again after requiring that Abraham sacrifice him—if God could do that to Isaac, who was in the line of the promised seed, then God could do that to his ultimate Son. The resurrection was no problem for Abraham. "We will go, we will worship, and we will come again." The import of that statement rests on the concept of the resurrection.

Please notice that it is in a context of the promise and the maintenance of the promise. This is my point: for if Abraham had plunged his knife into the heart of that boy and if there were no resurrection for those people who lived in Old Testament times, as some believe, then the promise is finished. It's all over. But there *is* a connection between the promise and the fear of God all the way back there. "Now I know that you fear God" is linked to the demonstration of belief in the reliability of the promise of the seed.

This is extremely important. The belief or trust in God equals the fear of God, which produces obedience because of trust in God's promise. That is what makes me think that the wisdom books are really the working out of the promise. It is law being put into the nitty gritty of life. It is the commandment of God which is the follow-through: "If you love me, if you believe me, then do what I say."

"Doing what he said" can be expressed in very practical terms: about families, about fathers, about sons, about mothers, about marriage, about work, about the use of the tongue, about the use of possessions. All who say that religion has lost its force in the real world where the nitty gritty exists, where the rubber meets the road, are probably yearning to study the wisdom literature, for it is terribly practical. In fact, it is so practical, they would probably soon say, Stop it! Let's go back to that abstract teaching again, because this is getting too personal!

There are, it seems to me, other demonstrations of the fear of the Lord than that which we see in the life of Abraham. Joseph manifested this same fear of God, as seen in Genesis 42:18: "On the third day, Joseph said to [his brothers], 'Do this and you will live ....'" (It sounds very similar to Leviticus 18:5.) "'Do this and you will live, for I fear God'" (NIV).

The display of the fear of the Lord also appears in the book of Job, which as we have noted takes place during the patriarchal age. In Job 1:1, we are told right from the very beginning that this man was altogether different from other men. That is why he was singled out to be tested by God. For it says there was in the land of Uz a man whose name was Job. "This man was blameless and upright; he feared God and shunned evil." The text goes on to say, "The LORD said to Satan, 'Have you considered my servant Job? There is no one on earth like him; he is blameless and upright, a man who fears God and shuns evil.'" Satan said, "Does Job fear God for nothing?" (Job 1:8-9). Again in Job 2:3 the Lord—still talking about the fear of the Lord—repeated the same words to Satan: "Have you considered my servant Job? There is no one on earth like him; he is blameless and upright, a man who fears God and shuns evil" (NIV).

Another reference to the fear of the Lord can be found in Exodus 1:17, where the text says that the midwives in Egypt, because they feared God, did not take the lives of any of the male descendants. Later, the Israelites "feared the LORD and put their trust in him" when they saw his power at the Red Sea (Ex 14:31). What about the Egyptians? In Exodus 9:20 we are told that some of them feared God and, therefore, when they were told one of the plagues was coming, they put their cattle indoors, and they too were spared. No wonder then in Exodus 12:38 the text says that when Israel went out of Egypt, a "mixed multitude" (AV) went out with them. That mixed multitude indicates that some Egyptians believed, for they feared God!

The Lord was Israel's God; therefore the injunction to "always fear God" appears repeatedly (Lev 19:14, 32; 25:17, 36, 43). "Always fear God and live," says the biblical text. Deuteronomy made the fear of the Lord one of the central points in its teaching. For example, in my book, *Toward an Old Testament Theology*, page 169, I have given a long list of over a dozen references to the fear of the Lord (Deut 4:10; 5:29; 6:2, 13, 24; chapters 8, 10, 13, etc.).

So this concept, *the fear of God*, did not begin with the wisdom books; it was already embedded in earlier narratives. In my opinion, a textually-derived linkage can be seen in the promise and the fear of God. Now, it's true the wisdom books do not stop to give us historical linkage. There is none whatsoever. There is no theological linkage, except the use of this one phrase, "the fear of the Lord." That's the beginning of everything!

## The Message of the Wisdom Books

What then is the message of these wisdom books?

### Ecclesiastes

Let's take Ecclesiastes, first of all. For a number of years I taught that Ecclesiastes is a book which tells us what not to do. It tells us in gory detail how bad sin is. The major part of the book is saying, "This is what *not* to do," with a little comment tacked on the end, "Now I see our time is up, so please remember this word from the Lord: 'Read your Bible and pray'!" That is the way most people read the book of Ecclesiastes; they see twelve chapters on vanity given by the Spirit of God, *vanity* repeated forty times. What is vanity?

'Vanity' is the word given to the second child born in the Bible, Abel, *Hebel*. *Hebel* means vapor, smoke, or what can be seen on a cold day. It really could be translated *zero, zilch, nil*. The NIV translates it as "meaningless, meaningless, everything is meaningless." I'm not so sure about this translation. The question is, what does it mean in context?

There are several ways to find the meaning and purpose of a book. One way we understand a book is to read the prologue. As a matter of fact, some authors want so badly for us to read the prologue that they actually label it "To Be Read." And in fact it is tempting to skip over the pages marked with small Roman numerals. But the prologue of Ecclesiastes is important because it does seem to say what the book is about: "The words of the Teacher, the son of David, king in Jerusalem: Vanity of vanities, all is vanity."

The phrase "vanity of vanities" is an example of the superlative in Hebrew which is shown by the connecting 'of': vanity of vanities is the most vain of all. Other common superlatives are King of kings, Lord of lords, heaven of heavens. The Holy of Holies means the most holy place; the heaven of heavens is the highest heaven.

Now let's check the conclusion of the book. That's another way to find out what a book is about, especially if it's a mystery. Who done it? Was it the butler or not? We can go all the way to the end of the book and see what Solomon says: "Here's the conclusion to the whole matter. Fear God." Oh, no! you say. I didn't get that at all! Well, like in Monopoly: go to Jail, pay the $200 fine, do not pass Go. You need to start all over again!

Another way to read a book is to look for repeated refrains. Eleven times the text in Ecclesiastes says, "For this is the gift of God, from the hand of God." There is also the refrain in Ecclesiastes 2:24: "A man can do nothing better than to eat and drink and find satisfaction in his work. This too, I see, is from the hand of God" (NIV). At the end of chapter 5 we find the same kind of phrase, which some have called the Epicurean phrase: "Eat, drink, and be merry, for tomorrow we kick the bucket." I admit that it doesn't say that here, but it does say to eat and drink: "Then I realized that it is good and proper for a person to eat and drink, and to find satisfaction in his toilsome labor under the sun, for this also is given by God" (Eccl 5:18-19). The same refrain is found in Ecclesiastes 8:15: "So I commend the enjoyment of life, because nothing is better for a man under the sun than to eat and drink and be glad. Then joy will accompany him in his work all the days of the life God has given him under the sun" (NIV). All that occupies a person's life is given by God, and therefore life can be lived with gladness in the heart.

We can look at this book as having four *colophons*: inscriptions placed at the end of a section or a book, giving facts pertaining to its publication or a summary of the section. This rhetorical device can be seen in the four sections of the book: chapters 1–2, chapters 3–5, chapters 6–8, and then chapters 9–12.

So what is vanity? Vanity, I think, is simply this: No one good thing in God's good world can supply the key to the meaning of life. Some people search for meaning in one direction while others look in another. A person could go for broke on wisdom, but the text says he'll get a headache from studying: "Of the making of books there is no end" (Eccl 12:12). Studying is not the *summum bonum*, the peak of everything. So Solomon says, "Don't make studying and the acquiring of degrees the meaning of life." Then he suggests that a person could go with pleasure. One could say, "I'm just going to go out on the golf links and stay there all day long. Yes, that's for me!" Again, Solomon warns, "Listen, that won't explain life either." And then a person could say, "Yes, but nature! Ah, the meaning of life is found in nature. If only I could go backpacking, just get out on the Appalachian trail and walk and walk. Just listen to the birds." And Solomon says, "No one good thing in God's good world can supply the answer"—because the key to the whole thing is in Ecclesiastes 3:11. He says, "God has made everything beautiful in its time, but he has also put eternity into the heart of man."

This Hebrew word *'olam* means God put eternity into the heart of man. It is not "world," as translated in some of the older texts.

We could illustrate this with a Valentine heart and put an A on one side of the heart and a Z on the opposite side. The text says that even though God has made everything beautiful in its time, and even though he has set eternity in the hearts of men, yet men cannot fathom what God has done from beginning to end, from A to Z. Here lies the great dilemma for mankind: There is a *capacity* and a *hunger* to know. And it is as big as all outdoors—eternity—because men and women are made in the image of God. Believers and unbelievers alike are hungry to know how all of life fits together.

Yet God has kept the beginning from the end, so that life does not make sense. It doesn't compute. And why won't it compute? Because it won't until the individual comes to know and to fear God, to believe God. That is the conclusion to the whole thing: Fear God.

That is also the beginning. Now we have made it to first base. Only when we fear God can we begin to get a glimmer of how the beginning fits with the end. Only then can some of the capacity for the hunger in our hearts be filled. In some sense, this is like Augustine's confession as he starts out: "Thou hast made us for Thyself, and our hearts are restless until they find their rest in Thee." Augustine got that from reading Romans when he had his great Garden Encounter. But he could just as well have been reading Ecclesiastes 3:11.

Solomon, out of that context, goes on to talk about the gifts of God—the basic gifts of life. Eating: a gift from God! It is not secular or mundane.

Drinking: a gift from God! Earning a paycheck and the ability to work: a gift from God! The concept of work is joy. Possessions: a gift from God! He talks about that in Ecclesiastes 6. It's an interesting thing, though, that God keeps the gifts of possessions separate from the power to enjoy them; a person can enjoy them when he comes to know God (Eccl 6:2).

Well, Ecclesiastes contains a whole theology of God/culture and the believing/fearing response from those who know God and are participants in the benefits of the promise. It is very practical.

### Song of Solomon and Proverbs

What about Song of Solomon? The Song of Solomon, which, I think, was also written by Solomon, is straightforward. And it also must be interpreted according to its conclusion. What conclusion does he come to? "Place me like a seal over your heart, like a seal on your arm" (SS 8:6, NIV). The bride wants a signet seal to be rolled over the bridegroom's heart, leaving an imprint of ownership. "For love is as strong as death, its jealousy as unyielding as the grave. It burns like a blazing fire, like a flame of Yah."

Love is a flame from *Yahweh*: this is the message of this book. The NIV translates this as 'mighty flame', which I do not think is correct. Flame of God, or flame of the Lord, as the NAS version translates it, is better. The Hebrew text says it is the flame from God. So here is a passion, which is physical and emotional as well as spiritual. And where does it come from? Not from instinct or from animal lust, but from God. So it ought to be taught. He goes on to say, "Many waters cannot quench love; rivers cannot wash it away. If one were to give all the wealth of his house for love, it would be utterly scorned" (NIV). This is what this book, which I think was written by Solomon, teaches.

Remember the story in which Solomon sees the Shunammite maiden. She came from Shunem, which is across the valley from the summer palace of the northern kingdom at Jezreel; low, flat, beautiful farmland in a kind of triangle. If we look over at the eleven o'clock position, we see Nazareth. The cliff there, the escarpment, is probably where Jesus played. If we look over in the one o'clock position from Jezreel, there is the Hill of Moreh, and on the side is the little village of Shunem, home of the Shunammite maiden.

Now, this girl is made to take care of the vineyards by her brothers and to work in the nut orchard. One day, apparently, according to chapter 6, there is a commotion, so she goes down to see what it's all about. Then she realizes that she is among the royal chariots of her people (SS 6:12). King Solomon is going by, his palanquin being borne by sixty men. Imagine all the pageantry, with incense burners preceding the king. And they are all startled to see this girl watching them. They look at the Shunammite girl and say, "Come back with us; come back with us to Jerusalem." In taking her to Jerusalem, they tear her away from her shepherd boyfriend back home, who is one of the three characters in the book. There is tremendous pressure on her by those who are part of the harem. They keep saying to her, "You've got it made in the shade! Name it—furs, money, expenses, food—and you can have it!" And she says simply, "All I want is my boyfriend. I'm engaged to him back home." The king keeps saying, "You are most ravishing, oh wonderful woman, my subject, my future wife!" He is trying hard to win her, but the text says that he can't do it.

This love is a flame from God! Many waters cannot quench it; rivers will not wash it away. It cannot be purchased with all the wealth of the kingdom. The psalmist also said, "I learned that. It's a gift from God." And so he speaks out of his own traumatic experience.

You say, Are you sure of that interpretation? The church has said that this is an allegory about Christ. Yes, we've said everything about this book! Of course, the problem is to find the evidence for it in the book itself, since we do believe that Scripture is inspired. You say, how shall we figure it out?

We can begin to understand the Song of Solomon by looking at another piece written by the same author. Proverbs 5:15-20 enlightens us, where the author uses metaphors and theology seen also in the Song of Solomon. Solomon says, "Drink water from your own cistern, running water from your own well" (NIV). How can this be interpreted? Is it saying that, if you're not hooked up to city water, you should drink water out of your own well? Should your springs overflow in the streets? Is this an ecological note here?

No, be careful! It's saying, Save the water; keep the springs for yourself. Let them be yours alone, not shared with strangers. The text goes on to say, "May your fountain be blessed, and may you rejoice in the wife of your youth" (NIV). We say, Wife of your youth? Beg your pardon? How did that get in here? "A loving doe, a graceful deer—may her breasts satisfy you always, may you ever be captivated by her love" (Prov 5:18-19, NIV). All of a sudden, this passage begins to make sense.

He is talking here about a fountain as being the marriage act; he's talking about unfaithfulness and fidelity within marriage. And he says that this is to be blessed; it is from God. So, "Why be captivated, my son, by an adulteress? Why embrace the bosom of another man's wife? For a man's ways are in full view of the LORD" (Prov 5:20-21, NIV). In other words, God inspects the marital bedroom. He calls it good if it is in the context of fidelity. The fountain is not to be shared with others in adultery.

Notice the theme of the garden, the theme of the fountain, as we go back to Song of Solomon; it is the same writer and the same period of time. He writes, for example, not in a crass way but it still is there, "You are a garden locked up, my sister, my bride; you are a spring enclosed, a sealed fountain" (SS 4:12, NIV). And again, "I have come into my garden, my sister, my bride" (SS 5:1, NIV).

I believe this clue helps us get into the text and interpret it. We have here a marriage manual which is to help us to understand that marriage for those who fear God is a gift from Jehovah. It is to be used with fidelity to the pledged partner and with great physical and aesthetic and emotional and spiritual joy.

So we conclude this chapter on the wisdom books, which embrace not only Proverbs, Ecclesiastes, and the Song of Songs, but also the Psalms. Psalm 1 is a wisdom psalm; Psalms 32, 34, 37, and 49 speak of life after death; then there are Psalms 78, 111, 112, 119—the longest psalm of all, 127, 128, 133. All of them have the same basic thematic content and stylistic criteria, such as alphabetic structure or numerical sayings or better sayings or blessed sayings or proverbial sayings. These tell us that we are dealing with wisdom literature.

In conclusion, what is the point of wisdom literature? It is simply this: we are being given Life in the Promise, and we are shown how practical life can be lived in that promise.

# Chapter Twelve

# The Promise and the Prophets

We are moving right along, coming now to the prophets. Keep in mind, as we deal with the promise and the prophets, that from the biblical standpoint we are talking not only about the sixteen writing prophets, but also about four earlier prophets. The sixteen writing prophets include the major prophets: Isaiah, Jeremiah, Ezekiel, and Daniel; and then the twelve minor prophets. Being classified as minor prophets does not mean they were in the minor leagues. This was not "bush league prophecy"; rather, 'minor' refers to size—the bulk of material written.

In addition to the major and minor prophets, we have the earlier prophetic books of Joshua, Judges, Samuel, and Kings. These are not just historical books; they are also prophetic in content, where the word of God is constantly being fulfilled. A prophecy is given; then the text says, "This took place that it might be fulfilled which was spoken by the prophets." Gerhard Von Rad in his *Old Testament Theology* gives some two dozen references of these fulfillments of prophecy.

Now we turn to the worldwide focus of the promise-plan of God and the prophets. The promise-plan already existed in germ form in Genesis 12:3: "And in your seed shall all the nations of the earth be blessed." *All the nations* refers to the seventy nations in Genesis 10, giving it an international perspective.

While the prophet is ready now to turn primarily to the worldwide aspect, he still must deal with Israel's penchant for running away from God, corporately as well as individually. So Israel's sin and failure must, alas, occupy a good portion of the prophetic material. Thus the genius of the promise doctrine was its twofold character. As Willis J. Beecher taught, "It was a standing prediction of the time to come, and it was an available religious doctrine for the time being" (*The Prophets and the Promise* [1905; reprint ed., Grand Rapids: Baker Book House, 1975], p. 242).

In previous chapters we have seen that the promise-plan included an heir, an inheritance, a rest, and a people who would be God's firstborn.

We noted the concepts of his treasure, his kingdom of priests, and a place where God's name would dwell. Although we have yet to talk about it, chronologically a king has come in the Davidic line who was given a dynasty, a house, a throne, and a kingdom. All this foreshadows the first and second coming of our Lord. It foreshadows Christmas and Easter and that great day which we are still looking forward to, when our Lord Jesus will come again.

Now as we come to the prophets, we will consider them in at least two main categories: prophets as *forthtellers* who tell forth the word of God, and then prophets as *foretellers*. The *pro* in prophecy can be temporal: to speak ahead of time. The *pro* can also mean to set forth the word of God. Both aspects are here. Interestingly, we generally think of prophecy as mainly predictive, when actually this was true for only about a third of prophecy. The other two-thirds consisted of warnings, the forthtelling of a preacher of righteousness to his generation and his culture. "Listen, we had better turn back to God. If we don't, there is nothing but trouble up ahead for us."

So we have prophets as forthtellers and as foretellers. Then thirdly, we want to talk about prophets as the *revealers* of the word of God, for the prophet was really the person who specialized in the word of God.

## The Prophets as Forthtellers

First of all, let's talk about the prophet as the *forthteller* who urged repentance and revival for all.

### They Urged Repentance and Revival for All

The most telling term in all the prophets is the simple word *shub* (with the *b* pronounced as a *v*). The text says over and over again, *Shub, shub*—turn, turn back, return, or repent. This is the Old Testament word for repentance. Repeatedly the prophet says, "You are headed in the wrong direction; you are headed toward sin, toward self, and toward the anti-God. Turn all the way around! Do not stop at 90 degrees, but turn 180 degrees and head back to the man of promise."

This turning usually has two parts, like our word *conversion*: a turning from and a turning to. Frequently this turning is needed within the believing body, too. For example, four of the seven letters to the churches in Revelation say, Repent! Repent! Repent! And this is being said to those assumed to be good people. God says, "Turn!"

So the first 90 degrees in conversion is to turn *from*: Turn from sin; turn from that which is against the Law or the will of God. The second 90 degrees is to turn *to*, and that is faith. The conversion process is broken down into repentance and faith. We say faith is the more necessary because it is the more proximate; it is that which is closer to the final goal.

Some people confess their sins, tearfully admitting to God, "Yes, I goofed. This is awful. I did that against you." But there it ends. I saw this happen in a missions outreach on Skid Row in Philadelphia, where I met a man who had been a surgeon, was a graduate of Columbia University, but now carried all his possessions under his arm. At one time he had been a surgeon at one of the country's top hospitals. Then his wife was killed in an automobile accident. He lost his daughter. He began drinking; he lost his practice; he lost everything.

I said to him, "Would you like to talk to God? Did you ever talk to him before?"

"No, I never have."

I said, "Then pray. It's just like talking to him."

So he did. Very simply, he prayed, "Oh God, I've never talked to you before, but I really have messed up. I've sinned." As he talked to God, he was in tears; it was a very touching time. Then he stopped.

So I said, "Now, why don't you just reach out and accept him. The Bible says, Believe. Accept him."

He said, "I can't do it."

"Why not?"

He answered, "Didn't you just hear the kind of person I am? I just can't!"

This man could turn *from*, but he wouldn't turn *to*. And without faith, it is impossible to please God. "He that comes to God must believe that he is, and that he is a rewarder of those that diligently seek him," says Hebrews 11:6. Some turn *from* but they don't turn *to*. That is why we say faith is the more necessary.

On the other hand, some would like to have faith without repentance. Every once in a while we hear someone say, "The New Testament doesn't talk about repentance." Of course, that is not true. Corinthians talks about repentance, and so do other portions of Scripture such as I have just quoted to you.

Where can you find that this is the summation of the prophets' message, besides finding the word *shub* so frequently? One of the last prophets, Zechariah, summarizes it this way: "Do not be like your forefathers, to whom the earlier prophets proclaimed ..." (Zech 1:4). Who were the earlier prophets? These happen to be the fourteen prophets who have already been on the scene, from among the four major and twelve latter prophets. He says, "Did not the prophets come to you saying, 'Turn from your evil ways and your evil practices'? Wasn't their basic message: Turn! Turn! Turn!"

I once participated in a Jewish-evangelical dialogue with rabbis on one side and pastors on the other. One rabbi said to me, "You evangelicals make us angry. You're always trying to convert us Jews and make us Gentiles."

"I'm not trying to convert you at all," I said. "As a matter of fact, I wouldn't use the word *convert* as you are using it. I don't believe in conversion of that sort. And I'm not trying to make you a Gentile."

To which one of my fellow evangelical colleagues of the evening said to me, "Yes, we are! We are trying to convert them."

I said to my friend, "Wait, I'll get back to you. I've got enough problems on my hands." So I went on to say to the rabbi, "Look, do you mean by *convert* that you lose your Jewishness and you become Gentile?"

"Yes," he said. "That's what I mean."

I said, "No, what I'm trying to tell you is the same thing the Jewish prophets said, the same thing the *Torah* said. There's one word: Turn! Turn around! *Shub!*"

Zechariah says, "Did not all the former prophets come saying, 'Turn ye'?" This phrase appears in the major revivals in the Old Testament. It occurs in the well-known verse in 2 Chronicles 7:14 which begins, "If my people ...." Here some might react, Uh oh, look out! This is specialized mail. Isn't that the same phrase we have seen used in "You will be my people"? "I will be your God; you shall be my people." So this does look as if it's addressed only to the Jews: "If my people ...."

But he then goes on to say, adding in apposition almost as a warning not to limit this to Israel: "I mean those over whom I've called my name— 'my people, who are called by my name.'" This phrase says to us, Do not make this uniquely Jewish mail. The expression is very literal, "to call God's name over," and is found frequently in the Bible—for instance in 2 Samuel 12:26-28. David's nephew, Joab, fought against Rabbah of the children of Ammon and took the city. Then he sent for David, urging him to come with more soldiers to take the citadel, so that the city would be called after David and not after himself, Joab. When David did just that, he owned the city.

When God called his name over the temple, he owned the temple. When God calls his name over a person, he owns that person. So this theme of calling them by his name—"my people, who are called by my name"— does not indicate that it is for pagans; that is not revival. Rather it means that it is a family affair; he's talking to believers. "If my people, who are called by my name, will humble themselves and pray and seek my face and *turn from their wicked ways*, then will I hear from heaven and will forgive their sin and will heal their land" (NIV).

This becomes a programmatic statement for the whole book of 2 Chronicles, making it the second or third most theological book in the Old Testament. I would put Chronicles alongside Isaiah and Exodus, for out of it come five of the ten major Old Testament revivals.

About half of the book of 2 Chronicles deals with one revival or another. Five revivals pick up the four aspects of 2 Chronicles 7:14: humble yourselves, pray, seek, turn. These words are not treated in order, but the first and the fifth revivals use the phrase "humble yourself." The first revival is a partial one under Rehoboam, right after the division of the kingdom. God says, "Because you have humbled yourselves towards me, therefore I will give you some relief" (2 Chron 12:7). God stops the advance of Pharaoh Shishak, even though he is right on Rehoboam's doorstep and has already taken some cities. Why does God do this? Because Rehoboam humbles himself. The last of the five revivals is one in which King Josiah humbles himself. The text will say five, six, seven, eight times, "he humbled himself."

The phrase "seek my face" is used in the story about King Asa. Seeking the face of God comes up about a dozen times in the space of three chapters in 2 Chronicles 14–16.

There's another revival under the reign of Jehoshophat, who learns how to pray. He stands "in the congregation of Judah and Jerusalem, in the house of the LORD" (2 Chron 20:5, AV). And he prays to the Lord, saying in essence, "If my people who are called by my name will humble themselves and pray and seek my face ...."

Then in 2 Chronicles 30, during the reign of Hezekiah, we find repeatedly the concept of "turning from their wicked ways" in phrases like "return to the LORD" and "return to him."

So here we have the prophet as a *forthteller* involved in all these revivals. During the reign of Asa, for example, four prophets—not the writing prophets, but four of the great galaxy of non-writing prophets—keep saying, "Turn, brother! Turn, people! Turn back to the Lord! We've got to repent, because if we don't, there's disaster up ahead for us."

Now, since it is put in a proverbial way, "My people, who are called by my name," I think this is also a text which must be preached today. In my book, *Quest for Renewal*, I urge men and women to announce this same news. By humbling ourselves, by praying and seeking God's face, and by turning to God, we, too, can bring an effect upon the land. Yes, I believe this is true. The prophets constantly made the connection between the condition of the hearts of the people and the condition of the environment or of the crops or of the fields.

Why is this? The answer goes back to an informing theology in Genesis 3. When man fell, when sin came into the world, nature also was affected. And nature continues to groan in travail, says Romans 8:22-23: It continues to groan, "waiting for the adoption," waiting for the redemption which is found in Christ Jesus our Lord. The whole of creation is waiting for its release. Streams, the air, the entire environment, all are saying, "How long? How long?"

Meanwhile, substantial healing is possible. It would not be right to rejoice and say, "The whole thing's gone to pot. Hallelujah! Crooks are in charge now, but let's not bother them. Maybe things will get so bad that the Lord will come sooner." The biblical text does not encourage that kind of cop-out. Rather, it says: Present the Lord Jesus much more boldly and forthrightly, and by so doing, speed up the day of the Lord. We cannot hurry up the day of the Lord with evil. That is exactly 180 degrees different from the Bible, so I warn you, do not so teach and preach! The biblical text says, "Announce Christ." That is the way we hurry up the day of the Lord (2 Pet 3:11-12).

While creation is waiting for its release, we do see that the condition of the people's hearts has an effect on nature. So when we see a people doing well, then we will see the crops come in. We will see the economy booming. We will see that the currency—the kopek, the franc, the yen, the dollar—has greater value.

But when we see a people in trouble morally, ethically, and spiritually, we will likewise see consequences. When we see even the remnant, the moral minority, fighting with each other in the household of God, then I fully expect a drought. I expect we will see inflation or depression. I expect we will see a high rate of unemployment. I expect the figures of the gross national product will be way off. There is a connection—not on a one-to-one ratio, but as a contributing factor.

Haggai is one of the clearest examples that I can think of in this connection. Haggai 1:5-9 says in essence, "Give careful thought to this. Think on this if you will. Are you eating more and enjoying it less? Are you drinking more and finding it less satisfying? Are you putting on more clothes but you're not warm? Are you earning money only to put it into a purse with holes in it?"

You might react to this by saying, Don't get so personal! Well, I didn't get personal. It was Haggai. Haggai's point is, "Listen, brethren, we came back sixteen years ago and got started on the temple. You remember?" Now, just a word of warning here: this text is not appropriate for use when there's a temple fund drive or a building fund drive. It's a call to renew the work of God. The temple building is only an illustration of the greater principle of putting God's work before our work, of putting God's ways before our ways. It's a matter of priority.

And so Haggai says, "Have you noticed how the crops have really dwindled? Have you noticed that your productivity is down? If you want to become more productive—right now—then I tell you we need to come back to God." And he gives a call for repentance. "Turn!" he says. "Turn! Turn!" Now, that is great prophetic preaching!

Although we desperately need that, and the biblical text cries for this to be said, some do not have enough courage to preach it. Some will excuse themselves by saying, "Yes, but it's not repeated in the New Testament."

Well, how many times does God have to say something before it is true? God wants us to realize that, "If my people"—if my Christians, if my denomination, if my school—"who are called by my name, will humble themselves and pray and seek my face and turn from their wicked ways, then will I hear. Then will I answer from heaven. I will forgive their sins, and I will heal the United States of America. I will heal Guatemala. I will heal Venezuela. I will heal the Ukraine." If we believe the word of God, I urge that we come to terms with that biblical word as did the prophets as forthtellers.

### They Were a Different Type of Revolutionary

The prophets were also revolutionaries in a sense. They were not our kind of revolutionaries with clenched fists, shaking them menacingly toward heaven. They did want change, yes; but they wanted changed lives, changed individuals. For them, changing society was not to be accomplished by signing petitions and marching against some particular institution or group. Instead, for them, changing society was, "Change your hearts! Change, you men and women! Change, you boys and girls!" That was the revolutionary thing about the Old Testament prophet.

Let me give you the best example of the revolutionary in action. We have the famous Temple Gate Message in Jeremiah 7. Here's a prophet who stands outside the church as people are going in and favors them with a pre-service. He says, "Hear, all you people that go into the house of the LORD!" He tells the people to listen to what God has to say. "You people keep saying all the time, 'the house of the LORD, the house of the LORD, the temple of God, the temple of God, the temple of God.' You're using those words like a rabbit's foot. You're repeating the words as if they were a talisman, a good luck charm" (vv. 2-4).

It's like what we American Christians say constantly, "God bless America! God will never bring judgment upon us. If he did, what would he do for money? Where would he get fundamentalists and evangelicals? They would all be gone. God bless America! He won't threaten to bring his wrath down on us. Why, there are more mission societies—in a straight line from Fort Wayne up to Grand Rapids, over through Chicago, up through Minneapolis, Winnipeg, and fifty miles on either side—than you can shake a stick at! Now, there is a real Bible belt! And God will never do anything against the U.S.A. for the sake of that new Bible belt. What would he do for all those Christian publishing houses? They would all be gone. What would he do for Bible institutes and for colleges and for mission organizations?"

We say "the temple of the Lord ... the temple of the Lord ... the temple of the Lord." That's just rabbit's foot theology, Jeremiah says. You want to bet that if you constantly repeat that, God won't do anything to us?

God says, "Reform your ways and your deeds, and *then* I'll come and live in this place. Don't trust in deceptive words and say 'the temple of the Lord, the temple of the Lord, the temple of the Lord.' If you really change your ways and your actions and deal with each other justly; if you do not oppress the alien and the fatherless and the widow and do not shed innocent blood; if you do not follow after other gods, then I will let you live in this place. Then ...." Some might think this sounds like social gospel. No, it's not social gospel at all. All these good deeds are simply signs of a full theology of trust and belief in the word of God.

God is saying, "If you say that I am Savior, then why don't you do what I say? It is impossible to say, 'Lord, Lord' and not do the things that I say." Jesus has said, "In the final day, a lot of people will say, 'Hey, Lord, remember me?'" In that day the Lord will answer, "Yes, I remember you. I saw what you did. Good-bye." It's quite clear there will be no salvation for these people. So here in this text, Jeremiah is communicating this same message in his prophecy outside the temple. He says, "You are trusting in deceptive words that are worthless. Will you steal and murder, and commit adultery and perjury, burn incense to Baal and follow other gods, and then come and stand before me in this house and say, 'We are delivered so that we can do these things'? Is that what you're going to do?" (Jer 7:8-10).

This is very stern preaching! The audience is people who have come to the house of God, so already that is an indication that they should be from the "better" group; they are not out on the golf links. Jeremiah is saying, "Attendance at the house of God is no substitute for a real meeting with him. Merely showing up is not the real McCoy." God wants the real McCoy. There are no substitutes for real faith. God says in Jeremiah 7:21-23: "I didn't speak to you for the sake of offering some sacrifices, but this is the command I gave you: Obey me, and I will be your God and you will be my people. Walk in all I have said." In other words, here once again, we cannot fool God. There is no substitute for a real meeting with God. Mere attendance will not do it. Religious ceremony is no substitute for a change of heart.

God says, "I didn't speak to you for the sake of sacrifices. Remember, I own the cattle on a thousand hills. I don't need to say to you, Feed me! Feed me with sacrifices! Rather, what I want is you. *I want you.*" Samuel had to remind Saul of that. In 1 Samuel 15:22, he said, "Obedience is better than sacrifice, and to hearken than the fat of rams." Basically, it is put into proverbial form. Samuel does not say, Do this and forget that. He does not say, Just obey, and forget sacrifices. But he says, What's the use of sacrifice when there's no obedience from the heart? What's the use of B when there's no A?

Let's go back to our narrative in Jeremiah 8. The prophet continues. He is not finished; this man is wound up like a corkscrew! He goes on to say, "Even the stork in the sky knows her appointed times, and the dove, the swift and the thrush observe the time of their migration" (Jer 8:7). He is saying, "You don't see the birds sitting out on the telegraph line, thinking, Fall is coming. Some say it's time to go south. But all this flap, flap, flap about going south is for the birds! We're not going to go this year. It won't get that bad. We'll just stay."

Jeremiah says, "Have you noticed how all of God's creation obeys the times and the seasons? But my people, what about them? My people are made in the image of God. But even with their high IQs, do you know what they do? They go merrily along, whistling, saying that disaster won't happen here. They know logically that disaster must come, but they continue insisting that it won't." So this is what Jeremiah is saying. "The birds get out of town when winter comes. They go south. But God's people just continue to sit on the wire and whistle!"

You're looking at me as if to say, Where does it say that! Well, it's in the margin—a wide margin, I admit, but it's still there. Jeremiah 8:8 says, "How can you say, 'We are wise, for we have the law of the Lord'?" (NIV). He says, "Actually the pen of the scribe is false." ('False' is my word; you might have the word 'vain'.) He says, They kept preaching "Peace! Peace!" and *"Shalom! Shalom!* Happy days are here again! Things are really going to get better." If you don't mind my grammar, he is saying, "Times are getting gooder and gooder!"

Verse 12 says, "Are they ashamed? No! Not at all. My word didn't even make them blush." So possession of God's word is no substitute for a response to it. We can say we have the Word of the Lord—the inerrant Word of God, the infallible, inspired Word of God. Jeremiah would say, "Bully for you! You are so-o-o orthodox; you are as straight as an arrow. But I'll tell you what: you're also in trouble, because you haven't responded to that Word. You want to fight over the doctrine of it, but you don't want to listen and do what it says. So what's the good? What's the use?"

It's as Kierkegaard said with sarcasm and irony about the state church in Denmark: There is a state church in Denmark. Christians are in the state church. Everything belongs to the state. Even the cows, the pigs, and the chickens are Christians since they belong to the state, too! It's all Christian. That seems to be the direction in which Jeremiah is going. He is saying, "Come on there, folks! Where did you get the idea that God wouldn't punish us for our sins?"

Compare the message of Amos to the women of his day. I mean, this really gets touchy when we start preaching like this! I don't necessarily advise you to follow his style; his spirit, yes, perhaps. He lived in a great culture, a luxurious time in history, with each family having its summer home and its winter home. A Harvard University excavation demonstrated that there were ivory etchings all over the palace of Samaria; beds and furniture were inlaid with ivory—beautiful furniture!

So Amos says, "You lie on beds inlaid with ivory and lounge on your couches. You dine on choice lambs and fatted calves. You strum away on your harps like David …" (Amos 6:4, NIV). To put it into today's language, he says, "You have filet mignon for supper. Then you play your stereo and improvise on your musical instruments; you have that wonderful electric guitar. You drink Mogen David by the bowlful and you use Chanel No. 5, but you are not grieved over the ruin of the U.S.A."

What's his point? Is he making a statement about society? No, his whole point is that we should turn back to God. All of these other things are only symptoms of a problem. Some people say, "Oh, okay. I won't use any more ointments or Chanel No. 5. I'll use something less expensive. You know, a little dab'll do ya." But Amos says, "That's not the point. The point is that we need to turn back to the living God."

Also in Amos 4, notice the principle of increasingly severe judgments on a nation as God tries to get its attention. In verse 6 God says through the prophet, "I sent you famine —empty stomachs—in every city and lack of bread, yet you didn't return to me." Then God tried to get their attention through another judgment: "I withheld the rain from you when the harvest was only three months away. And I sent too much rain in one city and not enough in another, yet you did not return to me" (Amos 4:7-8).

Verse 9 recounts another judgment: "And then, I struck your gardens and vineyards, and I gave you blight and mildew and locusts, and yet you did not return to me." There is yet another judgment in verse 10: "I sent you plagues as I did down in Egypt. I killed some of your young men with the sword, yet you did not return to me." A fifth attention-getter is found in verse 11: "I overthrew some of you as I overthrew Sodom and Gomorrah, and yet you did not return to me."

One, two, three, four, five times: each time God has to admit, "And yet, you did not return to me." Finally he says, "Therefore this is what I will do, and because I will do this, prepare to meet your God, O Israel" (v. 12). We have all seen the big sign as we drive through the countryside, "Prepare to meet your God." We think it is evangelistic, and I suppose it can be. But in context, it's not. In context, it is that the nation has been given one, two, three, four, five chances to repent and turn, but then that's it! Down comes Samaria. In 722 BC it was good-bye to the northern kingdom!

The people do hear the word, but they do not listen. Their response is, "Oh, words! words! words! Just another televangelist; just another preacher teaching us the word of the Lord. We've had enough!"

"Okay," God says. "I do love you. I have spoken to you through famine. I have spoken to you through drought. I have spoken to you through blight. I have spoken to you through sickness. I have spoken to you through war. But you didn't catch on. You didn't even know it was me. You haven't even said, 'Oh, Lord!' Misery hasn't even found a voice. 'Oh, God!' So, this is what I will do …."

The other principle in judgment is that God's justice or mercy to any nation depends on that nation's response to God's moral standards. In Jeremiah 18, we have, "Whenever I say to a kingdom or nation"—not just Israel, but any nation—"that I will bless you ..."—if that kingdom or nation turns away from God, then God will repent. He will change the direction of what he said he would do. The opposite is also true: If a nation repents when God has said, "I'm going to bring this nation down. They are godless; they are wicked," then God repents of his judgment.

Remember Jonah, who did not want to go to Nineveh to preach revival and give them a chance to repent. Finally he was willing to preach at Nineveh, but still he said, "I hope no one understands that there is a hidden 'unless' in this: unless they repent. I hope no one comes forward in my revival services." But they did! They repented en masse. So God said, "I'll change the judgment that I said I'd bring against that nation." And so we ought to teach. Wherever I am, no matter what country I'm in as I travel internationally, I call for that response: Turn!

## The Prophets as Foretellers

We have seen the prophets as *forthtellers*; now let's look at them as *foretellers*.

### Foretelling the Immediate Future

In many instances a prophet foretold the immediate future. For example, in 2 Kings 1, the prophet Elijah says the king is not going to get well. King Ahaziah has fallen through the lattice or from the roof gallery of his palace in Samaria, so he sends his messengers to consult the idol Baal-Zebub to find out whether he will recover from his injury. But an angel of the Lord tells Elijah to meet these messengers and give them the answer, "The king will surely die." And so the king dies.

Let's look at Daniel 4:24-25. Nebuchadnezzar has had a dream and needs an interpretation. So Daniel explains what God is telling him: "There are going to be seven years when you will not be rational." And so it is. He lives out-of-doors with the beasts and with the dew of heaven falling upon him, according to this prediction of the immediate future.

### Foretelling the Distant Future

In other instances the more distant—but not-too-far-distant—future is predicted. In Ezekiel 26, Ezekiel speaks of the prophecy of Tyre: The city on the mainland would be scraped, and its stones, its timbers, and its dust would be thrown into the sea to fill in a causeway. That is exactly what happened when Alexander the Great came 200 years later. He found that he needed to build a causeway, so he said to himself, "There's only one way I'm going to take that city. I'll take the old ruin, the one Nebuchadnezzar wrecked in the 580s BC, and I'll push that out into the sea." And so he did. He literally built a causeway jutting a half mile out into the sea, and his army marched out on this strip of land to get to the island-nation of Tyre. That's what the prophet had called for in Ezekiel 26:12.

Prophets would foretell the far distant future, too. The prophet Daniel speaks of the coming kingdom of God which will go on forever and ever, using this word picture: "That stone which fell on the great image and filled the whole earth." All the kingdoms of men—the Babylonian Kingdom, the Medo-Persian Empire, the Greco-Macedonian Empire, and the Roman or Western Empire—will come crashing down and God will set up a kingdom of stone which will never fall (Dan 2:35, 44-45).

Daniel 7:13-14 foretells an event much farther off in history, the handing of the kingdom over to the Son of Man, who comes to the Ancient of Days and is given the kingdom.

In Isaiah 24:21-22 we have an interesting passage: "In that day the LORD will punish the powers in the heavens above and the kings on the earth below. They will be herded together like prisoners bound in a dungeon; they will be shut up in prison and be punished after many days" (NIV). What are the "many days" here? I think Revelation 20:2-3 answers this: the "many days" is one of the references in the Old Testament to the Millennium, and Satan and all his crowd being boxed up and shut in prison for almost a thousand years. So here is a prediction of a very distant future, just as in Isaiah 65–66 we have the prediction of new heavens and a new earth. These prophets did a lot of foretelling in the Bible.

## The Prophets as Revealers of the Word of God

Thirdly, we come to the prophets as *revealers* of the word of God.

### Their Contest with False Prophets

The prophets were constantly having problems with false prophets. In Elijah's day, they were the prophets of Baal who were false because they pledged their allegiance to another god. There were also false prophets of Jehovah who did not get their message from God.

How can we tell a false prophet from a prophet of God? Jeremiah brings four charges against the false prophets in Jeremiah 23:9-39. He charges, first of all, that these false prophets are immoral, for they "commit adultery and live a lie" (Jer 23:14, NIV).

Secondly, they are popularity seekers; they say what people want to hear. Verse 17 tells us: "They keep saying to those who despise me, 'The

LORD says: You will have peace'" (NIV). They keep on saying, "All will be well. Come on, let's not be gloomy. Let's not be pessimistic. It will all work out in the end."

The third charge Jeremiah makes against these false prophets is that they distort the word of God. Verse 28 says that they confuse their own dream with the dream that God gave to his real prophets. Using a proverb, Jeremiah says, "What does straw have to do with wheat?" How does your dream compare to God's dream? In verse 36 he says, "Every man's own word becomes his oracle and so you distort the words of the living God."

The fourth charge against them is that they're just plain plagiarists. "'Therefore,' says the LORD, 'I am against the prophets who steal from one another words supposedly from me'" (v. 30).

### Their Method of Receiving God's Word, Jeremiah 36

What then is the method of receiving the word of God? The way in which God speaks his word to men is by a living assimilation of the truth. First Corinthians 2:6-16, I think, is a great neglected passage on inspiration. In verse 13 Paul says that it is in words *taught* by the Holy Spirit. Therefore, it was not a mechanical dictation, a whispering into the ear of the prophet, or any automatic writing. The full personality, gifts, and abilities of the prophet (or apostle) were used and brought into a living harmony and an assimilation with precisely what the mind of God communicated to these prophets by the work of the Holy Spirit.

Let's look at Jeremiah 36, where we are given the method of receiving the word of God. Here the prophet was told to write down all the words that God had spoken to him. Particularly in Jeremiah 36:2, he gives the best explanation I've ever seen in all Scripture: "Take a roll of a book and write therein all the words that I have spoken unto you ...."

These are words verbalized, not merely mechanically dictated. For example, it is not as if the Spirit of God said to Peter, "Propitiation," and Peter said, "How do you spell it?" Or that the Spirit of God took his arm and moved it involuntarily. It is not as if God dictated to Isaiah and he had to check to see what he had written. If you had asked Isaiah, "What does it say?" he would not have answered, "Beats me! I'm a 'non-prophet' organization." This would be merely mechanical. But in the text, it seems to me, what is indicated is quite different. We have God speaking his words to the prophet.

The prophet then dictated these words to an amanuensis; for example, Jeremiah dictated to Baruch (vv. 4, 18). Then the prophet, after receiving revelation from God, communicated God's words to the people.

The prophets, then, were forthtellers, foretellers, and revealers of the word of God, urging God's people to repent and turn back to him.

# Chapter Thirteen

# The Theology of the Messiah in the Old Testament

In this chapter, The Theology of the Messiah, we come to the heart of the promise-plan of God in the Old Testament. As said in previous chapters, the promise doctrine is the organizing plan of the Old Testament. While we do not believe in a Christo-exclusive theme, we do believe in a Christocentric theme: the Messiah is central. However, this promise theme includes more than a simple prediction or a series of predictions which have distant fulfillments in the first or second coming of Christ. We do not believe that when we have talked about the Messiah, we have said all there is to say. If we think that since we have seen the coming of our Lord Jesus in the New Testament, we can safely put away the Old Testament, that is just not true.

In *Toward Rediscovering the Old Testament* (p. 101), I cite some statistics from Alfred Edersheim's *Life and Times of Jesus the Messiah:* "according to some 558 separate citations in rabbinical writings, there are 456 OT passages that refer ... to the Messiah or to messianic times." These rabbinical writings span the several centuries before and after the start of the Christian faith. That is quite an impressive list! However, not all these Old Testament passages, given a grammatical historical exegesis, yield a messianic interpretation. I must say that some of them are very fanciful. But even if we have only half to three-fourths of these 456 texts left, we still have an enormous collection of texts.

It is interesting to note that when Jewish faith came into conflict with Christianity after AD 30, many rabbis hedged on some of those affirmations of the Messiah in the Old Testament. During the early part of the first century, Christianity was considered one of the branches of the Jewish faith. Some have estimated that one to two million Jews were part of those who affirmed Jesus of Nazareth to be the Messiah. This whole area needs to be explored much more. We have found seventy centers in Palestine itself where Jesus of Nazareth was the central figure in the Jewish affirmation and worship. But very quickly this degenerated into confrontation and antagonism, resulting in arguments rather than unity in worship.

However, with rabbis accepting this number of Old Testament texts as referring to the Messiah, it is no wonder that our Lord Jesus scolded the two disciples on the road to Emmaus. In Luke 24:25-27 he said: "O fools, and slow of heart to believe all that the prophets have said concerning me. ... And beginning with Moses and all the prophets, he began to show them all things concerning himself." When we add the Psalms to the books of Moses and the Prophets, we understand these to be the three sections of the Old Testament. I am sure that some of these 456 passages were among those referred to by our Lord.

In the final day, our Lord will also chastise the present-day church, including many evangelical, fundamental, conservative, orthodox Christians because they, too, are slow to believe all that was written about our Lord. He especially wants those of us who are proclaimers and Bible teachers to understand that the Word does speak concerning himself: his first coming, his second coming, and detailed acts and events in his life.

## The Modern Misunderstanding of the Messianic Doctrine

There is a fantastic table of reference to be found in *The Life and Times of Jesus the Messiah*, by Alfred Edersheim. This two-volume set, sometimes published as one volume, contains a table of messianic texts in the Old Testament and the New Testament; it goes through each event in the life of our Lord, listing each by category with the Old Testament reference on the left and the New Testament fulfillment on the other side. Indeed, it is a fabulous collection.

How aware were Old Testament writers of the Messiah? All too frequently, unbelieving and, I must say sadly, believing scholars have remained extremely skeptical about how aware Old Testament writers were of the Messiah in the Old Testament.

### The Attempt to Place Messianic Expectation in the Old Testament

First, I think it is important that we take up the modern misunderstanding of the doctrine of the Messiah: that is, a messianic doctrine which involves an attempt to place the messianic consciousness quite late in the second century BC. Therefore this messianic awareness would have come after the close of the Old Testament canon, about 400 BC, rather than during the time of Moses and the prophets.

Joachim Becker, for example, states this in his book, *Messianic Expectation in the Old Testament*: "There is no evidence for true messianism until the second century BC" (Philadelphia: Fortress Press, 1980, p. 50). We ask, No evidence? No evidence, he says. (I love the humility of such writers!)

Of course, he qualifies his statement with the word *true*. Becker continues, "It is on the threshold of the New Testament that we first encounter a real messianism" (p. 87).

This conclusion contradicts the most central thesis of the New Testament, which insists that messianism is taught with unprecedented frequency, intensity, and unanimity in the Old Testament. John, Peter, and Paul announced over and over again that Christ was proclaimed in advance in the Old Testament. They announced that what they were seeing in their day was what they should be expecting if they had read the prophets and if they had listened. These New Testament men were saying that if we read the Old Testament, we will be like the Christians in Berea when they were told about the Good News—about the gospel, about the kingdom of our Lord Jesus Christ. What did they do? They turned to the Scriptures—which for them were the words of the Old Testament—to see if these things were so or not.

They did not turn to a New Testament guidebook; nor did they turn to a glossary of terms or even to a collection of New Testament verses, a so-called *Testimonium* book, which is a very popular thesis now that we have found in the Dead Sea Scrolls a collection of a half dozen texts from the Old Testament said to be a *Testimonium* book. This may well be, but it would still be a collection of Old Testament verses. It would not be a new canon; at least, not yet prior to the first century AD.

One method the Jewish communities used to understand the Old Testament was a new type of exegesis called *pesher* exegesis. While *pesher* exegesis is technically somewhat different from what we call *midrash*, they tended to blend together to say that the words of the Old Testament prophets were secret. They were full of secrets and hidden meanings. It was only when Christ came that the hidden meaning—the so-called *raz*, using the Aramaic word from Daniel which means 'mystery'—came to fruition and was understood.

These hidden meanings of the prophets, as I say in *Toward Rediscovering the Old Testament* (p. 102), were "assumed to be allusions to events that were to take place at the end of time." Since, for the prophets and the New Testament writers, the time of the end was near, these prophecies were directly applied to the interpreter's generation. Therefore the Dead Sea Scrolls community, for example, which existed in the Dead Sea area a century to a century and a half before our Lord Jesus came, interpreted from the book of Joel that there would come a *Teacher of Righteousness*. They understood a special reading there which I think probably is valid: a *teacher* of righteousness and not that God would *rain* righteousness. The word for teacher and the word for rain are very similar, *moreh*. The Dead Sea Scrolls community interpreted this teacher of righteousness to be their own teacher, the head of the Qumran community; but it was this equating of their human leader with the coming Messiah as "teacher" that was incorrect. Reading in the book of Habakkuk of the Babylonians, they interpreted the "Babylonians/Chaldeans" as meaning the Romans of their own day. They began giving modern equivalents for all of the ancient values in the Old Testament, saying, "This is what is happening in our day." This is called *pesher* exegesis. *Pesher* comes from the Aramaic word meaning explanation, but it takes on the aura of giving a contemporary explanation for hidden values that are in the text. Thus the Christian community gave contemporary values to hidden Old Testament truths.

Now, I cannot subscribe to this method. I do not think we should take external data and make it normative for biblical interpretation. Large numbers of New Testament scholars today are in error, in my judgment, because they depend more upon intertestamental studies than they do upon Old Testament studies for interpreting the New Testament. Personally, I prefer to take God's word over that of modern interpreters. I think his revelation is to be taken more as normative than that of any others. Therefore, we can say that looking at the pseudepigrapha is helpful, but that it is only a cognate, or indirectly related, study. Looking at the Dead Sea Scrolls community is helpful but it is secondary. The same is true when looking at other materials such as Gnostic documents: they are helpful, but not definitive. So we need to see here that the *pesher* exegesis leads us in a very dangerous direction, confusing, as it were, the text with the notes in the margin.

As a matter of fact, Becker surprises us with his candor. He says that we may attach messianic meaning to an Old Testament passage, but he says frankly that to do so poses an "embarrassment." The New Testament writers do this by *pesher*—by finding hidden meanings; but, of course, he says, we cannot find messianic meaning there under normal rules of interpretation. To impose a doctrine of Messiah in the Old Testament is "arbitrary." And then in a wild moment of candor he even says that this will pose for us a "schizophrenic act of intellectual violence." Wow! That is all I can say. I can't believe it! He says it will turn us into schiz. We say the New Testament says that it is there in the Old Testament.

What would our Lord say to Becker? "O fool, and slow of heart to believe all that was written of me." He would not say "all that was *pesher* of me," or "all that was hidden about me." He says, "Didn't you know it was there? You could, you should, you ought to have seen that it was there." And he is still saying that to the twentieth century evangelical, fundamental Christian. Selah!

This first point is the important teaching of this chapter. Attempting to place a messianic doctrine no earlier than in the second century BC or even later in the early Christian consciousness would be like putting an overlay on the Old Testament. This, I think, is cheating!

Before I leave this point, let's see how it is argued convincingly by modern Jewish interpreters David Berger and Michael Wyschogrod in their book *Jews and "Jewish Christianity"* (New York: Ktav, 1978, p. 36). These two Jewish writers say:

> Christians can argue that the Hebrew Bible has hidden, profound meanings which are accessible once certain truths are already known from other sources. But let us be clear what this means. It means the verses we are talking about have a more obvious meaning which does not have anything to do with specifically Christian ideas. It means that they cannot be used to prove these ideas to someone who does not believe. ... If God wanted to teach such ideas clearly in the Hebrew Bible, he could have made them as clear as they are in the Gospels. It seems to follow that God wanted people to be able to read the Bible without seeing these beliefs. In that case, quoting verses to prove these doctrines [that is, the doctrine of the Messiah] to non-Christians doesn't appear to make sense.

Hooray for David and Michael! They understand better than the fundamentalist and the evangelical the significance of a non-argument, which I think is what we have for those who use *pesher* interpretation of the Old Testament rather than allowing the texts to make messianic claims in a natural, straightforward interpretation.

### *The Failure to Observe the Organic Unity of the Messianic Doctrine in the Old Testament*

Another liberal, Charles A. Briggs, wrote a magisterial work, *Messianic Prophecy*, published by Scribner in 1889. Although a liberal, he wrote this book before he moved too far away from a conservative doctrine of Scriptures. I'm quoting from pages 63-64:

> There is no section of Biblical doctrine which has been so little understood and so much abused as Messianic prophecy. [Right, I agree, Mr. Briggs!] The Scholastics have interpreted the Messianic passages in accordance with the Christian doctrine of the person and work of Christ, ... and they have ignored the organic system of Messianic prophecy.

As I said at the beginning of this chapter, they have not seen that the promise-doctrine hangs together and that there is more to it than just prediction and fulfillment. They are looking at these predictions as if they were disassociated one from the other. Mr. Briggs continues:

> They have seen neither the unity nor the variety of the organism. ... On the other hand, Rationalists have ignored the ideal element, and, in limiting the Messianic prediction to the local, temporal and circumstantial elements [that is, they made it all historical], determine the substance of the prediction by its external form, seeking in every way to exclude references to the Messiah ....

They have denied the doctrine of Messiah by their historical exclusivism.

How do we deal with this second misunderstanding of the messianic doctrine: the failure to observe the organic unity of the doctrine of the Messiah in the Old Testament? We must ask, first of all, *what is the best term to refer to this doctrine? Is Messiah the best term?* I would like to suggest that it be referred to as the "Servant of the LORD doctrine" rather than the messianic doctrine.

The word *Messiah* appears only thirty-nine times in the Old Testament. This doctrine of *mashiaḥ* (with a dot under the second 'h') is interesting because the word itself comes from the verb meaning 'to anoint'. Most of the thirty-nine times refer to the anointed persons: the Israelite kings, Saul, David, and Solomon, who are 'the anointed' of the Lord. In four other references, it is the priest who is 'the anointed'. So actually, at best, there are nine references to the coming person, the man of promise who will be 'the anointed' of God.

Even with these nine references, we have some problems. The clearest text, of course, is found in Psalm 2:2. This very clearly refers to the doctrine of our Lord as the coming person and Messiah. The psalm, in the magisterial terms of the King James Version, begins with: "Why do the heathen rage, and the people imagine a vain thing?" The NIV says, "Why do the nations conspire and the peoples plot in vain? The kings of the earth take their stand and the rulers gather together against the LORD"—against *Yahweh*—"and against his Anointed One" (Ps 2:1-2). And then what do the rulers do? They show their hostility with a picket sign bearing the slogan, "Let us break their chains and throw off their fetters" (v. 3). This is an embarrassment to the Jewish community. Why the plural suffix, 'their'? It is against Yahweh and against his anointed. The kings and rulers are saying, "Down with heaven! Down with God! And down with the anointed!" Who is the anointed? The anointed here, the *Mashiaḥ*, is to be accorded not only the office of the current ruling king, for example David, but more than that seems to be indicated: something much more magisterial, because this is the one whom the Lord has installed as king.

The nations have a slogan in verse 3, and God has one also in verse 6. He can picket, too! He carries a sign which says, "I have installed my King on Zion, my holy hill." And what will he say about this king in the investiture, the swearing-in scene? He will say, "You are my Son; *today* I have become your Father." What *day* was that? Paul will answer that question. You know the day when God threw down the gauntlet when he said, "Today, today!" In Acts 13 at Antioch of Pisidia, Paul says: "This day, the day of the resurrection." That is, the day when God threw down the gauntlet. Boom! That was it! That's the day in which he declared that the Messiah had become his Son. He gave him all power, all thrones, all dominion, all real estate, all wealth, all honor, all glory! It was a magnificent day, that day! Easter Sunday morning! No wonder we celebrate every seventh day. It is celebration day! The finest Savior earth has ever known! The finest day on planet earth! "Today!" Paul said, "I know the day you're talking about." He said, "We tell you the good news: What God promised our fathers he has fulfilled for us, their children, by raising up Jesus. As it is written in the second Psalm: 'You are my Son; [this] day I have become your Father.' The fact that God raised him from the dead, never to decay, is stated in these words: 'I will give you the holy and sure blessings promised to David.' So it is stated elsewhere: 'You will not let your Holy One see decay'" (Acts 13:32-35, NIV).

We can see a reference to this also in Daniel 9:25-26 in that great statement of the Messiah being "cut off, but not for himself" (AV). That is a difficult phrase, but nevertheless it is in a context which seems to be fairly clear. There is also a clear reference in Hannah's song in 1 Samuel 2:10.

But I think a better term than the anointed or the Messiah would be *Servant of the LORD*, which we will study in more detail in chapter 16. "Servant of the LORD" appears thirty-one times in Isaiah 40–66 alone. Also in these chapters, we have that same corporate or collective idea as we have seen previously in the word *seed*. We have said that seed is a singular, not a plural, but it is a collective singular, like deer. We don't say ten deers; we say ten deer or one deer. So with this collective singular, we can refer to the one who is the representative of the group or we can refer to the whole group. We find the same thing in Isaiah 40–53, where the word servant is used in the singular. In the middle of these twenty-seven chapters (Isaiah 40-66) we find the centerpiece of the argument in the fourteenth chapter: that is, in Isaiah 52:13 through Isaiah 53:12 we have a theological statement of Scripture on the nature of the atonement.

Up to this point, servant occurs twenty times, always in the singular. After the death of the Messiah on behalf of all the people—which, by the way, does not only pertain to Israel—the phrase is used in the plural, "servants of the LORD."

Once on the John Ankerberg show I faced Rabbi Pinchas Lapide in debate. In the middle of the debate he said, "My good friend Kaiser: Look, this is a reference to *us*—*we* are the ones who have suffered. This is a picture of Israel."

And I said, "My good friend Dr. Lapide: Look, this text is talking about the Messiah: 'There is no deceit; there is no guile in his mouth; he has done no wrong.' Of what Israelite is that true according to Isaiah's view?"

He said nothing in reply.

Now we know that God has said, "[All humanity] have gone their own way, and they have all sinned." So we cannot predicate a lack of deceit or guile of any Israelite except Messiah.

Eleven more times after Isaiah 53, 'servants' is found only in the plural. That makes a total of thirty-one times for the phrase "servants of the LORD." It is interesting how, as we move toward the atonement in the middle chapter, Isaiah 52–53, it is always "servant," "servant of the LORD."

After chapter 53, it is only in the plural, "servants of the LORD." There we see that same oscillation between the one and the many; between the whole group of those who believe, who are the servants, and yet, the one who is to come to serve all of them and to be the Servant of the LORD.

So I would suggest that Servant of the LORD is a very good name for this doctrine of the coming Christ. One of the drawbacks, however, is that the Servant of the LORD is very much connected with the suffering aspect, though not exclusively, because the last three verses of this fifty-third chapter is one of the clear statements of the resurrection of our Lord. However, the word *servant* tends to bring up images only of his death and his serving in the suffering capacity.

As to the concept of the unity of the doctrine, *we must also ask if the doctrine of the Messiah is the result of scattered predictions which unfold, or is there an organized plan to the whole doctrine?* In other words, are we dealing with predictions or a promise-plan? Which is it here? Is it Messiah or Servant? we ask. Do we have here in this doctrine a series of random predictions, or do we have a promise-plan? My answer is that prediction is a foretelling; in short, a type of prognostication. A prediction focuses mainly upon two things: It focuses on the word spoken prior to the event, and it focuses upon the fulfillment of the event itself. Now I think that is less than the doctrine of Messiah that is found in the Scriptures, for the promise-plan embraces three things: the *prediction or word spoken* before the event, the *fulfilling event* itself, and the *means* by which the word was maintained toward fulfillment. Therefore a third element to be considered is how the word was kept alive between the time when it was spoken and when it was ultimately fulfilled.

So a promise doctrine has three essential parts. We begin to see "unity arcs," as it were: arcs connecting son after son after son in the line of the seed. It is not that Abraham received the word and waited from 2000 BC patiently until the fulfillment came in AD 30; it is rather that Abraham received an earnest, a down payment. He received the reality itself when he saw Isaac; he saw it as if it were an engagement ring that usually is a promise of marriage.

It was part of reality which was yet to come. Isaac was not all that Christ was going to be, so this did not show all the reality that was to come. Isaac was still a sinner. Isaac had problems. But Isaac contained in his person all that was going to take place in the final day. This was true of each Judean king in the Davidic line. They too maintained the promise, and that is the way we should read the text. Therefore we can see that there is important organic unity here. There is an organization, a plan, that carries through. There are historical fulfillments, and as we go through history, we are seeing more and more of this great word being fulfilled.

Thirdly, we must ask the question: *How many peoples and how much material did this Old Testament doctrine embrace in its unity?* In other words, are these features separate or are they cumulative? We think that the messianic doctrine is part of the single promise-plan of God, and that it is cumulative rather than a series of isolated instances to be treated separately. It is a continuous plan, and each promise interfits—is interwoven, as it were—with the previous revelation on the subject. When we talk about Abraham's believing faith, we must understand why the Bible does not mention it until Genesis 15. This seems to be twenty-five years too late, because Abraham left Ur of the Chaldees when he was seventy-five, and now at one hundred he was talking about justification by faith. Why that twenty-five-year delay in speaking about his faith? We argue that this delay is textual until the issue of the seed is spelled out, so that it is clear that Abraham believed in the man of promise who was to come.

And there is no other name than the name of Jesus Christ given under heaven—none—whereby anyone ever was or ever could be saved in any dispensation at any time. No other name was ever given or will ever be found! So, it seems to me that we must see a continuous plan here.

And all nations are involved. It is cosmopolitan, not nationalistic nor exclusive in that sense. On the other hand, many Christian interpreters err in the other direction. They deny that the promise has anything left in it for national Israel now that the Christian era has arrived.

Willis J. Beecher, in the Stone Lectures given in 1904 at Princeton Theological Seminary, said, "If the Christian interpreter persists in excluding the ethnical Israel from his conception of the fulfillment, or in regarding Israel's part in the matter as merely preparatory and not eternal, then he comes into conflict with the plain witness of both testaments [and we might now add 'with history as well'] ..." (The Prophets and the Promise, 1905; reprint ed., Grand Rapids: Baker Book House, 1975, p. 383).

The plain witness of history—May 14, 1948—is hard to dispute. It will be harder for any of us than for John Calvin to stand before God as interpreters of the biblical record in the final day, having seen the state of Israel come into existence. When we stand in the presence of God it will be harder for those of us living today to find an excuse.

"Rightly interpreted," continued Beecher (p. 383),

> the biblical statements include in the fulfillment both Israel, the race with whom the covenant is eternal, and also the personal Christ and his mission, with the whole spiritual Israel of the redeemed in all ages. The New Testament teaches this as Christian doctrine, for leading men to repentance and for edification; and the Old Testament teaches it as Messianic doctrine .... The exclusive Jewish interpretation and the exclusive Christian interpretation are equally wrong. Each is correct in what it affirms, and incorrect in what it denies.

What a statement!

We must ask one more question: *Was the doctrine of the Messiah temporal or eternal?* And we answer, It was not limited to Old Testament times, nor was it simply futuristic; it included a "now and not yet." There were partial fulfillments along the way, with the climactic fulfillment to be in the first and second comings.

Let's go to the second main point in this chapter: the unfolding doctrine of the Messiah in the Old Testament.

## The Unfolding Doctrine of Messiah in the Old Testament

### The Promise-Plan and the Messiah

I just wish to make this point, first of all, about the promise-plan and the Messiah. E. Jenni has an interesting statement in his article, "Messiah, Jewish," in the *Interpreter's Dictionary of the Bible* (G. A. Buttrick, ed. [Nashville: Abingdon Press, 1962], vol. 3, p. 361): "The OT Messiah ... has no real counterpart in the ancient Near Eastern milieu. Its source must, therefore, be sought within the OT faith." There are no parallels for a doctrine of a Messiah anywhere in all of religious literature. It is unique! The best way to understand this doctrine is to see that the doctrine of Christ is at the heart of the whole of the plan of the promise and therefore it is an attempt to carry this out.

### The History of the Fulfillment and the Messianic Doctrine

Let's look at it in terms of the history of fulfillment. In this book we have put the promise-plan in proper sequence as it unfolds in the Old Testament and as it is being fulfilled. Now we find a veritable storehouse of texts and terms in the Old Testament itself which deal with anticipating and understanding the Messiah. We must know these if we are going to avoid the accusation given in Luke 24:25, 27, "O fools, and slow of heart." Let me quickly run through them.

There is the Messiah's forerunner, John the Baptist, referred to in Isaiah 40:3-5, which says there is a voice crying in the wilderness, "Prepare ye the way of the LORD." Get morally straight! Fill in the valleys and level out the plain and avoid the rough places. This text doesn't refer to road building or to LeTourneau equipment or to bulldozing. The prophet is saying, Get prepared; the Lord is coming! This is also found in Malachi 3:1 and 4:5.

The Messiah's birthplace was predicted in Micah 5:2 to be Bethlehem. That is why the wise men went there; they did not go there primarily because of the star. They went to Jerusalem and asked, "Where is he born, King of the Jews?" Had it not been for the book of Micah they would still be looking for the manger! They need not be an additional incentive for us to use horoscopes or astrology or any of that kind of thing. This text here is trying to talk about listening to the book, Micah 5:2.

Other references are to the Messiah and his betrayal price of thirty pieces of silver (Zech 11:12-13); to the Messiah's triumphal entry into Jerusalem (Zech 9:9); to the Messiah's anointing by the Spirit (Isa 61:1, "The Spirit of the LORD is upon me ... to preach good news ..., to set free the captives"). And there are references to the Messiah's resurrection, too, where David, foreseeing Christ's resurrection, spoke about him (Ps 16:8-10); and to the Messiah's second coming (Dan 7:13-14; 12:10-13).

So we conclude that there is a veritable storehouse of texts and terms and features of the Old Testament doctrine of Messiah. Those in Old Testament times were aware of them. We, too, can be aware and know that these texts are still being fulfilled as we look forward to the second coming of Messiah. (For more detail on sixty-five direct prophecies of Christ, see W. C. Kaiser, Jr., *The Messiah in the Old Testament* [Grand Rapids: Zondervan, 1995].)

# Chapter Fourteen

# The Theology of Messiah's Dynasty and Kingdom

Second Samuel 7 is the central showcase of the messianic doctrine. Here we find a new addition to God's promise-plan: God's blessing given to David. In previous chapters we have talked about the patriarchal-Mosaic promise and the premonarchical promise. Now we consider the connection between the previous promise doctrine and the promise made to David in 2 Samuel 7.

We find the third most significant moment of recorded Old Testament history in this passage. If we were to use mountain peaks to mark these key moments of the promise—not the totality of the doctrine, but its Christocentrism—then we would have Genesis 3:15 as the first peak, Genesis 12:2-3 as the second great peak, 2 Samuel 7 as the third, and Jeremiah 31:31-34 with the new covenant passage as the fourth great mountain peak. So if you feel overwhelmed by the detail involved in this study, just master these four mountain peaks and you will have gone a long way toward understanding it.

A great commentary on the third mountain peak of 2 Samuel 7 is found in Psalm 89, which celebrates the promise to David. "I will sing of the mercies of the LORD forever; with my mouth will I make known your faithfulness to all generations" (Ps 89:1). That word *ḥesed* that "I will sing of" is a most difficult and yet a most beautiful word. The translators of the Revised Standard Version reserved 248 spots for this word in the Old Testament. What English word, they wondered, will best interpret this Hebrew word *ḥesed*? After debating the issue, they finally decided that there was really no one single word to communicate its meaning, and so they settled on such terms as 'covenantal love' and 'loyal fidelity'. The old King James Version translated it 'mercy' or 'loving-kindness'. *Ḥesed* (with a dot under the 'h' to indicate the Hebrew 'ch') is basically the Old Testament word for grace: God's Riches At Christ's (Messiah's) Expense (G.R.A.C.E.). *Ḥesed* is also used for the covenantal love between Jonathan and David. But here David is using the word to describe the wonderful plan to all generations. "I will sing of the graces, of the mercies, of the unmerited favors of God; with my mouth will I make known thy faithfulness to all generations."

## The Connection between the Patriarchal-Mosaic Promise and the Promise to David

As we consider the contents of the promise made to David and the previous promises given to Abraham, to Isaac, to Jacob, to Moses, and to those who were the elders and judges in Israel, we find the promises to be the same in nine different areas.

### The 'Seed'

First, there is the promise of the seed. God said to David in 2 Samuel 7:12,14, "When your days are over and you rest with your fathers, I will raise up your seed to succeed you, who will come from your own body, and I will establish his kingdom. ... I will be his father, and he will be my son." I submit to you that this seed is the same one promised to Eve, to Abraham, to Isaac, and to Jacob. So we have continuity here. That word *seed* appears frequently in the Old Testament, beginning back in Genesis 3:15, then in Genesis 12:7, and is elaborated on particularly in the great chapter on justification by faith in Genesis 15, and then in the chapter on the sealing of the covenant in Genesis 17 (vv. 7-10, 19). This 'seed' is a collective singular word implying both *all who believe* in Messiah and the *one who represents the whole body of believers*: Messiah himself.

### Unconditional Promise

Secondly, as to content, this promise to David was unconditional, just as the promise made to Abraham was unconditional. God, as the smoking furnace, walked between the pieces of animals and obligated only himself in the covenant with Abraham; it was a unilateral and not a bilateral covenant.

One of the great royal psalms—also referred to as one of the "psalms of the ascent"—comments on this [covenant] in detail: "For the sake of David your servant, do not reject your messiah, your anointed one. The LORD swore an oath to David, a sure oath that he will not revoke: One of your own seed I will place on your throne" (Ps 132:10-11). That is the promise God made; his word was accompanied with an oath. And what was his oath that he cannot—he will not—revoke? It was: "One of your own seed I will place on your throne." It then goes on to speak of a kingdom and of a dynasty. Remember how Hebrews 6 says that by two immutable, unshakable, unchangeable things it was impossible for God to lie: i.e., his word and his oath; because of these two things the writer of Hebrews says we might have a strong consolation, a solid hope. We saw God giving his word in Genesis 12:1-3 and giving his oath in Genesis 22:15-18.

So, even though this promise to David in 2 Samuel 7 is not phrased the same way as in Genesis 22, it is unconditional. However there are a number of passages which might make us think there is an "iffiness" to it: there is a constant reminder about sin. For example, the passage we just read continues, "If your sons keep my covenant and the statutes I teach them, then their sons will sit on your throne for ever and ever" (Ps 132:12, NIV). But yet God has sworn with an oath; he will not revoke the promise. Why this condition of obedience when God has said it is irrevocable? Isn't this a contradiction? Having said, "God will not revoke it" (v. 11), then he says, "If your sons fail to keep this covenant, then they won't sit on the throne." How are we to explain that?

Let us also look at the greatest commentary on 2 Samuel 7. In Psalm 89:26-27 God says that the Son will call out to the Father, "'You are my Father, my God, the Rock, my Savior.' I will also appoint him my firstborn ...." (We have already seen the use of 'firstborn' back in Exodus 4:22.) God says, Israel is my son, my firstborn, "the most exalted of the kings of the earth. I will maintain my love to him forever, and my covenant with him will never fail" (Ps 89:27-28, NIV). There again, the text says the covenant is irrevocable. "I will establish his line forever, his throne as long as the heavens endure" (v. 29, NIV). But, "If his sons forsake my law and do not follow my statutes, if they violate my decrees and fail to keep my commands, I will punish their sin with a rod, their iniquity with flogging; but I will not take my love from him, nor will I ever betray my faithfulness. I will not violate my covenant or alter what my lips have spoken. Once for all I have sworn by my holiness—and I will not lie to David—that his line will continue forever and his throne endure before me like the sun; it will be established forever like the moon, the faithful witness in the sky. *Selah*" (vv. 30-37).

How then are we to understand this conditional aspect ("if his sons forsake my law and do not follow my statutes") being said in the context of "but I won't violate my covenant"? It seems to me that the answer must be that some members in the line can forfeit their participation in the benefits. Let's draw a long arrow to represent the line of David, the succession of seeds: David, Solomon, Rehoboam, all the way down to our Lord Jesus who comes from the house and the lineage of David. The text is saying that sin may, indeed, bring disastrous effects and may keep individuals from participating personally in the benefits. So below the line I will put: "They may not personally participate in the benefits because they lack believing faith or because they disobey." Here we have two conditions whereby the seed may fail personally to experience what it means to belong to the family of God or to experience a full life—what it means to be totally part of the family of God. Yet on the other hand, the seed must and will transmit the benefits to the succeeding seed. That seems to be the inviolable part of it: the benefits of the covenant must be passed on. Thus, above the line I will put: "All in the line of David must transmit the *promise* even if they do not personally participate in it by faith."

It seems to me that this is the correct way to understand this group of texts, of which I have given two samples. Probably there are between six and twelve places where the conditional and the unconditional are found in the same text. The easy way out would be to say that two different writers held two different points of view and to find one text showing the conditional aspects of the promise and another document showing the unconditional aspects. Hurrah for the person who takes up the challenge of the apparent contradiction and finds both in one text. Of course, another solution to the apparent contradiction could be to invent the hypothesis that a redactor smoothed it out and included both in the same context. But this is a "dead horse" type of solution which needs to be propped up continually.

### Kingly Line and a Kingdom

There is another aspect to the promise which says we are dealing with the same content; not only is it the same seed, but it is the same kingly line. In Genesis 17:6, 16, Abraham was told that kings would come out of his loins. It is also found in Genesis 35:11 and in the Balaam prophecies in Numbers 24:7. In Deuteronomy 17:14-20, it was God's intention to give Israel a king. This would fit in with the messianic plan previously announced in Genesis 17:6, 16 and Numbers 24:7.

In this magnificent text, 2 Samuel 7:12, 16, we are told again, "I will establish his kingdom." The Lord goes on to say that he would have a throne and a dynasty and a kingdom forever. The concept of a kingly line is expanded beyond the idea of authority and a throne. It includes also a sphere of authority, a reign, and a realm, otherwise known as the kingdom of God.

### A Promise Forever

There is a fourth similarity and connection with the previous promise doctrine: that is, the "foreverness," the eternal aspect of it. Doesn't Genesis 17 emphasize this concept? Numerous times—almost a half dozen times—the word comes to Abraham, "I have given you this covenant forever. It is an everlasting covenant. It is eternal." What word occurs over and over in 2 Samuel 7:13, 16, 24-26, 29? *Forever!* This blessing will be a blessing *forever*; this covenant will be a covenant *forever*; this seed will be a seed *forever*. It is an everlasting, eternal covenant of God.

## A Promise of Rest

A fifth similarity between the promises previously given to Abraham and now this one given to David in 2 Samuel 7 is the concept of rest. Second Samuel 7:1 says, "After the king was settled in his palace and the LORD had given him rest from all his enemies …," and verse 11 adds, "I will also give you rest from all your enemies" (NIV). Already in Deuteronomy 12:9-10 and in Deuteronomy 25:19 there was a clue that this promise would be restated at this time; that is, when Jehovah/Yahweh would cut off Israel's enemies, then he would give his people rest. Back then the Lord said, "You have not yet reached the resting place and the inheritance the LORD your God is giving you. But you will cross the Jordan and settle in the land the LORD your God is giving you as an inheritance, and he will give you rest from all your enemies around you so that you will live in safety" (Deut 12:9-10, NIV).

## Echoes in Phrasing

There is yet another similarity: there is continuity in the phraseology of the Abrahamic and Mosaic promises. We can't go into all of the similarities, but certainly we will see a thread of continuity in meaning here. For example, God says in 2 Samuel 7:24 that he has become their God. That reminds us of the tripartite formula: "I will be your God; you shall be my people; and I will dwell in the midst of you." That statement, "I will be your God," is first seen in Genesis 17:7-8, and is found multiple times— almost two dozen times—by the time we get here to 2 Samuel 7:24. God also says, "You shall be my people." And what does 2 Samuel 7:23 say? God has come to redeem a people for himself, to make him a name.

## Grammatical Echo

Look at the unusual construction in 2 Samuel 7:23. It is odd to those who read it in the original text. It says there, "And who is like your people Israel—the one nation on earth that God *have* gone to redeem a people for himself?" In order for you to hear what is in this text, I have committed the grammatical infelicity of using the plural verb 'have'. Why did the writer make this grammatical "mistake" at this point? It preserves the same oddity, if I may say so, that is found in Deuteronomy 4:7-8. Here is a deliberate connecting of ideas taken from two separate occasions—from the promise being given to David and from the Mosaic instruction. "What other nation is so great as to have Elohim/God drawing near them (plural) the way the LORD our God is near us whenever we pray to him? And what other nation is so great as to have such righteous decrees and laws as this body of laws I am setting before you today?" It is equivalent to saying: "So, what other nation is so great as our God who *have* gone …?" This is the same unusual construction repeated in 2 Samuel 7:23; thus the Davidic covenant echoed the older promises made to Israel.

### Adonai Yahweh

We want to mention two more oddities here: the unusual name, *Adonai YHWH*, and the concept of the fatherhood of God. In 2 Samuel 7 is found a word that is used only in this chapter; it is found nowhere else in 1 Samuel, 2 Samuel, or the rest of the historical books or Chronicles. The name is *Adonai Yahweh*: *Adonai* which means Lord in the lowercase and *Yahweh* which is generally written LORD in the uppercase. So we have Lord LORD: Adonai Yahweh. Interestingly enough, this word was the special word used by Abraham in Genesis 15:2, 8, when he had the Passing Between the Pieces vision from God. When the covenant was sealed with Abraham, he called God *Adonai Yahweh*. Now, when the covenant is being sealed with David, he calls God *Adonai Yahweh*. It is more than coincidental, since it is a word found in only five other passages in the entire Bible. So it is remarkable, and it links the Abrahamic and Davidic promises.

### Fatherhood of God

Then there is the ninth connection to the previous promises. Second Samuel 7:14 says, "I will be a father to him." That reminds us of "Israel is my son, my firstborn" (Ex 4:22-23). It reminds us, too, of the passage in Deuteronomy 1:31, where there is a legitimate aspect of the fatherhood of God: "There you saw how the LORD your God carried you, as a father carries his son ..." (NIV). Just as a father picks up his boy, just so Yahweh, the living God, does the same for Israel. In Deuteronomy 32:6, we again have a legitimate doctrine of fatherhood in the biblical sense, not in the outmoded liberal sense of "the fatherhood of God and the brotherhood of man." He says, "Is this the way you repay the LORD, O foolish and unwise people? Is he not your Father, your Creator, who made you and formed you?" (NIV). This is the doctrine of fatherhood because of creation and not because of redemption. The doctrine of the fatherhood of God because of redemption is found in the Exodus 4 passage.

## The Promise to David

Let's now go to the promise itself made to David. First of all, 2 Samuel 7 has a twin passage in 1 Chronicles 17. There are minor differences between the two accounts, but, so as not to confuse things, we will speak mainly about the outline of 2 Samuel 7.

### Its Outline in 2 Samuel 7

Probably the chronicler is writing in the post-exilic period; this is where most writers put him. Do keep in mind that there is a parallel passage in 1 Chronicles 17.

What is the occasion for the promise? Second Samuel 7:1-7 gives the scene, involving a conversation between David and the prophet, Nathan. (Let's call him Nate; we've studied this passage so frequently I think we can be on familiar terms.) King David is in his new home and he says to Nate, "Isn't this magnificent? I've just completed my palace, cedar and all. It is beautiful! But I've got a bad conscience. Why should God dwell in those dusty old curtains? He has been in them since 1400 and now it's 1000 BC. Those rugs are getting old. We really need to do something about it!" And so he exclaims, "You know what I'm going to do? I'm going to build a house for God!"

Nate responds, "Wonderful! Amen! Selah. That's great! Go and do all that's in your heart."

Now, don't forget that Nathan is speaking "off the cuff" here. Nathan, even though he is a prophet, at this point is speaking as a "non-prophet," for he is not speaking the word of the Lord.

That night the Lord appears to Nate and says, "Thus saith the LORD ...." There we have the prophetic formula; there we have revelation. That's the difference between a prophet as a regular kind of person giving his own wisdom (which in this case wasn't so wise!) and a prophet as a person who receives the word of the Lord. "Thus saith the LORD: Because his hands are filled with blood, he will not build the house for me, but I'll build a house out of him. I'll make a dynasty—the house of David, the dynasty of David—out of him." And so God has to correct Nathan for speaking out of turn.

In the morning Nate goes to see David to communicate what God has told him. He says, "David, I misspoke yesterday. I have a word from the LORD. Thus saith the LORD ...." And then he gives the revelation of God. That's the occasion in verses 1-7.

Then the promise itself is given in verses 8-16. We could divide the promise into two subpoints: (1) God's work in the past (vv. 8-9a); and (2) God's work in the future (vv. 9b-16). Here, God reviews how he took this boy from being just a shepherd boy following his flocks and made him to be a ruler over his people. God says that he has gone wherever David has gone; and he will go wherever David goes. He will make King David successful over his enemies, even as he already has.

God says, "I will make your name great" (v. 9). Here comes that promise which sounds terribly familiar. It sounds like Genesis 12:2! It sounds like what they were questing for in Genesis 6 before the flood: they wanted a *name*. It sounds like what they were questing for in Genesis 11 at the tower of Babel: they wanted to "make a name" for themselves.

God continues, "I'll provide a place for my people" (v. 10). A place? "A place for my name to dwell. And I'll plant them there, and I'll give them rest." That's what he was talking about in Deuteronomy 12 and other passages: bringing them into an inheritance and into a rest—spiritual as well as physical rest.

And then the Lord declares to David, "After your days, when you go to rest with your fathers, I'll raise up your seed to succeed you. I mean one that comes out of your own body" (v. 12). He's saying to David, "I want to be sure you understand, just as I told Abraham." Remember what God said to Abraham: "It won't be Eliezer your servant; I'm not going to have you adopt someone, such as an Arab from Damascus; I mean someone out of your own body." So when Abraham was as good as dead—already 100 years old—and his wife was 90 years old, God gave them the miraculous power of conception. And so God promises to David, "I will build a house for my name; I will establish the throne of his kingdom. I will be his daddy; he will be my son. And if he does wrong, I will punish him with the rod of men and with floggings inflicted by men. But my love will never be taken away from him" (2 Sam 7:13-15). Again this is an unconditional promise, even though there is the conditionality of a particular person in the line of David being able to participate in all the benefits.

Then we have the third main point in our outline of 2 Samuel 7: thanksgiving for the promise. In verses 18-19 David, after hearing God's promise of blessing, goes into the house of God and worships and prays. He says, "O LORD, who am I and what is my house, that you've done this thing for me? Don't you know that I'm from shepherd stock? I am not from the aristocracy!" He continues, "And more than that, look what you've done for me already. You've brought me this far. And as if that were not enough in your sight, you've also spoken about the future of my house. O LORD!" Unable to contain himself, he exclaims, "And this is the law for all humanity! What you have promised me is exactly what I've put my faith in. This is exactly what Abraham and Isaac and Jacob were trusting; they were trusting in this man of promise who is to come. Now you've told me this man of promise will have a kingdom and a dynasty and a throne and a people and an inheritance that will be forever and forever and forever!" He says, "O Lord, I just can't begin to grasp the whole thing! I just can't believe it!"

In verse 19 all the translations use a long phrase, "Is this your *usual way of dealing with* man?" All of that for *torah*. He just says, "*we-zo't torat ha-'adam.* This, the law of humanity!" I think it's an exclamation rather than a question. David is saying, "This! *Oy vey!* I can't believe the whole thing, that this is the law, the charter, for all humanity!" For he is conscious that what is being given to him is the gospel for all nations. This is missions; this is evangelistic; and this is universal!

So he thanks God for the promise *now*. Then he praises God for his favor in the *past* (vv. 22-24). He reviews the great acts of God in redemption and in bringing the children of Israel up out of Egypt. "Who is a God like you?" He uses that great expression: Michael or *miyka'el* or Michel or Micah. Whether it be in English or Russian—whatever language—this name just means "Who is like God? Who can compare to him?" The same phrase here speaks of the incomparability of God's person and of his power and of his attributes.

Then, finally, there is prayer for this promise in the *future*. For now, in verses 7:25-29, he turns to address the future, praying that God may complete his work even there.

### The Specific Content of the Davidic Promise

Now that we've discussed the outline of 2 Samuel 7, what about the specific content of the promise given in that chapter? It seems to me it focuses basically on four items. The first item is a *dynasty*, a house, a line, a lineage of David. Just as we have the famous houses in Europe—for example, the House of Hanover and the House of the Hohenzollerns—we have the great house of David, established by God.

Secondly, there is an *everlasting throne*, which speaks of the authority and the power which is given to David.

Thirdly, there is an *everlasting kingdom*. This speaks of a sphere, a realm, and a reign that is being given. When Jesus was on earth, the essence of his message was to announce the kingdom of God. On numerous occasions he said, "The kingdom of God is at hand. The kingdom of God is near." What does this mean? Many people have great difficulty with the phrase "the kingdom of God," and some have even been turned off by it because it previously was a term used more often by liberals in non-evangelical literature. But I want you to know that it is a biblical term, it is a term that was used by our Lord, so we should not be frightened by it. Then you might suggest, Why not make that the integrating theme for the Old Testament? Why not use the kingdom theme? In my books I have argued, as does Willis J. Beecher, that the kingdom is incorporated into the promise as one of its features. The best way to think of the kingdom of God is just to substitute the words "rule or realm of God." It is usually both, speaking of both the earthly and the heavenly, the terrestrial as well as the supra-terrestrial, where he rules and reigns. One day, when Jesus comes again the second time, he will be King of kings and Lord of lords and God of gods, and there will be no competition. None! Now, some become too narrow in their concept of God, making the "kingdom" only his heavenly or his earthly realm.

But there is the other aspect, the reign of God. Luke's Gospel says, "The kingdom of God is within you." That is why we also see an ingressive, an incipient form of the kingdom right now, in which God is reigning in the hearts of men. So the reign and realm of God form the third great feature of the promise.

The fourth great feature of the promise, I think, is its *missiological implications*. It is a *torah* or a charter (which is the word I would like to suggest for that Hebrew word *torah*) or an outline by which all humanity can come to the living God. It is the gospel by which all who believe in the person of promise who is to come will be saved, will have eternal life, and will enjoy the benefits of living life abundantly on earth. The *torat ha-'adam* is an amazing phrase that has been translated in a number of ways. Some Bibles just put ellipses at this point with the footnote, "Hebrew impossible" or "too difficult to translate." But I don't see that the word *torah* is too difficult; any lay person knows that it is the law. Then the word *'adam* is understood by most people to be the word for man or Adam or humanity. So it is simply saying "this law for humanity." What makes that Hebrew too difficult? What makes it too difficult is our own preconceptions, our sin, and our prejudices which say, "Don't let me see the obvious here."

Psalm 89 celebrates the specific content of the promise. So we need to see this in the terms of the psalmist. We have already introduced some of the great themes. He calls this the mercies, the *ḥesed*—the very graces of God. Psalm 89:4 tells us, "I will establish your line forever and make your throne firm through all generations. *Selah*" (NIV). Then he goes on to say that this one will have success. "I have found David my servant; with my sacred oil I have anointed him"—I have "messiahed" him (v. 20). That is the verbal root for the noun *messiah*. "I've anointed him." And he says, "My hand will sustain him ..." (v. 21). That is because he has God as his rock, as his Savior (v. 26).

Verse 27 tells us, "I will appoint him"—David and those in his line— "as my firstborn ...." We discussed the concept of the *firstborn* in a earlier chapter. The firstborn is not meant here in the sense of chronology, but it refers to rank and preeminence. David is not the eldest of his siblings, but eighth in birth order. Just as a point of interest, notice how by a factor of two we move away from the rights of inheritance of the eldest child. It wasn't Esau, who was the eldest, but it was the *second* son, Jacob, who was the "firstborn." It was Judah, the *fourth* in the family, not Reuben, the eldest, who was the "firstborn." In David's line, it was not the eldest son, but the *eighth* son who was the "firstborn." So we have two, four, eight. Now, obviously, we can't keep this up with sixteen, thirty-two! And so Psalm 89 goes on to celebrate this great theme.

### The Promise to David in Its Future Development

We turn, finally, to the promise to David in its future development. Notice all those metaphors which are used for David's seed. Isaiah 11:1 speaks of this person who will come from David as a shoot out of the stump of Jesse. Here are two metaphors: a *shoot* that comes from a *stump*—a cut-off stump. There are people who are not personally participating in the benefits of the promise; they have been chopped off, but the root still has life in it. It's like a big Dutch elm tree. When it is cut off about a foot above the ground, and when it gets lots of rain, it springs back in a year or two as an elm bush. This is like "a shoot out of dry ground." There is also another metaphor of the "Branch" of the Lord, in Jeremiah 23:5, used for Messiah.

There is Shiloh (not Johnny Shiloh of Civil War fame or some other kind of Shiloh) found in Genesis 49:10, "until Shiloh come," which is interpreted in Ezekiel 21:27 as "the one whose right it is," the one to whom it belongs. There is the horn of David, speaking of power; there is the scepter of David, the symbol of authority. There is the lion of David; there is the star of David. There is the ruler's staff; and there is the lamb of David.

We conclude this chapter by pointing to a number of royal psalms which pick up this theme. Psalm 2 is a great psalm that speaks of the king and his investiture. In Psalm 110 the Psalmist is apparently reading of Abraham's victory over the four kings from Mesopotamia, recounted in Genesis 14. By reading of the victory God gave Abraham, David realizes God's presence with him and feels refreshed, for he says it's "like a drink of cool water ..." (Ps 110:7). He begins the psalm with, "The LORD says to my Lord, Sit thou at my right hand ...." So we have A speaking to C about B: the LORD speaking to me about my Lord; i.e., the LORD God speaking to David about a third person whom he calls "my Lord." And then there are Psalms 45, 72, 89, and 132—all being royal psalms given to David about the coming Messiah.

So the theme of the Davidic kingdom and the promise made to David is one of the great doctrines of the Old Testament.

# Chapter Fifteen

# The Theology of the Day of the Lord

This chapter begins the study of the prophets. From now on, we will be dealing with the sixteen writing prophets, where the amount of material equals the bulk of the entire New Testament—an enormous amount of material! For the sake of convenience, these prophets are best studied in each of their centuries. Remember, when we talk about BC, the ninth century BC would be in the 800s, the eighth century BC would be in the 700s, the seventh century BC would be in the 600s, and so forth. Here flow five centuries of history with prophetic materials in each.

First, we will study Joel and Obadiah, whom we will place in the ninth century BC, although there is no point of orthodoxy which says we must put them in the ninth century. Yet it would appear that, on the basis of their message, they could have lived this early. Another option is to put them as late as 586 BC, just before or right after the fall of Jerusalem. I agree with those writers who put them in the ninth century, where they come shortly after the ministries of the two great prophets, Elijah and Elisha, who bring us into the ninth century BC, having accomplished the work which God gave them to do.

That great calamity of the division of the kingdom precedes all this, in 931 BC. Edwin Thiele in his doctoral dissertation at the University of Chicago determined this date to be 931 BC, rather than 922 BC, which is the Albright date and probably the more accepted date these days. I agree with Ed Thiele's date in his dissertation, *The Mysterious Numbers of the Hebrew Kings*, which was later published by the University of Chicago Press.

Thiele spent five years on the dissertation alone. At first his teacher said that he was not impressed by this particular problem. His teacher said that he had found 500 specific errors in the synchronisms between the kings of the north and the kings of the south in the Bible. In the end, his professor wrote a forward to the published book, saying he was convinced that the work of his student was valid, with the conclusions being based on external sources. Only one problem remained for him: the synchronism with King Hezekiah. He conceded that Thiele had explained everything else, mainly by using the cuneiform Khorsabad King List and the Assyrian Eponym List, which was something like *Time* magazine's Man of the Year list. (Eponym comes from the Greek, meaning 'name'.) Also, records of astrological observations were used in determining the dates of these synchronisms involving the north and the south. For instance, on June 15, 763 BC, there was a full eclipse of the sun; this can be correlated with astronomical observations. We can determine when on our Julian calendar that occurred. Counting back from that, we can date other events, for example, a battle with King Jehu; Ahaz is also mentioned. Thus, by using these two kings, we can get a "fix" on dating other Old Testament events.

So, I think that Ed Thiele's work stands on its external basis: It shows that 931 BC was the great moment in history when the two southern tribes, Judah and Benjamin, separated from the ten northern tribes, which will hereafter be known as Ephraim or Israel in contradistinction to the two southern tribes known as Judah.

To these two kingdoms, God sends a host of prophetic seers, warning them to repent and to abandon their ruinous course. The storm clouds of divine judgment gather, but the two nations continue in their sin, just as defiant and adamant as they can be. Thus, they have to face judgment before they can experience God's deliverance. This is a microcosm of the great judgment to come in the final day, the little judgments on Judah and Israel mirroring the great judgments that are to come, almost in typological form (like type and anti-type; like the Old Testament prediction and the New Testament fulfillment).

Suddenly Elijah comes on the scene in the ninth century BC; this is the first signal to the northern kingdom in God's order of warnings. First Kings 17 begins with, "Now Elijah the Tishbite, from the inhabitants of Gilead," went to the palace of Ahab .... And we say, Beg your pardon? Who is this man, Elijah? We have not been prepared for him. Elijah comes from the outback, from the boonies, from Gilead, which is way over on the east side of the Sea of Galilee. It's just a rocky, backwoodsy kind of place. This doesn't keep him from walking right into King Ahab's palace in Jezreel—the equivalent of the Queen of England's summer palace of Windsor—and saying, "Thus saith the LORD: As the LORD my God lives, in whose presence I stand, there will be neither dew nor rain these next years except by my word." Then he is gone. That's the way we are introduced to this man Elijah. And as he has said, for the next three and a half years, there is no rain!

Lest we make a plaster saint out of him, the book of James warns, "Now, friends, this man was a man of like passions as we are. He was made out of the same stuff. But this man prayed and it didn't rain. He prayed again, and it rained" (James 5:17-18). So what is the message for us? Pray! We ought to learn something from these prophets' lives. They were intercessors, praying on behalf of their people. But they also were bellwethers, just as the male sheep, with bells hung from their necks, are the leaders of the flock. These prophets ran out in front of the pack, saying, "Here's what is coming!" They were harbingers; forerunners. They were like one of the first flowers of the spring, like the crocus, letting people know what was ahead.

One example of this, found in 1 Kings 18:16ff, is when Elijah spoke at Mount Carmel at a face-off between the 450 prophets of Baal and the true God. He said, "Come on, people! How long are you going to waver between two opinions?" The word there is 'fence sitter'. These people were syncretists, combining a little bit of the culture (in a bad sense) and a little bit of God, mixing them up, and then trying to live by the mixture. There was an old political party in the 1800s—therefore it's safe to mention now!— which was a break-off from the Republican Party, called the Mugwumps. These were people who sat on the fence; they couldn't make up their mind. That's what the people were doing in 1 Kings 18; they were "mugwumping" between God and Baal.

Therefore the urgent message of the prophet from this time on would be, "If God is God, then let's serve him; but if Baal is god, then let's serve him. But the God who answers by fire, let him be God." Each group would set up a sacrifice of a bull on top of wood, but first Elijah said, "You call on the name of your god, and I will call on the name of the LORD. The god who answers by fire—he is God" (1 Kings 18:24, NIV). We might wonder, Why fire? The three and a half years of drought had been enough heat! Why did they need heat? It should be whoever sent rain first was God. They didn't need fire; they needed rain! But, no! Before the mercy of God could intervene so that he could send rain, the people had to experience the theology of sacrifice. There must be a substitute; there must be forgiveness; there must be something that intervenes which attracts the mercy of God. So that is what was happening here.

What did Elijah say in 1 Kings 18? "Your name shall be Israel" (v. 31). He was reminding the people of what God had said, "Don't you remember your name [Gen 35:2, 10] when I said, 'Put away your foreign gods; you shall no longer be called Jacob, your name shall be called Israel'? Don't you remember that revival—one of the first times I called you back to repentance? Come on, people, we're back there again." And so we have a good picture here of the prophets' work.

The ministry of Elijah was the first signal in God's order of warnings to the north, followed by that of Elisha. Elisha's ministry begins in 2 Kings 2:14, when he asks, "Where now is the LORD, the God of Elijah?" Where is this same God who manifested his power and all of his force? Elijah stood for the declaration of the power of God and the judgment of God on sin. But we see in Elisha the moderating, the mitigating, words of mercy and the accompanying themes of deliverance, repentance, and salvation.

## The Day of the Lord

Just after the days of Elijah and Elisha—perhaps even overlapping with Elisha—we find Obadiah and Joel at work in the ninth century, the 800s BC. The emphasis of their message is to be on the Day of the Lord, stimulated by a local locust plague, in Joel's case, and, in Obadiah's case, by the indifference of Edom, who are descendants of Esau, Jacob's brother. When Edom sees Judah under attack, the people just stand by and say, "None of our business. We're not going to get involved." They don't do a thing to help. So there is judgment on them for standing to one side when they could have come to their brothers' rescue. A modern parallel would be when President Eisenhower did nothing, although he had the power to help Hungary when that country was attacked. The book of Obadiah announces judgment upon those who do not exercise their ability to hear the cry of the oppressed.

### Its Key Theological Themes

What are the key theological themes of the Day of the Lord, which is brought up in the books of Joel and Obadiah? The Day of the Lord, *yom Yahweh*, comes from the Hebrew *yom* for 'day' and *Yahweh*, which is probably the correct pronunciation for the tetragrammaton YHWH. It is most certainly mispronounced in "Jehovah," which takes the consonants YHWH and inserts the vowels of *'adonai*. That makes about as much sense as taking the consonants of Grand Rapids, inserting the vowels of Villa Nova, and making a new name for the city. But that's exactly how we got the word Jehovah.

The first key theological theme involved in the Day of the Lord is that it is a time of divine reckoning for all nations, all countries. It will be a future time of divine accounting, a divine adding up, and so we speak of it as a reckoning.

Secondly, it announces the Day of Jehovah, *yom Yahweh*, as the day of God's supremacy over all nature and nations. That supremacy, that lordship, will be demonstrated.

There is a third theological theme. At this time and in connection with these events, there is to be a downpour, an outpouring, of the Holy Spirit on all the people of God. This theme is found in that great passage of Joel 2:28-32. Not just a shower; this is to be a tropical cloudburst of the Holy Spirit!

Fourthly, it is a time when a universal call will be issued by all nations to come up against Israel to settle the Jewish question (Joel 3). This will be permitted by God, but will be directly sponsored by every nation on Planet Earth, as I understand it. The nations will say, Let's settle the Jewish question once and for all! But God will join in the fray as judge over all nations, and will be the deliverer of Israel in that day.

A fifth theme in this study is that the Day of the Lord results in a revived Zion where God personally dwells in the midst of Israel. This is much like what the promise doctrine has said repeatedly: "I will be your God; you shall be my people; and I will dwell in the midst of you."

These are the five theological themes, then, in this great topic of the Day of the Lord: a divine reckoning on all countries; a demonstration of God's supremacy over all nature and nations; an outpouring of the Holy Spirit; a divinely permitted call given by all the nations in which they go up against Israel to settle the Jewish question, but in which God finally joins in the fray as judge of all nations and deliverer of the remnant of Israel; a revived Zion with the Lord personally dwelling in the midst.

Now we need to look at some of these passages in particular. But first notice the name *Joel*, which is thoroughly *theophoric*, meaning both aspects of his name are divine names: *Jo* is a shortened form of *Yahweh* and *el* is the second form of *'elohim*. Basically his name means "Jehovah is God" or perhaps "Jehovah is my God" (*Jo-el-i*).

### Its Character

Notice the structure of the book of Joel. There is an impressive beginning to this book, with the description of a fantastic plague that comes upon the people. It is a secondary issue whether Joel 1:4 refers to four different locusts or four waves of locusts or even to something else which the four types of locusts represent. The point is, some kind of agricultural tragedy is taking place. This is followed by a drought in which, when the farmers go to plant, the seeds dry up and waste away under the clods of dirt.

This is the occasion for the first call to repentance (Joel 1:13-14). What is the target of Joel's call? It is not the social institutions of his day. The prophets are reformers, but they see that the way to change society is to change individuals. So they go to the leaders—the priests—first, for indeed, as the saying goes, "Water can only rise as high as its source." Joel says, "Put on sackcloth, O priests, and mourn; wail, you who minister before the altar. Come, spend the night in sackcloth, you who minister before my God" (NIV). Then Joel goes on to say, "Declare a holy fast; call a sacred assembly. Summon the elders and all who live in the land to the house of the LORD your God, and cry out to the LORD" (NIV). That is his first call to repentance. And why should they do that, according to Joel 1:15? Because it will be a dreadful day—that Day of the LORD which "is near." The Day of the Lord "will come like destruction from the Almighty."

Well, Joel continues, in chapter 2, talking about the Day of the Lord: "Let all who live in the land tremble, for the day of the LORD is coming. It is close at hand" (2:1). He speaks of it using similes. He likens it to a storm: "a day of darkness and gloom, a day of clouds and blackness" (2:2). That's quite a storm! In verse 3 he says it is like a fire. This is because the Arabic word *yarad* means to 'scrape' or to 'clean'. The word for locust is 'scraper' or 'cleaner'. Imagine a locust plague. Everything in the path of the locusts that was previously green is gone: the grass, the leaves, the bark, everything! There is no stopping these locusts; they don't leave a scrap behind. They march ahead, shoulder to shoulder. Stamping on them, torching them, putting buildings in their path: nothing stops them, because there are always more locusts to fill in the ranks. When they come to a building, they eat the last blade of grass touching the base, march up the wall, over the roof, down the other side, and pick up the first blade of grass on the other side of the building.

They are very, very thorough. They are scrapers; they leave the landscape clean. The Latin word *locust* means 'burners': burners of the land. When the locusts go through it, it looks as if a forest fire has been through it. So it is no wonder that Joel uses the analogy of fire (v. 3). Then in verse 4, he says they look like horses. In a nature movie the camera could zoom in on one of these exotic creatures, so that the head would fill up the whole screen and really could look like a horse's head, when actually it is just a locust magnified many times. Verse 7 says they are also like an invading army.

All this leads to a second call to repentance (Joel 2:12-14). Joel says in verse 13, "Rend your heart." Everyone is to pour dust on his head and say, "*Oy vey!* This is terrible!" A typical expression of grief in that culture was to rip one's garment in front. God is saying, "Rip your heart instead!" Now, this does not mean to quickly open up a person as in preparation for heart surgery, even massaging the heart if there is no pulse. This does not mean to take the pericardium, the sack surrounding the heart, and rip it apart and then say, "Now I've kept that commandment." We understand this is speaking figuratively: Why are you ripping your garments? Instead rip your hearts in repentance. "Rend your heart .... Return to the LORD your God ...." Then Joel gives this great word: "... for he is gracious and compassionate, slow to anger and abounding in *hesed*"—abounding in love (v. 13). Now, there's a great word: *grace*, used 248 times in the Old Testament! Here it is translated love. It is also translated mercy, lovingkindness, covenantal love, loyal fidelity, and covenantal fidelity. It is all of these things and more!

And of course, it comes out of Exodus 34:6-7. This Exodus passage is quoted ten times in the Old Testament. God was causing his name—causing all of his goodness—to pass before Moses there on Mount Sinai. God was angry with Israel and he said, "I'll tell you what my name is. I'll tell you what my character is." His character is gracious and compassionate. He is full of grace and truth. As a matter of fact, this quotation is found in the Gospel of John: "The Word became flesh and made his dwelling among us" (1:14, NIV). The Word "pup-tented"; it tabernacled; it "shekinahed" in the midst of us. In the New Testament it is expressed as "grace and truth":

that Word was "full of grace and truth" (John 1:14), just as Yahweh's name was full of *ḥesed we-emet* in Exodus 34:6, 7. So what Jesus Christ is in his person is exactly what was expressed by the name that passed before Moses there on the mountain. This is a very astute theological point made by John.

I think we have not fully realized that John 1 is loaded with Old Testament references. Jesus said, "The law through Moses was *delivered* ..." (John 1:17). The verse does not go on to say, *"but* grace and truth ..." as I've heard people say frequently. That is not in the Greek or the English text at all. It is rather, "The law through Moses was delivered; grace and truth in Jesus Christ happened." *Happened.* The difference is in the verbs; it is not in the quality. It is a major faux pas in understanding the Old Testament not to make the distinction between Moses and Jesus. For John was saying, Here's Moses: he was a servant who merely delivered the law; but here is Jesus Christ who embodied it. That's what he was in his character: grace and truth; exactly the character of God, revealed in Exodus 34:6-7.

The text also says, with John the Baptist speaking, "The one who comes after me is actually greater than me, because he was here before me" (John 1:15). Not because "he is to be preferred before me." *Emprosthen*, used thirty times in the New Testament, is always a temporal thing: "He was here *before* me." The point is, he was here before me because *he always was.* He is the eternal God who appeared in Christophanies in the Old Testament and who has now come in the incarnation in the New Testament: the beautiful theology of the Word taking on flesh and dwelling amongst us. It is a connection between the Old and New Testament in a very beautiful form.

Well, Joel gave this call to repentance. Did the people repent? Yes, they did, but the text does not tell us in so many words. Joel 2:18-19 says, "Then the LORD *was jealous* for the land; the LORD *pitied* his people. The LORD *answered* and *said* ...." All the verbs in that particular form, the *waw* conversive imperfect form of the verb in Hebrew, should always be translated in the past tense, like *wa-yomer*, "and he said." Of all the discussion of tenses in the Hebrew text, this one is the clearest—the only one that is clear. And it is the narrative past tense. The NIV and the NASB do not translate it that way. They translate it as if the Lord *will* be jealous; the Lord *will* take pity; he *will* reply to them and *will* say to them. But no! This is the interpretive clue here; everything in the book moves up to this point, Joel 2:18. There was one call to repentance in Joel 1:13-14, and a second call to repentance in Joel 2:12-17. And did the people repent? Did they do anything? As we have noted, the text does not tell us in so many words that they repented, but it does say the Lord was jealous; he did have pity; he did hear; he did answer. This means the people did call on the name of the Lord; they did repent. The narrative past tenses of the four verbs here indicate that they did so. And what flowed from that? There was immediate blessing!

Substantial healing can come whenever revival breaks out. For the text says that it did rain, and God did do great things for them.

"Surely" (that word in Joel 2:20 becomes part of the psalmist's word in a psalm of ascent: "Surely we were as men that had dreamed," as dreamers) "Surely the LORD has done great things for us" (Joel 2:20b). The pastures turned green; the trees bore fruit again. They yielded their fruit because the "teacher of righteousness" had been given (v. 23). And he sent abundant showers and the autumn and spring rains as before. Notice that phrase at the end of verse 23, *ba-ri'shon*, which is like the phrase "in the beginning," *be-re'shit*, with which the Hebrew Bible begins in Genesis. "In the beginning" God sent autumn and spring rains (v. 23). "Now afterward ..." (v. 28). After what? After the beginning of the blessings, which came immediately after the people repented. Verse 28 says, "And afterward, I will send my Holy Spirit ...." These are distant blessings. So, from Joel 2:28 through chapter 3, we have distant blessings and the work of God, based upon this turning back to God.

In Joel 3 we find a statement about the Day of the Lord. When will it be? It will be when God restores the fortunes of Judah and Jerusalem. Upon whom will it come? It will come upon all nations (v. 2).

Where will it be? In the Valley of Jehoshaphat (v. 2). Jehoshaphat means "Yahweh will judge." He will judge. Where is the Valley of Jehoshaphat? Is this the Kidron Valley? I hardly think so. That eastern valley between the Mount of Olives and the Temple Mount is hardly large enough for a couple of good football teams, much less armies. Many have said that this is probably at Armageddon, the Valley of Megiddo near *har*, 'mountain', of Megiddo. It could be there, but we are only guessing. Then, where will it be? The text simply says that it will be in the Valley of Jehoshaphat.

Upon whom will the Day of the Lord be? All nations. Why will it be? Because they have "scattered my people"; they have parceled up the land; they have divided Israel" (v. 2). And because they have "sold my people for prostitutes and for a drink of wine" (vv. 3, 6). It is also because they took the dedicated vessels in the temple (v. 5), and they have—remember in the book of Daniel—drunk wine to their gods. So they scattered Israel; they partitioned the land; they made slaves of the people; and they carried away the sacred vessels. The text says, "Multitudes, multitudes in the valley of decision! For the day of the LORD is near in the valley of decision" (v. 14, NIV).

This brings us to a discussion of the character of the Day of the Lord: it will be a time of judgment; it will be universal, involving all nations. Joel 2:11 says, "The LORD thunders at the head of his army .... The day of the LORD is great; it is dreadful. Who can endure it?" That's the question! Who is going to be able to endure it? We can almost hear the strains of Handel's *Messiah* interpreting some of this, and also Joel 3:14-15: "Multitudes, multitudes in the valley of decision." He goes on to speak of universal involvement. Joel 3:2 states that all nations will be gathered together. It will be inescapable.

Later on, another prophet, Amos, will give us a little parable as an answer to the question, What is the Day of the Lord? (Amos 5:18-20). Some people say, "I wish the Lord were here" (v. 18), wishing it as a cop-out. Amos is saying, "Wait a minute! Only those people who are prepared for what will come should wish that. Can you imagine what it will be like?" And he goes on to give a parable, which I picture with the Roadrunner who is hurrying along down the road. Beep! Beep! All of a sudden, he comes to a screeching halt. There's a lion in the middle of the road, so he walks carefully around it, fixing his eyes on the lion. Then off he goes again: Beep! Beep! He beat the system with the lion. He's so proud of himself! Then all of a sudden, he comes to another screeching halt, for there is a bear in his path this time. So he goes carefully around the bear, gently moving to the other side. And he's off again: Beep! Beep! Into his house he goes and slams the door, leaning against the wall. (My marginal notes say he's panting, panting, panting!) The text says he escaped the lion and the bear "only to have a snake bite him" (Amos 5:19). That is what the Day of the Lord is like: it is inescapable. Any who keep saying, "I wish the Lord were here" had better be ready for it. Isaiah 13:11 says, "I will punish the world for its evil, the wicked for their sins" (NIV).

It is retributive, too. Obadiah 15 (*verse* 15, that is, since Obadiah has only one chapter) says, "The day of the LORD is near for all nations. As you have done, it will be done to you; your deeds will return upon your own head" (NIV). It says there that it will be retributive.

Another feature of its character is that it is a time of salvation as well as of judgment. Joel speaks of this in 2:32: "Whoever will call upon the name of the LORD will be delivered; for on Mount Zion in Jerusalem there will be deliverance." This is the great word that Peter uses on the day of Pentecost (Acts 2:17-21). "Come on, people; call on the name of the Lord!"

It is also a day of discrimination, of deciding and of discriminating between the righteous and the unrighteous. We turn to Malachi 3:1-3 where the prophet speaks of the righteous and the unrighteous. A day is coming when fire will expose and refine true faith. Malachi is referring to what happens to slag and to pure metals in a furnace. A heated furnace doesn't frighten silver and gold, for they have nothing to fear. It's like with fullers' soap: clothes have nothing to worry about when soap is used on them. But for the dirt in the clothes, it's a different story. The soap will get the dirt out of those duds, say the ads. So it will be a day of discrimination between the righteous and the unrighteous in general, and between the righteous and the unrighteous in Israel, too. Malachi 3:1 says, "I will send my messenger, who will prepare the way before me. Then suddenly the LORD you are seeking will come to his temple" (NIV). They *are* seeking, in a way. They are saying, "Where is the God of justice? Where is he?" Malachi says, "The LORD whom you seek"—sort of—"will come suddenly." *Suddenly*. And he "will come to his temple, even the messenger of the covenant." This is Christological, of course. The messenger owns the temple and he will come. Also, God, the first person, speaking about God, the second person, says, "I will send my messenger, even the messenger of the covenant." This is another great Christological reference.

So the Day of the Lord is a day of discrimination not only between the righteous and the unrighteous in general, and between the righteous and unrighteous in Israel, but also between Israel and the nations. Joel 3:16 tells us, "The LORD will roar from Zion and thunder from Jerusalem; the earth and the sky will tremble. But the LORD will be a refuge for his people, a stronghold for the people of Israel" (NIV).

## The Time of the Day of the Lord

When is the time of this coming?

### It Is "At Hand"—Imminent

The time of the coming, it seems to me, is always "at hand," in the sense that it is imminent. The prophets stress this great theme ten times: the Day of the Lord is *qarob*; it is near. This little adverb, which comes also from a verbal root, means to be near, to be at hand, to be pending. It is at the door! The interesting thing is that already four times in the ninth century BC, it is said to be *near* (Obad 15; Joel 1:15; 2:1; 3:14). Then Isaiah comes along and knowing, I would think, about Obadiah's and Joel's message, he too says that it is near (Isa 13:6). In the next century, the seventh century BC, Zephaniah also says that the Day of the Lord is near (Zeph 1:7, 14). Then Ezekiel comes along in the next century, and he too says that the Day of the Lord is imminent; it is near (Ezek 30:3). Do you begin to get the flavor of this doctrine of imminency? The Day of the Lord is near. It is pending, threatening. "Whoever has this hope in himself/herself," says 1 John 3:3, "purifies himself/herself." So we have here five prophets in the space of four centuries saying, The Day of the Lord is near; it is imminent; it is at hand.

### It Will Be Future—"It Comes"

Yet, although it is imminent, it is also a Day that will come. The verb is *ba'* in Hebrew, which means 'it comes'. The Day of the Lord will come; it is yet in the future. It is pending; it is both at hand and it is near.

It is a Day that is future; a date that is not specified. It does not matter whether this Day is one we can identify with a twenty-four-hour day; it is probably not to be put in any twenty-four-hour configuration. Rather, it seems to be a whole complex of events that surrounds the conclusion to history as we know it, or that introduces some of the climactic events that are on the border between history and eternity. So in this sense, God is now completing in time what he began in time.

There are three great moments of *tetelestai*: "It is done; it is finished!" One comes on the Sabbath, which marks the break between God's work in creation and God's work in providence. God was still working, but it was a different work. That comes in Genesis. Then, on the cross, the second "It is finished!" marks the point between God's promise to bring his salvation and his provision of it. And in the book of Revelation, there comes the end to the historical process; and once more, *tetelestai*, "It is done! It is finished!" This marks the division between history, God's work in time, and God's work in eternity. There are continuities that cross over these two time periods, but of course there are discontinuities too.

So the Day of the Lord is the great theme that brings together all of God's work of judgment and concluding work in the future. It is the Day of the Lord when God vindicates himself by great works, which all men must recognize as divine. As a rule, these works are described as direct acts of God, although providential works of such magnitude are included that God must be recognized as their author.

To summarize, the Day of the Lord is the Day of God's vindication. An examination of the passages listed for the "day of the Lord" in any exhaustive concordance will furnish abundant evidence for this characterization. The prophets longed for such a day as this, because they saw God's name and God's people being put to shame, without any complete answer from Yahweh. This will be the Day in which God gives his finale, his final wrap-up, his final answer. The two books that epitomize this for us are the books of Joel and Obadiah, where the centerpiece is Joel 2:28; for it is at this time that God will not only judge, but he will also mercifully deliver, and send a downpour of his Holy Spirit such as we have never seen before! This, then, will be the Day of the Lord.

# Chapter Sixteen

# The Theology of the Servant of the Lord

We have been talking about the prophets, how they viewed the calling of Abraham from Ur of the Chaldees as the beginning of Israel's history. When Jewish history is narrated, it begins with "When God called our forefather Abraham out of Ur down in southern Mesopotamia ...." The story goes on to say that the promise to Abraham was renewed when Israel became a nation. Later, when the people of Israel were in desperate straits in Egypt, God remembered his covenant with Abraham, Isaac, and Jacob (Ex 2:23-25). The demonstration of his remembering that covenant can be seen in the way in which he brought them out of the land of Egypt and formed them into a nation and into a people. Once again, God renewed this great promise with David when he called him to be on center stage: he gave him a kingdom, formed a line of kings, gave a throne, and created a dynasty. Up to this point there seems to be a passing of the torch, as it were, from one to another; a meshing—an interlinking—of the promise.

In order to elaborate on this doctrine of the promise, we have noted a host of terms which have taken on a quasi-technical sense, especially those personal terms denoting the seed or offspring through which the promise and its benefits were to come. We have seen 'my son', 'my firstborn', 'my chosen one'. We have also seen the word translated 'my Holy One', *hasid*, in Psalm 16:10, for example. We have seen 'my Branch'. The terms multiply: we have seen the 'Shoot' and the 'stem out of Jesse'. Then more recently we have noted the terms 'Messiah' and the 'Servant of the Lord'. By the very usage and context of these terms, they begin to build up a whole environment which takes on a quasi-technical status.

These terms relate to personal history and to the person who would be the man of promise at the center of that history, but there are other terms which relate the promise doctrine to history itself and to the great work that God is going to do abroad. Here we have the 'last days' or the 'latter days'. This develops after Genesis 49, where the text speaks of the latter days. We will also have the 'kingdom' or the 'kingdom of God', when we get to the book of Daniel. There are terms, too, like the 'Day of the Lord', which we discussed previously. These are terms, as I say, that relate the promise doctrine to human history, while others relate it to the person who is at the head of that history.

## 'Servant of the Lord' as a Term of Corporate Solidarity

The most prominent term of all, and the best fitted to describe the personal aspect of the promise—yet also linking it with human history—is the term 'Servant of the LORD'. We argued in chapter 13 that the words *messianic* or *Messiah*, while having come to designate the promise of the coming of our Lord Jesus Christ, refer to the Lord only nine out of thirty-nine times. In my view, the greatest term is this one: the *Servant of the LORD*.

### 'Servant' as a Corporate Solidarity

Let's look, first of all, at Servant of the LORD as a term of corporate solidarity. What do we mean here when we speak of corporate solidarity? I do hope that introducing the somewhat novel idea of corporate solidarity will not impede your study of this topic. I don't mean corporate personality. Rather, what I mean is something we can see in the business world of our culture; we can see illustrations of what was meant in Near Eastern culture. In business law, a fictional person is created so that corporations are treated as if they were single individuals. For example, if you buy a "lemon" from one of the Detroit automakers, you will try to settle the problem through legitimate channels—complaining, talking, pleading, praying—with the car dealer. But if, eventually, you don't get satisfaction, you will take the company to court. The court case will read, "[Your name] versus GMAC." For the purposes of that court case, a legal fiction will be created in which all of General Motors Corporation is treated as one individual versus you, one individual. For the duration of the trial the whole company is treated as if it were a single person, even though behind it is a management team, and behind that is probably a board of directors, and behind that are employees by the thousands, and behind them are stockholders. That is what we mean by corporate solidarity, in which the whole group is represented by one.

I think I have just such a situation here, where the whole group is represented by the one; that is, in the phrase *Servant of the LORD*. We have already seen that the word *seed* is not a plural and is not a singular, but is a collective singular. We miss the whole point unless we understand that it is a collective singular. 'Servant of the LORD' is a different situation. It is not exactly a collective singular; it is a pure singular: a servant of the LORD, which would seem to indicate one individual. What seems to come into play, however, is corporate solidarity. This is not corporate personality, something brought out by H. Wheeler Robinson in his article at the turn of the century on human psychology, which was another point of view altogether. This corporate solidarity is not to be confused with collectivism of a totalitarian sort, where the individual is sacrificed for social ends. Nor is it to be confused with the corporate personality, where the individual has no consciousness of being an individual, or where the individual is incapable of being distinguished from objective reality. Rather, it seems to me, the individual is able here to implicate the whole group, either for blessing or for reprobation. To say it positively, the whole group is able to function as a single individual through one of its members.

This can be seen, for example, in Joshua 7, where Achan's sin brings judgment on a whole nation. He steals a Babylonian garment and some gold and puts them in his tent. The spoils from Ai were things dedicated to the Lord and should not have been taken. And when Achan takes them, the biblical text says, "Israel has sinned." It doesn't say, "Achan has sinned"; it says, "Israel has sinned," because one individual is able to implicate the whole group.

We in the Western world find this hard to assimilate. We don't understand it, except, of course, when blessing is involved. We do like to receive all the benefits from our forefathers. We say, "Amen!" to that. When it comes to the debit side, however, we say, "Not fair!" We protest. But the individual is able to implicate the whole group either for blessing or for reprobation, and the group is able to function as a single individual through one of its members, much like a court case in which GMAC functions legally as a single individual.

We have numerous examples of blessing which comes because of corporate solidarity: to Isaac for Abraham's sake; there is blessing passed on. And to Obed-Edom's household for the sake of the Ark. We have examples, too, of judgment and of cursing which come because of solidarity. The nation experiences difficulty because of Saul's violation of the Gibeonite treaty in 2 Samuel. Cities fall because of wicked men and the lack of a sufficient number of righteous men, as in Genesis 18–19 with Sodom and Gomorrah. So we have the interchangeable nature of a group and the representative of that particular group.

### Frequency of the Use of the Term 'Servant'

Looking at the term *servant*, we note how frequently it is used. First, let us look in the New Testament, in Acts 3. Peter and John, you remember, go up to the temple to pray at three in the afternoon; they meet a man, crippled from birth, at the temple gate called Beautiful. After telling him that they don't have any silver and gold but such as they have, they will give to him, they address the crippled man: "In the name of Jesus, get up and walk." And the man begins running and jumping and praising God.

Once this is taken care of, Peter uses the occasion to give a little message. He exhorts: "Repent, therefore, so that the times of refreshing may come from the LORD" (v. 19). Then he goes on to say, in verse 25, "And you are heirs of the prophets and of the covenant God made with your fathers" (NIV). He is saying, "You people standing here, I want you to know that you are the beneficiaries and the heirs, at least potentially, of the promise that God made to Abraham, Isaac, Jacob, David, and Jeremiah." Remember, God said long before to Abraham, "Through your seed all peoples on the earth will be blessed."

The prophets and the apostles *do* love to preach that Genesis 12:3 text! They know it is central. For them, Genesis 12:3 is like John 3:16, "For God so loved the world ...." They repeat it over and over again, such as in Galatians 3:8: "In your seed shall all the nations of the earth be blessed." That's good news; that's gospel; that's central here.

I want to call your attention to the word *servant* in Acts 3:26: "When God raised up his servant, he sent him first to you to bless you by turning each of you from your wicked ways" (NIV). Notice the phrase, "When God raised up his servant." This great theme is not expressed in the words, "When he raised up his Messiah," but rather by "When he raised up his servant." So notice that we have an example of a New Testament usage of this term *servant*.

Back in the Old Testament, the word *servant* (or servants) occurs thirty-one times in that great theological section of Isaiah 40–66. In the first fourteen of these twenty-seven chapters (40–53) it occurs twenty times, each time in the singular. This I have pointed out before. But in the last thirteen of the twenty-seven chapters (54–66), the word *servants* occurs eleven times, each time in the plural. So when we come to the high point chapter, the pivotal chapter 53—which is the fourteenth and middle chapter of these twenty-seven—we find the singular usage changing to a plural usage. We will come back to that.

Quite apart from the book of Isaiah, there are other passages where servant is used. In Zechariah 3:8 we find the connection of two messianic words which take on a quasi-technical status: the Branch, which is the Messiah, and the Servant, who is the Messiah; he puts them together, "my servant, the Branch." Frequently we find "Jacob my servant" (Jer 46:27-28; Ezek 28:25; 37:25). We find even more frequently "David my servant" (Jer 33:21-22, 26; Ezek 34:23-24; 37:24-25). Then, there is another example, in Haggai 2:23, where we have "my servant Zerubbabel." Zerubbabel was in the Davidic line also. My point is that the word *servant* is used much more frequently to refer to the coming person, the man of promise, than is the term Messiah.

If I had my "druthers," I would name this doctrine not the messianic doctrine but rather the Servant doctrine. Servant, then, is a term that is used frequently, and it functions as a corporate solidarity in which the one is able to implicate the many, and the many can be represented by the one.

## 'Servant' as the Key Messianic Term in Isaiah

Let's look more in depth at *servant* as a key messianic term in Isaiah. We already have said it appears thirty-one times in Isaiah 40–66. Even with this frequency of use, however, we have problems with its meaning. What could the meaning of this term be? Many are put off by the fact that, in the text itself, the word *servant* seems to be used in so many different ways. First of all, in twelve of the twenty instances where it occurs in the singular (Isa 40–53), it does clearly refer to all Israel. There are so many such passages that it is difficult to avoid that particular conclusion. And in the eleven plural instances, it definitely denotes all of Israel. For example, in Isaiah 41:8, "But you, O Israel, my servant," it is clear that "my servant" is used in apposition: "O Israel, my servant, Jacob, whom I have chosen." To whom is he speaking? He is speaking to Jacob; that is, to Israel; that is, to the nation. No wonder, then, that the Jewish response to much of Christian exegesis is, "Look! Look who the servant is! *We* are the servant." They will point to a passage like this, and on that, they are dead right. There can be no debate.

Now look in Isaiah 44:1-3: "But now listen, O Jacob, my servant, Israel, whom I have chosen." So we have "my chosen one" and we have "my servant," which we said have quasi-technical form: he is referring to the many, not to the one—not to the Messiah or the Christ who is to come. That is very clear. Later in this chapter, the same theme will come up: "Remember these things, O Jacob, for you are my servant, O Israel" (v. 21). It seems to be in such clear appositional form that it would be difficult to miss. He goes on to say, "I have made you, for you are my servant." So twice in this verse "my servant" occurs, referring to the whole nation—to all the people. Again, we see this in Isaiah 45:4: "For the sake of Jacob my servant, of Israel my chosen, I call you by name and bestow on you a title of honor, even though you do not acknowledge me." That verse is even more interesting: he says they (e.g., Cyrus, to whom this passage is addressed) are called the servant even though others do not acknowledge him.

Note, then, that this reference to Israel as the servant is not merely to Israel as an ethnic aggregation, but to Israel as the people upon whom the promise has been bestowed; Israel as the people of the covenant who carry in their midst—in the heart of the nation—this great affirmation from God. That is the point that is being made, it seems to me. So, the first meaning of servant is that it functions for the whole nation as recipients of the great promise of God. The nation must transmit that promise, even though certain individuals may not themselves personally participate in it because of lack of faith and belief in the promise, as we pointed out earlier. There is a difference between the requirement to transmit it (hence its unconditionality) and the participation in it by faith (hence its conditionality). There is a conditional sense which requires accepting, receiving, and taking; the individual does not automatically benefit from the promise.

But there is a second meaning which, for the sake of our topic, we are more interested in: *the servant as an individual*. It is quite clear that the servant also has a ministry to all of the people. This becomes even more enigmatic; how can we put this puzzle together? If all of Israel is the servant, how can they be their own grandpa? How can they turn around and minister to themselves?—for this is the way we must understand some of the texts unless our suggestion of corporate solidarity is at work here. With corporate solidarity, the whole group can be represented and implicated both by the many and the one. We think that is what is happening.

Let's go back to Isaiah 42:1 ff., for example: "Here is my servant, whom I uphold, my chosen one in whom I delight" (NIV). Notice again the concatenation of terms: "my chosen" and "my servant." We have seen this linking of terms before. The passage continues: "I will put my Spirit on him and he will bring justice to the nations. He will not shout or cry out, or raise his voice in the streets. A bruised reed he will not break, and a smoldering wick he will not snuff out. In faithfulness he will bring forth justice; he will not falter or be discouraged till he establishes justice on earth"— or until he establishes the rule of God on earth. "In his law the islands"— the distant countries—"will put their hope." And so he goes on to say, in verse 6: "I, the LORD, have called you in righteousness ...." I think he is still talking here about "my servant." "I will take hold of your hand." *Raq ḥazaq* (e.g., Josh 1:7) means "only be strong." He is saying, I will take hold, I will be strong with your hand. "I will keep you and will make you to be a covenant for the people and a light for the Gentiles, to open eyes that are blind, to free captives from prison and to release from the dungeon those who sit in darkness" (NIV). Well, this seems to be an *individual*. It is quite clear here that the servant is now given a ministry to the nations. He is given a ministry to be a light to the Gentiles and to be a covenant for the people or the peoples. He is gentle, too, with people who are down and out: he does not break the bruised reed off and he does not snuff out a smoldering candle—that is, a wick that has become smudgy and is about ready to go out. There is a gentleness in the way he handles people.

Now that we have established that the servant looks like an individual (the third masculine singular pronoun is used; *he* and *him* and *his* occur frequently), let's turn over to Matthew 12:15-21 where we see the use of this passage in Isaiah. Jesus is aware that the Pharisees are plotting how to kill him, so he withdraws from that place. Many follow him, and he heals all their sick, warning them not to tell who he is. "This was to fulfill what was spoken through the prophet Isaiah: 'Here is my servant whom I have chosen, the one I love, in whom I delight; I will put my Spirit on him, and he will proclaim justice to the nations. He will not quarrel or cry out; no one will hear his voice in the streets . ...'" In other words, there will be no big billboard which says, Hear ye! Hear ye! Come hear Jesus! "A bruised reed he will not break, and a smoldering wick he will not snuff out, till he leads justice to victory. In his name the nations will put their hope" (NIV). This is the quotation from Isaiah 42.

One major interpretation of Matthew is that this passage is a turning point in the offer of the kingdom made by our Lord. Those who hold this position feel that the Lord senses the Pharisees are out to kill him, so he takes back the offer of the kingdom. It is postponed until a later date. Hence follow the parables of the mystery of the kingdom. I don't subscribe to that; but I think you should be aware of the way some use this passage.

It is quite clear that Jesus saw the person referred to in Isaiah as himself. It is also quite clear from the text that he is an individual, and that he has some linkage to the seed of Abraham, Isaac, and Jacob—yes, even to the seed of the woman.

## The Work of the Servant of the Lord in Isaiah 52:13–53:12

Let's turn to another passage, Isaiah 52:13–53:12, which is directly cited at least nine times in six New Testament books: the Gospels of Luke and John, Acts, Romans, Galatians, and 1 Peter. So this is quite a passage! There are even more than these nine citations, if we consider passages alluding to, but not citing, Isaiah 52:13–53:12. This chapter was loved by the early church. (I call it a chapter because it seems to me that the chapter division is wrongly placed: I feel that instead of dividing the chapter at 53:1, it should have been moved back three verses to begin at 52:13.)

The most familiar treatment of Isaiah 52:13–53:12 in the New Testament, of course, is in Acts 8 where the Ethiopian eunuch is on his way home when the evangelist Philip finds him having devotions along the side of the road. Philip says, "What are you reading?"

He replies, "I'm reading from the prophet Isaiah, where it says ...." And the Ethiopian eunuch quotes Isaiah 53:7-8: "'He was led like a sheep to the slaughter, and as a lamb before the shearer is silent, so he did not open his mouth. In his humiliation he was deprived of justice. Who can speak of his descendants? For his life was taken from the earth.'" (Acts 8:32-33, NIV). Then the Ethiopian eunuch shows he is very perceptive when he asks, "Of whom does the prophet speak?" (v. 34). That's interesting; he asks the right question. There's a great theologian and a great exegete in the making! If you can ask the right questions, even if you cannot answer them, you are on the right track. And he did ask the right question: "Of whom does he speak; of himself or someone else? I really can't understand. How can I understand unless someone helps me?"

This man did not have the advantage which the disciples had. Remember, the Lord had said to them on the road to Emmaus, "Look, fellows, you should, you could, and you ought to be able to understand this. You really should!" The eunuch did not have their background in the Old Testament, but he was close to understanding the passage. "Of whom does he speak?" He knew it was someone. It's rather interesting that he did not put the question in terms of the nation, but in terms of some individual. And then, you remember, in Acts 8:35 Philip began to explain to him about Jesus from this passage in Isaiah.

Therefore I would like to take a close-up look at the work of the servant as outlined in Isaiah 52:13–53:12. It will help us to understand this text which was so significant in the life of the early church and also so important in the life of the believing community during Old Testament times. The passage divides itself very nicely into five parts of three verses each, treating the mystery, the rejection, the atonement, the submission, and the exaltation of the Servant.

### The Mystery of the Servant, 52:13-15

Beginning in 52:13-15, the mystery of the Servant is put very simply and yet very profoundly: showing that "my servant shall have success." God does not want us to bite our fingernails, as it were, wondering how this thing is going to come out. The Lord starts out by saying, "Behold, my servant shall ...." I don't think that "my servant shall act *wisely*" is a good translation. This is the same Hebrew word as in Joshua 1:8 where the Lord says that Joshua will win or that he will have success. ("Do not let this Book of the Law depart from your mouth; meditate on it day and night, so that you may be careful to do everything written in it. Then you will be prosperous and successful" [NIV].) What we must understand is that "my servant will have success."

If we would want to put a conference banner over the front of the auditorium expressing this, it would be: *My servant will win!* "He will be raised and lifted up and highly exalted" (v. 13, NIV). Some interpret these three verbs to mean the death, the burial, and the resurrection. I think that's a little too much myself; but at any rate, there are at least three wonderful things here; an accumulation in the exaltation, the jubilation, the happy glee of a victor who has come back home. When a local team comes back as a success, people who weren't even sports fans previously turn out to greet the sports heroes. They join in the welcome, feeling that honor has come to their city. Honor has even come to their household, because the team has been successful. We have the same thing in this case. Our Lord has been successful! "Behold, my servant will have success."

But in verses 14 and 15 we have a comparison. We cannot separate these two verses: "Just as ... so ...." These verses make up the mystery. Here is the conundrum. "Just as many were appalled at him—his appearance was so disfigured beyond that of any man and his form marred beyond human likeness—" Here, I think we are basically talking about his suffering in his first Advent. He looks as if he is being trounced; he is being beaten;

he is being mauled. That's the mystery of it.

Verse 15 says, "... so he will startle many nations." I know most of the texts read "sprinkle" here. The LXX, the Septuagint, actually makes it quite clear: *thaumazo*. "He will startle many nations." *Nazah* is the word that occurs twenty-three times in the Old Testament, and it has an Arabic cognate which means 'to leap' or 'to cause to leap'. Hence, we would speculate "startle." It is certain that we are not talking about sprinkling as in a discussion on baptism. This is definitely something that will happen to many nations, "and kings will shut their mouths because of him." That's the expression there. "For what had not been told them, they will see; and what they have not heard, they will understand." What is this? It is the glory of the Lord; it is his second Advent.

I don't think the writer Isaiah knew that these were the first and second Advents, but he did write of a mystery here. He knew the servant would win; he said so in verse 13. He knew, too, that two things would come, and he even seems to have known the right order: first of all, suffering; secondly, glory. That's the way 1 Peter 1:10-12 puts it, too. We can now label them the first Advent (52:14) and the second Advent (52:15).

### The Rejection of the Servant, 53:1-3

Next, in Isaiah 53:1-3, there comes the rejection of the Servant. There is first the rejection of his message: "Who has believed our report? To whom is the arm of the LORD revealed?" Who has seen the power or the might of God? Power like baking powder which explodes when put in a cake. There's power there! The arm of the Lord! The might of the Lord!

The people rejected first his message, then his person. They said, "Aw, he's too backwoodsy. He's a tender shoot out of dry ground. He's like a branch on the corn stalk that must be stripped off because it's bleeding the main stalk." That's just what they thought. "He comes from Galilee. What good can come from there?" Therefore, they rejected his person.

Then emphatically the text says, "He was despised and rejected by men, a man of sorrows, and familiar with suffering. Like one from whom men hide their faces he was despised, and we esteemed him not" (v. 3, NIV). They did not put any value in him at all. So there was a rejection of his message, a rejection of his person, and a total rejection of him.

### The Atonement of the Servant, 53:4-6

But then comes the atonement. The central part of this teaching is found in Isaiah 53:4-6. It says here, "Surely he took our infirmities; he carried our grief. Yet we considered him stricken by God." So probably very much like Job's comforters, the people said, "Look! He must have done something wrong. Why is he on that cross? He must have sinned.

That's why he's there." But he had not sinned; he was there because of *our* infirmities; it was *our* sorrows. "He was pierced for our transgressions; he was bruised for our iniquities. And the punishment that brought us peace was upon him, and by his wounds we are healed" (v. 5). He got the electric chair when it was *our* due. That's what Isaiah is saying. And then the confession: "All we, like sheep, have gone astray." There is the herd instinct—"like sheep [we] have [all] gone astray"; this is depravity. But there is individual sin, too: "Each one of us has turned to his own way." So we have depravity and we have individual guilt. "Yet the LORD has laid on him the iniquity of us all."

### The Submission of the Servant, 53:7-9

Then we come to the submission of the Servant. Look how he submits. He submits, first of all, in his suffering. "He was led like a lamb to the slaughter; as a sheep before her shearers is silent, so he opened not his mouth" (v. 7). In death he submits: "By oppression and judgment he was taken away" (v. 8). Taken away—*snatched away*—in death; life was yanked out from under him. And "he was cut off from the land of the living; for the transgression of my people he was stricken" (v. 8). Finally, even in his burial he submits: "He was assigned a grave with the wicked [note: the word is plural, for he was hung between two thieves], and with the rich [note: the word is singular, for he was put in Joseph of Arimathea's grave] in his death" (v. 9, NIV). And indeed, in the first Advent, he was on the cross with the wicked; and Joseph of Arimathea, the rich man, provided his tomb.

### The Exaltation of the Servant, 53:10-12

Finally, we have the exaltation of the Servant. Look how he is exalted. Isaiah says that on account of his labor, "He will see the light of life and be satisfied; ... by his sweat"—I would translate that word *da'at* as if it were *za'at*, which is a good cognate here—"by his work my righteous servant will justify many" (v. 11). It goes on to speak of his resurrection: "Therefore I will give him a portion among the great, and he will divide the spoils with the strong, because he poured out his life unto death, and was numbered with the transgressors. For he bore the sins of many and made intercession for the transgressors" (53:12, NIV).

So we conclude this statement on the great prophet Isaiah, the promise theologian who has also given to us the doctrine of the servant: the *Servant of the LORD*.

# Chapter Seventeen

# Isaiah, the Promise Theologian

Along with tracing the promise doctrine in the Old Testament, we are studying the development of prophecy. This can be shown clearly on a step diagram. The first step begins in the ninth century, where Joel and Obadiah were the prophets, with the great themes being the Day of the Lord and the outpouring of the Holy Spirit. From there we step up in time into the next century, which produces Isaiah, with the motivating theme of the Servant of promise or the Servant of the LORD. Here, along with Isaiah, we have such books as Hosea, Amos, Micah, and Jonah.

Isaiah is the great theologian of the Old Testament. Chapters 40–66 of his book have been referred to by some as the New Testament within the Old Testament or as the book of Romans of the Old Testament. It really is great theology! There are several good Bible trivia questions here: What book of the Bible has the same number of chapters as there are books in the entire Bible? (*Isaiah*) How many chapters does the special section of Isaiah have, which is also the number of books in the New Testament? (*27; chapters 40–66*) This would give us, by process of elimination, How many books are there in the Old Testament? (*39*)

Isaiah 40 begins with the announcement of John the Baptist: a voice that is crying in the wilderness, "Prepare the way of the LORD." Very few miss the point that this is a reference to John. From this beginning with John, we make a big leap over to the central chapter of these twenty-seven chapters: Isaiah 52:13–53:12. (Let's just simplify and call it Isaiah 53.) Here is the greatest statement on the nature of the atonement, but from this high point on, the text does not fade out. No, it actually leaps to even dizzier heights as we come to Isaiah 65–66 with the new heavens and the new earth. These twenty-seven chapters cover, in short, the whole scope of the New Testament, moving from the very beginning to the very end of its twenty-seven books. Indeed, this section starts, as do the Gospels, with a voice crying in the wilderness; then we have a great statement of the death, burial, and resurrection of our Lord, as at the end of each of the Gospels.

We go on to read of the new heavens and the new earth in Isaiah 65–66, which provides much material for Revelation 20–21. This has great promise for us.

In addition, the outline for the last twenty-seven chapters of this sixty-six-chapter book divides neatly into three enneads, three groups of nine chapters. These three are: Isaiah 40–48, 49–57, and 58–66. We know this division is more than accidental, because the concluding verses of the first two enneads are the same: compare Isaiah 48:22 with Isaiah 57:21. In other words, we have a rhetorical device serving as a seam at a breaking point in the argument. What is that rhetorical device? It is the quotation, "'There is no peace,' says the LORD, 'for the wicked.'" That phrase is repeated in effect at the end of chapter 66 also; although these exact words are not used, the idea is given by description. We have here perhaps the greatest statement from which our Lord borrows most of his terminology when he discusses the problem of the afterlife and particularly the suffering of the wicked in hell.

## Yahweh, the God Over All
## Isaiah 40–48

Let us investigate the theological themes of these magnificent chapters. What we find in the first nine chapters is a discussion of God the Father, whereas in the second ennead, Isaiah 49–57, God the Son is discussed. God the Holy Spirit is mentioned in the third ennead. So the three persons of the Trinity are stressed here and the great works of each person of the Trinity are noted. In this second half of Isaiah, there is a shift in emphasis; whereas chapters 1–39 were keyed mainly to judgment, the emphasis now turns to a theme of comfort. Isaiah 40:1 says, "Comfort ye, comfort ye my people ... Speak tenderly to Jerusalem and tell her that her warfare has been accomplished." This major theme of comfort is introduced and then a voice cries out and says, "Look, get ready! Make ready a highway." A highway metaphor is used for the spiritual and moral preparation for his coming. This is one of those epiphanies, or a *parousia*. When a king comes to a town, the town submerges itself in preparation. When a president comes to a city we can be sure that crews will work all night. All the junk piles will either be covered over or removed; dilapidated houses will be fixed up. Even spots where there is no grass will be sprayed with green paint in order to look nice. I have seen it happen. Why? Because the king, or the president, is coming to town. In this case, God is coming to town. The visit requires *moral* preparation, not a beautification program. Get ready!

Then "a voice says, 'Cry out.' And I said, 'What shall I cry?'" Isaiah 40:6 continues, saying in effect, Don't you know that people are like grass? People are beautiful; we all have moments in which we flower and bloom and blossom, but then we fade. "But," he says, "the word of our God stands forever" (v. 8). "You who announce good news"—you who announce the gospel—"get up on a high mountain ... lift up your voice ... do not be afraid; say unto the cities of Judah, 'Behold your God!'" (v. 9). I can almost hear that in terms of Handel's scansion. But this is more than just a Jewish message. The message is: Say to the cities of America, say to the cities of the world, say to all of them, cry aloud, "Come on, buddies! Take a long look at our God." There comes our theme, "Behold your God." Behold our God! These chapters are an invitation to investigate a God who cannot be compared; he goes beyond all comparison. God the Father who is God of all!

### The Incomparable One

In Isaiah 40:10-11 the theme opens up somewhat as an overture opens up with the theme of a pastoral symphony. The great statement of this chapter is put in the form of a question: "To whom, then, will you liken God?" That is the rhetorical question; the answer is in the paragraphs which follow. In verses 12-17, though the question does not appear as such, it would seem that the theme of the incomparability of God is there, since the following set of verses (vv. 18 ff.) begins with "To whom, then, will you compare God?" referring to the preceding verses. "What image will you compare him to?" And beginning the third major section in this chapter, the question appears again: "To whom will you compare me? Or who is my equal?" (v. 25). Our proper names like Michael or Michelle or Micah, or Mickael in Russian, all mean the same thing: they are asking, To whom or to what is God equal? The answer, of course, is that there is nothing; there is no one who compares to him. So we are given an analysis of the situation by taking a long look—an investigative look—at God. "Say to the cities of Judah, 'Behold your God!'"

Three statements are made about our God which provide a lead-in for the rest of the chapter. "See, the Sovereign LORD comes with power, and his arm rules for him." His arm signifies his power and might; his muscles show his force when he goes into action. The overture continues, God is incomparably great in his person: "See, his reward is with him, and his recompense accompanies him" (v. 10). He is a loving person. He can reward. He is also incomparably great in his pastoral care, in his provision. Look how he takes care of his flock like a shepherd, gathering lambs into his arms. Little people and people who are hurting are important to this incomparably great God. He is not so transcendent that he has become the Force; he is personal in that he cares for hurting people—the little lambs. "See, his reward is with him, and his recompense accompanies him. He tends his flock like a shepherd: He gathers the lambs in his arms and carries them close to his heart; he gently leads those that have young" (v. 11, NIV). So we have a development here of a God who is incomparably great: he is the God over all. These three statements concerning the power, person, and pastoral care of God are elaborated on in the rest of the chapter.

This main statement on the incomparability of God's power is further developed when compared to nature (v. 12). He says, Do you have in mind the trinitarian God who is above all other gods? If you do, then the seven seas with all their tremendous volume of water are just like a handful of water in comparison. It is like putting all the waters in the hollow of his hand. If you compare the immensity of all the planets and of the universe itself, it is just like the span of a man's hand from his thumb to his little finger. That's all the universe is in comparison to God. Think how great God is! All that he has made is teeny-weeny. It is small. It is peanuts, compared to him. Then Isaiah says, How about the dust of the earth? Why, it's just a third of a bushel in comparison to God. How about the mountains? They are no big deal at all!

So much for the comparison of nature to God. And even when we consider the intelligence of man, who has understood the Spirit of the Lord? Who has instructed him (vv. 13-14)? Has the Lord ever come to you or to me and said, "Walter, I've got a tough one. What am I going to do? I have no idea. Have you read the newspapers? What will I do with Iran and Iraq? Do you have any ideas about what to do with the problems in El Salvador or Nicaragua?" I don't ever remember the Lord coming to me. Maybe he has come to you, but he has never asked me anything. Never! As a matter of fact, he's the one who gives wisdom. He gives understanding. And yet sometimes we act as though we need to inform God. We have all heard people give God the whole story and all the bits of information in their prayers. The truth of the matter is, the Lord does not need to hear any of that information. He already knows it all.

How great is he in his power compared to nations? He says, "Surely the nations are like a drop in a bucket ..." (v. 15, NIV). All the military power of the U.S.A. and Russia put together is truly like a drop in the bucket by comparison.

The text goes on to say that the nations, even the islands, "are regarded as dust of the scales." By *islands*, Isaiah always means the distant ones that go out into the Mediterranean Sea. Those remote countries, too, are like fine dust. About this point, we say, I understand! I've got the big picture. But Isaiah continues: "Lebanon is not sufficient for altar fires, nor its animals enough for burnt offerings. Before him all the nations are as nothing; they are regarded by him as worthless and less than nothing" (vv. 16-17, NIV). Even the idea of cutting down all the cedar trees of Lebanon to make an altar in order to offer as a sacrifice all the animals of that country would not be sufficient. This would be like cutting down all the redwood forest and building an altar seventy-five miles long by fifty miles wide by a hundred miles high on which to sacrifice all the longhorns from Texas. Can you imagine all those cattle and burgers when it is lighted! But the biblical text says, "That's inadequate. That's puny! Where did you get such a small view of God?" We say, But look, brother. That's redwood; that's cedar. I want you to know there is an awful lot of hamburger up there. The text says, "No, that's inadequate! His power exceeds all of that."

What was said of God's power in Isaiah 40:12-17 is true concerning his person (vv. 18-24): "To whom, then, will you compare God?" Don't think of God as if he were an idol. You say, I'm not into idolatry. The text says, Yes, but remember that if what you regard as being significant and the mainspring of your lives is equal to or higher than God, you must name it Baal. It is an idol. It may be golf, baseball, football. Perhaps it's some idea, some person, some commitment, some institution, some goal. It is the same stuff that idolatry is made of. He taunts them here, "If you are going to make an idol, at least put some gold over it. Give it some worth. And put some chains on it too. The idols need jewelry. Oh, you are too poor? Well, at least select your wood carefully. Look it over. It would be embarrassing to have your god eaten by termites. And get a skilled craftsman, too. Some people couldn't make a god if their lives depended on it! And another thing: nail it down. You don't want your god tipping over!" He is surely smiling at this point. I think this text is saying, Look, God is a living person. He is not dead like an idol, like some sort of gold image people pursue.

Isaiah goes on to say that he is a greater person even than princes and rulers (vv. 23-24). Have you ever noticed that no sooner do we hear of some important people than they are gone? We say, What happened to them? God says, "I blew on them. It's all over. That's it. *Finis!*" And they wither and are gone.

When it comes to God in his pastoral care, the third section in Isaiah 40 (vv. 25-31), verses 25-26 say, "'To whom will you compare me? Or who is my equal?' says the Holy One. Lift up your eyes and look to the heavens: Who created all these? He who brings out the starry host one by one, and calls them each by name. Because of his great power and mighty strength, not one of them is missing" (NIV). He's saying, Look up at those heavens. I want to ask you, Are there more stars or more people in the world? We say, That is easy. By billions, there are more stars. God knows each star by name. And we know that when he calls things by name, it means he owns them; he made them. We can give names to the kids down the street, but these names won't stick. It is only our own children whom we can name. God named the stars because he owns them and he created them.

Isaiah 40:27 says, "Why do you say, O Jacob, and complain, O Israel? Why do you say in your heart, it is not fair? My rights have been disregarded by my God." God answers, "I heard you. I know what you are saying, you despondent people. You finite people, I know your case. Don't you know that the Lord is the one who gives strength? He is the one who renews those who are tired and those who are weak. Don't you know those are the ones who will soar on wings like eagles?" So we have the great statement here about the God who is Lord over all.

## Creator of All

As God shows how great he is, the book of Isaiah stresses the theme of creation. Some twenty times, three Hebrew synonyms for 'to create' are used: *bara'*, 'to create out of nothing', which is uniquely and always used with God as its subject; *'asah*, 'to make'; and *yatsar*, 'to form' and 'to shape' like a potter. (*Yotsar* is the word for potter, the one who forms.) All three of these forms occur very frequently. For example, in Isaiah 44:24 he makes this statement, "This is what the LORD says—your Redeemer, who formed you in the womb: 'I am the LORD, *who* has made all things, *who* alone stretched out the heavens, *who* spread out the earth by myself ....'" There in three statements beginning with *who* he describes what he means by these self-asseverations, this word of self-predication, "I am Jehovah. *Yahweh.*"

## Revealer of All

Not only is God the *creator* of all, but he is also the *revealer* of all. In this section which discusses God the Father, we have a doctrine of incomparability, a doctrine of creation, and also a doctrine of revelation. There is a constant challenge to the gods: Come on, you gods, say something! Don't just stand there. Say *something*, whether good or bad. It would be wonderful if you could say anything.

Isaiah 41:21-23 is an example: "'Present your case,' says the LORD [to these idols]. 'Set forth your arguments,' says Jacob's King. 'Bring in your idols to tell us what is going to happen. Tell us what the former things were, so that we may consider them and know their final outcome. Or declare to us the things to come, tell us what the future holds, so that we may know that you are gods. Do something, whether good or bad, so that we will be dismayed and filled with fear.'" He continues, "'But you are less than nothing.'"

There are about a dozen passages like that in this section. For instance, in Isaiah 41:28-29 he picks up this same theme. And in Isaiah 44:7-8: "Who then is like me? Let him proclaim it. Let him predict something—foretell as I did." Also Isaiah 44:26b-28 says: I am the God "... who says of Jerusalem, 'It shall be inhabited,' of the towns of Judah, 'They shall be built,' and of their ruins, 'I will restore them,' who says to the watery deep [of the Tigris and Euphrates], 'Be dry, ...' who says of Cyrus, 'He is my shepherd and will accomplish all that I please; he will say of Jerusalem, "Let it be rebuilt," and of the temple, "Let its foundations be laid"'" (NIV). God is saying, I am the Lord who called the shots 200 years before Cyrus was born. Before his mother named him Cyrus, I called him that. Through Cyrus, my policy will be to allow the people to be repatriated after having been in exile. My policy, too, will be that they should have a chapel fund so that they can build their own temple. God is saying, I'm telling you all this 200 or 250 years before it takes place. Now, you idols, it's your turn! Say something about the past; say something about the present; say something about the future. Say *something!* God is the God who talks and he is the God who can speak. That is what revelation is about. God has not been silent. That is the great theme of this section.

### Guide of All History

God also is the God of *providence*, the *guide of all history*. Isaiah 41 has a marvelous statement of how God called a man from the east to do his will. We are not told in this chapter who this man from the east is, but there is the statement, "I have stirred up one from the north, and he comes—one from the rising sun who calls on my name" (Isa 41:25, NIV). In Isaiah 44 he goes on to say what this man from the east is going to do. He is then revealed to be Cyrus. So God is in charge of history.

This first ennead, Isaiah 40–48, is a marvelous section setting forth the sovereignty of God the Father, who is incomparable. We have noted the doctrine of creation, the doctrine of revelation, and the doctrine of providence.

## The Redeemer of All
## Isaiah 49–57

In the middle section, Isaiah 49–57, we have the centrality of redemption. In the preceding chapter we looked at the great chapter of Isaiah 52:13–53:12. Here God acts as the kinsman-redeemer. He is the one who is the *go'el*, restoring what has been broken and redeeming what is in debt. God becomes the kinsman-redeemer, the *go'el*. This is like Boaz who is a relative, a kinsman, who goes to redeem the inheritance of his deceased relative and therefore takes over his land and also marries the widow, Ruth. Though there are many other statements here, the high point can be found in the fifty-third chapter. This person, who is the Servant of the Lord, ministers to Israel, as we have said, but he cannot be equated with Israel because the text says "he had done no violence, nor was any deceit in his mouth" (v. 9, NIV). This is hardly a description of the nation of Israel.

God, through the prophet Isaiah, goes on in Isaiah 55:1-2 to give the invitation to salvation: "Anybody who is thirsty, come. Come without money; come, buy and eat. Come, buy wine and milk. I don't mean regular milk. I don't mean regular food. I'm talking about soul food." In verse 3 he says, "Give ear and come to me; hear me, that your soul may live." He invites us to salvation, a salvation that is based on the promise: "I will make an everlasting covenant with you, my faithful love promised to David" (NIV). God says, the covenant substance promised to David is what I'm talking about. Hey, anybody thirsty? You all come! Whosoever believes in the mercies given to David will receive life to their souls.

He goes on to say, "Surely you will summon nations you know not, and nations that do not know you will hasten to you" (v. 5, NIV). Again we have the missiological emphasis, opening this up to the Gentiles—an expansion of the message.

It is even plainer in Isaiah 55:6-7, where he says, "Seek the LORD while he may be found; call on him while he is near. Let the wicked forsake his way and the evil man his thoughts. Let him turn to the LORD, and he will have mercy on him, and to our God, for he will abundantly pardon" (NIV). There are many words for 'forgive' and 'pardon' in the Old Testament, but the word here for pardon is one used exclusively with God as the subject: *salah* means that God will super-abundantly, freely, graciously pardon as a gift. It is like that letter we all hope to receive in our mailbox announcing, "You have definitely won!" It rarely happens to any of us, but here we have definitely won a free salvation.

Then he adds, as if knowing exactly what we are going to say: "I don't think the way you think. I don't act the way you act." You know how we can react when people do something against us. We think, I'll take my good old time in forgiving you. You really hurt me, and I'm going to think about this for a while. But this is not the way God thinks. This is not the way God acts. He doesn't say, "Well, well, well! Look who we have here! It's Kaiser. It's about time." God doesn't make us sit there, waiting for a telephone connection to heaven because all the lines are filled at the moment! That is not what God does here at all. He says, Listen! "As the heavens are higher than the earth, so are my ways higher than your ways and my thoughts than your thoughts" (v. 9, NIV). I will abundantly, freely, immediately pardon and forgive you.

We might say, Yes, I know he pardons, but he remembers too; this is, after all, the Old Testament. But what did the Psalmist say in Psalm 103:12? "As far as the east is from the west, so far has he removed our transgressions from us" (NIV). It is not biblical to say that in the Old Testament God forgave sins but still remembered them. We might say, How can that be? I thought that God knew everything. How can he forget my sins and still be omniscient? I must admit that the question really troubled me at one time. But then I remembered to quote the full verse. "He remembers them against us no more." Every time we come back to the Lord it is not as if he says, "Well, well, well! Look who's here—the big sinner!" He doesn't say that; he says, "I have deliberately made a decision not to put that on your account and not to remember it against you anymore." These are wonderful words!

Can we be sure about this? Is it really for sure? Yes, it is as sure as that "the rain and the snow come down from heaven and do not return to it" until they have finished the job which they are sent to do. My word "will not return to me empty" (Isa 55:11). God is saying, I give you my word. You will be abundantly and freely pardoned and it will not be remembered against you. Come, I want you to receive some food and water that will make your souls rich.

This is a wonderful section on redemption, on God the Son, and particularly on his great invitation in Isaiah 53 and 55.

## The End of All History
## Isaiah 58–66

The last section, on God the Holy Spirit, stresses more than the theme of redemption; it stresses the end of all history.

### Age of the Holy Spirit

The first ennead (40–48) talks about God over all in his sovereignty; the second ennead presents the Redeemer of all (49–57); the third ennead, the last nine chapters (58–66), stresses the end of all history.

This is stated clearly in Isaiah 61:1: "The Spirit of the Sovereign LORD is on me, because the LORD has anointed me to preach good news ..." (NIV). Here we have *meshiaḥ*, the Messiah in a verbal form, anointed with the Spirit and proclaiming the news of the day of the Lord's vengeance. Remember how Jesus, in Luke 4:16-21, when given an opportunity to read in the synagogue, selected this passage as the reading for the day. He got up and read it and then took his seat as was the custom. The substance of his exposition was simply this, "This day is this text fulfilled in your hearing; you are seeing what the prophet promised here." It is pointed out by many that he read the passage only up to the point where it says, "The day of vengeance of our God" (Isa 61:2). He did not continue reading past the middle of verse 2 of the Isaiah passage. He read verses 1 through 2a and said, It is fulfilled up to that point. He deliberately kept the *now* from the *not yet*: the second Advent had not yet been fulfilled, for it was still the age of the Holy Spirit.

Two of the three references in the Old Testament where the Holy Spirit is mentioned are to be found in Isaiah 63:7 and following. There it is in a trinitarian statement: "In all their distress he too was distressed, and the angel of his presence saved them. In his love and mercy he redeemed them; he lifted them up and carried them all the days of old. Yet they rebelled and grieved his Holy Spirit" (Isa 63:9-10, NIV). This is probably the greatest trinitarian statement in the whole Old Testament, for we have "the angel of his presence," which is a Christophany; we have the Father speaking; and we also have the Holy Spirit. Again in verses 11b-12a there is mention of the Holy Spirit: "Where is he who set his Holy Spirit among them, who sent his glorious arm of power to be at Moses' right hand?"

## Revelation of the Glory of the Lord to All Nations

The end of history is more than just the age of the Holy Spirit; it is the revelation of the glory of the Lord to all nations (Isa 60). And there's a great statement, "Arise, shine, for your light has come, and the glory of the LORD rises upon you" (v. 1, NIV). So the revelation of the glory of the Lord appears to all nations, and it becomes one of the great themes associated with the nations.

## 'New Things'

This section also lists a number of new things. There is the new Jerusalem (Isa 60), the new heavens and new earth (Isa 65–66), and the new sincere repentance (Isa 58–59). Let me comment on these chapters, for they are exceedingly practical. Having talked about the sovereignty of God and about the provision of the atonement through the suffering Servant and the risen Servant, he then says in Isaiah 58, "Shout it aloud, do not hold back. Raise your voice like a trumpet. Declare to my people their rebellion and to the house of Jacob their sins" (v. 1, NIV). And what is their sin? "For day after day they seek me out; they seem eager to know my ways, as if they were a nation that does what is right and has not forsaken the commands of its God" (v. 2, NIV). God's people pretend to have correct practices, correct knowledge, correct habits, even correct desires. Isaiah 58 continues, "They ask me for just decisions and seem eager for God to come near them" (NIV). We wish the Lord were here, they say. They have their own interpretation of the doctrine of the coming of the Lord.

And then, "'Why have we fasted,' they say, 'and you have not seen it? Why have we humbled ourselves, and you have not noticed?'" (v. 3, NIV). Lord, aren't you impressed with our religiosity? Aren't we better than other people? Can't you just see the pride sticking out all over the place. People can be so proud of the fact that they are kosher, that they are orthodox—they have orthopraxy and orthodoxy and ortho-everything! But God says, "Yet on the day of your fasting, you do as you please and exploit all your workers" (v. 3). He is saying, You set up all kinds of fast days to remember this and to remember that. Do you realize that this puts a big burden on people? I gave you only one fast day, that being the Day of Atonement. On your various fast days, what do you do? You can't even set them aside for me. You keep thinking about yourselves: "How can I make another buck?"—or, excuse me, "shekel." Your mind is always on business. And you also are saying, "How can I get more out of my workers and pay them less?" And so he adds, "Your fasting ends in quarreling and strife, and in striking each other with wicked fists. You cannot fast as you do today and expect your voice to be heard on high" (v. 4, NIV).

The Lord says, Do you want to fast? Okay, I'll give you something worthwhile to do. And we're not talking social gospel here; we're talking about a command from the Lord. He is saying, Listen, you want to do something? I'll tell you some things to do. "Is not this the kind of fasting I have chosen: to loose the chains of injustice and untie the cords of the yoke, to set the oppressed free and break every yoke?" (v. 6, NIV). How about that? What about some of those fraudulent contracts? What about some of you in service industries who say, "Yeah, I guarantee it" until the car gets to the street and then falls apart. Do you say, "Well, business is business"? God says, You're a believer and you're doing that! Then you say that you want to fast? I'll give you a fast to do. How about this? And is this not the kind of fasting I have chosen? "Is it not to share your food with the hungry?" Is it not "to provide the poor wanderer with shelter?" How about "when you see the naked, to clothe him, and not to turn away from your own flesh and blood" (v. 7, NIV)? Before getting on to inner city work, how about your own relatives—like Uncle Louie? What about him? You say, he's the black sheep of the family. I wouldn't give him a plugged nickel. God is saying, Well, if you want a fast, there's one. Do something for Uncle Louie!

"Then your light will break forth like the dawn, and your healing will quickly appear" (v. 8, NIV). Some of you might wonder why you have some very bad health problems. He says, That could be part of it. "Then your righteousness will go before you, and the glory of the LORD will be your rear guard" (v. 8, NIV). Just as God protected and led the people of Israel in the wilderness with a pillar of cloud that preceded them and a pillar of cloud that followed them like a vanguard and a rear guard, verse 9 says, "Then you will call, and the LORD will answer; you will cry for help, and he will say: Here am I" (NIV). The Lord will say, "*Hinneni*, here am I." Now don't forget, he is saying that if you do away with the yoke of oppression, the pointing of the finger, and the malicious talk, if you give of yourselves on behalf of the needy, *then* your light will break out and you will be like a well-watered garden.

What a fantastic passage! Each time I've preached on that passage, you could hear a pin drop in the church, because it's just so practical, it's so biblical, and it must be highlighted.

## Reference to the Previous Promise-Plan
## Isaiah 40–66

Finally, what about the frequency of reference in Isaiah 40–66 to the promises previously given? We have already noted creation and the part that it has played with the numerous references from Genesis. We find references to Genesis peppered throughout these twenty-seven chapters of Isaiah. We have referred to the verbs *bara'* 'to create', *yatsar* 'to form', and *'asah*, 'to make'.

Let's look at several references to Abraham. For example, in Isaiah 41:8: "But you, O Israel, my servant, Jacob, whom I have chosen, you seed of

Abraham my friend ...." And in Isaiah 51:2: "Look to Abraham, your father, and to Sarah, who gave you birth. When I called him he was but one, and I blessed him and made him many" (NIV). Again, Isaiah 63:16 says, "But you are our Father, though Abraham does not know us or Israel acknowledge us; you, O LORD, are our Father, our Redeemer from of old is your name" (NIV).

There are also references to the covenant: a covenant for the people. In Isaiah 42:6 and 49:8, he speaks of God making "you to be a covenant for the people." In Isaiah 54:10 the text speaks of "a covenant of peace" and in Isaiah 55:3 and 61:8, of "an everlasting covenant." "My covenant" appears in Isaiah 56:4, 6 and 59:21. These are among the seventeen references to the new covenant, where only once is it actually called "new covenant." The other times it is called "my covenant" or an "everlasting covenant" or "covenant of peace" or "new heart" or "new spirit." There are references to the seed too: "The seed of Abraham my friend" (Isa 41:8); "I will bring my seed from the east" (Isa 43:5); "I will pour out my Spirit on my seed" (Isa 44:3); "to Jacob's seed" (Isa 45:19); "all the seed of Israel" (Isa 45:25). All these bring back themes we have talked about previously.

And then there is the everlasting aspect of the promise: thirty-four times he calls this promise, this covenant of God, everlasting. Then too we note that this promise is for the nations just as God said to Abraham, "and in your seed shall all the nations of the earth be blessed." The nations figure thirty-six times in Isaiah 40–66 (for example, 42:1, 6; 49:6; 52:15).

So we conclude by saying that the book of Isaiah is a mini-theology of the whole Old Testament. It is also like the book of Romans in that the prophet summarizes his case and tries to show that God still honors the promise made over the centuries to Abraham, Isaac, Jacob, and David. Before we conclude this chapter, let's step back and take a moment for theological reflection as we get the overview of the book of Isaiah: God over all, Redeemer of all, and then the end of all as history comes to its conclusion. All of this is communicated in three sections of nine chapters each: God the Father, God the Son, and God the Holy Spirit.

# Chapter Eighteen

# The Theology of the Inclusion of the Gentiles
## Jonah, Micah, Hosea, and Amos

What a great section of the Old Testament this is! Along with the study of Isaiah, who is the major prophet of the eighth-century group, we will consider Jonah, Micah, Hosea, and Amos.

Jonah, although an unwilling one, is the great missionary to the Gentiles. He does not mind preaching to the people of Israel about the expansion of their borders. But when God tells him to go to Israel's major enemy and preach the Good News to them, he decides it is time to take a vacation in Hawaii! He takes off in the Mediterranean for warmer climate, heading for Spain. He has a whale of an experience, but comes back to deliver his message to Nineveh: "In forty days and forty nights, it is all going to go! Nineveh is going to go. Assyria is going to go. You brutal people!" They *were* brutal people, too. In battle, they would chop off the hands, literally keeping a hand count on how many people they had killed. They also skinned their victims and used the skin for wallpaper. Just by looking at a corpse it was obvious if the person had been killed by the Assyrians. When the Assyrians were not in battle, they were out shooting up the area, sporting a macho man image. They would get into a chariot, find a bunch of lions, and go riding right out in the middle of them. When the lions jumped up, attacking the chariot, the Assyrians would wait until they could look down the lions' throats and then would drop the arrows in. This proved they were real men! It's no wonder Jonah says, "Who? I should go talk to *those* fellows?"

So he takes off in the opposite direction. But God rescues him from his fish trip and tells him again to go preach at Nineveh. This time he obeys. Of course, he still doesn't want anyone to come forward in the Nineveh Revival Meetings; he wants no results, for he knows that there is an underlying *unless* to his message: "*Unless* you repent." To his great consternation, the citizens of Nineveh do repent! The warning from God is more effective at this time than it is to be later on in the book of Nahum. This twin book, Nahum, comes in the seventh century with the Jeremiah group. On this second occasion, 100 years after Jonah, the Assyrians are again told to repent; this time they respond, "Oh, we've heard that before. We heard tragedy was coming before, but it never did come." The point is that in the book of Jonah, punishment was avoided because they repented.

Along with Jonah, we have the prophet Hosea, the great teacher of the heart and holiness of God. Can we imagine a greater picture of abuse of love than in this narrative where, after bearing Hosea's three children, his wife decides to leave him? Hosea tries to preach in the same town where his wife is working in the red light district. In open-air evangelism, he tells the people, "God loves you, and you need to come to him."

Imagine the catcalls: "Hey, preacher! Hey, prophet! I saw your wife down here on the strip. Some babe!" (Of course, I am getting all this from the margins, but basically I think that is the general tenor of the situation.)

And he says, "Who said that?"

We can almost imagine the conversation. A man says, "I did. So what?"

Hosea says, "Listen! If you see her, tell her that I love her! She's my wife. I've been trying to get in contact with her, and I would take her back anytime. I don't care how many men have abused her."

Imagine the crowd. "Wow! This guy is an idiot! He should just let her go!"

But with that, the prophet turns around and says, "Listen! You have pulled the same deal on God, for he is married to you. You are his wife. And I want you to know that he still loves you and will have you back. I don't care how many times you've been abused by a pagan culture."

What an amazing thing, the heart and holiness of God! No wonder the book of Hosea is called the Gospel of John of the Old Testament. God loves in a most amazing way. We see this in Hosea 11:1, 3 where God says, "... out of Egypt I called my son." My *son*. "When you were a little child, I took you by the arms and taught you how to walk."

I remember teaching our youngsters to walk. For our first child, we tried from the time he was four or five months of age. At that age, babies don't look natural, but rather monkey-like, hanging there by their little fingers. We put his toes down and pushed his feet along, encouraging him, Walk, walk! Just so we could say, "Look! The kid is a child prodigy, just like his mother! He is really going to walk early."

Now, that's cheating just a bit. I don't think the Lord cheated, but he did take his people by the hand; he did teach them how to walk. And just as a distraught parent puts his arms out and says, Where did we go wrong? What did your mother and I do wrong? God asks the question in chapter 11: "O Ephraim! O Israel! What am I going to do with you?" That is the picture here. The Lord says, "How can I give you up, Ephraim? How can I turn you over, Israel?" The Lord uses a very strong figure of speech:

"My stomach is turned within me" (v. 8). He is saying, I think that I am going to get sick when I think that I might possibly give you up. I cannot! I will not! For I am the Holy God of Israel, not a man. I won't let you go (v. 9).

Love? Oh, yes! The everlasting, freely-given love of God. Hosea is a wonderful, helpful book in that it gives both the prophet's own life experience and his message to the people. God says, "I can't give you up, Ephraim. I can't make you like Admah. I can't make you like Zeboiim" (v. 8). We say, I beg your pardon? What is Admah? What is Zeboiim? They are Sodom and Gomorrah, two of the five cities of the plain. And just so we don't miss the message, let me suggest how we might put it in modern terms here. God is saying, How can I give you up? How can I make you like Nagasaki? How can I make you like Hiroshima? When we think of it in terms of these modern tragedies of atomic devastation, we begin to get the sense of God's words.

But on the other hand, is the message of the prophets, especially these eighth-century prophets, nationalistic in character? Is God chauvinistic in his dealing with the Jews? Is he focusing in only on the Jews; Gentiles need not apply, at least not until New Testament times? No, Genesis 1–11 can hardly be called a nationalistic tract or pamphlet. Its scope was the seventy nations, and the message given to Abraham applied to all seventy nations: "Through your seed shall all of these families of the earth be blessed."

Herein lies the dilemma. Must we choose between a solely nationalistic interpretation of the Old Testament promise made to Abraham and David and a purely spiritual interpretation which puts them all together as the people of God? One evangelical group says that Acts 15:12-18, which recounts the first church council in Jerusalem, is the most important passage in the New Testament—a passage which, incidentally, cites Amos 9:11-15. Another group says, No, in that Acts 15 passage James is only showing that Peter's experience at Caesarea was consistent with God's intention to take from out of all peoples—Gentiles included—a people for his name.

We will look at the Amos 9 passage, but first we must raise three important questions concerning this whole concept of the rule and reign of God. How far did that rule and reign of God extend in the Old Testament? Did it include a spiritual body of all believers, or did it mainly focus on a political body, such as national Israel? Along with that comes the question of the time when that rule and reign of God commenced. Did it start with the Ascension? Did it commence with Pentecost? Will it commence with some future *parousia*, an epiphany? These are great questions. And then, what was the form of that rule and reign of God? Was it solely inward and, therefore, spiritual, beginning in the heart? Or was it solely external, having geo-political formations in that day? I think one of the great texts of the Bible is, indeed, Amos 9:11-12, with the context continuing through verse 15.

## The Gentiles in the Previous Promises

Let us first of all ask the question: Where do the Gentiles fit into the previous promises of God?

### The Same Gospel

We have already seen that the gospel given in the New Testament is the same gospel as is given in the Old Testament. I think we "cut the bologna too thin," to use the expression, when we try to distinguish between the gospel as presented in the New Testament and in the Old Testament. Rather, as Galatians 3:8 shows us, what Paul identifies as the gospel or the Good News is exactly what was preached and promised to Abraham in Genesis 12:3. In Galatians, Paul says that the Good News was pre-announced: "The Scripture foresaw that God would justify the Gentiles by faith, and announced the gospel in advance to Abraham: 'All nations will be blessed through you'" (NIV). That is a divine revelatory declaration equating the word *euangelion*, 'gospel', with this phrase found in Genesis 12:3.

We see this idea of the same gospel in another passage, Romans 10:5-10, a passage which needs to be appreciated by the church, for I think it is one of the great teaching passages. Paul is discussing his own preaching: this word that says, "with the mouth confession is made, and with the heart one believes." Paul says, "Do you know where that comes from? I got that from Moses." It is the same thing that Moses said in Deuteronomy 30:11-14: "Now what I am commanding you today is not too difficult for you or beyond your reach. It is not up in heaven, so that you have to ask, 'Who will ascend into heaven to get it and proclaim it to us so we may obey it?' Nor is it beyond the sea, so that you have to ask, 'Who will cross the sea to get it and proclaim it to us so we may obey it?' No, the word is very near you; it is in your mouth and in your heart so you may obey it" (NIV).

Before we discuss Paul's use of this Deuteronomy passage, let's back up just a bit to Romans 9:30, where Paul starts by saying, "What then shall we say?" *Ti oun?* This is Paul's way of introducing the subject: What now? What then? He is saying, How is it that "the Gentiles, who did not pursue righteousness, have obtained it"? Isn't it ironic? These fellows didn't set out on a quest for it, but they got it—"a righteousness that is by faith." How ironic that "Israel, who made a law out of righteousness, did not attain it"! The Greek word order there is that they made a law out of righteousness.

No one can do it the "Smith-Barney way," earning it the old-fashioned way, as the investment firm advertises. It can't be done by works. Paul says, "They stumbled over the stumbling stone. As it is written: 'See, I lay in Zion a stone that causes men to stumble and a rock that makes them fall, and the one who trusts in him will never be put to shame'" (Rom 9:32-33).

Here we have a contrast: works and faith. The Gentiles did it by faith and received God's righteousness; many of the Jews did it by works, and did not attain it because they made a law out of righteousness, either in the Midrash or the Talmud or in the whole oral tradition which they built up around that law—not the Old Testament law but that overlay that they put on the Old Testament law.

What about zeal? Do we get points for zeal? I suppose so; but there are no points in God's eyes for salvation. Paul says in Romans 10:2, "For I ... testify about them that they are zealous for God, but their zeal is not based on knowledge" (NIV). Yes, zealous, indeed! Give them points for zeal. But this is not zeal according to the knowledge of the Bible.

He says they did not know the righteousness that comes from God (v. 3). Of the Jewish people whom Paul is talking about, he says: Here they have a law, but it is their own law, it is a homemade law. They have a righteousness, but it is their own homemade righteousness: *ten idian,* "their own." So we have works righteousness, making a law out of righteousness; trying to be zealous, with a homemade, do-it-yourself job!

The fact of the matter is that Christ is the goal of the Law. He is the *telos.* He is the goal post. Don't understand this to mean that Christ's coming was the conclusion of the Law, that it was the last car of the train, the caboose. Jesus said, "I didn't come to put an end to the Law." So don't say, Aha! That is the end of it! For Paul says, "Christ is the end of the law so that there may be righteousness for everyone who believes. Moses describes in this way the righteousness that is by the law: 'The man who does these things will live by them'" (Rom 10:4-5, NIV). The word *by* here is locative rather than instrumental: "to live *in the sphere of* them," not "to live *by means of* them." This is not an alternate route to salvation; he says that works are an impossible route.

Notice the Greek construction in Romans 10:5-6: *gar ... de.* It is the same as the construction we will have later on: "For with the mouth ... and with the heart." It is not "for with the mouth ... *but* with the heart"; it is "for with the mouth ... *and* with the heart." Moses describes a righteousness which is by the biblical law of God; that is, "'The man who does these things will live in the sphere of them.' And the righteousness that is by faith says ... (vv. 5-6).

Paul continues in Romans 10:6, referring to Deuteronomy 30. What does Deuteronomy 30:12 say? It says, "Don't say in your heart 'Who will ascend into heaven?' [Paul clarifies by adding,] (that is, to bring Christ down), or 'Who will descend into the deep?' [Again Paul adds,] (that is, to bring Christ up from the dead.) But what does it say? 'The word is near you; it is in your mouth and in your heart.'" Here he is still quoting Moses and then adds in Romans 10:8: "... that is, the word of faith we are proclaiming: that if you confess with your mouth, 'Jesus is Lord,' and believe in your heart ..." (NIV). In this text Paul is confirming that it is the same gospel. However, Romans 10:16-18 says, "But not all the Israelites accepted the good news. For Isaiah says, 'LORD, who has believed our message?' Consequently, faith comes from hearing the message, and the message is heard through the word of Christ. But I ask: Did they not hear? Of course they did" (NIV).

Another passage underlines for us that it is the same gospel. Hebrews 3:15-17 talks about those who rebelled: "Don't harden your hearts like those who hardened their hearts in the day of provocation, whose carcasses/ bodies fell in the wilderness." The writer of Hebrews goes on, "Therefore, since the promise of entering his rest still stands, let us be careful that none of you be found to have fallen short of it. For we also have had the gospel preached to us, just as they did; but the message they heard was of no value to them, because those who heard did not combine it with faith" (Heb 4:1-2, NIV). "They" and "them"? Who? What is the antecedent of *them*? The bodies/carcasses that fell in the wilderness. "Therefore the gospel is preached unto *us*, as well as the gospel is preached unto *them*." This is the same gospel, the same preaching.

Christ went and preached through Noah while the ark was in preparation—the ark that was to save Noah and his family from drowning (1 Pet 3:18-22). Christ also went and preached through Moses while the people of Israel were wandering around in the wilderness. It is the same word: it is the word that is "in your mouth"; it is the word that is on your tongue. It is that same word of faith preached in Old Testament times to the Jewish nation and preached centuries later in New Testament times. Selah.

### The Same Extent

Well, I could get excited about it, and probably I have! But you can see the theme here of reaching out to all peoples. There is the Table of Nations in Genesis 10, referred to in Genesis 12:3, "In your seed shall all those"— all those that are in the seventy nations—"be blessed." Furthermore, large sections of the prophetic books are addressed to the Gentiles: Isaiah 13–23, Jeremiah 45–51, Ezekiel 25–32. In fact, we have 680 verses in these twenty-five chapters of biblical word. Wilbur Smith says that in the 100 years of the *International Lessons*, never once did the lessons deal with these 680 verses. This series purported to take believers through every chapter in the Bible, yet never once were these chapters treated! These chapters are God's word to the Gentiles.

Note the dozen references to the plagues in Egypt, beginning in Exodus 7:5. God sent those plagues. Why? So that the Egyptians, including Pharaoh, might know and might believe that "I am God." In other words, the point of the plagues in Egypt was not primarily to zap the people; the goal was to provoke the Egyptians to faith! God wanted them to see that *he* was capable of doing these things (Ex 8:10, 19-20; 9:16, 20, 30; 14:4, 18).

We might think that this word to the Gentiles did not work, that it did not result in believers. Oh, yes it did! For Exodus 12:38 says a great multitude went out from Egypt, a mixed multitude. That means that Jews and Egyptians went out together. So already we have a people of God being formed in the Old Testament.

We can mention here just a few of the many Gentiles who believed the Lord: Melchizedek, the local Canaanite priest-king; Jethro, Moses' father-in-law; Zipporah, Moses' "Ladybird" herself; Balaam, who actually was not quite as bright as his donkey; Rahab, a local barmaid; Ruth, a Moabite. The Gibeonites, too, who were hewers of wood and drawers of water; they became proselytes. The nation of Nineveh repented en masse. They even put sackcloth on their cows! (Not that the cows were saved, but massive obedience is certainly seen here.)

What about the Recabites? Jeremiah 35 narrates how that prophet was told by the Lord to invite the Recabites "into one of the side rooms of the house of the Lord and give them wine to drink." Now, we cannot interpret this passage as advocating teetotaling. It is simply a lesson on the subject, Why do people obey a human command and yet "my people" cannot keep a divine word (Jer 35:13-16). For the Recabites would not drink wine, because their great-great-great-great-great-grandfather said, "Fellows, stay away from vineyards, and don't settle down! Keep on the move, and live a simple nomadic life. We don't want to lose our edge in the iron-working industry; therefore, I don't want you to settle down." And the Recabites obeyed this human command.

### The Remaining Questions

Whole books feature the Gentiles: Obadiah, Jonah, Nahum, and Ruth. But questions still remain. For one thing, did the prophets predict the church in any form or shape? Concerning the prophets, 1 Peter 1:12 says, "It was revealed to them that they were not serving themselves but you, when they spoke of the things that have now been told you by those who have preached the gospel to you by the Holy Spirit sent from heaven" (NIV). ('Revealed', *apocalupto*, is in the aorist tense, meaning that it occurred at a single point in the past.) True, there is no doctrine of the church here, but it certainly indicates something that goes beyond the people of Israel of that day. That is very definitely taught.

Were the Gentile believers a parenthesis in the plan of God, a gap left in mystery form due to Israel's rejection of the kingdom? I have studied this and feel that there is a gap, but the gap is really with Israel. The people of Israel are the ones who have been lopped off. And so, "until the times of the Gentiles be fulfilled," there is a hiatus as far as Israel is concerned; but not with regard to the plan of God.

Have the promises of Israel been transferred to a "new Israel," the church? I do not see any transfer going on here. What I see is an enlargement in the progress of revelation, an enlargement that was already anticipated in the Old Testament.

This brings us to our great passage concerning the Gentiles in Amos 9, which we shall look at in more detail.

## The Gentiles in Amos 9:11-15

Amos is very beautifully divided up by several rhetorical devices: (1) "For three, yea, for four transgressions ...."; (2) "Hear ...."; (3) "Woe to ....."; and (4) "The LORD showed me ...." In the first two chapters, the repetition of "For three, yea, for four transgressions ...." does not mean "three or four," or "three plus four," or "I don't know," or "give or take." It means, "This is the last straw!" These words are intended to show nation after nation that God holds them all to the same standards. For example, in chapter 2, when Moab took the king of Edom and threw his bones into a lime barrel and desecrated them, God held it against the Moabites because they did not observe the sanctity of the human person. These two chapters bring out various crimes committed by a number of nations, including Israel, Moab, and Edom. And God is saying, This is the last straw!

Then in Amos 3–5 we have the great *shema'* sections. Each one begins with 'Hear,' *shema'*. "Hear this word the LORD has spoken against you, O people of Israel" (Amos 3:1, NIV). God is saying, You think you are so great because I have chosen you, but I have something to say to you! And then, "Hear this word, you cows of Bashan on Mount Samaria, you women who oppress the poor and crush the needy and say to your husbands, 'Bring us some drinks!'" (Amos 4:1, NIV). A word delicately put to the women! And then in 5:1, "Hear this word, O house of Israel, this lament I take up concerning you: 'Fallen is Virgin Israel, never to rise again.'" Then follows a number of verses where God is giving the great invitation, "Seek me and live," (v. 4), along with the warning that "If you don't, 722 BC is coming!" And indeed it did come. The people said, "It will never happen. It will never come." Here is a call to repentance because God wants to prevent the fall of Samaria.

Then comes the section of woes: "Woe to you people ...." Amos 5:18 says, "Woe to you who long for the day of the LORD!" You people who keep saying, Oh, I wish the Day of the Lord were here! Well, woe to you! Can you understand what the Day of the Lord is? It is like a man who meets a lion on his path. He gets away from that, and then he meets a bear. He gets away from that, only to be bitten by a snake when he returns to his own home. That is what the Day of the Lord is like! And, "Woe to you who are complacent in Zion, and to you who feel secure on Mount Samaria, you notable men of the foremost nation, to whom the people of Israel come!" (Amos 6:1, NIV). He is saying, "Woe to you!" to those people who put their pinky in the air and say, "Is there any Mogen David in the refrigerator?"; to those who sit around listening to instruments such as harps—those who love stereophonics; to those who have the finest ointments and who anoint themselves with Chanel No. 5; to those who do not grieve over the hurt of "my people," Jacob and Joseph. To those people, God says, "Woe to you!"

Then in Amos 7–9, there come five visions: "This is what the Sovereign LORD showed me .... The LORD showed me .... The LORD showed me ...." As I wrote in *Toward an Old Testament Theology* (p. 193), Amos "received five visions, offering at first some escape but then hardening into no way of escape except for God's eschatological offer of hope vis-à-vis the present certain doom." We find these words, "the LORD showed me," in Amos 7:1, 7:4, 7:7, and 8:1. Then we come to the last vision, in Amos 9:1-10, which has the Lord standing by the altar, destroying the places of religious ceremony, because they are empty of any meaning for the people.

However, in that day, the prophet did not just leave the people on a note of gloom. It is too bad that modern scholarship cannot understand that the same prophet can deliver a message of both judgment and hope. Modern scholars put these in two different buckets; they say either he is a prophet of judgment or he is a prophet of hope. It is a fact that these prophets did read the riot act to those who must turn to the Lord immediately. If the people did not repent, there would be judgment one, judgment two, judgment three, judgment four .... However, the prophets added, Turn to the Lord and there is deliverance! Even in that day, the prophet would look way beyond the present and would see an eschatological rosy-tinted glow to the future, in which he saw God's program triumphing.

God is going to accomplish his plan, no matter what. In any event, God is not dependent on any one nation to accomplish his purpose. I should say this more dramatically: God is not dependent on fundamentalism or on America! He can raise up from the People's Republic of China and from Russia a whole new people for his name tomorrow. He does not need us! American Christianity can go kaput and he will still triumph! That is the point of the prophets.

### The Fallen Hut of David

Amos reports God's message of an eventual restoration of Israel in Amos 9:11: "In that day I will restore David's fallen hut." The word *fallen* is a Hebrew active participle, which can describe either the present condition, a "falling" hut, or its imminent condition, a hut "about to fall." What on earth is this? We have heard of the *house* of David in 2 Samuel 7. But what is this dilapidated, ramshackle hut? I would like to suggest that the dynasty of David and his house are in disrepair. It looks as if the promise of God needs repair, too! The dynasty of David will suffer, but God will bring it back from its ruined condition, for he promised David that his was an eternal house. God says, "I will raise it up. I will restore it in that day"— the Day of the Lord; the latter day; the last day.

That is the great phrase which connects the promise of God with his plan in world history! The latter days. In that day. So the stately house of David mentioned in 2 Samuel 7:5, 11 is now in the process (present participle) of falling down and being reduced to a booth. The word *sukkah* means hut or booth, such as in the Feast of Booths. It is not equated with the Mosaic tabernacle, which is a *miskan*. Nor is it a messianic branch that will raise up a *sukkah*, as some rabbis read it. Rather, God is talking about David's stately house: it is in disrepair.

### Three Suffixes in Amos 9:11

In Amos 9:11b we find three suffixes which we need to consider. God says here that he will restore David's fallen booth or hut or tent: "I will repair *its* broken places, restore *its* ruins, and build *it* as it used to be." This is the way the translators of the New American Standard Version, as well as the New International Version and the King James, render this verse. They do not, as far as I can see, understand that the first suffix is a feminine plural: "I will repair *their* (feminine plural) broken places." Why is it a feminine plural? What could possibly be the antecedent of the "broken places" or of that which is distorted and twisted and now in ruin?

I suggest to you that the feminine plural refers back to the implicit kingdoms—the northern and the southern kingdoms. That is the only feminine plural that I can think of. When God puts the house of David back together, he will also put back together the northern kingdom and the southern kingdom. Translating this with a neuter indefinite form is not sufficient. This is to fail to understand what is being said.

Ezekiel 37:15-28 talks about deliberately taking two sticks, the stick of Joseph and the stick of Judah, putting them together, and making them into one stick: one people, one name, one God, one Lord, one kingdom. This is not the Mormon teaching on the lost tribes of Israel; this is something else. He is talking about the northern and the southern kingdoms. So my suggestion is that the feminine plural suffix on the end of "broken places"—or however we want to translate that word of ruins—is a reference to the ten northern tribes and the two southern tribes. These had been divided in 931 BC and to this day have never been put back together.

Secondly, God says, "I will restore *his* ruins." This word *ruins* has a masculine singular suffix, which I think refers to David himself. It cannot refer to David's booth or hut, because that would require a feminine suffix. The natural explanation would be that the suffix refers to David—and to the messianic person coming later in his line. Throughout the Maccabean and intertestamental times, it looks as if the Messiah has been forgotten. But God says, "I am able to restore his ruins"—the ruins of that one in the line of David, the Messiah who will come from that seed.

The third suffix is: "I will build *her*." This feminine singular suffix refers to the fallen-down hut. A booth in those days was used as temporary housing at the great Jewish festival of the Feast of Booths/Tabernacles. For the week of the festival, people would make a rough pup-tent from the lower branches of trees. This is what David's house looked like; it was no longer a stately cedar home for royalty, but simply looked like bramble bushes, cut down to keep the dew off people while sleeping in the fields.

So when we look at these three suffixes, I say, Hooray for dispensational thought on the first suffix: "I will repair *their* broken places." This is a feminine plural meaning the northern and southern kingdoms will be restored. This is a geopolitical concept of bringing the nation of Israel back together. Secondly, God will restore *his* (David's, and the Messiah's) ruins. Hooray for covenant and dispensational theology! Both are agreed here. Then, God will rebuild *her*, as the text says here; that is, the fallen booth or hut. This is to take the throne, the dynasty, the house of David and to restore it to a full house. It will no longer be a lean-to.

### The Possession of Edom/Mankind, Amos 9:12

Notice that he follows these three statements of restoration by saying "as it used to be" or "as in the days of old." Amos 9:11 says God will repair, restore, and build "as it used to be, so that...." There is a deliberate reference to a house for David, mentioned in 2 Samuel 7:11-12, 16. Amos 9:11-12 says God will do these things—repair, restore, and build as it used to be— "so that they may possess the remnant of Edom and all the nations that bear my name" (NIV). What does the possession of Edom have to do with it? God is saying, That is why I am going to raise up David. That is why I am going to restore the northern and southern kingdoms. That is why I am going to raise up the hut and also repair David's ruins: so that they may possess—take possession of—the *remnant* of Edom. But why Edom?

Edom was the worst of enemies in the Old Testament; the Edomites were harassers of God's people. They were much like the Amalekites of the early days. In Exodus 17 the people are presented in such a way as to divide them into the good guys and the bad guys, or a kingdom of God and a kingdom of men. When the Amalekites challenged Joshua down on the plains, the Israelites succeeded in battle only as long as Moses held up his hands in prayer. The people of God opposed the people of this world, the Amalekites (see Ex 17:14). Later on it was the Edomites, close relatives through Esau, who assumed that particular position. But here Amos says that a remnant from Edom, along with believers from the other nations, will be brought under the reign of the future Davidic king.

Take this great word *remnant*. In Amos, for example, it is used in three different ways. (1) It is used in a way that makes clear that it does not refer to all Israel. That point is made in Amos 3:12, 4:1-3, 5:3, 6:9-10, and 9:1-4. (2) It is used to describe a true remnant from Israel in the *eschaton*, in the last day. That is in Amos 5:4-6 and other places. (3) It is used to include the "remnant of Edom" as well as the neighboring nations as beneficiaries of God's promise to David. Edom is used in a representative role.

The remnant is made up of a believing group in Israel and a believing group of Gentiles. We know that because of the appositional phrase after Edom: "that they may possess the remnant of Edom, *even* all the nations that bear my name" (Amos 9:12). (I would translate the 'and' there in an epexegetical way.) So, that is the nature of Edom and the remnant here: "*even* all the Gentiles who have my name called over them."

The 'remnant', then, is the term for those who come under the ownership and belief of the living Lord. That phrase is used in the Old and the New Testaments simply of those who are part of the believing body of God. In Genesis 17:5 Abraham was told that he was going to be a father of a multitude of nations—not an assemblage, but a multitude of nations. The message is the same here.

### Gentiles, No Less than Israel, as the People of God

Let us look in Acts 15 to see how this passage was used at one of the great crisis times in the early church. It is no small dissension in Acts 15; the church is involved in a royal battle. We can almost hear it.

"Mr. Chairman! Mr. Chairman!"

"Oh, be quiet! I had the floor first."

Depravity is certainly manifesting itself in this business meeting. The real issue is: Unless the Gentiles are circumcised according to the custom taught by Moses, they cannot be saved. It is a clash between Jewish and Gentile cultures.

What to do? They use relational theology: some get up and tell their experiences.

Peter tells of what happened with Cornie. He says, "Boy, you wouldn't believe it! I saw this big sheet. Wow!" And he gives his testimony.

They say, "Thanks a lot, but that is only your personal experience and solution."

Paul says, "Yes, but I've been traveling all over the place. I've had Barnie along with me, and we've had great results on our trips. I must tell you, it's a different world out there!"

They are battling back and forth, making no progress, until James stands up and wants the floor. "Brothers," he says, "listen to me. Simon has described to us how God at first showed his concern by taking from the Gentiles a people for himself" (Acts 15:13-14, NIV). Notice he says "how God *at first*." Now, some understand this by inserting a word, "how God in the first era. ..." But there is no such word there. That is adding to the Bible, and I would say, No, no, no! Don't do that! James does not mean in the first era; rather he is saying, chronologically speaking, "Simon has described to us how God at first showed his concern by taking from the Gentiles a people for himself. The words of the prophets are in agreement with this, as it is written ...." He then quotes Amos 9:11-12, quoting not merely the gist of what the prophet Amos says, but the very words.

Some say, Yes, but this is not your formula for citing the Old Testament in the New. On the other hand, there is no regular formula for citation from the Old Testament in the whole New Testament, much less in the book of Acts. He is saying, "Look, that is what Amos said. 'After this I will return and repair, restore and rebuild.'" Some say this means "after this gospel dispensation." But that is not fair either, because the text does not say "after this gospel dispensation." James is trying to replicate the words in Amos, where Amos says that, "first," God would visit them with judgment; then, "after this I will return."

Some say that "I will return" refers to the second coming. *Anastrepho* for second coming? This would be the only place in the Bible where *anastrepho* is used for the second coming. No! *Nein! Nix! Non! Nyet!* I think that it is saying here, "After this I will return and rebuild David's fallen tent. Its ruins I will rebuild, and I will restore it, that the remnant of mankind may seek the LORD."

Look what James does here when quoting the Amos passage: *'edom* (Edom) has become *'adam*. In one of the Dead Sea scrolls there is a text that supports *'edom*—Edom—becoming *'adam*, since the Hebrew consonants are the same and the vowels are understood, but often not written in the older and modern Hebrew. But it may be that James is giving a general interpretation: using Edom to represent all *mankind*. So he gives the substance of it. "... that the remnant of mankind may seek the LORD, even all the Gentiles who bear my name, says the LORD, who does these things that have been known for ages."

When the Christians in Acts 15 hear this passage quoted, they say, "Okay. The plan of God in the Old Testament—the promise doctrine of God given to Abraham, Isaac, Jacob, and David—includes the Gentiles. And in the house of David—the kingdom of David, the dynasty of David— there were Gentiles as well. Why are we fighting? Now we will make certain recommendations." They give four recommendations for their brethren: abstain from food polluted by idols, from sexual immorality, from the meat of strangled animals and from blood (v. 20). We can imagine that the church council then sings the song, "I'm So Glad I'm a Part of the Family of God," and they conclude their meeting. They have decided that Jews and Gentiles do belong together.

Notice then Acts 15:14: God would take a people, *laos*, from the Gentiles for himself. They are no less his people than is Israel. He would take them and regard them as people of God, "my people." So although we have different aspects, we have a single people of God. Yes, God did include the Gentiles in his plan!

# Chapter Nineteen

# Jeremiah, Theologian of the Word of God

In this chapter we take a close look at Jeremiah, the theologian of the Word of God. The 600s BC—the seventh century—mark one of the most critical periods in the whole history of the nation of Israel. Habakkuk was written somewhere around 625 BC, shortly before the awful days which preceded the fall of Jerusalem. Daniel the prophet and his three friends were captured in about 606 BC; Ezekiel was deported with King Jehoiachin to Babylon about 597 BC; and ten years later the city of Jerusalem fell in 586 BC. We will be studying Ezekiel and Daniel in succeeding chapters. But these were certainly unsettled days.

In spite of the best preaching of Jeremiah, Zephaniah, Habakkuk, and Nahum, the nation of Judah tottered on the brink of national destruction and, indeed, went over the edge. All the words of the prophets were to no avail. Words were in vain also when the prophet Nahum went among the Ninevites and the people of Assyria. One hundred years earlier his compatriot, Jonah, had gone to these same people but had met with success. Others who preached to the ten northern tribes in the Isaiah era—the eighth century or 700s BC—did not find a positive response to their message. At least, their warnings did not seem to be effective. Yet, God mercifully sent a whole wave of proclaimers who said, "Listen to the words so that I won't have to teach you with the sword." Instead they responded, "Judgment won't come." But it did come.

Judgment came to Samaria, the capital of the northern ten tribes; it fell in 721 BC. But Judah seemed to be none the wiser for this lesson from the northern kingdom. She, too, was plunging headlong into disaster as the nation teeter-tottered right on the brink of national destruction, courting God's judgment at every turn. So on the seventh-century step of the prophet diagram, we are dealing with the southern two tribes.

During this century, the key prophet is Jeremiah. But we should say just a word about his companion-prophets, Zephaniah, Habakkuk, and Nahum, and about the emphases of their ministries. Zephaniah revives once again the topic of the Day of the Lord. The same topic we saw in the ninth century, with Obadiah and Joel, becomes the hallmark of Zephaniah's ministry, too. "A day of destruction is coming, before we can experience salvation, if we do not repent."

The prophet Habakkuk begins with a question: "Lord God, why do you make me so sensitive to evil? Why do the people of Judah seem to be getting away with bloody murder—literally?"

The answer of the Lord is, "They are not going to get away with it; I am going to bring chastisement, and there will be a response. I will use the Babylonians" (Hab 1:5-6).

This startles Habakkuk: "How can you use those people?" Why would God use them? It just does not make sense at all. His question remains on the table.

In Habakkuk 2 he says in essence, "All right, I will take my stand upon my watchtower and I shall wait to see what God will do, because the Lord says the just really live, but they 'live by faith'" (Hab 2:1-4). This is the great announcement which becomes the hallmark of the Reformation. It is repeated three times in the New Testament, each time with stress put on a different part of the verse. In Romans 1:17 the emphasis is upon *who* the *just* person is. What is the definition of the just? In Galatians 3:11, the emphasis is on *shall live*. But another passage in Galatians says, "I am crucified with Christ; nevertheless, I live" (Gal 2:20). So we might say, Wait a minute! Which is it, dead or alive? Paul answers that by saying, "I am crucified; nevertheless, I live, but the life which I now live, I live by the Son of God, who loved me and gave himself for me." In the original text, it is as if it were "the-Son-of-God-who-loved-me-gave-himself-for-me faith"—that is how I live! And then, of course, the book of Hebrews quotes the Habakkuk passage one more time, and the emphasis here is *faith*. So we have the *just* in Romans, the *shall live* in Galatians, and the *faith* in Hebrews. That is the great lesson we learn from the book of Habakkuk.

The book closes with a wonderful prayer-song where Habakkuk says in effect, "I will tell you the truth: I do not look forward to the days which apparently we must face. The Babylonians are coming down upon us; yes, they are so wicked; they worship the 'net,' their military might; they go after gods like Marduk and others, the sun and moon gods. The Babylonians and days of judgment must come. It feels as if my bones are coming apart, as if rottenness is coming into my soul." But the song concludes: "... yet I will rejoice in the LORD, I will be joyful in God my Savior. The Sovereign LORD is my strength; he makes my feet like the feet of a deer, he enables me to go on the heights" (Hab 3:18-19, NIV). He speaks of a deep, settled inward joy, while outwardly he says, Frankly, I am disturbed! This is the theme of the book of Habakkuk.

These are the compatriots who ministered with Jeremiah, but Jeremiah is the most outstanding of them all. He is the prophet and the theologian of the word, whose message may be best summarized by three theological assertions: the theology of the word, the theology of the Branch, and the theology of the new covenant.

## The Theology of the Word

First, notice the theology of the word. We note how frequently the phrase, "the word of the LORD," appears in Jeremiah. Out of the 349 occurrences in the Old Testament of the phrase, "Thus says the LORD," or a similar phrase, 157 are found in the book of Jeremiah. That is quite a record! Jeremiah contains almost half of these references. By this he is saying, "The message that I'm giving to you came from God." From the very beginning he establishes his authority to speak: "Then the LORD reached out his hand and touched my mouth and said to me, 'Now, I have put my words in your mouth'" (Jer 1:9, NIV). Obviously, the text is speaking in a figurative modality, for the Lord does not have hands in that literal sense. But certainly, if we ask what reality the words point to, we must admit that there is some kind of directness between the Lord and the message received by this man. "Behold, I have put my words in your mouth." But more than source and directness of source, there is authority here: Jeremiah is underlining the fact that he did not dream this up; he got this from God.

Although we have already looked at his method of recording the words "put in his mouth," let's review here for the sake of completeness. Jeremiah was in the habit, says chapter 3, of dictating to his secretary, his amanuensis, Baruch, either after the Lord gave him the word or after he gave the message publicly. Baruch would take down, as I understand it, a synopsis, or at least key points of the message. This man, Baruch, is very upset, understandably, when after he has written down all the prophecies delivered by Jeremiah, King Jehoiakim cuts up the scroll as each section is read to him and destroys it by throwing it into the fire. So in Jeremiah 45, Baruch is going through a real depression; a mid-life crisis perhaps. He says, "Woe is me!" (I think in order to do this justice, we must read it dramatically with real emotion.) "Woe is me! I've had it! Here I've put my whole life into writing these scrolls. My brother is the king's chamberlain; he is Secretary of State. And what am I? I'm just a book printer, and now my book is in the flames. It will never see the light of day."

How does the Lord answer Baruch's moaning and groaning? He says, "Should you then seek great things for yourself? Seek them not!" (Jer 45:5). In effect, the Lord is saying to Baruch, "You think you have problems? Well, so do I! What I've put together over the last millennium and a half, I must now tear down and pull apart. If you think you've got big problems, you ought to see mine!" This is a message about the pride of seeking great things for oneself; this may also help us in a day of great wealth, health, and prosperity when we hear a message of "name it and claim it." God did not say that to Baruch. He had another word of advice: "Name it and forget it!"

So we have here the theme of the word of God. But the word of God is more than an objective revelation. Jeremiah says that "when your words came, I ate them; they were my joy and my heart's delight, for I bear your name, O LORD God Almighty" (Jer 15:16, NIV). He genuinely delighted in it. If only we, who have the great privilege of announcing the Word of God, would treat it with seriousness and beyond that also find great delight in it! If only this delight and joy would be communicated! There is an indefinable something—a dimension to communication and teaching and preaching—which exceeds the exact content of what is being said. If enthusiasm and great joy are not projected to the listeners, what we have found and expressed will never be contagious. I don't know what it is, but there is that certain something about some speakers which enables them to get their message across to people as they teach and preach the Word of God. The audience reaction might be, "Well, I don't know all that that person is saying, but I'll tell you what: the speaker surely does seem excited about it. It's fun to watch and it must be important. I'm going to try to find out what it is." If nothing else, we ought to be able to communicate some Sunday school enthusiasm and some joy about our message.

That's what this man did. Jeremiah 15:16 says that the word of God was the joy and the rejoicing of his heart. It was his heart's delight when God's words came to him. If I may put it into modern English, he is saying, I have eaten them, and I've found that they are finger-lickin' good! He likes the word of God.

But there is more to it than that. Teaching and preaching is not all joy. God's words produced conflict in Jeremiah. There are some portions of the Word of God that, when announced to a contemporary generation or in certain theological settings, cause cinders in the stomach. It's upsetting to announce the horrible results of our sins—not because the Word is bad, but because the preacher or teacher is going up against a wall. Marathon participants find that in the twentieth or twenty-first mile they "hit the wall." To continue seems impossible. The runner tells his feet, "Go," and his feet say, "We're stopping; we've had enough; twenty miles of pounding the pavement is enough." Well, that same experience happens to speakers: they hit the wall. They feel it is just impossible to keep preaching their message. To be sure, there are safe topics, certain old rallying topics which all audiences can tolerate and will respond to with an "Amen," "Praise the Lord," "Uh-huh," "Preach it, Brother!" (One man who sat behind me even said, "Mess it up, Brother, mess it up!") But the point here is that the Word of God, instead of convicting the hearers, can turn on the speaker and, in a strange sort of way, become a source of reproach for him.

Jeremiah finds this, in Jeremiah 20:7-8: "O LORD, you deceived me, and I was deceived; you overpowered me and prevailed. I am ridiculed all day long; everyone mocks me. Whenever I speak, I cry out proclaiming violence and destruction. So the word of the LORD has brought me insult and reproach all day long" (NIV). The words "violence and destruction" become the hallmark of this man's ministry. I can assure you that the people were saying, "Here he comes, old two-pointer. He's easy to take notes on. Point No. 1: Violence! Point No. 2: Destruction!" These two points could easily describe the essence of Jeremiah's ministry.

This is a man who wept for his people, too. We even have an English word today which derives from this prophet's experience: 'jeremiad', meaning a long tale of woe.

The Word is a word of joy, but it also is a word of reproach; it is a word that must involve a stinging reminder. A person who speaks prophetically must let the chips fall where they may; he is not speaking editorially. The *Saturday Evening Post* spoke out on the issues, too, and is now defunct. We don't need people to speak out editorially on issues in the Bible, giving their opinions. We need people to hold their finger on the text and to gesture with the other hand, always calling people back to the text, "The Bible says ...," and to remind them, "Is that not true?" The message is not, "You have in the Bible in general ...." Too many people are preaching "in general." We need to teach specific paragraph after paragraph, chapter after chapter, book after book if we are going to end a famine of the Word of God, for a lot of junk preaching and junk theology is abroad in the land, even in our best fundamental, evangelical circles. Sometimes the more evangelical and the more fundamental the circle, the more general is the preaching. It does not necessarily go together, but it does happen.

For Jeremiah, this word of God becomes a source of reproach, and the ministry seems to be fruitless. Not only do people call him "Old Two-Pointer: Violence-and-Destruction," but Jeremiah 20:10 says, "I hear many whispering 'Terror on every side! Report him! Let's report him!'" (NIV). This expression, *magor-missabib*, came about in an interesting way. Jeremiah uses it first in connection with Pashur, who is the priest, the chief officer in the temple. Upon hearing of Jeremiah's prophecies, Pashur has Jeremiah beaten and put in stocks in the Upper Gate of Benjamin at the Lord's temple, but releases him the next day. At that time, Jeremiah says to him, "The LORD's name for you is not Pashur"—which means "to be fruitful"—"but Magor-Missabib"—which means "terror on every side" (Jer 20:3-4). However, the people turn this around and apply the name to Jeremiah instead of to that false prophet.

We can almost hear the people chanting "*magor-missabib, magor-missabib!*" This is the kind of thing children will pick up from their parents, and chant as they dance around. They are saying in a sing-song way, "Terror on Every Side, Terror on Every Side." It is in this ambiance that Jeremiah continues to try to preach and warn the people. To use a modern analogy, this man sees terrorists all over the place. They are coming out of the woodwork. He sees Babylonians here, Babylonians there; terror, terror everywhere! So we have the phrase, "terror on every side" (Jer 6:25; 20:10; 46:5; 49:29).

Conflict is produced by Jeremiah's message: "Repent, or else we are going to go into captivity!" He is misunderstood and people say, "That is not a very patriotic way to preach. Where is your patriotism?" But Jeremiah refuses to espouse civil religion which says, "My country, right or wrong." There are some who are so busy waving their flag that they forget it is not "My country, right or wrong." Whether to obey God or to obey men is not in question, for Acts 5:29 says we must obey God rather than men when it comes to a moral decision, an ethical decision that forces us to choose between the two. Citizens should be loyal but not to the point of violating their conscience, not at the expense of going against what God has taught. So Jeremiah has to preach this warning.

Now we come to the Confessions of Jeremiah. (I've called them this, having in mind the *Confessions* of Augustine.) There are about six of these confessions, these conflicts in Jeremiah's mind and heart. In fact, the prophet is in such conflict that he wants to stop preaching. The first confession is found in Jeremiah 11:18-20. Here he is exposed to a plot against him where it would seem that his own brothers and sisters say, "Listen, our brother is crazy; we've got to get rid of him!" So he cries out to God to help him to persist in his preaching.

Then in Jeremiah 12:1-4 he begins his second confession with this word: "You are always righteous, O LORD, when I bring a case before you." The way we would express that today is, "You are always *in the right*." That's the way he begins, but he goes on to say, "Yet I would speak with you about your justice: Why does the way of the wicked prosper? Why do all the faithless live at ease?" (v. 1, NIV). Like Job, who questioned the meaning of his suffering, Jeremiah wonders, Why am I the target of all the zaps of my culture just like a lightning rod? (Like Jeremiah, some of God's ministers have also attracted the thunderbolts of their day and generation. I do not think we ought to go around in a masochistic way looking for trouble; there is no sense trying to become a martyr. Do wait until the Lord gives you the gift for this.)

There is a third confession in Jeremiah 15:10-18, a fourth confession in Jeremiah 17:14-18, a fifth confession in Jeremiah 18:18-23, and then, finally, a sixth one in Jeremiah 20:7-18, which is probably the most severe of all. He finally breaks down and says, "O Lord, I think you tricked me; I think you called me into this ministry, but why is it every time I announce your word, I get such poor results? And the people keep saying, 'Here comes old Violence and Destruction, old *Magor-Missabib*—Mr. 'Terror on Every Side.' That's all we hear from this bird.'" Jeremiah says, "Lord, why is that?"

What we are hearing from Jeremiah is the theology of the word: the joy of the word, the conflict of the word, and the authority of the word.

## The Theology of the Branch

We must also take note of another great theme of this man, another theological assertion: the theology of the Branch (Jer 23). The word *branch* is a technical name for Messiah: *tsemaḥ*. It is a very important title in the biblical text, and as we begin this study of the Branch, we need to see that there are four facets of the Branch which occur in three of the prophetic books. Each is reminiscent of one of the four Gospels.

### Four Pictures of Messiah, the Branch

There is, first of all, the branch of David, found here in Jeremiah 23:5-6: "'The days are coming,' declares the LORD, 'when I will raise up to David a righteous Branch, a King who will reign wisely and do what is just and right in the land. In his days,'" Jeremiah continues, "'Judah will be saved and Israel will live in safety. This is the name by which he will be called: The LORD Our Righteousness'" (NIV). We'll come back to this name in just a minute. But let's talk here, first of all, about the Branch of David. Most say that the Branch of David in these verses is a picture like that of the Gospel of Matthew, which was aimed at a Jewish audience and stressed Messiah's *Davidic roots*.

A second facet of the Branch is found in Zechariah 3:8, one of the later prophets. There he says, "Listen, O high priest Joshua and your associates seated before you, who are men symbolic of things to come: I am going to bring my servant, the Branch" (NIV). We have here the great theme which we have already seen, the Servant of the Lord, my servant, the Branch. In this case, we have a second picture, which was likened in the early church to the Gospel of Mark, because the *servanthood* of Jesus is stressed in this wonderful Gospel. Mark was probably aimed at the Roman culture. It is a fast-paced Gospel which reads somewhat like a script for a movie, panning from one event to another. There is frequent use of the word *immediately*. For example, "... Jesus reached out his hand and touched the man. ... Immediately the leprosy left him and he was cured" (Mark 1:41-42, NIV). So whereas Matthew gives a Jewish portrait, Mark zeros in on one scene after another, using little dialogue.

A third facet of the Branch is found in Zechariah 6:12: "Tell him this is what the LORD Almighty says: 'Here is the man whose name is the Branch, and he will branch out from his place and build the temple of the LORD'" (NIV). So we have this third picture: the man who is the Branch. Here, instead of the Davidic aspect of the Branch or the servant aspect of the Branch, we have his humanity. This can be likened to the Gospel of Luke, where the *humanity* of our Lord is stressed.

Then finally, in Isaiah's great message in Isaiah 4:2, we have a fourth and final facet of the Branch. The text says, "In that day the Branch of the LORD will be beautiful and glorious, and the fruit of the land will be the pride and glory of the survivors in Israel" (NIV). The Branch of the LORD, the branch of Yahweh, stresses his divine origins and roots. This is the Johannine emphasis; John's Gospel, like this fourth picture of the Messiah the Branch, points to his *deity*.

### The Branch as the LORD Our Righteousness, Jeremiah 23:5-6

Now let's examine Jeremiah 23 in particular, for the Branch here is given a distinctive name, and that name is just plain outright a divine name: "The LORD Our Righteousness." It is not "The LORD *Is* Our Righteousness," for it does not have the verb "to be" in the middle there. Instead, this is the name he will be called: "The LORD Our Righteousness." I would understand this to mean that his name refers to his character; to speak of his name is to speak of his character and the nature by which he will be known. The nature and character of the Branch, who will be born in the line of the seed of Abraham, Isaac, Jacob, and David, will be divine. For he will be called "The LORD Our Righteousness." Yahweh, Jehovah, LORD (spelled with capital letters) denotes his divine nature; 'Our Righteousness' denotes his divine work on our behalf. In this name we have both his divine nature and his divine work: The LORD Our Righteousness.

This idea of the Branch—or the sprouting out, if we want to take the verbal root—goes back to at least two sources which we have seen previously. The first reference to the idea of God causing a branch to sprout or to branch out from David (it is the same verb, *tsemaḥ*) can be seen at the early stage where the Lord gives this promise to David. In 2 Samuel 23:5 David says, "Is not my house right with God? Has he not made with me an everlasting covenant, arranged and secured in every part? Will he not bring to fruition my salvation and grant me my every desire?" (NIV). There is the first reference to the branching out: Will he not sprout? Will he not branch out, or cause to branch out, my salvation?

There is another reference that seems to lie behind this great theme of the Branch. Psalm 132:17 says, "Here I will make a horn grow for David ...." The NIV renders the word *grow*, but it is a growing which means 'to branch out' or 'to sprout': *tsemaḥ*. David is called the 'horn', which symbolizes the power of an animal. God says, "I will make a horn to sprout—to branch out—from David ...." So here we have the concept of horn, Messiah, and branch all brought together within the scope of one verse, through verbal ideas, certainly in Psalm 132:17. Then God continues, "I set up a lamp for my anointed one." Lamp, horn, anointed one, and Branch: four metaphors for the Messiah brought together in the scope of one verse.

This Branch has its origin in the LORD. I understand the Branch of the LORD that appears in Isaiah 4:2 to be a genitive of source, the Branch that is *from* the LORD. It is *of* the LORD: *of*, in the sense of source, *from which* he comes. So this is his name: The LORD Our Righteousness. We can also see it treated later on in Jeremiah, for Jeremiah 23:5-6 is not the only passage where we see this name. In Jeremiah 33:14-15, he uses this same name once again: "'The days are coming,' declares the LORD, 'when I will fulfill the gracious promise I made to the house of Israel and to the house of Judah. "In those days and at that time I will make a righteous Branch sprout from David's line; he will do what is just and right in the land. In those days Judah will be saved and Jerusalem will live in safety. This is the name by which [he] will be called: The LORD Our Righteousness"'" (NIV).

So the theology of the Branch is important, just as is the theology of the word. Then, finally, a third theological assertion that we want to treat here—and, of course, the great one in Jeremiah—which is the theology of the new covenant.

## The Theology of the New Covenant
## Jeremiah 31:31-34

The theology of the new covenant appears in that magnificent text which we described in a previous chapter as being the fourth greatest mountain peak in Old Testament revelation, Jeremiah 31:31-34. This passage is cited *in extenso* in Hebrews 8, and again cited almost totally in Hebrews 10, making it the longest single quote of any passage from the Old Testament in the New. This in itself ought to signal its importance.

### The Theological Problem

Yet, there are several theological problems we must speak of as we discuss this theology of the new covenant. First, why call the covenant *new*, when a good deal of it takes up topics given in the previous covenants and promises of God? Why call *new* that which is in substance basically a repetition? What is new about repetition?

The second problem that we must deal with here is: What are the essentially new features? Jeremiah 31:32 says that there are certain things that are *not* like "the covenant I made with their forefathers." What is it that is not like the old covenant? Also, Jeremiah 31:34 says, "No longer ...." Twice in that 34th verse the Lord says that. So what are the things that have been jettisoned and deleted?

There is a third theological problem: What is the "better covenant" spoken of here (these words seem to be in quotes). What is the "better covenant" of Hebrews 8:6-13? Better than what? What was the first one? And in what sense has that been made obsolete, or in what sense is the "better" to be understood? These are the theological problems, as I see it, with the new covenant.

## Features of the Previous Covenants in the New Covenant

What are the features of the previous Old Testament covenants that can be found in the new? Here we need to deal with a number of features. First of all, there is the feature of *inwardness*. We see this in the previous covenants, in Deuteronomy 6:6, "These commandments that I give you today are to be upon your hearts." God said he would write the Torah on the heart. Psalm 37:31 says, also illustrating inwardness, "The law of his God is in his heart; his feet do not slip." We've seen it, too, in other places.

A second feature that is shared with the previous promises of God is *fellowship*. Genesis 17:7 tells us, "I will establish my covenant as an everlasting covenant between me and you and your descendants after you for the generations to come, to be your God and the God of your descendants after you" (NIV). That same promise is repeated here in the new covenant. Again it is stated in Exodus 6:7: "I will take you as my own people, and I will be your God. Then you will know that I am the LORD your God, who brought you out from under the yoke of the Egyptians" (NIV). There are a number of other passages on fellowship which we cannot deal with here.

A third feature shared by the two covenants is *individualism*. In Exodus 29:45-46, there was that word, "Then I will dwell among the Israelites and be their God. They will know that I am the LORD their God, who brought them out of Egypt so that I might dwell among them. I am the LORD their God." It seems to me that here we have the theme of individualism.

*Forgiveness* is a fourth theme that is shared with the Abrahamic and Davidic covenants and that is found also in the new covenant. For example, in Psalm 86:15 and in about ten other verses, that phrase is quoted from Exodus 34:6-7, "The LORD is a merciful, gracious God, slow to anger, and abounding in steadfast love and faithfulness, and keeping steadfast love for thousands, and forgiving iniquity and forgiving transgression and forgiving sin." So this theme of forgiveness had been found earlier in the Mosaic covenant, as well.

Then there is the Torah. God said he would write his Torah upon the hearts, but he did not say, "I will write a *new* Torah upon the heart." He said, "I will write *Law* on their hearts." I don't think we have understood that; we have missed that in thinking about the new covenant. So there are a number of features that are shared: inwardness, fellowship, individualism, and forgiveness.

## Other Names for the New Covenant

Now we must also take up briefly other names for the new covenant. Seven times the new covenant is called the "everlasting covenant" (Isa 24:5; 55:3). An everlasting covenant is the same thing as the new covenant. It is also called "a new heart and a new spirit," especially in Ezekiel (Ezek 11:19).

If we count the Greek translation of Jeremiah 32:39, it occurs four times. It is called the "covenant of peace" three times (Isa 54:10). Then four times it's called "my covenant," or simply "covenant" (Hos 2:18-20; Isa 42:6). In the New Testament, of course, the "better covenant" is mentioned in Hebrews 8:6 and is equated with the Abrahamic promise and the new covenant. There are seventeen major places where the new covenant is discussed in addition to Jeremiah 31:31-34.

### The Fault of the Mosaic or First Covenant

Now for the great problem here: What was wrong with the first covenant? And just exactly what is the first covenant? It was probably the Mosaic covenant, because it was the first to be put into practice, even though, chronologically, Abraham's came before that of Moses. But where was the fault or problem with that first, or prior, covenant? Whose fault was it that a new covenant needed to replace the first covenant? Was the fault with God? With his revelation? Was it with his terms? The answer is *No!* The biblical text says the fault was with *them*, not with *it*. Hebrews 8:7-8 tells us, "For if there had been nothing wrong with that first covenant, no place would have been sought for another. But God found fault *with the people* and said: 'The time is coming, declares the Lord, when I will make a new covenant ...'" (NIV). And then the writer of Hebrews goes on quoting from the Jeremiah 31:31-34 passage: "It will not be like the covenant I made with their forefathers ..., because they did not remain faithful to my covenant .... This is the covenant I will make with the house of Israel after that time, declares the Lord" (NIV). That is why there is need of a new covenant. Our argument, then, is that the new covenant is a *renewed* covenant, for the Hebrew word for 'new' can also mean 'to renew'. Hebrew does not have two separate words for 'new' and 'renew' as Greek, English, and Indo-European languages possess. It also points to a renewal since so much of its contents are repeated from the earlier Abrahamic and Davidic covenants.

### Some New Developments in the New Covenant

Finally, there are some new developments in the new covenant. What are the things that go beyond what we have seen before? We can quickly list at least six things. (1) There's the universal knowledge of God. Jeremiah 31:34 says that everyone will know the Lord. (2) There will also be universal peace in nature and in the nations (Hos 2:18). This will be a time when there is no more war; a time, too, when problems with ecology have been settled. (3) There will be universal material prosperity. The health/wealth people are slightly ahead of schedule, for Isaiah 61:7-8 indicates universal material prosperity. (4) It will be the age of the Spirit, an outpouring of the Holy Spirit, as the prophet Joel promised in Joel 2:28. (5) The sanctuary of God will be in the midst of Israel (Ezek 37:26-28). (6) There will be a capacity to keep the law of God, for God will write it on the inside, on the interior, of his men and women (Jer 31:33).

Yes, the theology of the new covenant is the centerpiece of the seventh century. It is the centerpiece of Christianity, too, for we participate in the new covenant; we are ministers of the new covenant; we drink the blood of the new covenant. And we now share some of these fine results, as well. So, we conclude, then, with the study of Jeremiah, the theologian of the Word of God, the great prophet of the seventh century BC.

# Chapter Twenty

# The Theology of the Holy Spirit in the Old Testament

We now want to take up the theme of the work and ministry of the Holy Spirit. Having just considered the great message of Jeremiah and the new covenant, it seems the proper time to look at the words of Ezekiel, one of the great prophets of the Holy Spirit.

Since the new covenant introduces the age of the Spirit—at least the idea of a downpour of the Holy Spirit—this raises the question, What was the Old Testament believer's experience of the Holy Spirit? At this point in the Old Testament, people were looking forward to the time when the Holy Spirit would be poured out abundantly, like a downpour. On the other hand, this is not to say that there were not already showers or sprinkles. What was the nature of these sprinkles?

Very few scholars have written on this subject, but there is a landmark work in the field: *The Doctrine of the Holy Spirit*, by Abraham Kuyper. This book needs to be published again. Also, Professor Leon J. Wood was one of the first to dedicate a monograph to this topic, and it is the best known recent work in the United States: *The Holy Spirit in the Old Testament*, published by Zondervan in 1976. One article that I have found to be extremely helpful was done by Geoffrey Grogan, "The Experience of Salvation in the Old and New Testaments." This appeared in the London Bible College magazine, *Vox Evangelica* (Vol. 5, 1967, pp 12-17). In this, Grogan mentions a lecture series given at the London Bible College in 1961 by J. C. J. Waite, titled, *The Activity of the Holy Spirit within the Old Testament Period* (London, 1961).

Several other people have written on this topic, but actually very, very few have studied in depth the ministry of the Holy Spirit in the Old Testament. So let us examine this subject. Let us begin with those areas which are the easiest and where there is agreement.

## The Holy Spirit as Creator of the World

First, we will examine the Holy Spirit as Creator of the world. The text here, of course, is Genesis 1:2, where the Spirit moved over the face of the deep. We believe that it is proper to understand this to be the Holy Spirit, although it is true that it can be translated 'wind' or 'breath' or 'spirit'. Not all scholars agree that it is 'Spirit'.

One of my professors, Harry Orlinsky, the only Jewish translator on the Revised Standard Version committee, said, "Look, it is clear here that this is the *wind* of God that moved over the face of the deep."

"Why is that?" I asked.

He said, "It is clear because that is what it is in the Babylonian tablets, and therefore translating it as 'Spirit' is sheer eisegesis."

Then he told us how the Revised Standard Version committee came to the choice of 'Spirit'. He said, "The first day this came up, we spent all day long arguing over whether this should be 'wind' or 'spirit'. Then someone reminded us, 'It is five o'clock. Let's take a break.' So after arguing all day, the vote was 8 to 7 in favor of 'spirit'. Then someone said, 'How shall we spell it? Should it be with a capital 'S' or a small 's'?' So we argued that question all the next day, with a vote finally of 8 to 7 in favor of capital 'S'. Do you know what that is? That is eisegesis! Eisegesis! That is reading into the text. There is nothing there." The truth of the matter is that there is something to be said for that.

E. J. Young countered, even before Orlinsky had made those objections to me in class: "In the Babylonian story it is an evil wind. And it is not one wind; there are seven winds." Supporting the idea of the ministry of the Holy Spirit being present at the creation is an allusion to this which we find in Isaiah's writings. Isaiah 32:15 says, "… till the Spirit is poured upon us from on high, and the desert becomes a fertile field …." (By the way, all three persons of the Trinity are said to have been involved in the creation of the world.) Another verse concerning the Spirit is Job 26:13: "By his Spirit the skies became fair; his hand pierced the gliding serpent." Here we have God depicted as overcoming the mythological figures of the literature of that early period. I don't think this verse is giving credence to their existence, but it is saying that God, in his creation, conquered all that represented the force of negativism and evil. So the interpretation of these texts, it seems to me, clearly establishes that the Holy Spirit was involved as the Creator of the world.

Certainly we do not want to get tangled up in the Arian heresy, held by the Jehovah's Witnesses and others: that God existed first and then he created Jesus. I guess we would have to say then that the Holy Spirit was created, too. And then out of that came the creation of the world. There is no evidence for such a thesis. The Son and Holy Spirit are just as eternal as is the Father, according to Scripture.

## The Holy Spirit as Sustainer of the Created Order

There is a second area where the work of the Holy Spirit is seen in the Old Testament: the Holy Spirit as *Sustainer* of the created order. We see this in texts like Job 34:14-15: "If it were his intention and he withdrew his Spirit and breath, all mankind would perish together." It is God who sustains and maintains and upholds the universe. This is seen also in the great creation psalm, Psalm 104: "When you send your Spirit, they are created, and you renew the face of the earth" (v. 30, NIV). The interpretation of these texts is that the Holy Spirit's work and ministry is not only in the making of the world, but also in the maintaining, upholding, and sustaining of the world.

## The Old Testament Believer's Experience of the Holy Spirit

But we come to a more critical issue. Let us look more directly at the Old Testament believer's experience of the Holy Spirit.

### For the Writing of the Old Testament Scriptures

We could speak of the Holy Spirit's role in the ministry of revelation and in the giving of the Word—that ministry for believers in the writing of Scripture. Frequently, the writer says that he is being prompted by the Spirit of God. Ezekiel, one of the men carted off into captivity in Babylon, speaks under the inspiration of the Holy Spirit (Ezek 2:2; 3:24). Daniel, also (Dan 4:8-9, 18). Daniel is taken off with Meshach, Shadrach, and Abednego. (If the Babylonian names given to these three men are hard for you to remember, here is a trick: My shack, your shack, and a bungalow.)

Micah 3:8 is also quite an important text in this regard. "But as for me, I am filled with power, with the Spirit of the LORD, and with justice and might, to declare to Jacob his transgression, to Israel his sin." Micah is the great prophet who contrasts those who really do minister the Word of God with those false prophets who are unable to minister and to say anything authoritative. In this chapter, Micah says that those who abuse position, proclamation, and privilege will receive no answer from the Lord. I believe this is the way to principle-ize this theme for today's teaching. In verses 1-4, Micah speaks of the rulers of the house of Israel who abuse their *position*. Verse 4 says, "Then they will cry out to the LORD, but he will not answer them."

Micah 3:5-8 speaks of those who abuse *proclamation*. The Lord says in verse 5, "As for the prophets who lead my people astray, if one feeds them, they say 'Shalom.'" In other words, if we give the prophets or teachers a good honorarium they will say anything we want them to say. They will say, "What do you want me to say? Shall I say, *Shalom*? Okay, *shalom*! Sure, peace. Whatever!" Verse 5b continues, "If he does not, they prepare to wage war against him." So if we give them a small honorarium, they will let us have it full barrel—there is trouble up ahead! "Therefore night will come over you, without visions, and darkness, without divination. The sun will set for the prophets, and the day will go dark for them" (v. 6, NIV). The sun has set for some prophets today—and for some preachers, too! The sun has set, and the day will grow dark for them. "The seers will be ashamed and the diviners disgraced. They will all cover their faces because there is no answer from God" (NIV). This is the second time in this chapter that it says, "no answer." Then Micah goes on to say, "But as for me, I am filled with power, with the Spirit of the LORD" (NIV). I think that this refers to the Holy Spirit, the Spirit that comes from the Lord.

So this passage speaks of those who abuse both position and proclamation. Micah goes on to speak, finally, in 3:9-12, of those who abuse *privilege*. Again, the passage implies that there is no answer from God. But what about those who really trust God? "As for me," Micah says, "I am filled with power, with the Holy Spirit." So, it is "not by might, nor by power, but by my Spirit, says the LORD." Zechariah will say that, too. This is the great theme of the experience of the Old Testament believer in writing Scripture.

Thus far, we are still on common ground where everybody can agree and say, "Amen!" But now let us go on to the question of regenerating unbelievers.

### For Regenerating Unbelievers

What is the ministry of the Holy Spirit in the regeneration of unbelievers in Old Testament times? We do believe, as stated in New Testament terms, that it is "not of works, lest any man should boast"—should *ever* boast! Salvation is not of works; it is the gift of God. And if it is the gift of God, then this implies that there really is a regenerating work of the Holy Spirit. Where is that regenerating work?

John's Gospel seems to me to be the best reference to check on this subject, for, you will recall, the environment is still an Old Testament one. Christ has not yet died; Good Friday has not yet been enacted; Easter Sunday morning has not yet occurred. Nevertheless, we have a man of good credentials named Nicodemus, a Pharisee, a member of the Jewish ruling council, who has a question which puzzles him. He must see Jesus, but he must see Jesus at night in secret. I would, too. I would not take too many risks in that particular environment, especially with the radical kind of situation that existed with this Jesus of Nazareth being around. Nicodemus says to Jesus, "You are a teacher come from God, for no one can perform the works that you are doing." This is marvelous endorsement on the part of Nicodemus. He starts the conversation with more than a nice, "Hello, how are you? I think an awful lot of your work!" It is more than that. He is saying, "You must be from God. You are divinely authenticated by what you do."

Nicodemus is more than pre-evangelized; he is far down the road toward becoming a believer. But something is still baffling him. And that is, "What am I going to do about this whole matter of eternal life?" This seems to be his problem.

Jesus answers, "You must be born again, and that is the work of the Holy Spirit."

Now, Nicodemus is surprised at that answer. He says, "No! How can that be? I didn't know this at all. Would you run that by me again?" (I'm giving you the expanded translation here!)

Basically, Jesus says, "I'll tell you again; you've got to be born again." In John 3:10 he says, "You're a teacher in Israel, and yet you don't understand these things. Where did you go to school? Who taught you?" That seems to be what our Lord is saying here. How can Nicodemus be a teacher of the Jews, held in high respect in the Jewish community, teaching the Old Testament, and yet not know anything about (a) being born again and (b) the work of the Holy Spirit?

I find this passage to be extremely challenging, for Jesus is a very authoritative teacher and his teaching should be normative for us. We should not argue with the text. Where our theology runs counter to what he says, we should capitulate; he is the norm. Now, his norm here is that he thought Nicodemus ought, could, and should have known about these things. It was the same for those two disciples on the road to Emmaus who could have, who should have, who ought to have known about Jesus' suffering and his coming back again. What he said about them was, "O fools, and slow of heart to believe all that the prophets have said concerning me." Here he is saying in effect to Nicodemus, "O fool and slow of heart. What is wrong with you? Don't you know anything about salvation? Don't you know anything about eternal life? Don't you know anything about being born again? Don't you know anything about the Holy Spirit?"

Some of us would want to tap the Lord on the shoulder and say, "Pssst, Lord. This is pre-Cross. Wait! You are getting ahead of yourself— ahead of your super-duper plan. This will come after John 21—you are only in John 3. Wait up! You are giving him the wrong dispensation." But there is no hint of that here. He says, "I tell you the truth." Where would poor Nicodemus have learned these things? My answer is that he should have been able to understand them from Ezekiel 36:26-27, where there was a promise of a new heart and a new spirit. There he was talking about a new birth and about the work of God's Holy Spirit. Nicodemus, as a teacher of the Jews, a Pharisee, one of the ruling party, should have been familiar with Ezekiel 36:26-27. So this is probably the text our Lord had in mind during his conversation with Nicodemus. This, I think, gives us some background to help us understand the work and ministry of the Holy Spirit. Yet not all our questions are answered.

## The Coming of the Holy Spirit in New Testament Times

How do we understand Jesus when he says, "It is necessary that I go away in order that the Comforter may come"? If the Comforter is to come, how can it be said that he is already here? I mean, either he is or he isn't here. And either our Lord must go away or he does not have to go away. If it is necessary that he go away in order for the Comforter to come, what do these texts mean?

To help clarify the question, we will be looking at a number of New Testament texts mentioning the Holy Spirit which can be put into some kind of pattern. In order to classify these texts, let us number them here. John's Gospel is especially rich in this subject. They are:

1. Matthew 3:11, which has its parallels in other Gospels;
2. John 1:33;
3. John 7:37-39;
4. John 14:16-17;
5. John 14:26;
6. John 15:26;
7. John 16:7;
8. John 16:13-15;
9. John 20:22, where he breathed on them and said, "Receive the Holy Spirit";
10. Acts 1:5, "Not many days hence you will be baptized by the Holy Spirit";
11. Acts 11:15-16;
12. Acts 15:8. What happens in Acts 15 is the great Jerusalem council where there is no slight disagreement; this is the chapter we discussed in connection with that great word in Amos 9.

How shall we interpret these texts? We can break this short list down into three groups for our purposes: Group A includes 1, 2, 10, 11, and 12; Group B includes 5, 6, and 8; and Group C includes 3, 4, and 7.

### Baptism of the Holy Spirit

In Group A we have five texts which deal with a unique work of the Holy Spirit which he did for the first time when all believers were incorporated into one universal body at Pentecost. The text refers to this as a *baptism* of the Holy Spirit. Perhaps the best way to picture the chronology of these verses is to draw a line on which Matthew 3:11 ("He *will* baptize you with the Holy Spirit") appears on the left, followed by an arrow pointing to the reference in the center, Acts 1:5 ("*Not many days hence* there is going to come the baptism of the Holy Spirit.") This should be followed by a short arrow facing the previous two texts on the line. The reference we will put on the right end of the line is not one of the twelve listed for you: 1 Corinthians 12:13 ("For we *were* all baptized by one Spirit into one body"). Here we need to put an arrow pointing back to Acts 1:5, which is in the middle. We think that what took place is that the universal body of believers was created in some new beginning. Whatever these texts in the Gospels referred to as an anticipated event and what the book of Acts tells us was "not many days hence," Paul says in Corinthians, "It took place" prior to AD 54, when Paul wrote 1 Corinthians.

I suspect that Acts 2 with the Jewish Pentecost, Acts 8 with the Samaritan Pentecost, and Acts 10 with what some call the Gentile Pentecost teach the forming of a new group: the universal Church, the universal body of Christ. And therefore, these are explanations of the "you were" (past tense of completed action) in 1 Corinthians 12. So we have the anticipation of the baptism of the Holy Spirit in the Gospels and in the book of Acts, and then we have the event itself somewhere between Acts 1:5 and 1 Corinthians 12. Although this is not our main point here in this study, it does remove five of the twelve texts from our list.

### The Holy Spirit and the New Testament Canon

Now, for Group B, we can pull out of those remaining texts (5) John 14:26, (6) John 15:26, and (8) John 16:13-15. The church has experienced a lot of difficulty with these verses. Almost every cult to come along has, in one way or another, appealed to these particular texts. Unfortunately, I have found that the evangelical body appeals to them, too. I do not know how many times I have seen this in our literature, but I think it is dead wrong. In John 14:25, 26 Jesus is quoted as saying, "All this I have spoken while still with you. But the Counselor, the Holy Spirit, whom the Father will send in my name, will teach you all things" (NIV). Many take this as a personal promise that the Holy Spirit will teach them all things. As a matter of fact, the Roman Catholic Church took this as a promise in recent centuries when they declared the infallibility of the Pope. While it is true that the idea of infallibility is not found in the Scriptures, the leaders of the Church decided that the Holy Spirit would teach them all things and this was one of those things that he was teaching them! The Book of Mormon claims this also, that he is teaching them all things and leading them to all truth. I do not know of any new religion or cult that claims to be somewhat related to Christianity that has not used this verse.

But may I go on to point out that Jesus finishes the sentence by saying, "... and he will remind you of everything I have said to you." There seems to be a "calling to mind" here. I think this is the answer to the synoptic problem in the Gospels. Why is there so much similarity in these books, and how could these men be reminded of so much? Because it was the Holy Spirit who recalled everything to the mind of the disciples who had been present with the Lord. This is a promise of the New Testament canon; it is not a promise to the individual believer. (There is a promise similar to this for individual believers in 1 John 2. However, I do not think that passage has a place in this study.)

So in John 14 Jesus says that the disciples have heard everything that he has said. John 15:26-27 also says, "When the Counselor comes, whom I will send to you from the Father, the Spirit of truth who goes out from the Father, he will testify about me. And you also must testify, for you have been with me from the beginning" (NIV). You and I were not with our Lord from the beginning; the disciples were. Therefore it seems to me that there is an exclusionary clause: "You were with me from the beginning." This is not only like the last passage, in the authentication for the synoptic problem, but it is now a promise of doctrine that God would teach them things, and testify about himself.

Then in John 16:12-15, Jesus continues talking to his disciples: "I have much more to say to you, more than you can now bear. But when he, the Spirit of truth, comes, he will guide you into all truth" (NIV). Is Jesus saying that the Spirit will guide all of us? I don't think so in this context. He continues, "He will not speak on his own; he will speak only what he hears, and he will tell you what is yet to come"—so there is future here. "He will bring glory to me by taking from what is mine"—the doctrine of God— "and making it known to you" (NIV). I take it that this is a third promise of the New Testament canon. Our Lord is saying, "I have a lot to tell you men, but you are not able to bear it right now. But when I go away, I will send my Holy Spirit, and he is going to tell you about things in the future. He is going to tell you about doctrine. He is going to testify about me. He is going to call all things to your remembrance. And you are going to recall episodes and incidents of our three years of ministry together."

### The Old Testament Believer and the Holy Spirit

With the elimination of the texts in Groups A and B, we now come to the verses which deal with the question, What is the experience of the Holy Spirit in the life of the Old Testament believer? In Group C we have (3) John 7:37-39, (4) John 14:16-17, and (7) John 16:7. These are the key passages. I am setting to one side for the moment John 20:22. Remember, we are still in Old Testament times as our Lord deals with the church in this matter.

The Holy Spirit, in the key text of John 14:16-17, is said to be with the believer. Jesus says, "I will ask the Father, and he will give you another Counselor to be with you forever—the Spirit of truth. The world cannot accept him, because it neither sees him nor knows him. But you know him, for he lives with you and is in you." I would like to comment on two key phrases here. First, he is *para*; he is *with* you. We need to ask, What is the sense of the "withness"? Then we need to notice, "he is in you" (or "he will be in you," as most of the texts are translated). First, the preposition here, *para* or *with*, does not denote a fluctuating relationship. The oldest teaching on this matter of the Holy Spirit in the Old Testament is that the Holy Spirit came on a believer for a particular time, such as in the book of Judges, for example, where the Holy Spirit came on Samson and Samson did something or other. So it is said that for special people at special times there was a special ministry of the Holy Spirit. But the truth of the matter is that, if we look at the prepositions in the Old Testament, we will find almost all of them used. We will have the Holy Spirit coming *to* people; we will have the Holy Spirit coming *upon* them; we will have the Holy Spirit being *in* them. So if we were going to do just a prepositional study of the work and ministry of the Holy Spirit, we would find that ministry to be more than just a temporary clothing or bathing of Old Testament believers.

This is no different than in the New Testament, where we will have an indwelling as opposed to a baptism or as opposed to an infilling, or a special enduement at a special time for a special work. "Then Stephen, being filled with the Holy Spirit, stood up and said ...." "Then Peter, being filled with the Holy Spirit ...." That is a very special enduement at a special moment in time for a unique ministry of God.

In the John 14 passage we note that the same preposition, 'with', is used again a few verses later: "My Father will love him, and we will come to him and make our home with him" (v. 23, NIV). That tells us that this "withness" of the Holy Spirit to the Old Testament believer was not a fluctuating experience, but rather was a "making one's home with." That is a rather permanent thing: an abiding of the Father and the Son already with the believer. So we argue that this 'with' is not just a loose association.

Then there is the other key phrase we want to look at. There is a choice of translations: the Holy Spirit 'will be' in them or 'is' in them. We think the best text support is for the present tense rather than for the future tense here. The best manuscripts and the earliest manuscripts say not only that "He lives with you, and will be in you," but, "He is in you already." And I would argue further that the present tense is less likely to be a correction. That was B. F. Westcott's interpretation, too. If a scholar must choose between two readings, he usually chooses the more difficult reading; the more difficult reading here is the present tense, rather than the future tense.

Furthermore, the Holy Spirit was with the disciples prior to the resurrection of Christ, for when he sent them out, he said that his Holy Spirit would go with them, for he was in them. (See Matthew 10:20 and parallel passages; also Luke 11:13; 12:12.) In Luke 12:11 the disciples were told not to worry when they were brought before synagogues, rulers, and authorities. For "in the same hour" the Holy Spirit who was with them would teach them what to say. We have several pre-Cross situations where we see the abiding work of the Holy Spirit.

So we think that regeneration is not a work of an individual in the Old Testament, but is a work of the Holy Spirit there, as well. The convincing and convicting of sin and bringing the gospel before people's eyes was as much the work of the Holy Spirit then as it is now. And there is this sense in which the Holy Spirit, after the work of regeneration, was also in the work of sanctification—was *in* the believers and not just *on* them for special works.

This leaves one more great question: Why was Pentecost necessary? What is the significance of Pentecost? *Was* it necessary? The answer is *Yes!* Here I think George Smeaton is helpful in his excellent work, *The Doctrine of the Holy Spirit* (2d ed., Edinburgh: T. & T. Clark, 1889, p. 53; citing T. Goodwin, *Works*, Edinburgh, 1861, 6:8). This work is long since out of print. He said, "[The Holy Spirit] must have a coming in state, in a solemn and visible manner, accompanied with visible effects as well as Christ had and whereof all the Jews should be, and were, witnesses." This is to say that in the Old Testament there were those who enjoyed proleptically the benefits of Christ's death: there were converted individuals who waited for the benefits that were to come from the cross of Christ. He says here, if I understand the argument, that all the benefits of the Holy Spirit that are being seen in the Old Testament are necessary because, without Pentecost, without his coming in state, without his visualizing here—an outward newness to it, and some advance over it—all that had been experienced of the Old Testament with the work and ministry of the Holy Spirit, like those who were counting for their salvation based on the death of Christ, would not have been validated either. I find this to be an intriguing and wonderful answer to a response that shows that there is something new and that there is an advance in Pentecost; but indeed there is also something which I think helps us to understand that some basic seminal ideas were already there, too.

Something seems to be deficient in the traditional dialectic: that in the Old Testament the Holy Spirit came on people temporarily for special moments, but in the New Testament the Holy Spirit is *in* us. The most important text in this whole discussion is John 14:17. The other passages, it seems to me, will then fall in line and we will see that it was necessary for the Holy Spirit to come. Our Lord had to go away and he had to have the Comforter—the Holy Spirit—come, for without the visualizing of that for all to see, there would be no basis for what they had experienced already in the Old Testament.

Is there nothing new to it? There is much that is new. For example, this work of the Holy Spirit in which he forms believers into one body—the baptism of the Holy Spirit—and the uniqueness there seems to be an intensification. But I can see how our Lord could have urged upon Nicodemus the fact that he ought to have known, and he should have taught, and he should have personally realized, that there was already in the Old Testament the possibility of the new birth and the work of the Holy Spirit. This can be found in passages like Ezekiel 36 which speaks of a "new heart and new spirit."

So we conclude by saying that, while this doctrine is not stressed in the Old Testament, it certainly is there, and it grows as we move through the text. The emphasis in the Old Testament, of course, is upon the incomparable God and upon the coming of the Messiah. What takes lesser precedence is the work and the ministry of the Holy Spirit. But just as in the doctrine of the Messiah we look forward to Calvary, so with the doctrine of the Holy Spirit we are looking forward to Pentecost. Smeaton's work here is extremely important and very useful. Also I would urge you to look at the discussion, "What Was the OT Believer's Experience of the Holy Spirit?" in my book *Toward Rediscovering the Old Testament*, pages 135-141.

Our summary of the experience of the Old Testament believer's participation in the ministry of the Holy Spirit cannot be put any better than Geoffrey Grogan did. He said, in "The Experience of Salvation in the Old and New Testaments," page 17:

> Hence we may say that the *full* N.T. experience of the Spirit as the Spirit of Christ from Pentecost onwards is at one with that of the true saints of the O.T. in that it was always a regenerating experience, bringing men to newness of life, but that there is an important difference. It is not simply that the Spirit now operates on the basis of the perfect character of Jesus. Presumably [the Spirit] had already done this in anticipation even in the OT. Rather it is that [the Spirit] operates on the basis of that character *as now revealed historically* and so held before the minds of those who now experienced His activity in their hearts. For example, men in OT days had the command of God to love Him and to love their neighbor. However, our Lord had said "a new commandment I give you, that you love one another ..." (John xiii.34). There was ... a partial realisation of it [in the OT]. ... Now, however, the standard has been perfectly revealed in [Christ].

Just so, we conclude that in the Old Testament the Holy Spirit regenerated people and was in the Old Testament believer. But it was necessary that he come visibly and formally to validate all that had been proleptically experienced in the Old Testament in anticipation of Pentecost, just as Calvary was necessary to validate all that had been offered in the name of the coming sacrifice and atonement of Christ. This is our teaching on the question of the experience of the Holy Spirit in the life of the Old Testament believer.

# Chapter Twenty-One

# Ezekiel, Theologian of the Glory of God

The worst has taken place. Jerusalem fell in 586 BC. Down came the walls; down came the Davidic line; down came the throne; down came even the Temple where the shekinah glory dwelt. It has really been bad news!

But in the midst of this, the prophet Ezekiel continues to minister long-distance, even sending his message back to Jerusalem after he is deported. Because what he has to say to the people back home is so meticulously dated, it is easy to plot his book. Ezekiel is the epitome of organization, probably the most organized of the prophets, whereas Jeremiah is probably the most disorganized. This makes Jeremiah a hard man to take notes on! By contrast, Ezekiel's book contains three great moments; it divides itself into three major segments: before, during, and after the siege and fall of Jerusalem. These divisions are fitting not only for a survey of the book, but also for the theology of the book.

The first section of the book of Ezekiel (chaps. 1–24) takes place before the siege, while there is still time for the people to repent. We recall from the book of Jonah that the prophet preached repentance to Nineveh up until the last minute, up until the fortieth day.

In the second movement of Ezekiel (chaps. 25–32), the siege of one and a half years takes place. Nebuchadnezzar sits outside Jerusalem, waiting for the people to surrender. In this section there are messages for those nations who were basically saying, "Aha! The nation of Israel deserves what it is getting." The word of the Lord came to Ezekiel with prophecies against Ammon, Moab, Edom, Philistia, Tyre, Sidon, and Egypt.

In the third section (chaps. 33–48), after the siege, what does the subject matter turn to? After the siege and the fall of the city, it turns to eschatology. With the deportations, the people lose hope and are forced to think eschatologically. It is my view that there were three different times when the Babylonians came to Jerusalem and took people back home with them. In 606-605 BC, Daniel was taken along with Meshach, Shadrach, and Abed-nego. Then in 597 BC, just a decade before the city fell, Ezekiel was taken

231

in a second deportation. Most scholars do not want to accept the first and second deportations, or they at least rule out 606-605 BC. But I think there is good biblical evidence as well as external evidence for their occurrences.

At the time of the third deportation, Nebuchadnezzar came. This time he put up a siege around the city and was going for broke. And this time down it came! There was nothing left but a ruin and a mess. The invaders would taunt the children of Israel as they passed by the house of God, "You say that is where your God lives. Look at it! It's just a burned-down building. ..." We can imagine it looking like one of the great European cathedrals after a World War II bombing raid: nothing left but a burned-out shell, with an empty circle where the rose stained glass window used to be. The Hebrew tells us in typically dramatic fashion that the invaders would hiss at the Jewish people. This was a real put-down, a loss of face. In the West, we don't realize the full import of this, but in the Near East and the Far East, the worst thing that can happen to a person is to lose face. He must never do that! We would do well to apply this cultural knowledge to diplomatic negotiations with these countries.

The old order was gone, the Davidic throne and kingdom and dynasty were removed, and there was now only one way to go. That was forward to the new David with his throne and his kingdom. This forced Israel to think eschatologically. What about the great promise of God? He had said that it was eternal. What about the great promise to David that there would be a new David in the succeeding lines of David? What about the throne of David? There would be one coming who would sit upon the throne and who would never have an end. And what about his kingdom? There would come a kingdom that would never have an end. We can see that eschatology was forced upon them.

Even in our own preaching and thinking, have you ever noticed how we begin to think apocalyptically when things turn sour? It is hard to preach on Daniel and Revelation when things are going well, when the economy is healthy, and when there are no international threats. But just wait till we get into a world war, and, suddenly, out come the prophecy notes again. There are many people who have no tolerance for prophecy, who normally say, "That stuff turns me off. I want to hear about fulfilled life. I want to hear about 'positive thinking' and 'possibility thinking.'" But when the evil days come, they turn around and say, "Talk to us about the future." And so it was in Ezekiel's day.

## The Glory of the Lord

What are the theological themes of Ezekiel? The first theological theme has to be the glory of God, the glory of the Lord, for that is the dominant scene that actually begins the book.

## The Dominant Scene: The Throne of God, Ezekiel 1:4-28

When I took a course on the book of Revelation, my teacher, Merrill C. Tenney, required that we start our study by going home and getting out an 8.5 by 11 inch piece of paper. We were to draw a picture of chapters 4 and 5 of Revelation. In spite of our protests that we were not artists, he said, "I want you to be able to visualize, to see, to feel, to think color. Draw that throne scene!"

That Revelation scene is, of course, a reflection of the throne scene in Ezekiel 1. Could you paint this in your mind's eye? If not, get out some crayons or some oils and try to draw it. There's the crystal-clear platform which is simply a clear 'expanse'. The word used in Genesis 1 is also used here in Ezekiel 1. In fact, it is one of the few places where *raqiya‘* occurs. *Raqiya‘* is generally translated as an 'expanse', although in the Greek translation and the Latin Vulgate it is 'firmament'. But it simply means an expanse. This is not a hard canopy, a shell, with holes poked through it. It is not a three-part universe, which was that misleading concept, that red herring, in antiquity. It was merely an expanse.

On this expanse is a marvelous throne in sapphire. Someone *like* the son of man or *like* one of the gods is seated on the throne. Many similes appear in this first chapter of Ezekiel. Surrounding the entire scene is a rainbow of many colors. And there are flashes of lightning and thunder, so you will need to draw some thunder bolts in the picture. Verse 28 says, "Like the appearance of a rainbow in the clouds on a rainy day, so was the radiance around him" (NIV).

Supporting the platform which holds the throne are four living creatures, the seraphim and cherubim. We need to imagine or draw these four living creatures with their wings spread out under the platform: two of their wings are spread at right angles around each corner underneath the clear crystal, as if they are holding it up. This probably looks somewhat like Oriental furniture. With their other two wings, they seem to cover their bodies. This is happening at all four corners.

These four creatures are standing on a wheel in the middle of a wheel. It must be that they are standing on the axle. The wheel in the middle of the wheel must be something like modern desk furniture wheels which are able to turn in any direction. The important thing is that there is no steering mechanism; this is God's heavenly thronemobile! Rather than a popemobile, we have here a thronemobile which can go anywhere.

As we have said, a huge rainbow comes all the way around. Crashing in on the sides are thunder bolts and lightning. Someone is seated on the throne, though it is not quite clear who it is; it is sort of like the Son of the Lord. "This whole scene was the appearance of the likeness of the glory of the LORD" (Ezek 1:28). What does Ezekiel mean? He is talking about the 'thereness' of God. The glory of God is not just a phrase in our theological terminology, so that because it sounds good, we say the glo-o-o-ry of the Lord! No, it is much more than that. The verbal root of the word is *kabed*, which means 'to be heavy'. It indicates the sheer gravity, the weight of his presence. He is there: the *thereness* of God.

What is God telling Ezekiel by all this? "Ezekiel, go! I am sending you; but don't forget: it is I, the LORD of the universe, who am now in session. I, the LORD, am seated on the circle of the earth; and the point is that where you go, I can go. This thing can go off on an angle; it can go left, right, backward, forward, any direction, because it's solid: a wheel in the middle of a wheel. It doesn't even need to be steered around or backed up. The point is, where you go, I will go." It is *Emmanuel*: God with Ezekiel!

So the glory of God is one of the great points here, and this very descriptive scene in Ezekiel 1:4-28 is extremely important: the sapphire throne, the crystal platform, the display of thunder and lightning and color and sound, the graphics, the maneuverability of the thronemobile. Ezekiel 1:28 tells us the meaning: it was the likeness of the glory of God. He tells us its significance: God would be with his prophet and his people wherever they went.

So Ezekiel, who is in exile, writes back to his people in Jerusalem. "We've got to go through a lot of deep waters. Do you know what really stirs me? It's not the idea of going back home. It's not nationalism. It's not a new kind of politics and a new institution for our people. And it's not an end-time Babylonian party: Down with these people who are Gentiles! What really stirs me is the concept of the *glory of God*." That is the dominant scene here in Ezekiel 1 with its meaning and its significance.

### The Removal of the Glory of God from a Sinful People

Secondly, this book is about the removal of the glory of God, which occurs in Ezekiel 8. This chapter is a most discouraging chapter, for here Ezekiel is transported, by way of a vision, back to his homeland during the final hours before the siege is successful and the country is taken by Nebuchadnezzar. What does he see going on? He sees a country, Judah, which is ripe for judgment. Otherwise how can we explain what is taking place? In his vision, what does he see at the temple of God? Verse 3 says he looks and sees that an idol or image 'that provokes to jealousy' has been erected in the temple of God. What is this? Probably a symbol—a sexual symbol at that—representing the goddess Asherah, from what we can gather. This goddess, a Canaanite deity, with all of its religious prostitution, is set up in the house of God! We know this from Ugaritic materials. I did my doctoral dissertation on the Canaanite Ugaritic pantheon, and I must tell you that what is going on here is straight porno. It is certainly not devotional reading. This image of 'provoking to jealousy' is not very nice.

In the vision, Ezekiel was brought to the entrance of the court. What did he see? He saw that the house of God was also being used for animal worship. "So I went in and looked, and I saw portrayed all over the walls all kinds of crawling things and detestable animals and all the idols of the house of Israel" (Ezek 8:10). Perhaps this was leftover Egyptian influence, where the cat and crocodile and other things were set up and worshipped.

Then verse 14 says Ezekiel was brought "to the entrance to the north gate of the house of the LORD" (NIV), and what did he see there but women weeping for Tammuz. Tammuz? Oh, yes. He was the Sumerian god of vegetation. Tammuz supposedly died every fall and reappeared in the spring. In the house of God, there was weeping in sympathy for Tammuz in the fall, as part of the death, burial, and rising god theme from the Near East. I don't know that there is any evidence for an annual resurrection of Tammuz. I've worked in the Sumerian documents and have taken a course from Samuel Noah Kramer of the University of Pennsylvania. Now deceased, he was probably the most distinguished man in this field. We went through the text that supposedly said Tammuz was resurrected. One of my friends, Ed Yamauchi, wrote an article published in the *Journal of Biblical Literature* (*JBL*), refuting that he was resurrected. But the truth of the matter is that it was much like Frazer's *Golden Bough*, mimicking the rhythm in nature where we see the leaves dying in the fall and the rising and coming back to life in the spring. So these women of Ezekiel's day felt that by weeping for the god who could bring life back again in the spring, they could bring fertility to the land. What were these women doing? They were practicing a religious kind of syncretism and religious prostitution with Tammuz. And that was going on in the house of God as well.

We have Asherah with the image of jealousy; we have animal worship; we have people weeping for Tammuz. And now verse 16ff tells us that the elders—twenty-five men—were facing east and worshipping the sun from the house of God. So the people were into sun worship, too. Well, if by now we don't think the people of Judah were ripe for judgment, we have missed the point! And if we don't think their false worship was being authorized, then what was it doing in the Temple? We must realize that this was about as much authentication and authorization as was possible in that culture.

The Temple was to be set apart for the worship of God. What would you do in this situation if you were God and this was the place where people were to worship you? There was only one thing to do, and that was to get out!—which is exactly what God did. Ezekiel 9:3 says, "Now the glory of the God of Israel went up from above the cherubim ...." This was in the Holy of Holies, where God was said to be seated, enthroned between the cherubim. There he dwelt; he tabernacled; he pup-tented among the people. But now God moved from there to the threshold—out to the doorway of the temple. This was the first stage in the removal of the glory of God. Notice the repetition in Ezekiel 10:4: "Then the glory of the LORD rose from above the cherubim and moved to the threshold of the temple" (NIV).

Ezekiel 10:19 goes on to tell us of the next stage: the Lord moved from the doorway over to the entrance to the east gate of the Lord's house. He moved out to Stephen's Gate, or it could be the Lion Gate, which was right alongside. It was either that East Gate, or the East Gate that remains blocked up to this day and tradition says that it won't be reopened until the Messiah comes back. You've seen that in the East Portico of the city of Jerusalem. So the glory of God was now on the edge of town, as it were.

But that was not the last stage. In Ezekiel 11:23 the glory of the Lord moved once again and left town altogether. "The glory of the LORD went up from within the city and stopped above the mountain east of it." This would be the Mount of Olives. The glory of the Lord left town by degrees. From the Mount of Olives the glory of God went up into heaven and was removed. We do not see it again until after the siege of Jerusalem in the eschatological portion of Ezekiel which deals with the last days.

Where in Ezekiel 33–48 do we find it again? Look in Ezekiel 43:5. In this vision of Ezekiel's, the glory of God came back to a temple which no one had ever seen before. There is a discussion of a temple which no one has ever seen before and which we think will possibly be built in a future day. We could assume that Ezekiel hoped this would be built, but it never was. Therefore it was a failed dream, which is the way most liberals treat it. Or we could assume, as some evangelicals do, that Ezekiel 40–48, where this temple is described, is symbolic, that it is allegorical. But if you take this position, I must tell you that this is quite an allegory! What can we say for these nine chapters that just go on and on with details: so many inches here, so many benches there, so many cornices here, and just so high and so wide? The detail is astounding. It seems to me that there is no other analogy like this. The description goes on for nine chapters. So it seems to me that it is something in the future.

Ezekiel 43:5 says, "Then the Spirit lifted me up and brought me into the inner court, and the glory of the LORD filled the temple" (NIV). And again, in 44:4, "I looked and saw the glory of the LORD filling the temple of the LORD ..." (NIV). This is not the restored temple, not the second temple that would come—Herod's temple, which was restored during the life of Jesus. Rather, it seems to me, this is the temple that is to come in the future. Because the temple will be there, God himself will be there. Ezekiel 48:35 tells us, "And the name of the city from that time on shall be: *Yahweh Shammah*, Jehovah is there." For he will come back once again to his people, to his land, and to a revived history, with the city's name now being *Yahweh Shammah*: the place where God is.

This brings us full circle in the theology of the glory of the Lord in Ezekiel. I understand this in a millennial sense: When the Lord is ruling and reigning from Jerusalem, the name of the city at that time will be *Yahweh Shammah*. The reason for his being there is that the glory of God has come back into town: the visible presence of the living God will dwell in

Jerusalem, just as he did in the days of the incarnation when Jesus walked on this earth for thirty years.

So we do have a rather interesting situation here. To review, visualize, if you can, the eastern portion of the town where the temple complex existed. Within the temple itself was the Holy of Holies. The Lord removed himself from the Holy of Holies where the cherubim were and went out to the doorway to the temple. From there, he went out to the gate on the east side of the city, and then over to the Mount of Olives, which was just across the valley. And there it was that he went up into heaven.

This is symbolic of the Luke narrative in the book of Acts. "You men of Galilee, why stand you here gazing into heaven?" I have always thought this to be an unfair question. What would you think if someone went up to heaven right in front of you? I mean, NASA at least checks out all the valves, weather reports, and so on, before blasting off. But not Jesus! He just goes right up in front of them. I think I would have stood there, too, staring up into heaven. So, the question must be rhetorical: "You men of Galilee, why stand you here gazing up into heaven?" I think I, too, would have stood there with my mouth wide open, watching, stammering, "Huh?" "This same Jesus will come in like manner as you have seen him go." It was a bodily ascension into heaven; he will come again bodily. And because of this passage in Ezekiel, and other passages, we believe the place will be on the Mount of Olives, just as Zechariah 14 indicates.

So, just as in the New Testament teaching, here in Ezekiel the glory of God goes up into heaven from the Mount of Olives, returns to the same location, and comes back into the city. The city will be known then as *Yahweh Shammah*, where God is: there he dwells. The Lord is there in the city!

The theology of the glory of the Lord: it's one of the great teachings about our God.

## The Theology of Knowing God

The second theological proposition in Ezekiel is the theology of knowing God.

### Ezekiel's Favorite Phrase

One of Ezekiel's most famous phrases is "that they may know that I am the LORD." *Knowing* here is not purely cognitive; it is not an intellectual, cerebral exercise. "That they may know that I am God" is experiential. It is that they may come to know God personally. This has a relational, experiential aspect to knowing, in the Hebrew Semitic sense. "That they may know that I am God" is much like the phrase which occurs during the plagues in the book of Exodus. Again, it is an invitation to salvation; it is a salvific and apologetic kind of verse. The phrase occurs *fifty-four times* in just this book of Ezekiel. If we add the eighteen times it exists in a slightly expanded form, we then count *seventy-two times*. It is a very, very important theme! This man's goal is communicating who God is and eliciting a corresponding action. So we have the name of God and the theme of his person coming forth in Ezekiel's favorite phrase in the theology of knowing God.

### Ezekiel's Description of the Rightful King

Included in the theology of knowing God, it seems to me, is Ezekiel's description of the rightful king, the legitimate king. As compared to the previous revelation of God, we learn something new about this 'rightful king' in Ezekiel 21. In this chapter, Ezekiel relates how Nebuchadnezzar is coming down out of the north, by the route he typically would take from Babylon. Ezekiel says in verses 18-21, "The word of the LORD came to me: 'Son of man, mark out two roads for the sword of the king of Babylon to take, both starting from the same country. Make a signpost where the road branches off to the city. Mark out one road for the sword to come against Rabbah of the Ammonites and another against Judah and fortified Jerusalem. For the king of Babylon will stop at the fork in the road, at the junction of the two roads, to seek an omen: He will cast lots with arrows ...'" (NIV).

This is an interesting passage, because while we have here someone using all kinds of non-approved means of getting direction, we still see the sovereign plan of God in operation. God is saying, The man is going to come to the fork in the road, where he must make a choice. Should he take the interstate that takes him over to the Ammonite territory east of the Dead Sea, or should he go down through Jerusalem? He doesn't know what to do, so he's going to try to get some direction from his god.

One method of getting direction is through *belomancy*: taking arrows, shaking them, and trying to get them to point in a direction. But then he goes on to also consult his idol, and so we see another method: *necromancy*, that of consulting the dead. Then, there is a third method of determining directions: *hepatoscopy*, that of examining a liver. This was a science among the Babylonians. They would take the liver out of a sheep destined for sacrifice and proceed to examine the shape of the liver. I have personally read some of the stone copies of livers with various directions written in cuneiform over them. If the liver is large on this side, it means this; if it has a dent here, it means this; if it's lined here, it means another thing. It could be compared to palm reading in our day, I suppose. They would not only do this with the liver of sheep, but they would also shoot down birds to examine them. This was to determine whether they were under the proper auspices. Our word *auspices* comes from the Latin which means 'to shoot down the birds'. There is irony in the situation when a good kosher, evangelical, fundamentalist organization says, This meeting is held under the auspices of ....

Well, Nebuchadnezzar uses belomancy, necromancy, and hepatoscopy, and even with all that, the Lord has already determined the way he will come. He says, You can mark it out, but I'll tell you what, he's going to come to Jerusalem. So we can see the overruling providence of God. Do you want to understand about the freedom of man? There it is. Put a big 'A' over Nebuchadnezzar's shaking the arrows, his consulting the idols, and his checking the liver. 'A' stands, not for adultery, but in this case for Arminius. Then put a big 'C' for Calvin over the fact that the text says he is coming to Jerusalem. We have here a "Calvaminian" verse in which the two currents 'A' and 'C' converge.

So Nebuchadnezzar comes to Jerusalem. What message does God give to Ezekiel concerning the last man ruling on the throne in Judah, the Davidic prince Zedekiah? "O profane and wicked prince of Israel, whose day has come, whose time of punishment has reached its climax, this is what the Sovereign LORD says: Take off the turban, remove the crown" (Ezek 21:25, NIV). He is saying, You, the high priest, you who are wearing the turban, the tiara, take that off! And you, the king wearing the crown, you take that off! "It will not be as it was: The lowly will be exalted and the exalted will be brought low. A ruin! A ruin! I will make it a ruin! It will not be restored until he comes to whom it rightfully belongs" (vv. 26-27, NIV). Until he comes whose right it is.

Who is this Mystery Person? As in the television show of the past, whoever he is, would he please sign in. Who is the person whose right it is to come? What does this mean? I think that it is a reflection and an expansion of Genesis 49:10: "The scepter will not depart from Judah, nor the ruler's staff from between his feet, until he comes to whom it belongs and the obedience of the nations is his" (NIV). Or "until Shiloh comes." It's in the same form here. If we take the word *Shiloh* apart, *Sh* probably reflects the relative pronoun 'which' or 'to whom'; *le* is the way to say 'he has', 'you have', or 'you possess'; *oh* would be 'to him' or 'belongs to him'. So the point is: until Shiloh comes—it is a cryptic word for the full expression which means "until he whose right it is comes." Ezekiel 21 is saying, Remove the scepter. Remove the crown from off the head of the king. Remove the turban from the head of the high priest until Shiloh comes—the true king, the true prophet, and the true priest—whose right it is. This is not Johnny Shiloh, of Civil War fame, nor the city Shiloh, but rather "he whose right it is." (See on this passage W. C. Kaiser, *The Messiah in the Old Testament* [Grand Rapids: Zondervan, 1995], pp 50-53.)

This is the theology, then, of the Messiah, the rightful one. The kingship and priesthood in Judah would remain abandoned until the one comes to whom it rightfully belongs. So Ezekiel's description of the rightful king is another way in which we can know God: "That they may know that I am God." He is the one who will come to whom all authority, all rulership, and all mediation of the priesthood belong. He is the one who has the right to wear the turban and the crown, symbols of the office of priest and king. It will belong to him. But take it off Zedekiah; take it off the high priest's head. They won't need those things, because here comes Nebuchadnezzar. Here comes the end, until the one comes to whom it rightfully belongs. Don't worry; God will still keep his promise. But on the other hand there will be some deviation and time lapse.

### Ezekiel's Description of the Good Shepherd

Under the heading, The Theology of Knowing God, we can put also Ezekiel's description of the good shepherd in Ezekiel 34. The comparison of God to the good shepherd is found elsewhere in the Bible, for example in the famous John 10 passage. "Therefore Jesus said again, 'I tell you the truth, I am the gate for the sheep. All who ever came before me were thieves and robbers, but the sheep did not listen to them. I am the gate; whoever enters through me will be saved. He will come in and go out, and find pasture. The thief comes only to steal and kill and destroy; I have come that they may have life and have it to the full. I am the good shepherd'" (John 10:7-11, NIV).

These words remind me of a story one of my teachers recounted about a memorable sermon he witnessed in England. A visiting, quite rotund preacher was awaited in the high pulpit that looks out over the congregation, as the pulpits do in old Church of England sanctuaries. He was late, but was to slip through the little doorway in the wall, climb the narrow stairway, and emerge at the pulpit. Try as he would, there was no way he could get up the stairway built for a parson half his size. There was only one thing to do: the janitor got a ladder twenty feet high and put it up to the front of the pulpit area, and the rotund speaker climbed up and over in as dignified a manner as possible. Then he announced his text from John 10: "A thief and a robber climbeth up some other way. ..."

It was quite a text for the occasion! But the substance really comes from Ezekiel 34, where the shepherd theme is well developed; this discussion of the good shepherd seeking his sheep is embodied in Ezekiel 34. "For this is what the Sovereign LORD says: I myself will search for my sheep and look after them. As a shepherd looks after his scattered flock when he is with them, so will I look after my sheep. I will rescue them from all the places where they were scattered on a day of clouds and darkness" (Ezek 34:11-12, NIV). You can see the parallels in these two texts for yourself.

## The Theology of the Reunited, Restored Israel

The third great theological theme in Ezekiel is the theology of a reunited, restored Israel, which comes up especially in Ezekiel 37. This chapter has two rather magnificent points to make: the resurrection of the nation itself and the reunification of Joseph and Judah.

### The Resurrection of the Nation

The first is that marvelous statement of the valley of dry bones. Ezekiel says that in a vision he was put in the midst of a valley full of bones. He says that he saw the whole floor of the valley just littered with bones. And the LORD asked Ezekiel, "Son of Man, can these bones live?"

In essence Ezekiel answered, "Lord, you're not going to get me on that one! You know whether they can live or not."

Then the Lord said to him, "Preach, preach. Prophesy. Prophesy to these bones and say, 'Dry bones, now hear the word of the Lord!'" It was like the spiritual says, "Dem bones, dem bones gonna walk around." But what is really the revivifying force that will give life to them? The word. The word of God.

Ezekiel continues, "Then he said to me, 'Prophesy to these bones and say to them, "Dry bones, hear the word of the Lord! This is what the Sovereign LORD says to these bones: ... I will attach tendons to you and make flesh come upon you and cover you with skin; ... Then you will know that I am the LORD"'" (Ezek 37:4-6, NIV). As we have it in the spiritual, "The knee bone connected to the thigh bone, the thigh bone connected to the hip bone. ... Now hear the Word of the Lord! Dem bones, dem bones gonna walk around." The spiritual celebrates it, but in the vision it was actually happening in front of Ezekiel's eyes.

God told him to prophesy and speak to 'dem bones' that were assembled into bodies. So he said to them, "This is what the Sovereign LORD says: 'O my people, I am going to open your graves and bring you up from them; I will bring you back to the land of Israel'" (v. 12, NIV). This is not a statement about life after death. It is not even an argument for the resurrection of the body. It is an argument for the resurrection of a nation, the nation of Israel.

The bones were reassembled into bodies, but they needed life. God said to Ezekiel, "Look, son of man, can these bones really live again? They're standing there like zombies. They've got flesh; their bones are back together again. Can they really live?"

And Ezekiel again responded, "Lord, you know that, too."

Ezekiel 37:9-10 tells us God's answer. "Then he said to me, 'Prophesy to the breath; prophesy, son of man, and say to it, "This is what the Sovereign LORD says: Come from the four winds, O breath, and breathe into these slain, that they may live"'" (NIV). Ezekiel prophesied the word and they began to breathe once again.

With this whole discussion here we have the promise of the future nation coming back together again. We must not forget that this was coming on the heels of one of the greatest tragedies ever suffered by the nation.

Judah was going out of business in 586 BC. We don't even hear of them or see them again as a nation until 14 May 1948. Is that the moment that God was speaking about? It does not seem that it has yet come about, but at least in our day and generation we have less excuse than anyone else in the long interim has ever had for not seeing how such a thing might take place. Indeed, we may already be seeing the beginning movements of such a thing.

### The Reunification of Joseph and Judah

This chapter is making the point of the *revivification* of the nation, and then there is the second point of the *unification* of the nation. In verses 15-16 Ezekiel was told to take two sticks of wood and write Judah on one stick and on the other, Ephraim or Joseph for the ten northern tribes. Then he was told in verse 17, "Join them together into one stick so that they will become one in your hand" (NIV). The explanation for this command comes in the following verses. "When your countrymen ask you, 'Won't you tell us what you mean by this?' say to them, '… This is what the Sovereign LORD says: I will take the Israelites out of the nations where they have gone. I will gather them from all around and bring them back into their own land'" (NIV). There will be one stick (vv. 16-19), one nation again (v. 22a); one king over them, 'my servant David' (v. 22b, 24), the new David. There will be one God (v. 23), one shepherd (v. 24). God says this will be part of his everlasting, eternal covenant (vv. 25-26). So on the heels of disaster, God promises still to remember his word and still to remember his covenant: we have the promise of the nation becoming one again, the glorious theology of a reunited, restored Israel.

We conclude with one more theme, in Ezekiel 40–48, a most difficult but important teaching of the restored new temple. There has never been a temple built with these proportions, but it looks as if there will be a real temple built in the middle of the land, possibly not on the same site where it is now (for it could well be positioned in the center of the land where Samaria once stood), and in a restored geography that looks more like a stepladder rather than the typical twelve tribes that we've seen before.

What about the sacrifices in that future day? Hasn't Hebrews made it clear that sacrifice has been put away once for all? The answer is, Of course. These sacrifices are either, as one school of thought says, a memorial, or they are, as I prefer to say, a way of speaking of worship in terms that the people of that day would comprehend. At that point in time, sacrifice stood for a way of praise and thanksgiving to God; so it was used to speak of the worship in that future day. Hence, just as future wars are spoken of in the Bible not with planes, tanks, submarines, and nuclear bombs, but with bows, arrows, swords, and spears (thereby implying the equivalent future hardware under the known hardware of the day), so future worship is spoken of in the Bible in terms of worship known in the day in which the writer wrote.

Ezekiel, the theologian of the glory of God, dwells on the great theme of God's wonderful work, his glorious work in the day to come.

# Chapter Twenty-Two

# Daniel, Theologian of the Kingdom of God

The kingdom of God is one of the great themes of Scripture, and Daniel is one of its great exegetes, so we will now consider Daniel, the theologian of the kingdom of God.

The doctrine of the kingdom of God is presented in the Old Testament as part of the promise-plan. A good number of evangelical scholars, some of whom are my best friends, critique me on this point. They say, "What in the world is wrong with you? Why don't you use the kingdom of God as the main theme instead of as part of the promise-plan? After all, didn't Jesus come announcing the kingdom of God? Isn't that the substance of what Paul is speaking about? Isn't that the substance of Ezekiel and Daniel especially?" Of course it is. I readily admit that. But I think that the kingdom is only an aspect of the larger promise-plan of God. Furthermore, the kingdom theme develops much later. For an overall theme, we need to go all the way back and begin from Genesis 1–11 and go through the patriarchal period. In those earlier sections of Scripture we find precious little about the kingdom of God, but we find an enormous amount on the promise-plan of God. So we subsume the kingdom theme under the promise-plan rather than vice versa.

As Willis J. Beecher remarked, "The most prominent thing in the New Testament is its proclamation of the Kingdom and its anointed King. But it is on the basis of the *divine promise* that its preachers proclaim the Kingdom, and when they appeal to the Old Testament in proof of Christian doctrine, they make the *promise* more prominent than the Kingdom itself" (*The Prophets and the Promise* [New York: Thomas Y. Crowell, 1905; reprinted 1963, 1975 by Baker Book House], pp 178-79).

## Introduction

We have already traced the development of the kingdom in the promise-plan, but let's review the main elements by way of introduction to this theme of the kingdom of God.

First, look at Genesis 17:6, 16, where God makes a covenant, promising that kings will come from Abraham, Sarah, and Jacob. "I will make you very fruitful; I will make nations of you, and kings will come from you" (NIV). So as early as Genesis 17 we are given a hint of the kingdom theme. Also we see it in Genesis 35:10-11. Of course, this means that the Ishmaelite kings, the Midianite kings, the Moabite kings would all come from Abraham's seed. That's for sure. But there would also be a royal line leading up to David. I think that is implicit in the promise.

A second fact in this development is that Moses looked forward to a king in Israel. Even before Samuel's great prayer, in which he was upset with the people for wanting a king, it had been God's plan and intention. This was true in patriarchal times, 2000-1800 BC, and in the time of Moses, 1400 BC. In Deuteronomy 17:14-20 God is saying, When you come into the land, I will set a king over you.

A third fact that should be put here is found in Hannah's song, in 1 Samuel 2. You remember, Mary, in the Magnificat, takes words right out of Hannah's song offered on the occasion of the dedication of Samuel: "My soul doth magnify the LORD." But I am thinking particularly of the last words of her song, in verse 10: "... those who oppose the LORD will be shattered. He will thunder against them from heaven; the LORD will judge the ends of the earth. He will give strength to his king and exalt the horn of [his Messiah,] his anointed" (NIV). Here we find 'horn', 'Messiah' and 'king' all used in one verse. As Hannah prayed in this song, we know that the Messiah who was to come would be triumphant. The anointed one would be a king.

A fourth fact is that God promised to give David a kingdom. In 2 Samuel 7 he was saying, "I'll make out of you a dynasty, a house, a throne, and a kingdom. Your son will be a king forever, and I'll be a father to him." With this great teaching, we go miles forward; we find that the promise now included not only a seed, but that seed would be a king who would have a throne and a dynasty and a realm—a kingdom—over which to reign.

So we do see that the Scriptures give a central and emphatic place to the kingdom in the promise doctrine. Psalm 89 is the greatest commentary on 2 Samuel 7 and 1 Chronicles 17. Psalm 89:25 tells us how widespread the kingdom of God will be. God says here, "I will set his hand"—the hand of my Messiah—"over the sea, his right hand over the rivers." He goes on to speak of the kingdom as being from "shore to shore."

As a matter of fact, it will also be eternal: "Till the moon shall wax no more" (Ps 72:5, 7). Isaac Watts used those words in his famous hymn:

Jesus shall reign where-e'er the sun
Does his successive journeys run;
His Kingdom stretch from shore to shore,
Till moons shall wax and wane no more.

That is taken out of Psalm 72; it is messianic, speaking of the extent of the kingdom of God. As far as the east is from the west, that is the extent of his kingdom. It is worldwide.

God's throne on earth promised to the seed of David is to be eternal, says Psalm 45:6 in a most startling way: "Thy throne, O God, is for ever and ever ...." This is speaking of God's throne on earth, not in heaven. Almost every commentator who tries to handle this reference finds it mind-boggling. How could the throne of David be called "thy throne, O God"? The person addressed in apposition to the throne is God; the one seated on the throne is accorded deity. He is addressed as God and he lasts forever and forever.

The seminal thoughts on the kingdom doctrine are in these passages we have just traced in the Old Testament, but then the kingdom doctrine becomes more explicit. It is Daniel who gives us one of the kingdom's fullest developments in the Old Testament. So we turn to Daniel, the theologian of the kingdom of God.

## The Kingdom of God Will Succeed the Empires of Men
## Daniel 2

The first assertion that Daniel makes is that the kingdom of God will succeed the kingdoms and empires of men. We find the kingdom of God and the kingdom of men placed in juxtaposition.

### Nebuchadnezzar's Dream of the Colossal Image

One of the great chapters demonstrating this is Nebuchadnezzar's dream of the colossal image in Daniel 2. Daniel was called in, somewhat belatedly, to interpret this dream. As we already know, Daniel and his three friends, Shadrach, Meshach, and Abednego, had been carted off to a pagan culture and had been given a pagan education in exile.

By the way, this seems to me to be one of the strongest arguments against environmental determinism. As believers, we should not buy into this idea which comes to the fore every once in a while. I am for Christian education and have spent most of my life in it, but we must not assume that the environment determines the child: that all we need is one good example and the kids will stay on the right track. That's like saying that what every hospital ward needs—especially an AIDS ward—is someone who is robust in health to sleep in the middle of that ward so that the others can get the idea of what a good healthy body is like. Or it's like saying that all a bushel of rotten apples needs is one good apple right in the center. If only the other apples could see a wonderful Michigan Winesap right in the middle of the bushel, they would shape up and say, "Let's get rid of our rottenness." There is something wrong with that illustration, I think.

But it's amazing how many Christians fall for that logic: that a good environment will do the trick. And they depend on it!

Daniel was in Babylon. There were some things Daniel would not do. He purposed in his heart to not defile himself; he took a separation stand. That is correct. On the one hand, he mastered all the arts and sciences and astrology of the Babylonian culture. But on the other hand, he kept his commitment clear to God. This is an interesting study in Christ and culture: deliberate involvement in the culture without compromise in the heart. I think we need to give more thought to this. Joseph would be another example of involvement in society. We would think that a boy, seventeen years of age—thrown into a pit, feeling bitterness against his brothers and then against God for not helping him, being repeatedly rebuffed in one situation after another—could have said after a while, "Look, God doesn't care. I think I'll go do my own thing. I'll capitulate to the Egyptian culture." But he didn't do that.

So here Daniel was called in because Nebuchadnezzar had had a dream and this time he was not going to put up with those charlatans around him. He suspected the fellows on his payroll were just spoofing him, telling him whatever he wanted to hear. And so he said, "Fellows, before you give me the interpretation, first tell me what I dreamed." That really shook them up! If the king would only tell them the essential elements of the dream, they could hand him a line of chatter. They could say, This means that. They had all kinds of devices for interpreting these things. Instead, Nebuchadnezzar said, "If you've got contact with the supernatural, then tell me what I dreamed. And, if not, I'm going to see that this whole university gets murdered!"

Now, this is really quite an examination! They hadn't faced one like this before. Finally, Daniel and his three friends were brought in. These three friends, whom we affectionately know as "Your Shack, My Shack, and a Bungalow," were also in trouble. And Daniel said, "My God is able to reveal the dream to me."

### The Interpretation of the Dream

As we recall, the dream was about a statue with a head of gold, shoulders and arms and chest made of silver, the body and the belly made of bronze or copper, and then two legs made of iron and clay mixed together. Daniel says, "Isn't that what you saw, O King?"

The king says, "Yes, that's right."

"And then you saw a stone. It was taken out of a great mountain, but it was cut without hands."

"Yes," he says, "that's right."

"Then the next thing you knew, it hit the feet of this thing, and the whole image—this colossal image—was crushed to powder. And then you saw the stone—that rock—grow and grow until it filled the whole earth."

Nebuchadnezzar says, "Go ahead, tell me what the meaning is, son. That was the vision. That's what's bothering me. I can't get to sleep at night; I keep thinking about my empire. What's going to happen?"

So Daniel explains, "I'll tell you what this means. Going from the head to the feet, that image is made of four metals of decreasing value and increasing brittleness and weakness. The image then becomes increasingly divided as it goes from one head down to ten toes." We must notice all of those things, from the head of gold, which is the most valuable material, all the way down to the feet of iron and clay. With the ten toes, there is bifurcation, division. This will become explicit later on.

"Let me give you the interpretation of it," Daniel says. "That rock, the rock that you saw cut out of the mountain but not with human hands, is in the time of the four successive empires of the human kings representing the kingdom of men. God is going to set up a kingdom that will never, never fail. You, O King, are the head of gold. You are the Babylonian Empire, magnificent in its standard, beautiful in its benevolent dictatorship. And after you will come another kingdom."

So we know that Nebuchadnezzar stands for the first kingdom. After him, though it is not defined here, it becomes clear that the second kingdom is Medo-Persia. Then as Daniel goes on through the succeeding chapters, we will find out that the bronze, the third part, is the Greco-Macedonian Empire set up by Philip and then enlarged by Alexander the Great— Alexander the Great, who at thirty-three years of age drank himself to death, mourning the fact that there were no more lands to conquer. He took everything from Europe all the way through the Middle East, right up to the Indus River in India, and that was it! He said, "It's all over. There's nothing more to conquer." He had marched his armies farther than any had ever gone before.

Finally, there comes the fourth empire, the Roman or Western Empire, which continues to the present day. Its final manifestation, as found in Daniel 7, will be ten kings in the Western confederation, over which will rise the little horn who is the Antichrist.

But at the moment we are not concerned with the identification of the Babylonian, Medo-Persian, Greco-Macedonian, and Roman Empires. We are more concerned about that rock or stone which will crush all of these previous empires. God will set up a kingdom which will never be destroyed. Daniel 2:44 says, "In the time of those kings, the God of heaven will set up a kingdom that will never be destroyed, nor will it be left to another people" (NIV).

So we have the main part of the interpretation about a kingdom that is coming: this rock, or stone, that is cut out of a mountain. But notice that it is not cut with human hands, so it does not come from human origins. Rather, it is supernatural. Daniel 2:35 says that this kingdom itself will become a huge mountain, and it will fill the whole earth. The fact is that the kingdom of God grows and extends beyond anything that Babylon or Medo-Persia or Alexander the Great was able to do, or even his four generals who succeeded him. Or even the whole Western civilization as we know it up to the present day. It grows into a huge mountain and fills the whole earth.

Now, when Nebuchadnezzar heard this, he fell down prostrate before Daniel and paid honor to him. He said to Daniel, "Surely your God is the God of gods and the LORD of kings and a revealer of mysteries, for you were able to reveal this mystery" (v. 47, NIV).

The theology of the kingdom of God signifies God's rule and God's reign and God's realm: rule, reign, and realm. The realm is worldwide: the whole earth. The rule includes all power, all authority, all dominion given over to him. This is a fantastic statement in and of itself!

Nebuchadnezzar would need to learn this lesson one more time. It was when he went mad, and for seven years was put out to pasture—literally! He was there with the ducks, roaming around with the dew of heaven coming down upon him. Finally, his senses were restored to him; he came back, and gave a wonderful affirmation of the majesty of God. It is interesting that a pagan king, under inspiration, is writing autobiographically in this chapter in Scripture. Daniel 4 recounts for us, "At the end of that time, I, Nebuchadnezzar, raised my eyes toward heaven, and my sanity was restored. Then I praised the Most High; I honored and glorified him who lives forever."

Now here's his reason: because "his dominion is an eternal dominion; his kingdom endures from generation to generation. All the peoples of the earth are regarded as nothing. He does as he pleases with the powers of heaven and the peoples of the earth. No one can hold back his hand or say to him: 'What have you done?'" (Dan 4:34-35, NIV). No one can say that! Not Mikhail Gorbachev in Russia. Not even Mr. Reagan or any other U.S. president. No one can say to him, What on earth are you doing? There's no one who can say that. His dominion, his authority, his providential rule will be without challenge anywhere, now and certainly in that day when manifested worldwide and when he crushes the last of the empires of man. This is a magnificent teaching on the kingdom of God and on the sovereignty of God!

## The Ancient of Days Will Give the Son of Man an Everlasting Kingdom
## Daniel 7

There is a second point that we must make here. We have already seen that the kingdom of God will succeed the empires of men and build itself into a worldwide dominion that will never be challenged. But now, in

Daniel 7, we see that the Ancient of Days will give to the Son of Man an everlasting kingdom. And once again, we come back to the same four empires of men which we saw earlier: Babylonian, Medo-Persian, Greco-Macedonian, and, finally, Roman or Western. This vision of Daniel's, we think, parallels the dream of Nebuchadnezzar in the second chapter.

### Daniel's Vision

We are given a picture here of four beasts which rise out of the churning sea. The great sea is in upheaval. Each beast is less stately, less majestic than its predecessor. We start with the king of the beasts, the lion, and the king of the bird realm, the eagle. So, what a lion is to animals and an eagle is to birds, what gold is to metal and the head is to the body, that is what Nebuchadnezzar and his kingdom, Babylon, are to all of the succeeding empires of men. Daniel watches the first beast until its wings are torn off, so that it stands on two feet like a man, "and the heart of a man was given to it" (Dan 7:4). This empire is vincible. It can be penetrated, as history proves.

But then he sees a second beast, a bear, which is "raised up on one of its sides." Modern scholarship dislikes making this second kingdom Medo-Persia. Scholars would prefer to consider Media the second kingdom, Persia the third, and the empire of Greece the fourth, feeling this is safer for prophetic and historical reasons. But they are wrong on every count, because we know that this empire was a combination empire. Remember, back in Daniel 2 we already saw its division into the chest and arms, into two parts. Now we have a bear that is raised up on one side; one side is more prominent. Of course, Persia is more prominent than Media, but the empire is a composite. It has in its mouth three ribs: it has already ripped off three major countries. Here in this vision of Daniel's, it is chomping on them.

The third kingdom is that of the leopard which has four wings of a bird. This beast has four heads. We can't confuse that, for here we have one, two, three, four: the Seleucids, the Ptolemaics, and the others who come from the four generals of Alexander the Great. If we start trying to divide Medo-Persia, we're going to miss the symbolism, and the whole thing is going to unravel on us.

The fourth beast is not described as a particular animal. Daniel says that the fourth beast is a terrifying and frightening and powerful thing. It has iron teeth; it crushes and it devours its victims; it tramples them under its feet. And it has ten horns. While the preceding image given in chapter 2 to Nebuchadnezzar in a dream did not stress the ten toes, we know that two feet have ten toes. So there is an implicit harmony here between the two passages. And while Daniel is looking, from the midst of those ten horns up comes another horn—a little one with a big mouth. This is Big Mouth–Little Horn. Big Mouth–Little Horn speaks blasphemous things against God, against men, and as we will find out, rips off three of the ten horns and makes himself to be the leader of the whole Western confederacy as history comes to a conclusion.

For the moment we are not interested in identifying these horns. It is the fourth beast that occupies Daniel's attention, with its terrifying power and its voracious appetite for conquest, with its division, its ten horns, and with the little horn that has a big mouth.

### The Ancient of Days

But the fourth beast is still not the central feature of the chapter. Rather, it is the Ancient of Days. In verse 9 Daniel saw the Ancient of Days take his seat: Court is now in session! Here comes the living God, for that is who we think this Ancient of Days is. "His clothing was as white as snow; his hair was white like wool. His throne was like a blazing fire, and its wheels were all ablaze. A river of fire was flowing out of it." We must not forget that this was not just a dream like the one Nebuchadnezzar had: this was a vision. Visions apparently come in scenes where action flows.

As Daniel continued watching, he saw 'thousands upon thousands' attending the Ancient of Days; "ten thousand times ten thousand stood before him. The court was seated, and the books were opened" (NIV). This is a dramatic moment in the judgment of God upon all the works of men and upon all the kingdoms of men and all the societies of men. God will now state what was done and whether it was done correctly or incorrectly. No more argument about what was right or wrong with the Sandinistas or the Contras or any other recent news story of national injustice and abuse of power. Court is now in session. The living God, who knows what is right, is going to declare what is right and what is wrong.

Daniel continued watching as Big Mouth spoke boastful words. "I kept looking until the beast was slain and its body destroyed and thrown into the blazing fire. (The other beasts had been stripped of their authority ....) In my vision at night I looked, and there before me was one like a son of man, coming with the clouds of heaven. He approached the Ancient of Days and was led into his presence" (vv. 11-13, NIV). So here comes one from heaven called the Son of Man, coming to present himself to the Ancient of Days.

Now we have a problem. For those who say in the great *shema'*, "Hear, O Israel: The LORD our God is one," this poses a similar problem. Which one is God? Well, we might say, the Ancient of Days is. Yes, but this other one comes from God. Here we have another hint of at least two of the three persons of the Trinity, for while being fully God, God the Father and God the Son are now brought into the presence of each other. "He approached the Ancient of Days and was led into his presence."

What did God give to this Son of Man? "He was given authority, glory and sovereign power; all peoples, nations and men of every language worshiped him. His dominion is an everlasting dominion that will not pass away, and his kingdom is one that will never be destroyed" (v. 14, NIV).

We are finding a fantastic development here, then, in this particular text! Notice the purity, the majesty, the 'awe-full'—full of awe—holiness of the living God. He appears with literally thousands upon thousands attending to him, who are called his ministering spirits and angels. God has armies like we can't imagine!

Elisha's servant had to be reminded of this in 2 Kings 6. In this text, the Syrian king was quite upset each time he planned an attack against Israel, for it seemed that the king of Israel had been warned and so avoided the spot where the Syrians would attack. "Time and time again Elisha warned the king, so that he was on his guard in such places" (v. 10, NIV). Finally the Syrian king discovered the information leak: Elisha. So he found out where Elisha and his servant were. "Then he sent horses and chariots and a strong force there. They went by night and surrounded the city" (v. 14, NIV). So here were Elisha and his servant surrounded in Dothan by all these Syrians. And the servant said, "Oh, my master, look out there! Look at all those Syrian troops. We've had it! This is going to be the day that we die." What to do?

"'Don't be afraid,' the prophet answered. 'Those who are with us are more than those who are with them.' And Elisha prayed, 'O LORD, open his eyes so he may see.' Then the LORD opened the servant's eyes, and he looked and saw the hills full of horses and chariots of fire all around Elisha" (vv. 16-17, NIV).

Sometimes I think that, although we believe in a theology of the presence and the power of God and in the ministry of angels, we forget the surrounding host of God that protects his servants and his work. Well, here in Daniel we have the living God standing with 'thousands upon thousands' attending him and doing his bidding. In front of him are myriads upon myriads, 'ten thousand times ten thousand'. We almost exhaust our language trying to express the enormity of the host.

And then we find the Ancient of Days opening the books. God keeps very careful books. Some people think that everything has to be reckoned with here in this life. That's not so. It's better just to let go of some things in which we can't get a fair shake. For example, some deacon, some elder may have ripped apart a servant of God. (You know, some of God's people bite, and they bite badly!) We may have done everything we could do, but there still is no fairness, no equity, no justice. Leave it on the books, for the biblical text says that God keeps everything there. We might wonder, Will this affect salvation? No, that record is kept in the Book of Life. It's much better to have our names in the Book of Life as having believed, for that determines our eternal destiny.

But this is important, because we have verses like 2 Corinthians 5:10, "For we must all appear"—Does this say *all*? Yes!—"we must all appear before the judgment seat of Christ to give an account of deeds done in the body, whether good or bad." We might ask, What is that for? It's for fruit inspection. God is going to inspect the fruits not only of the believer but also of the unbeliever. He is going to ask, "So what did you do with your three score and ten years? Or has it been four score or more? What did you do with your life?"

So here the books are opened. As the Son of Man approaches, the Ancient of Days gives to him all authority, all glory, all sovereign power, all peoples, all languages, all worship, all dominion, and a kingdom that will never be destroyed. I can't imagine a higher point in the teaching on the kingdom of God.

Daniel 7 tells us that Daniel was troubled in spirit and the visions passing through his mind disturbed him. So he approached one of those standing there and asked him the true meaning of all this. I'm so glad Daniel is a little dense at times. He says, "Huh?" That helps us enormously, because when Daniel was asked, "Do you understand?" he said, "No, my lord." And then he was given the explanation; it was revealed to him. That is why the first eight or nine chapters of Daniel are so easy; they are self-explaining.

That adds to my argument that the prophets did understand what they wrote. Otherwise, they did not have anything revealed, uncovered, made bare to them. That's the whole nature of revelation; it is a disclosure. Verses 16-17 say, "So he told me and gave me the interpretation of these things: 'The four great beasts are four kingdoms ...'" (NIV). Well, that settles that! I don't see how we can quibble with the text. And he says these kingdoms "will rise from the earth." That is why he saw them coming up out of the sea of men. "But the saints of the Most High will receive the kingdom and will possess it forever—yes, for ever and ever" (v. 18, NIV). That's clear, too.

In verse 20 Daniel is saying, "Then I wanted to know the true meaning of the fourth beast, and also I wanted to know about the ten horns, and about the other horn, and about the horn that looked more imposing than the others, that had eyes and a big mouth." Verse 21 continues, "As I watched, this horn was waging war against the saints and defeating them, until the Ancient of Days came and pronounced judgment in favor of the saints of the Most High, and the time came when they possessed the kingdom. He gave me this explanation ..." (NIV). Thank you! That will help me understand! "He gave me this explanation: 'The fourth beast is a fourth kingdom that will appear on earth.'" Oh, okay, it's not spiritual; it's real. "'It will be different from all the other kingdoms and will devour the whole earth ...'" (NIV). Does this text mean to say that Western economies will just take over the whole world situation, trampling it down and crushing it? It sounds that way.

What about the ten horns? "'The ten horns are ten kings who will come from this kingdom. After them another king will arise'"—oh, yeah,

Big Mouth—"'different from the earlier ones; he will subdue three kings. He will speak against the Most High and oppress his saints and try to change the set times and the laws'" (NIV). I take it he's going to try to get rid of Sunday. Economists note our heated-up economy which keeps on heating up and they can't figure out what's wrong with it. They don't know that it must be 'turned down' one day out of seven. That's the only way to keep an economy going. But we're going to keep on burning it out. Christians are not understanding that either.

"'The saints will be handed over to him for a time, times and half a time'" (v. 25, NIV). From our study of other passages, this sounds like three and a half years. It is probably near the end of the seventieth week, i.e., the last seven years before the whole thing collapses.

He says, "'But the court will sit, and his power will be taken away and completely destroyed forever. Then the sovereignty, power and greatness of the kingdoms under the whole heaven will be handed over to the saints, the people of the Most High. His kingdom will be an everlasting kingdom, and all rulers will worship and obey him'" (vv. 26-27, NIV). So stripped of his power, the little horn's sovereignty (i.e., Antichrist's sovereignty) and his greatness and his dominion will be handed over to believers, to the saints, to the people of the Most High, and this will be given to them as an everlasting kingdom. I understand this to mean that the Son of Man and the saints of the Most High will be given all authority, all power, all dominion. True worship will be received by God, as it was intended to be offered. And I take it that therefore all rulers and peoples on earth will worship and obey him.

## Conclusion

The conclusion to this has to be the same as the conclusion to that famous section at the end of 1 Chronicles: worship and thanksgiving for the kingdom of David's son, the Messiah. In the postexilic time, the chronicler wrote of the normativeness of David and Solomon as a pattern, a type, of what was to come in the kingdom of God. Second Chronicles, especially, is a great book of revivals. But more than that, if Isaiah is the most theological book in the Old Testament, and if Exodus is the second, I would put 1 and 2 Chronicles in third place as the third most theological books in the Old Testament.

We recall that in 1 Chronicles 29 David asked for voluntary offerings so Solomon could build the temple, and the people and their leaders gave generously; they gave way beyond what was expected of them. In verses 9-13,

> The people rejoiced .... David the king also rejoiced greatly. David praised the LORD in the presence of the whole assembly, saying,

"Praise be to you, O LORD, God of our father Israel, from everlasting to everlasting. Yours, O LORD, is the greatness and the power and the glory and the majesty and the splendor, for everything in heaven and earth is yours. Yours, O LORD, is the kingdom; you are exalted as head over all. Wealth and honor come from you; you are ruler of all things. In your hands are strength and power to exalt and give strength to all. Now, our God, we give you thanks, and praise your glorious name" (NIV).

We find mention of the kingdom right in the middle of this prayer.

As I wrote in *Toward an Old Testament Theology* (p. 261),

... the focus on the temple, the ordinances connected with the temple, and the emphasis on music and prayer in times of revival and worship were a fitting doxology to the one to whom the kingdom belonged and whose reign had already begun in believers but was yet to have its total sway over heaven and earth. That ancient prophetic word of promise had not failed, nor would it.

We conclude this teaching on Daniel, the theologian of the kingdom. Two great chapters give us the main thrust: Daniel 2 and Daniel 7. There's much more in Daniel, especially Nebuchadnezzar's experience at the end of Daniel 4, which we have linked with Daniel 2. But it is clear here that the kingdom of God speaks of the rule and the reign of God, which will be absolute and total. And thereby this indicates that it will be a realm, as well, which takes in everything. We conclude that God's kingdom is part of his everlasting promise-plan. God said a king would come. He said he would give a throne. He said he would give a dynasty. He said he would give a kingdom.

And now Daniel tells us how the kingdom of God will come suddenly. It will come as an 'inbursting'. We don't even see the action of the stone. To speak of the stone's falling would be incorrect; there is no indication of that at all. We just see it arrive. It hits the feet of the monster image—the colossal image—and destroys the whole thing! Then it grows and grows and grows until it fills, literally, the whole earth. This is the kingdom of God, as taught here in the book of Daniel. It is one of the great themes in the promise doctrine and is elaborated on in the New Testament. When Jesus came, this was the heart of his message: He came announcing and preaching that we should get ready, "for the kingdom of God is at hand."

# Chapter Twenty-Three

# Theologians of God's Coming Conquering Hero

## Haggai, Zechariah, Malachi

Haggai, Zechariah, and Malachi are the three post-exilic prophets sent by God during those days of pain, economic recovery, and sluggish progress of a defeated nation now returned from exile. To get a sense of how defeated the people were we must realize they had seen the majesty of the glory of Judah literally go up in smoke. It had seemed to them as if the promise of God had gone up in smoke, too, for the temple lay in ruins; the Davidic dynasty lay in ruins; the whole kingdom of God seemed to have come to a grinding halt. When Cyrus, in a most magnificent gesture, said, "Look, my policy is repatriation; let the people return to their land once again," the response was that very few went back to their land.

We come, then, to the final part in the scheme of the promise-plan of God. This program of God has many aspects, but it is seen as a single promise-plan and a single program, with one people of God. Even in the term 'people of God', which is single-fold, we will be able to distinguish multiple aspects, such as Israel and the church. We call this an *epangelical* (the Greek word for *promise*) scheme.

We can visualize this developing promise of God in the shape of a cornucopia, a horn of plenty. Starting at the small end with the seminal idea of Genesis 3:15 of the blessing of the seed of Eve, it then begins to widen. From the very beginning we are told that a few of the elements have a planned obsolescence; that these elements are only the models, shadows of things to come. Exodus 25:40 and other verses indicate that the tabernacle, its services, and the priesthood will have only limited duration; the symbols will pass away when the reality comes. "See that you make them according to the *pattern* shown you on the mountain" (NIV).

The cornucopia shape continues expanding as more elements of the promise-plan are detailed in each successive period of time, starting with the *Prolegomena to the Promise*, the pre-patriarchal era (Gen 1–11); moving through the Preparations or the *Provisions for the Promise* in the patriarchal period (Gen 12–50); on to the *People of the Promise* during the time of the Exodus; to the *Place of the Promise,* where God gave them a land, a rest, and an inheritance. History continues with the *King of Promise* during the days of David, when God gave a throne, a dynasty, a kingdom, and a charter— a law for all of humanity; and with *Life in the Promise,* during the time of Proverbs and Ecclesiastes, with its teaching about the fear of the Lord that was wisdom, that was life. Then, the *Day of Promise* focuses on the out-pouring of the Holy Spirit. The *Servant of the Promise,* with the Isaiah group of prophets, teaches us that God would raise up David's fallen hut once again. What had been the majestic house of David was now in a delapidated state, but God would raise it up. And even the Gentiles would come to it. The cornucopia continues expanding with the *Renewal of the Promise,* the new covenant, which we understand to be a renewal of the old covenant plus new additions to what God previously said. Habakkuk, along with Jeremiah and Zephaniah, promised once again the *Day of the Lord,* and the 'just shall live by faith'. The mouth of the cornucopia widens still more with the *Kingdom of the Promise,* the kingdom of God, where we have Ezekiel and Daniel in their days of exile.

This brings us up to the point where the exile is over. We want to talk, finally, about the *Triumph of the Promise.* During the post-exilic time we can see the one program and the one people of God. We can see that this word *epangelical* brings it all together: *epangelia,* the Greek word, means 'the promise of God'. The people of God have been given permission to return to their native land after seventy years of sitting in exile. Daniel and his three friends left their homeland in 606-605 BC; it is now 536 BC; it is time to go home!

We would expect a massive response to the possibility of going home, but the truth of the matter is that there was a very poor response. Zerubbabel led the first return about 536 BC, with just under 50,000 people. Most opted to stay in Babylon, saying, "Our roots are now in Babylon, Mesopotamia; we want to stay here in Iraq." So they stayed. There was a second return under Ezra in 457 BC. It too was, in comparison, a very small group. Then finally, Nehemiah himself gave up a very, very high post in government and led a third group in 445 BC. He was the king's cupbearer. He was not just the taster of the wine; he was secretary of state, second in command! And he gave up this position, at least for the moment, in order to go home.

On the first return, in 536 BC, the people were exceedingly happy; they couldn't have been more enthusiastic. The approximately 50,000 people dug in immediately and started to clear the burned-out shell of the temple and to set up the foundation. They agreed, "This is terrible; look at the temple!" But there was division in their house, as there is in most church meetings. Some of the older folks hesitated: "We're building too small.

We're building too early. I tell you, we should wait a bit." The younger folks said, "Let's get it going!" The 'to build' faction won and started building. The book of Ezra says that between the crying and the rejoicing, you couldn't tell which group was which. What a cacophony! Some were moaning and saying, "This is like a game of tiddlywinks; this temple is so rinky-dink in comparison to the one we knew years ago." Some of the people had seen Solomon's temple, and this was not going to be any Solomon's temple! This was a mere shadow of that one. So what did they do? They quit! They discouraged each other. The biblical phrase is they 'weakened the hands of each other', a phrase popularized during Jeremiah's days. And so, for sixteen years, they did nothing. There was no center of worship; there was no corporate worship. The people raised a whole generation of children who did not even know what the house of God was like. It would have been better had they stayed in Babylon where there was a synagogue, which had become the center and the start of what we call *Judaism*.

Don't confuse Old Testament theology and teaching with Judaism! They are two different things. Though there are continuities, there are some strong discontinuities which were introduced as a result of the exile. Judaism has the *synagogue* as the center rather than the temple. And whereas the Old Testament faith had the prophet and the priest as the center, now *the scribe* has become the center in Judaism.

For sixteen years the Jews did nothing about rebuilding the temple, and then God sent Haggai. The name *Haggai* is like the word *festival*, the same name in the feminine form as our Hilary; it means 'my feast'. God also sent Zechariah, whose name means 'God remembers'. These two men began their ministries in the year 520 BC and continued for two years, down to 518 BC. At least in the case of Zechariah this was true. Later on, perhaps about 450 BC, God sent Malachi, the last in the series of prophets and the one through whom he gave the last of Old Testament revelation.

## The Promise of God's Signet Ring

What shall we say about the ministry of these men? We will consider three theological affirmations. The first theological formulation we can make about the *Triumph of the Promise* of God is to be seen in Haggai. I think we can summarize the theology of Haggai as the promise of God's signet ring. The reference to the signet ring comes at the end of the book, Haggai 2:20-23.

### Haggai's Call to Renew the Work of God

But before we look more closely at the signet ring passage, let's look at a series of calls or messages in Haggai. This man gives four messages which are dated very precisely. The first message comes in the second year of King Darius on the first day of the sixth month. That translates on our Julian calendar as August 29, 520 BC. I don't know of any disagreement on this date among scholars. Notice that we have now moved away from dating things according to the people of God or to the kings of Judah, or even to the messianic line. We are now in *the times of the Gentiles*: it is in the second year of King Darius. That is one clue as to the date.

The second thing is that it is the New Moon; it's the first day. It is a time of celebrating and remembering, for it is the sixth month, which is the end of the harvest season. The harvest is past and the summer is gone. Without refrigeration, this means the end of the fruit that has come in. I think there also is a mournful note here, such as we find in the book of Jeremiah, where he says, "The summer is past and the harvest is over, and we are not saved." Or as we find in Amos 8, where Amos recounts how, in a vision, God showed him a basket of summer fruit at the end of the harvest season and asked him, "What do you see?" In the answer of Amos and in God's subsequent remark we find a pun in Hebrew; the Hebrew words for 'end' and 'fruit' sound alike. Amos replied, "A basket of summer fruit," *qayets* in Hebrew. "Then said the LORD unto me, The end is come upon my people of Israel; I will not again pass by them any more" (v. 2, AV). Here the Hebrew word for 'end' is *qets*. Indeed, the end has come; it is the second year of King Darius, 520 BC.

And so "In the second year of King Darius, on the first day of the sixth month, the word of the LORD came through the prophet Haggai to Zerubbabel son of Shealtiel, governor of Judah ..." (Hag 1:1, NIV). This Zerubbabel was in the Davidic line, so we are seeing here another reference to the promise made to Abraham, Isaac, Jacob, and David. God's word was still being propagated. Here was an earnest; here was a down payment on the one who was finally to come.

The word also came "to Joshua son of Jehozadak, the high priest: This is what the LORD of hosts says: 'These people say, "The time has not yet come for the LORD's house to be built"'" (NIV). When they used the word *time*, they were using a circumlocution. It was a roundabout way of saying that it was God's fault, but they didn't want to refer to him directly.

I would simply entitle Haggai's message "A Call to Renew the Work of God." It wasn't a call to start a building program. Often we get the message of Haggai out when the church is going to build a new auditorium or an extension to the Sunday school plant. But the point is that to build the temple or to build the house of God—or not to build it—is only symptomatic of what is happening in the heart with regard to worship of the living God. So I understand this passage to be about ways to renew the work of God.

*The first way to renew the work of God is to refuse to make excuses.* These people were making excuses. They were saying, "We have not normalized relations with the Persians yet. There is still inflation. There are all sorts of reasons why we shouldn't do this. Don't build! Don't build!" And God said, "'This people are saying"—or "these people are saying," if you want to look at them in the plural concept—"These people are saying, 'The time has not yet come ....'" They were using their own problems as the reason for having done nothing on the house of God for sixteen years. But this was only symptomatic of their spiritual condition.

*The second way to renew the work of God is by setting priorities* (vv. 3-6). "Then the word of the LORD came through the prophet Haggai: 'Is it a time for you yourselves to be living in your paneled houses, while this house remains a ruin?'" (NIV). This verse is not an occasion to take free shots at materialism. Materialism is a bad thing, but God's people can become schizophrenic by focusing too much on this. The point was not that they were in fine homes; that may or may not have been a problem. But the point was, "How is it that you are able to build your own homes, and you are not able to build God's house?" Some people when they look at a building project react, "This is going to cost $300,000! Or maybe even $500,000!" Now, it is curious that some of the people who react this way live in homes that cost that much or more. And they don't even see this cost being shared, corporately and collectively. Then, of course, we get the odd argument against building: "We're only going to use the building one day a week." To which I answer, What about the tabernacle? The Holy of Holies was used only one day a year; yet that project was probably something on the order of two billion dollars.

The priority here is, he says, "Now this is what the LORD of hosts says: 'Give careful thought to your ways'" (v. 5). He is saying, Think this one over; ponder this one in your heart. Are you planting more and harvesting less? Are you eating more and enjoying it less? Are you drinking more and finding it less filling? Are you putting on clothes but you are not warm? Are you earning wages only to put them in a purse with holes in it? Have you noticed that?

To which people say, "That's my own business." And God says, "No, I've been trying to get through to you. You say relations haven't normalized yet. You say that the living wage isn't up to par. You say that inflation is really a thief." (And of course, inflation is a form of thievery. In our day, now that we have moved off the gold standard, all we have to do is watch the papers for M1 and M2, the money supply, to understand how much thievery is going on. For when more dollars are printed in order to pay the bill of the government, I want you to understand, the government has dipped into the pockets of all the citizens. It is a form of theft.)

I understand this passage in Haggai 1 to be saying, "Hey! Set priorities." It should be God's work ahead of our work, God's house ahead of our house. So the Bible teaches. It needs to be proclaimed in our day and age. If we don't think so, then we have missed the point that there is a connection between our spiritual development and the way the natural world works!

When people get into trouble spiritually, the natural world starts getting into trouble, too; the productivity of the farm goes down. This is because when sin entered the world, there also came a judgment on the natural world. Romans 8 says that the whole creation is waiting for the final redemption that is found in Christ Jesus the Lord. There is to be a final, total victory which includes even the atmosphere, the elements, the productivity of the land. But in the meantime, substantial healing can come whenever God's people in a certain locale become serious about him. Blessing on the majority for the sake of the few comes when the moral remnant, the moral minority , responds to the preaching. So here Haggai was trying to urge people to renew the work of God.

Then God continued, helping the people get the point. "Because of my house, which remains a *hareb*—a ruin, while each of you is busy with his own house ... I called for a *horeb*—a drought—on the fields ..." (vv. 9-11). As a pun he used the other word for Mt. Sinai: Mt. Horeb, which means a dry, desolate place. A little bit of poetic justice here. It is not that God was vindictive, but rather, he wanted to get their attention. The love of God said, "You can't hear me! You're tone deaf. In sixteen years you've done nothing on the temple since laying the foundations in 536 BC? All right, I'll get your attention: the fields just won't yield much."

We might say, "The jet stream can explain that. That's all it is. The weather man can give us the reason why crops were not so good this year." I suppose so; but the biblical text in verse 9 tells us that God says, "You expected much, but see, it turned out to be little. What you brought home, I blew away. Why? ... Because of my house which remains a *hareb*—a ruin, while each of you is busy with his own house."

*The third way in which we renew the work of God is by getting involved* (vv. 7-11). We must refuse to make excuses, we must set priorities, and we must get involved. God said, "Hey, I want you to give careful thought to this once again. Think about this. Go up to the mountains and bring down timber and build the house, so that I may take pleasure in it and I may get honor to myself." There's an amazing thing in that verse! Why did they have to cut down more timber? Wasn't it true that sixteen years previously Cyrus had given them all the building materials they needed? What happened to those materials? I have two suggestions, neither of which I like. One is that they pilfered the lumber; that was where they got the material for their paneled homes. They stole off the job! The other possibility is that the wood rotted, and they had to get other timber.

Why did God tell them to build the temple? "Do this so that I may take pleasure in it, and I may get honor." The purpose of obedience and getting involved in the work of God is for his honor. We might wonder, What's the alternative? The alternative is in verse 9: "You expected it to be much, but, see, it turned out to be little." This alternative is pretty bad: shortages of time, shortages of material, shortages of everything. Why?

The Lord said, Because of my house, which is a ruin while you are busy, each of you, with your own home.

The lesson here is that the work of God should come before our work, before my work. The events of life, said old T. V. Moore, a Puritan commentator, are like hieroglyphics, the key to which can be found in Scripture. So the very events of life—droughts, a great corn or soybean crop, how things go this spring, this summer, this fall—are dependent to a great degree on the faithful preaching of the Word and the people's response. I submit this thought to you: to teach less is to be overly cautious and to understate the Word of God. So in this case God said, "I called for a drought on the fields and the mountains, on the grain, the new wine, the oil and whatever the ground produces, on men and cattle, and on the labor of your hands" (NIV). I don't believe that this message was meant for Israeli ears alone; God stated it in principle and universal form.

About this time we say, So that's what this passage is teaching: we must refuse to make excuses; we must set priorities; we must get involved. But if we conclude our study of this text here, we miss the point. Or if we say, "Boy, if only there were some gospel, some good news, some grace here," without much hope of finding that good news, we also miss the point. I must tell you that the good news is here! "Then Zerubbabel son of Shealtiel, Joshua son of Jehozadak, the high priest, and the whole remnant of the people obeyed the voice of the LORD their God and the message of the prophet Haggai, because the LORD their God had sent him. And the people feared the LORD" (NIV). And what was the basis for this fear of the Lord? In verse 13 we are told that the Lord said, "I am with you." I understand this text to say that *a fourth way we can renew the work of God is by receiving God's enablement*, because he promises, "I am with you." Emmanuel! "So the LORD stirred up the spirit of Zerubbabel son of Shealtiel, governor of Judah, and the spirit of Joshua son of Jehozadak, the high priest, and the spirit of the whole remnant of the people. They came and began to work on the house of the Lord Almighty, their God, on the twenty-fourth day of the sixth month in the second year of King Darius" (vv. 14-15, NIV). So it took only from August 29, 520 BC, to September 21, 520 BC, for the preaching to make an impact. That's actually pretty good! That's great preaching! And it was a great message from God.

### God's Promise of the Desire of the Nations

Another message from God is found in Haggai 2:1-9. This is God's promise about the *desire of the nations*, which is a messianic note. He says, "I will shake all nations, and the desire of all nations will come ...." Most people, as do most translations, avoid interpreting 'the desire' to be messianic because it is followed by a plural verb. It is generally translated, in several modern translations, as 'the valuable things' or 'the treasuries'.

But I must tell you that the word does occur in the plural when referring to one person. The plural is used in referring to Daniel, 'the desired one'. In other cases, it is in the singular. Here, the plural verb does not indicate that the subject should be plural, 'desired ones' or 'treasuries' or 'precious things', but rather that it is the one, 'the Desire' of all nations. This phrase has been made popular through Christmas hymns: "the Desire of the nations come." In the hymn "Come, Thou Long-expected Jesus," the first verse ends with "Dear Desire of every nation, Joy of every longing heart." I have tried to treat it in *The Hard Sayings of the Old Testament*, published by InterVarsity, and in my *Messiah in the Old Testament*. Contrary to most Bible translations, I think this means that God will bring his special person, the one whom the nations really desire and look for.

### Haggai's Warning that Holiness Was Not Catchy

Haggai goes on to give his third message: his warning that holiness is not contagious (2:10-19). He is saying, "You can't catch holiness. You can catch sin, but you can't catch holiness."

### God's Signet Ring

Then, finally, comes the great *signet ring* passage in Haggai 2, where the word of the Lord came a second time on December 18, 520 BC on our calendars. Lo and behold, verses 20-23 tell us, "The word of the LORD came to Haggai a second time on the twenty-fourth day of the month: 'Tell Zerubbabel governor of Judah that I will shake the heavens and the earth. I will overturn royal thrones and shatter the power of the foreign kingdoms. I will overthrow chariots and their drivers; horses and their riders will fall, each by the sword of his brother. "On that day," declares the LORD Almighty, "I will take you, my servant Zerubbabel son of Shealtiel," declares the LORD, "and I will make you like my signet ring, for I have chosen you," declares the LORD Almighty'" (NIV).

This great text has many allusions to past history. Notice how God talked about the future in terms of the past. Just as God had overthrown or overturned Sodom and Gomorrah in Deuteronomy 29:23, he said here, "I will overturn ...." When God said that the horses and the riders would go down, he was referring to the past experience in Exodus 15:1, Miriam's great song, "The horse and the rider will go down." I'm giving you the literal Hebrew translation.

Haggai spoke of the mass confusion that day would bring: "... each one by the sword of his brother." That is a reference straight out of Judges 7:22. He talked about the victory of God in the final day in terms of Gideon's victory over the Midianites. Gideon was told to choose three hundred soldiers and divide them into three companies. Each of the three hundred soldiers was given a trumpet and an empty jar with a lit torch inside. With these items, the Israelites were to fight the opposing army of 135,000 soldiers. "'Watch me,' [Gideon] told them. 'Follow my lead. When I get to the edge of the camp, do exactly as I do. When I and all who are with me blow our trumpets, then from all around the camp blow yours and shout, "For the LORD and for Gideon."' Gideon and the hundred men with him reached the edge of the camp at the beginning of the middle watch, just after they had changed the guard. They blew their trumpets and broke the jars that were in their hands" (Judg 7:17-19, NIV). And out of the jars the flames shone brightly, so that the Midianites thought there were three hundred columns when there were only three hundred men. The Midianites got up in the middle of the night, each looking for his sword and pointing out things to his companions in a lethal way. And so the text in Haggai says here, "Each will fall by the sword of his brother."

That's what the future battle of God is going to be like when he brings things to a climax in the final day. It will be like overthrowing Sodom and Gomorrah, like Pharaoh and his chariots drowning in the Red Sea, and like the day of Gideon, with the enemy falling by the sword of their own brothers.

On that day, the text continues, God Almighty will say that this is "my servant" (Hag 2:23). Do you notice the messianic term there? Then he connects that *Servant of the LORD* with a *signet ring*. The signet ring was the seal of authority, just as we use a seal for the President of the United States of America to indicate the authority of his person and his office. When the President speaks or appears in person, he is accompanied by the presidential seal. Here the seal was a signet ring. It was the signet ring that was taken from the line of David back in Jeremiah 22:24, where we have the Davidic king Jehoiachin. There was a line of descent from David to Solomon, coming through Rehoboam, all the way down to this fellow, Jehoiachin, where it came to an end, because God said, "Write this man childless." Actually, Jehoiachin had five sons, but they were all carried off into captivity and were made eunuchs (Isa 39:7). So there were no descendants of Jehoiachin.

However, the line continued through another of David's numerous sons, Nathan (not to be confused with Nathan the prophet). The line of descent swung over to Nathan's line, and we have this line now coming down through Zerubbabel. I won't trace all the details of the line of descent; it's a little difficult in spots. But that is essentially what was happening. And here God gives his servant the seal of authority which was taken abruptly from Jehoiachin in Jeremiah 22:24 and was given to another in the Davidic line. Thus God showed to the world that he intended to continue fulfilling his ancient promise. These are "the sure mercies of David," to use a phrase from Isaiah 55:3 (AV).

So Haggai is the prophet with whom we connect the signet ring and the messianic person who is the Messiah, who is God's victor in the final day.

## God's Final Day of Victory

Now we turn to the prophet Zechariah, where we have another theological formulation: God's victory in the final day. We find two 'burden' messages in Zechariah 9–14. In a number of Bible translations, the heading for Zechariah 9 and 12 is "An Oracle." But I don't like the translation of *massa* as 'oracle'. In all the references in my personal studies, *massa* is a *burden*; it is a weight; it is something difficult to pick up. Zechariah 9–11 deals with the first burden, generally with the first advent of our Lord. Then Zechariah 12–14 deals with the second coming of our Lord.

### The Two Burden Messages

We begin with the first burden message, starting out with Alexander the Great (Zech 9). Though it is not mentioned in the text, it is clear that he came through Damascus to Tyre, and cleaned up Tyre. We recall that Nebuchadnezzar, even after thirteen years, had not really been able to conquer Tyre. He had taken the mainland city; but the people just moved a half mile out into the Mediterranean Sea, set up the city of Tyre again, and kept on going. Then Alexander came along. Even he was unsuccessful in the first naval engagement; they defeated him. But Alexander was indomitable; he was not going to be beaten on this. So he took the remains of the old city, as the book of Ezekiel says, and he scraped the site clean and dumped the rubble into the Mediterranean Sea, using the rubble to build a causeway one-half mile out to sea—right out to the island. Then he marched his troops out on the causeway. Our text is talking about some of this in chapter 9. Alexander was victorious as part of God's judgment on the Gentile nations.

But the interesting thing is that in the midst of this military prowess, verse 9 says that Israel's true king, Messiah, will be inaugurated into office in the typical manner in which kings were installed in that day, by riding into town on a donkey. His character is given here as being righteous, as 'having salvation', as being gentle, meek, and humble. That is true. He is shown here as one being afflicted, which is somewhat similar to the Isaiah 53 passage. Even though this king in Zechariah 9:9 is the Messiah, and even though he comes in a very gentle, humble, yet righteous way, he will be victorious. He will destroy the implements of war. Zechariah 9:10 says, "I will take away the chariots from Ephraim and the war-horses from Jerusalem, and the battle bow will be broken" (NIV). But more than that, "He [the Messiah] will proclaim peace to the nations. His rule will extend from sea to sea and from the River [the Euphrates] to the ends of the earth" (NIV). That is a way of saying that there is no end: it goes all the way past the sunset. We are given an indication of his destruction of all implements of war and of a period of peace over the whole earth. *Shalom!* Down with war! This compares favorably with Isaiah 9 and 11, and also with Micah 5:2-5.

### Earth's Last Battle

Earth's last day battle comes in Zechariah 14, where we find a very interesting thing. It is now the Day of the Lord; we are getting ready for the final act: earth's worst moment. Winston Churchill is known for that famous phrase "their finest hour," but here we have "the worst moment" on earth. It is called the *Day of the Lord*, which is not a 24-hour day, but is that period of time when God concludes the whole eschatological epoch. Zechariah 14:2 says, "I will gather all nations to Jerusalem." We saw this in Joel 3, but now it is spelled out more fully. All nations will come to Jerusalem, I take it, to settle the Jewish question.

Secondly, God has selected this day as one in which he himself will personally intervene. For in that day, the text says, after half the city has gone into exile and has experienced the horror of war—houses ransacked, women raped, the city captured, the people terrified—"Then the LORD will go out and fight against those nations, as he fights in the day of battle. On that day his feet will stand on the Mount of Olives, east of Jerusalem." (vv. 3-4, NIV). Even the created order will recognize that the king of glory has come back, for as I understand it, the text is saying that the Mount of Olives will come unglued, literally. There exists a rift and a fault line which goes north and south; but this split goes east to west, and will extend, I take it, through Jerusalem itself, and some think perhaps out to the Mediterranean Sea. One thing is certain: it will open up a magnificent valley. Mount Scopas, on the north part of the Mount of Olives, with the Hebrew University and the Hadassah Hospital, will be split off to the north. The rest of the mountain will go south. The biblical text dares to call the shots before the event happens. If you have never read or heard about this before, remember that you heard it here first! One half of the mountain will move north and the other half will move south.

Now, I have been to Israel several times, and I've checked this out; it is still together, all in one piece. This has not yet happened. Although the prophet wrote the prophecy in 518 BC, we must still wait. But it is sure to happen. So if you have problems with the hermeneutics here and you wonder how a prophecy given over two thousand years ago should be treated, just remember that if indeed you do hear a news flash that this thing is dividing, then you know the great Day of the Lord is happening. "On that day there will be no light, no cold or frost. It will be a unique day, without daytime or nighttime—a day known to the LORD. When evening comes, there will be light. On that day living water will flow out from Jerusalem, half to the eastern sea and half to the western sea ..." (vv. 6-8, NIV). That is a body of water we have never seen before; there's a division with a stream running out. It sounds something like what we read in Ezekiel, too.

We read the most amazing thing in Zechariah 14:9: "The LORD will be king over the whole earth." Period. *Shalom!* What a day that will be!

And "On that day there will be one LORD, and his name the only name" (NIV). His will be the only name. *The only name.*

This is a fantastic statement about the day when the Messiah will return to the Mount of Olives! As the angels said in Acts, "You men of Galilee, why stand ye here gazing? This same Jesus shall come again in like manner." Tourist guides to the Mount of Olives will point out the footprints of Jesus as he left the earth. Actually, I think concrete came into use a bit too late for them to get his footprints! But indeed, they think they can show you the exact spot on the Mount of Olives where he left this earth. This text is also talking about the fact that he will come back, and that he will come to this place; and he will be king over the whole earth.

## The Messenger of the Covenant

The third theological affirmation is from the prophet Malachi, the messenger of the covenant.

### The Search for the God of Justice Is Ended

The book of Malachi is a delightful book because it asks the questions we would want to ask. There is audience participation: "Who, us? We did that? When did we ever do that?" It reminds me of when my wife and I were house-parents for thirteen students the first year we were married. We shared a bath with five of them. And I remember, about February, there was such a great clatter over my head about 2:00 a.m. that I sprang to my feet to see what was the matter. I got up to the bathroom only to see balloons and water all over the place, and the wallpaper coming off! I said to the thirteen, "Gentlemen, gentlemen! Who did this?" They all seemed to be as concerned as I was. "Yeah, who did this?"

Now, this was a Christian school and they were saying, "Who, us?" They didn't say, "We didn't do it." That would have been lying. But they did want to join in my concern. That's what I think of when I look at this book of Malachi. "Who, us? We did this?" In Malachi 2:17 the text says, "You have wearied the LORD with your words." And the people said in essence, "Who, us? We've wearied him? How have we wearied him? Have we wearied him by saying, 'All who do evil are good in the eyes of the LORD, and he is pleased with them'? or 'Where is the God of justice?'"

The answer is given in chapter 3. "'See, I will send my messenger, who will prepare the way before me. Then suddenly the LORD you are seeking will come to his temple; the messenger of the covenant, whom you desire, will come,' says the LORD Almighty" (Mal 3:1, NIV). Basically the text is saying, You say you are looking for the God of justice? You're not really, you know; but if you want to pretend that you're looking, behold, he will come! And so we will have the search for the God of justice which ends with the Lord Jesus coming to his temple. He will be preceded by a messenger, John the Baptist, who will prepare the way before him. He is also the owner of the temple; he is the Lord; he is called the messenger of the covenant. And so, we have here again another great prophecy of the Messiah in the Lord Jesus.

### The Distinctions on the Day of the Lord

The text tells us, from Malachi 3:16 through the end of the book, that distinctions will be made in the Day of the Lord between those who fear him and those who do not serve the Lord. "'Surely the day is coming; it will burn like a furnace. All the arrogant and every evildoer will be stubble, and that day that is coming will set them on fire,' says the LORD Almighty. 'Not a root or a branch will be left to them'" (Mal 4:1, NIV). Verse 2 says, "But for you who revere my name, the sun of righteousness will rise with healing in its wings. And you will go out and leap like calves released from the stall" (NIV). The people will rejoice like calves going out to pasture for the first time in the spring. They'll kick up their heels! Look out!

Just as John the Baptist was a forerunner of the Messiah in the first coming, the book ends with a reference to Elijah the prophet as a forerunner of the second coming. As I say in *Toward an Old Testament Theology* (pp. 257-58):

> The forerunner is first presented as a "messenger" (3:1) and then as "Elijah the prophet" (4:5). Probably we are not to think of Elijah the Tishbite, a fact sometimes encouraged by Elijah's translation into heaven without experiencing death. But after the analogy of that new or second David, so there was to be a new or second Elijah. He would be a man in the "spirit and power" of Elijah, even as Jesus pointed to John the Baptist and said that he was Elijah, for he came in the "spirit and power of Elijah."

Yes, Haggai, Zechariah, and Malachi are those theologians who are announcers of God's coming conquering hero, even the Son of God.

# Chapter Twenty-Four

# The Continuation of the Old Testament Promise in the New Testament

I have titled this chapter "The Continuation of the Old Testament Promise in the New Testament" because the greatest fulfillment of the promise is the person and work of Jesus Christ. The argument of these chapters, and I believe of the Old Testament and New Testament, too, is that when Jehovah, or *Yahweh*, called Abraham, he gave a promise through him to the whole human race. "In your seed shall all the nations of the earth be blessed" (Gen 12:3). The history of Israel is an unfolding of that promise. So it is not just a prediction which will wait for fulfillment. Rather, the very means by which God will keep that promise alive is seen in the history of Israel. The promise was renewed with David and preached by all the prophets. It is not just a prediction, but it is also a principle by which men can live, for it is to result in a holiness of life. This is much like Peter's position when he argues, With the coming of the Lord, what sort of holy people ought we to be? So it is with the prophets. Immediately after the promise is made, it begins to be fulfilled. There is never a time lag which sees no fulfillments; it is being progressively fulfilled, even as it waits for its ultimate fulfillment. It continues to be fulfilled, and will be until the final day.

As we have said, the greatest fulfillment of the promise-plan is in the person and work of Jesus Christ. Even through all eternity, this will be the *everlasting* promise-plan of God. This promise doctrine is the sum of what the prophets teach in the Scriptures. Now I've given to you, in its substance, a quote from Willis J. Beecher in *The Prophets and the Promise*, page 195 (New York: Thomas Crowell, 1905; reprint, Grand Rapids: Baker, 1963), where he pulls the whole thing together.

What observations can we make about the theological connections between the Old and New Testaments, and how will these observations help us in determining the great question of the relevancy of the Old Testament for the believer today?

## Cheap and Facile Contrasts between the Two Testaments

First, we have to recognize that many cheap, facile contrasts are made between the two Testaments; they are as abundant as they are wrong-headed. For example, we note attempts to excise the Old Testament from the canon.

### Attempts to Excise the Old Testament from the Church's Canon

Marcion was one individual who tried to do this, and he remains the bad guy ever since he split off from the church in AD 144. A wealthy merchant, born in Pontus on the Black Sea, he broke away from the church with his own sect. His sect continued until it was stopped by the Edict of Constantine in the fourth century. Remnants of the sect continued until the tenth century, and ghosts of Marcion are around even to the present day. What did he teach? His teaching was that the God of the Old Testament was a demi-god, a harsh, cruel kind of God, irreconcilable with the God revealed in the New Testament. He said that Jesus came down to earth like a phantom, without any earthly antecedents—no Davidic, no Abrahamic roots. Therefore, Marcion felt that all references to the Old Testament should be erased from the New Testament. Consequently, he took the 300 major direct quotes from the Old Testament and deleted them.

There is a problem with that: it's a never-ending game, because in the New Testament there are a minimum of 1,400 indirect citations or allusions to the Old Testament and a maximum of some 4,000 allusions to the Old Testament. Deleting all these references might result in a mighty small book which we could soon put on a postage stamp! That is where Marcion's Bible was headed: to a very, very small volume. Most of the New Testament references to the Jews and to the law were deleted from his canon. For example, he would not allow a verse like Romans 1:16 to stand: "For I am not ashamed of the gospel of Christ: for it is the power of God … to the Jew first …" (AV). Oops! That's no good, because the Jews are mentioned. So he took that out, as well as all references to the law. Take, for example, Romans 3:31–4:25. Out that had to go, because he said, "Are we not finished with the law?" Paul says, "No; by faith we establish the law!" But Marcion insisted that, yes, we are finished with the law. Marcion still has some would-be converts, even to the present day, who are not aware that he is their father.

Schleiermacher comes in the same vanguard. There's Adolf Harnack, too, who deliberately went back to Marcion, as many of his quotes show. The morbid Dane, Sören Kierkegaard, also agreed with cutting the Old Testament quotes out of the New Testament text, as did Friedrich Delitzsch (this is the younger Delitzsch, not the father Franz).

### Attempts to Draw Simplistic and Overdrawn Contrasts

Then there are other attempts which make simplistic, over-drawn contrasts. I give to you a very bad piece of writing from Dr. Harry Emerson Fosdick, who is not too popular in our circles. (I would guess he is not too popular with the Lord either, from what he says here.) In *Christianity and Progress* (New York: Fleming H. Revell Co., 1922, p. 209-210), he said:

> From Sinai to Calvary—was ever a record of progressive revelation more plain or more convincing? The development begins with Jehovah discovered in a thunder-storm on a desert mountain, and it ends with Christ saying: "God is a Spirit: and they that worship him must worship in spirit and truth;" it begins with a war-god leading his partisans to victory and it ends with men saying, "God is love; and he that abideth in love abideth in God, and God abideth in him;" it begins with a provincial deity loving his tribe and hating its enemies and it ends with the God of the whole earth worshiped by "a great multitude, which no man could number, out of every nation and of all tribes and peoples and tongues;" it begins with a God who commands the slaying of the Amalekites, "both man and woman, infant and suckling," and it ends with a Father whose will it is that not "one of these little ones should perish;" it begins with God's people standing afar off ... lest they die and it ends with men going into their inner chambers and, having shut the door, praying to their Father who is in secret.

Well, thus endeth that miserable quote, in which Fosdick takes cheap shots at the God of the Old Testament and the actions of the Old Testament.

With a quote like that, it was rightly deserved when a Jewish author, Claude G. Montefiore, in *The Synoptic Gospels*, answered him in the same literary style: "Very good. No doubt such a series can be arranged. Let me now arrange a similar series" (Claude G. Montefiore, ed. [London: Macmillan, 1927], 2:326). Here is a quote from Montefiore (2:326-327):

> From Old Testament to New Testament—was ever a record of retrogression more plain ...? It begins with, "Have I any pleasure at all in the death of him that dieth?"; it ends with, "Begone from me, ye doers of wickedness." It begins with, "The Lord is slow to anger and plenteous in mercy"; it ends with, "Fear him who is able to destroy both body and soul in gehenna." It begins with, "I dwell with him that is of a contrite spirit to revive it"; it ends with, "Narrow is the way which leads to life, and few there be who find it." It begins with, "I will not contend forever; I will not be always wroth"; it ends with, "Depart, ye cursed, into the everlasting fire." It begins with, "Should not I have pity upon Nineveh, that great city?"; it ends with, "It will be more endurable for Sodom on the day of Judgment than for that town." It begins with, "The Lord is good to all, and near to all who call upon him"; it ends with, "Whoever speaks against the Holy Spirit, there is no forgiveness for him whether in this world or in the next." It begins with, "The Lord will wipe away all tears from off all faces; he will

destroy death forever" [Isaiah]; it ends with, "They will throw them into the furnace of fire; there is the weeping and the gnashing of teeth."

This man argues that "the one series would be as misleading as the other" (p. 327). I say, *Touché!* At any rate, I think we have to be careful about simplistic, over-drawn contrasts between the two Testaments.

## More Recent Scholarly Solutions to the Problem of the Relationship between the Testaments

What about more recent scholarly solutions to the problem of the relationship between the Old Testament and the New? We find David Leslie Baker's 1975 doctoral dissertation helpful, in which he proposes several kinds of solutions. This was published by InterVarsity Press in 1976, but is now out of print. *Two Testaments: One Bible* is the substance of his doctoral dissertation in which he reviews three different solutions for us.

### Old Testament Solutions

For example, Arnold A. van Ruler has a suggestion: The Old Testament is the real Bible, says Ruler in *The Christian Church and the Old Testament* (Grand Rapids: Eerdmans, 1971); the New Testament is its glossary of terms. Now, I think that's unbalanced; he has gone too far in the other direction.

I should add, however, that Ruler says that the Old Testament is necessary for the church in six ways. Let me give you his six points; they are very simple:

(1) *Legitimation.* The Old Testament legitimates what Christ claimed. His claim is found in the Word that preceded it. That's a good point; I buy that.

(2) *Foundation* is the second way in which the Old Testament is necessary to the church. The basis for the church, the work of our Lord, and the Messiah who is to come is found in the Old Testament.

(3) *Interpretation.* Ruler said that the New Testament is to be found in the historical base of what God began to do in Israel with Abraham, Isaac, Jacob, and David, continuing to the Messiah.

(4) *Illustration.* Ruler said it is impossible to understand the images, the language, and the interpretation of the New Testament without understanding the background that comes from the Old.

(5) *Historicization.* Jesus the real person of history comes from the history of salvation of the Old Testament.

(6) *Eschatolization.* That is the particular kind of eschatology which operates in the Old Testament, where all time and the entire world are found in God's massive plan that concludes in the Messiah who is to come.

The list is not bad, actually, but I think Ruler undervalues the New Testament too much. When he says that the Old Testament is the real Bible and the New Testament is really an appendix or glossary of terms, he has certainly missed the progress of revelation. But he has surely found the roots of biblical revelation, all right.

Then there is also Kornelis H. Miskotte, who wrote *When the Gods Are Silent*, published in Dutch in 1956 and in English in 1967. Miskotte said that the Old Testament is an independent witness to the Name, and the New Testament is merely its sequel. Both Ruler and Miskotte give answers that put too much emphasis on the Old Testament and give too little weight to the New Testament.

### New Testament Solutions

What about New Testament solutions? This is the second of David Baker's suggestions. We turn to two other men, Rudolf Bultmann and Friedrich Baumgartel. Bultmann says that the New Testament is the essential Bible, and the Old Testament is its non-essential Christian presupposition. Baumgartel says the New Testament shows the Old Testament to be a witness to the promise of God. Yet he ends up by saying that the Old Testament is also a history of failure; it is a negative lesson.

Both of these men, Bultmann and Baumgartel, undervalue the Old Testament. In comparing the two men, we find that Bultmann would put his accent on and would preach out of the New Testament. And at least for the thirty minutes he preached each week he would say that the Bible is inspired. You understand, I'm painting with a broad brush, so in no sense should you think that the existential view Bultmann held is a view similar to mine. When he was out of the pulpit, he lived and taught as if the Bible were not inspired in the evangelical sense.

So there are some who emphasize the Old Testament to the disregard or the repudiation of the New, and there are others who emphasize the New Testament to the disregard or the repudiation of the Old. What then about other solutions? Is there a third possibility?

### Other Solutions

Well, there's Wilhelm Vischer, who says that every Old Testament text —and he does mean every one—points to some aspect of Christ's person, work, or ministry. He makes a type out of everything! In 1939 and following, he began writing from the continent, proving a typological base for every verse in the Old Testament. This he taught in his multi-volume set. I think the problem there is that he cannot show the divine designation for all of his types; and he has come up with some strange, unusual things.

Then there is the typological approach in general, which is based on the concept of *analogy* more than on the principle of Scripture. This goes back to Greek thought with the 'downstairs' (i.e., earthly) view which is supposed to be reflective of what is 'upstairs' (i.e., heavenly) by way of analogy. And so the point is that everything happening on earth in the history of mankind is a type; it is *as* or *like* something; it is an expressed comparison or an analogy. The problem there again is, Who is building the analogy? If it is *our* analogy, then it must fit *our* grid.

There is also the *history of salvation* approach in which the Old Testament was actualized in the New Testament. This approach was very popular, especially with the conservative movement, at the end of the nineteenth century. The conservative movement on the continent talked about a *heilsgeschichte*, a history of salvation. Here, the Old Testament and the New Testament form one history of the plan of salvation; and therefore, most of the biblical theologies of that period (1860s to 1890s) tried to demonstrate exactly that point.

# An Evangelical Solution to the Problem of the Relationship between the Testaments

Having considered these various possibilities, we now need to find an evangelical solution to the relationship problem of the two Testaments. Here is my attempt to be creative. My solution does not appear to fit easily into any single one of the previous three categories we have looked at. I realize it's one thing to take easy, quick, historical reviews and pot-shots, and to say, "Too much here; too little there. Selah." And then conclude with a poem and say that we have done our work.

## The Promise Continues in the New Testament

In order to present my solution, it might be helpful to attempt to put the apostolic writings in chronological order. Basically, I think we would see that James comes first; then perhaps the Synoptic Gospels; then Paul, or at least the earlier Paul in his writings up to the Prison Epistles; then the Petrine material; and finally the Johannine materials. That would cover it, basically, although some Catholic epistles are not there. The order would be: James, the Synoptics, Paul, Peter, John. Charles Ryrie has treated this a bit in his earlier work on the theology of the New Testament. I think putting it in that historical order will help us to continue what he touched on.

What would be a provisional outline for New Testament theology, if we were to extend the promise outline of this course on the Old Testament? I would like to suggest an outline, at least in seminal, provisional form.

I would start with *The Perfect Law and the Promise* as seen in Acts 15 and the book of James. The book of James, of course, is built on a homily from the law of holiness, Leviticus 19:12-18. We all know the verse on the royal law of love (James 2:8). What few people recognize is that James was doing an exegesis; indeed, the whole book of James has at least seven other verses from that same section of Leviticus. He was giving a series of lessons based on these passages. Every verse from Leviticus 19:12-18 is commented on in James, except verse 14. In my book, *The Uses of the Old Testament in the New*, you can study this more.

From The Perfect Law and the Promise, I would move to the Synoptics, with *The Kingdom of God and the Promise*. Jesus came, along with John the Baptist, proclaiming that "the kingdom of God is at hand."

Thirdly, continuing with our outline of the promise theme in the New Testament, I would title the study in the book of Acts, *The Ministry of the Holy Spirit in the Apostles of the Promise*. We will want to see the preaching of the early church there in the life of the apostles.

Then we could move on to the writings of Paul, at least up through the Prison Epistles. This I would title *The Church and the Promise*.

Then, in the Petrine literature, especially in 1 Peter, we would find the basis for *The Suffering of Believers and the Promise*.

The Johannine materials, found in the Gospel of John, the three epistles of John, and the book of Revelation, would give us *The Gospel of the Kingdom and the Promise*.

I do not have it all worked out yet, but we can see how the promise-plan of God continues with references to the perfect law of love, the kingdom of God, the Church, the ministry, the Holy Spirit, suffering, and the gospel of the kingdom.

### Key New Testament Concepts and Passages on the Promise Theme

What are some of the key New Testament concepts and passages on the promise theme, and how would we begin to develop this? *One key New Testament theme is that the promise includes the Gentiles.* We have already seen this in connection with Amos 9 and Acts 15. It seems to me that we would have to treat Acts 15 in detail. We would need to deal with a passage like Romans 15, where Paul takes pains to ground his message in the Old Testament. He takes this up as the concluding factor of the so-called soteriological tract, the book of Romans. He says in Romans 15:8-9, "For I tell you that Christ has become a servant of the Jews on behalf of God's truth, to confirm the promises made to the patriarchs so that the Gentiles may glorify God for his mercy ..." (NIV). Paul is saying, "Don't you understand what has happened here? Christ has become a servant to his people Israel, the Jews; and this is on behalf of confirming the truth that God gave to Abraham, Isaac, and Jacob about that promise-plan, so that specifically, in that seed, all the nations of the earth might be blessed." He is still harkening back to Genesis 12:3. He gives a philosophy of ministry and forms a whole biblical theology there. And then he says, "... so that the Gentiles may glorify God for his mercy."

He continues in Romans 15:9, "… as it is written …:" and he quotes from the following Old Testament texts: 2 Samuel 22:50, Psalm 18:49, Deuteronomy 32:43, Psalm 117:1, and Isaiah 11:10. He strings together these five texts, all trying to say, Don't you get my point about the *goyim*, the Gentiles? "'Therefore I will praise you among the Gentiles, O LORD; I will sing praises, I will sing hymns to your name' [2 Sam 22:50; Ps 18:49]. Again, it says, 'Rejoice, O Gentiles, with his people' [Deut 32:43]." The Gentiles join with God's people in worship and praise to his name. "And again, 'Praise the Lord, all you Gentiles, and sing praises to him, all you peoples' [Ps 117:1]. And again, Isaiah says, 'The Root of Jesse will spring up, one who will arise to rule over the *goyim*, the nations; the Gentiles will hope in him' [Isa 11:1, 10]" (NIV).

So here in Romans 15 Paul is saying, Don't you get my point? This Gentile thing is not some sort of *ab extra*, an addition. This is God working and becoming a servant of the Jews (I find that very interesting), a servant of the circumcision, on behalf of God's truth, which truth was to confirm the promise made to the patriarchs. And that is so that the Gentiles may accept him. A fantastic statement: the promise of God includes the Gentiles! as we have seen in Romans 15:7-13 and Acts 15.

*Secondly, the promise establishes rather than nullifies the law.* It is not that the Old Testament law was a troublesome burden. Paul speaks to this issue when he asks plainly in Romans 3:31, "Do we, then, nullify the law by this faith?" (NIV). Does the law run counter, or contrary, to the promise? Does the text permit us to speak of a law-gospel dichotomy? The text says, You may not! *Nein! Nix! Non! Nyet!* Not at all! The King James translation even swears: "God forbid!" NO! That is as strong as Paul can make it at this point: God forbid! *Mé genoito!* We can imagine someone saying this, stamping his foot for extra emphasis. "No, no, no! Rather, we *establish* the law by faith." This is very, very interesting, and Paul goes on to discuss it.

This is tricky. There are some real difficulties here, and I am aware of the most difficult passage in Galatians 3:15ff. It is tough going. I still think the church is going to want a seminar on law when we get to heaven, because I don't think we have been able to understand it properly. There are some tough things there to understand; there are things that have been sloughed off, that have been jettisoned because they were temporal. But on the other hand, it seems to me that we must understand what is permanent and abiding in the law.

Romans 9:30-10:15 is another passage which touches on this difficult subject of law and promise and how they function together. "What then?" asks Paul in Romans 9:30. "Are we to say that the Gentiles, who did not pursue righteousness, obtained it?" How can it be that a people who were not really interested in rightness before God were the ones to get it—a righteousness which, by the way, they got through faith? The interesting thing is that Israel, who made a law out of righteousness, did not obtain it.

I would submit to you that this is the proper way to translate Romans 9:31, *nomon dikaiosunes*: 'a law *out of* righteousness'. How is it that the people who were not really looking for it exercised faith and got it, and the people who were looking for it made a law out of it, their own law, yet missed it? It's legalism, in that sense. So they didn't get it. Notice the little Greek expression there which shows how futile it is: 'as if it were possible' to get it by works.

Paul says they stumbled. What did they stumble over? They stumbled over the Stone of offense, that Stone being messianic. They stumbled over the identity of the person. They didn't put their trust, their faith, in the proper object. The object of faith in the Old Testament, as in the New Testament, is the Son of God. So they stumbled over it. But on the other hand, did they have zeal? Oh, yes, yes, yes! Give them points for zeal, but no points for salvation. These were the real Avis people; they did try harder, much harder—so hard that it hurt! But this is not really what the text is about. For Paul goes on to say there that they also tried to achieve a righteousness which was their own (Rom 10:3). Here we have a home-made righteousness, a works righteousness, a law out of righteousness—and all three failed. All three failed, faced with the means that God offered all along in the Old Testament.

In Romans 10:5-6 Paul refers to two Old Testament verses where Moses described that kind of righteousness that is by the law. First, Paul quotes Leviticus 18:5, "The man that does these things shall live in them." I think in this verse, *in* is locative of place: "live *in the sphere of* them," not "*by means of* them." Romans continues, "But the righteousness that is by faith ...." No, we need to understand that phrase, which is a quote from Deuteronomy 30, as, "*And* the righteousness that is by faith." Paul is saying, That is the same word of faith that we are preaching: that whosoever will really confess with their mouth and believe in their heart that God hath raised him from the dead, they shall be saved. So that is the principle of the righteousness taught by Moses in the law, and the righteousness taught by faith, and the righteousness taught by Paul. Selah. That's a great section, and it seems to me very, very necessary.

*Thirdly, the promise continues with the same gospel to our day.* In Galatians 3:8, Paul tells us that Abraham was pre-evangelized when he received the good news, "In your seed shall all the nations of the earth be blessed." And Romans 1:2-4 speaks of "the gospel he promised beforehand through his prophets in the Holy Scriptures regarding his Son, who as to his human nature was a descendant of David, and who through the Spirit of holiness was declared with power to be the Son of God by his resurrection from the dead: Jesus Christ our Lord" (NIV).

The text in Hebrews 3:17–4:2 is talking about those people who hardened their hearts in the wilderness, where their carcasses fell. "Let us, therefore, be careful lest a word of faith or belief being given to us, we too should fail; for the gospel is being preached unto us as well as the gospel was preached unto them" (Heb 4:1-2). I understand this to mean that the gospel is the same. The promise continues in the provision of the new covenant; the promise continues in the provision of the people of God; the promise continues in the program of God. Even though we can distinguish various aspects within the promise program and the people of God, it is a single program and promise, a single people.

### Concepts that Have Been Jettisoned from the Old Testament

This leads us to the question: What concepts have been jettisoned from the Old Testament law? What is dissimilar? There are three areas which are different. First, the ritual ceremonies and the sacrifices are very dissimilar, just as the Old Testament itself had warned by using the word *pattern* over and over again, beginning in Exodus 25:40. "Moses, you are being shown this only as a sample. This is only an illustration. These are only symbols. You are asked to make this after the model." This is the interpretive word that there is divine designation of a type, there is divine designation of a symbol. The type points away from itself to the reality of what was reserved in heaven for a later disclosure.

Secondly, it seems to me that the Aaronic priesthood with all of its institutions, its ceremonies, and its sacrifices were to be jettisoned. The priesthood—at least the Aaronic priesthood—was established on that basis. The interesting thing is that the priesthood itself, the institution of priest and mediator, is perpetual and everlasting. The word given to Eli in 1 Samuel 2 was that it would be a perpetual, eternal priesthood, even though it would not be maintained with Zadok or with Aaron or with any of these others. The priesthood of Christ is after the order of Melchizedek, whose father and whose mother we do not know, whose birth and whose death are unknown. That makes a divinely designated picture; it is a type of the priesthood of Christ. So the Aaronic priesthood comes to an end, but the office of mediator continues with the Messiah.

The same thing is true with the theocracy and its earthly line of Davidic monarchs. Those men themselves passed away, and with them passed the form of government. But a kingdom, a dynasty, a throne, an office, and an officeholder would come from them. It is clear in the text that he would succeed and transcend them. These are types or illustrations of concepts that have been dropped off from the Old Testament and therefore illustrate for us its dissimilarities.

### Calvin's Fivefold Dissimilarity between the Two Testaments

In Calvin's *Institutes of the Christian Religion*, Book 2, chapter 11, he speaks of a fivefold dissimilarity between the Old and the New Testaments. He speaks first of all, as we have, of the spiritual blessings of the Mosaic economy which were regulated by temporal conditions. This, he says, is the first dissimilarity. His argument here is much the same as mine. Secondly, he says, the truth in the Mosaic economy was set forth by numerous symbols and ceremonies typifying Christ. That is dissimilar, for when Christ came, the symbol and the ceremony were no longer necessary. Thirdly, the Old Testament focused on the literal letter; the New Testament is spiritual. I am not so happy with Calvin's third distinction, which can be misunderstood. It can be construed to mean that the New Testament does not have literal letter or that the Old Testament does not have any spiritual truth. We know that Calvin is not saying this, because in his commentaries he makes this clear. However, in the long discussion in the *Institutes* he does make this his third point, and it seems to me that it needs to be qualified a little bit more.

His fourth point is that there was bondage under the old order but freedom under the new: bondage under the old order because the functioning of the form could substitute for the reality of the heart. Set procedures in a high church form might result in such bondage, but this can be true under the low church form, too: the mere attendance at the house of God, the mere giving of an offering, the mere singing of hymns. Some might think, I've paid my dues, so I'm paid up for the week; I've done my part. That misses the internal reality as well. So we need to look at this fourth one with some qualification and understanding.

Fifthly, Calvin says another dissimilarity between the two Testaments is that the covenant administration was restricted to one nation under the old, but extends to all nations under the new. Now again, Calvin's point needs some modification, because, as we have seen, missions is the heart of the promise-plan from the very beginning. God has all nations—all the families of the earth—on his mind, after that universal section of Genesis 1–11. "For in your seed shall all those seventy nations be blessed." And this continues to be the great point of the rest of the Testaments. Several recently-published books [i.e., since the 1980s] have stressed this theme of missions as being part of the Old Testament theme.

Well, these are some of the ways that people have attempted to put the Old Testament back into the hands of the church.

## Summary

To summarize, we have six current answers.

(1) The Old Testament is a waste and a pagan religion. Those who hold this position are the Marcions, the Schleiermachers, the Harnacks, the younger Delitzsches.

(2) The Old Testament is a negative lesson: we can learn what *not* to do. This is somewhat the way many people read the book of Ecclesiastes: its twelve chapters tell us what not to do. Then at the end of the book, there

are two final words: "Don't forget, *fear God*, and keep his commandments." This is a very simplistic and, I think, incorrect way of understanding Ecclesiastes. For Solomon is saying, These two words are my whole point and if you don't get that, go back to the beginning and start over. Many think that is the way we should read the Old Testament, too: it's just a history of failure. It's a negative lesson. We can't buy that either.

(3) Another attempt at relevancy is to say that the Old Testament is indispensable for New Testament background. We need to understand this in order to have historical appreciation. But it has no word for us; it is a word that prepares us for the later revelation. Some read it that way. This makes the Old Testament like the preface to a book; it tells us where the book is going.

(4) The Old Testament is a providential preparation for Christ and the Church. We accept the greats acts of God (i.e., his events) in his providence, but we don't take his Word (i.e., his revelatory word and message found in the Old Testament). I think that we're getting closer to an answer; that is part of the answer.

(5) The Old Testament is typologically or allegorically useful to illustrate or to teach Christian doctrine by way of analogy. That's getting closer to an answer, too.

(6) My final recommendation to you is that we need to take the Old Testament as *God's everlasting plan.*

This is the best way to look at it. Let me again define it for you. Simply, the promise is God's everlasting plan to be and to do something for Israel—for Abraham, Isaac, Jacob, and then the whole nation of Israel—and thereby to be and to do something for *all the nations* on the face of the earth. And, I might add, his plan is to speak, too—to speak his Word for all nations upon the face of the earth. *The everlasting promise-plan of God:* I recommend to you that this is the way to read the Old and New Testaments.

# Bibliography

Abba, Raymond. "The Origin and Significance of Hebrew Sacrifice." *Biblical Theology Bulletin* 7 (1977): 123-38.

Achtemeier, Elizabeth. *The Old Testament and the Proclamation of the Gospel.* Philadelphia: Westminster, 1973.

___ "The Relevance of the Old Testament for Christian Preaching." In *A Light Unto My Path,* ed. Howard N. Bream, Ralph D. Heim, and Carey A. Moore, 3-24. Philadelphia: Temple University, 1974.

Ackroyd, P. R. "The Old Testament in the Christian Church." *Theology* 66 (1963): 46-52.

___ "The Place of the Old Testament in the Church's Teaching and Worship." *Expository Times* 74 (1963): 164-67.

Alonso-Schokel, L. "The Old Testament, a Christian Book." *Biblica* 44 (1963): 210-16.

Amsler, S. *L'ancien testament dans l'église.* Neuchâtel, 1960.

Anderson, Bernhard W. "Introduction: The Old Testament as a Christian Problem." In *The Old Testament and Christian Faith,* ed. Bernhard W. Anderson. New York: Harper and Row, 1963.

Anderson, G. N. "Canonical and Non-Canonical." In *The Cambridge History of the Bible.* Vol. 1, *From the Beginning to Jerome,* ed. Peter R. Ackroyd and C. F. Evans, 113-59. Cambridge: Cambridge University Press, 1970.

Armerding, Carl. "The Holy Spirit in the Old Testament." *Bibliotheca Sacra* 92 (1935): 277-91; 433-41.

___ *The Old Testament and Criticism.* Grand Rapids: Eerdmans, 1983.

Atkinson, B. F. C. *The Christian's Use of the Old Testament.* London: InterVarsity, 1952.

Auray, Paul. *L'ancien testament et les chrétiens.* Paris: Les Éditions du Cerf, 1951.

Bahnsen, Greg L. *Theonomy in Christian Ethics.* Phillipsburg: Presbyterian and Reformed, 1984.

Baker, D. L. *Two Testaments: One Bible.* Downers Grove: InterVarsity, 1976.

Baker, David W. "The Old Testament and Criticism." *Journal of Theological Studies* 48 (1984): 13-20.

Baldwin, Joyce G. "Is there Pseudonymity in the Old Testament?" *Themelios* 4 (1978): 6-12.

Barker, Kenneth L. "False Dichotomies between the Testaments." *Journal of the Evangelical Theological Society* 25 (1982): 3-16.

Baron, David. *Rays of Messiah's Glory: Christ in the Old Testament.* 1886. Reprint. Grand Rapids: Zondervan, n.d.

Barr, James. *Old and New in Interpretation: A Study of the Two Testaments.* London: SCM, 1966.

Barre, M. L. "A Note on Job XIX. 25." *Vetus Testamentum* 29 (1979): 107-10.

Barry, G. R. "The Old Testament: A Liability or an Asset?" *Colgate Rochester Divinity School Bulletin* (1930): 8-22.

Bartling, Victor A. "Christ's Use of the Old Testament with Special Reference to the Pentateuch." *Concordia Theological Monthly* 36 (1965): 567-76.

Barton, John. "Approaches to Ethics in the Old Testament." In *Beginning Old Testament Study,* ed. John Rogerson, 113-30. Philadelphia: Westminster, 1982.

___ *Reading the Old Testament: Method in Biblical Study.* Philadelphia: Westminster, 1984.

___ "Understanding Old Testament Ethics." *Journal for the Study of the Old Testament* 9 (1978): 44-64.

Baumgärtel, Friederich. *Verheissung: Zur Frage des evangelischen Verständnisses des Alten Testaments.* Gütersloh: C. Bertelsmann, 1952.

Becker, Joachim. *Messianic Expectation in the Old Testament.* Trans. David E. Green. Philadelphia: Fortress, 1980.

___ "Das historische Bild der messianischen Erwartung im Alten Testament." In *Testimonium veritati,* ed. Hans Wolter. *Frankfurter theologische Studien* 7 (1971): 125-41.

Beecher, Willis J. *The Prophets and the Promise.* Grand Rapids: Baker, 1976.

Bennett, W. H. *The Value of the Old Testament for the Religion of Today.* London: 1914.

Bentzen, A. "The Old Testament and the New Covenant." *Hervormde Teologiese Studies* 7 (1950): 1-15.

Best, E. "The Literal Meaning of Scripture, the Historical-Critical Method and the Interpretation of Scripture." *Proceedings of the Irish Biblical Association* 5 (1981): 14-35.

Betz, Otto. "The Problem of Variety and Unity in the New Testament." *Horizons in Biblical Theology* 2 (1980): 3-14.

Bewer, J. A. "The Christian Minister and the Old Testament." *Journal of Religion* 10 (1930): 16-21.

___ "The Authority of the Old Testament." *Journal of Religion* 16 (1936): 1-9.

Birkeland, Harris. "Belief in the Resurrection of the Dead in the Old Testament." *Studia Theologica* 3 (1950): 60-78.

Bjornard, R. B. "Christian Preaching from the Old Testament." *Review and Expositor* 56 (1959): 8-19.

Blackman, E. C. *Marcion and His Influence.* London: SPCK, 1948.

Blenkinsopp, Joseph. "The Documentary Hypothesis in Trouble." *Bible Review* 1 (1985): 22-32.

Blumenthal, David R. "A Play on Words in the Nineteenth Chapter of Job." *Vetus Testamentum* 16 (1966): 497-501.

Blythin, Islwyn. "The Patriarchs and the Promise." *Scottish Journal of Theology* 21 (1968): 56-73.

Bock, Darrell L. "Evangelicals and the Use of the Old Testament in the New." *Bibliotheca Sacra* 142 (1985): 209-23, 306-19.

Boisset, J., et al. *Le problème Biblique dans le Protestantisme.* Paris: Presses Universitaires de France, 1955.

Borland, James A. *Christ in the Old Testament.* Chicago: Moody, 1978.

Bosman, H. L. "Taking Stock of Old Testament Ethics." *Old Testament Essays* 1 (1983): 97-104.

Bowden, John. *What About the Old Testament?* London: SCM, 1969.

Box, G. H. "The Value and Significance of the Old Testament in Relation to the New." In *The People and the Book,* ed. A. S. Peake. Cambridge: Clarendon, 1925.

Boyer, P. J. "The Value of the Old Testament: A German Estimate." *The Interpreter* 1 (1905): 258-63.

Briggs, Charles Augustus. *Messianic Prophecy.* New York: Scribner, 1889.

Bright, John. *The Authority of the Old Testament.* Nashville: Abingdon, 1967.

___ *Covenant and Promise: The Future in the Preaching of the Pre-Exilic Prophets.* Philadelphia: Westminster, 1976.

Bromiley, G. W. "History and Truth: A Study of the Axiom of Lessing." *Evangelical Quarterly* 18 (1946): 191-98.

Brown, Colin, ed. *History, Criticism and Faith.* 2d ed. Downers Grove: InterVarsity, 1977.

Brown, John. *The Sufferings and Glories of the Messiah.* Byron Center, MI: Sovereign Grace, 1970.

Bruce, F. F. *The Christian Approach to the Old Testament.* London: InterVarsity, 1955.

Brueggemann, W. "Canon and Dialectic." In *God and His Temple,* ed. L. E. Frizzell, 20-29. South Orange, NJ: Institute of Judaeo-Christian Studies, 1981.

Brunner, Emil. "The Significance of the Old Testament for Our Faith." In *The Old Testament and Christian Faith,* ed. Bernhard W. Anderson, 243-64. New York: Harper and Row, 1963.

Buhl, F. *Canon and Text of the Old Testament.* Trans. J. McPherson. Edinburgh, 1892.

Bultmann, Rudolf. "The Significance of the Old Testament for the Christian Faith." In *The Old Testament and Christian Faith,* ed. Bernhard W. Anderson, 8-35. New York: Harper and Row, 1963.

Burney, C. F. *The Gospel in the Old Testament.* Edinburgh, 1921.

Campenhausen, Hans von. *The Formation of the Christian Bible.* Philadelphia: Fortress, 1977.

Caquot, André. "Peut-on parlez de messianisme dans l'oeuvre du Chroniste?" *Revue de theologie et de philosophie* 99 (1966): 110-20.

Cate, Robert L. *Old Testament Roots for Christian Faith.* Nashville: Broadman, 1982.

Cazelles, H. "The Unity of the Bible and the People of God." *Scripture* 18 (1966): 1-10.

Childs, Brevard S. "The Hebrew Scriptures and the Hebrew Bible." In *Introduction to the Old Testament as Scripture,* 659-761. Philadelphia: Fortress, 1979.

___ "The Old Testament as Scripture of the Church." *Concordia Theological Monthly* 43 (1972): 709-22.

Christie, W. M. "The Jamnia Period in Jewish History." *Journal of Theological Studies* 1 (1950): 135-54.

Clements, Ronald E. "History and Theology in Biblical Narrative." *Horizons in Biblical Theology* 4 (1982): 45-60.

Clines, David J. A. *The Theme of the Pentateuch.* Sheffield, England: University of Sheffield, 1978.

Clowney, Edmund P. *Preaching and Biblical Theology.* Grand Rapids: Eerdmans, 1961.

Congar, Y. M. J. "The Old Testament as a Witness to Christ." In *The Revelation of God,* 8-15. New York: Herder and Herder, 1968.

Cooper, David L. *Messiah: His First Coming Scheduled.* Los Angeles: Biblical Research Society, 1939.

Coppens, J. *Vom christlichen Verstandnis des Alten Testaments.* Louvain: Publications Universitaires de Louvain, 1952.

Coppens, Joseph. *Le messianisme royal. Lectio divina 54.* Paris: Éditions du Cerf, 1968.

___ "La relève du messianisme royal." *Ephemerides theologicae Louvanienses* 47 (1971): 117-43.

Dahood, Mitchell. "Death, Resurrection and Immortality." In *The Anchor Bible: Psalms III (101–150),* xli-lii. Garden City: Doubleday, 1970.

Davidson, A. B. "The Uses of the Old Testament for Edification." *Expositor,* 6th ser., 1 (1900): 1-18.

Davis, John D. "The Future Life in Hebrew Thought." *Princeton Theological Review* 6 (1908): 246-68.

DeGraff, A. H. and C. G. Seerveld. *Understanding the Scriptures: How to Read and How Not to Read the Bible.* Toronto: Association for the Advancement of Christian Scholarship, 1968.

Dentan, Robert C. "The Unity of the Old Testament." *Interpretation* 5 (1951): 153-73.

Denton, D. R. "The Biblical Basis of Hope." *Themelios* 5 (1980): 19-27.

Dexinger, Ferdinand. "Die Entwicklung des jüdisch-christlichen Messianismus." *Bibel and Liturgie* 47 (1974): 5-31, 239-66.

Dillenberger, J. "Revelational Discernment and the Problem of the Two Testaments." In *The Old Testament and Christian Faith,* ed. Bernhard W. Anderson, 159-75. New York: Harper and Row, 1963.

Dreyfus, F. "L'actualisation à l'interieur de la Bible." *Revue Biblique* 83 (1976): 161-202.

Driver, S. R. "The Moral and Devotional Value of the Old Testament." *Expository Times* 4 (1892): 110-13.

___ "The Permanent Religious Value of the Old Testament." *The Interpreter* 1 (1905): 10-21.

Duesberg, Hilaire. "He Opened Their Minds to Understand the Scriptures." In *How Does the Christian Confront the Old Testament?* ed. Pierre Benoit, Roland E. Murphy, and Bastiaan van Iersel, 111-21. New York: Paulist, 1967.

___ "He Opened Their Minds to Understand the Scriptures." *Concilium* 10 (1967): 56-61.

Dunbar, David G. "The Biblical Canon." In *Hermeneutics, Authority, and Canon,* ed. D. A. Carson and John D. Woodbridge, 299-360. Grand Rapids: Zondervan, 1986.

Dunn, James D. G. "Levels of Canonical Authority." *Bible Translator* 4 (1982): 13-60.

Ebeling, G. "The Significance of the Critical Historical Method for Church and Theology in Protestantism." In *Word and Faith,* 17-61. London, 1963.

Edwards, O. C. "Historical-Critical Method's Failure of Nerve and a Prescription for a Tonic." *Anglican Theological Review* 59 (1977): 115-34.

Ellison, H. L. *The Centrality of the Messianic Idea for the Old Testament.* London: Tyndale, 1957.

Erlandsson, Seth. "Faith in the Old and New Testaments: Harmony or Disagreement?" *Concordia Theological Quarterly* 47 (1983): 1-14.

Eybers, Ian H. *Historical Evidence on the Canon of the Old Testament with Special Reference to the Qumran Sect.* Ann Arbor: University Microfilms, 1966.

Fensham, F. C. "The Covenant as Giving Expression to the Relationship between Old Testament and New Testament." *Tyndale Bulletin* 22 (1971): 82-94.

___ "Covenant, Promise and Expectation in the Bible." *Theologische Zeitschrift* 5 (1967): 305-22.

Filson, Floyd V. "The Unity of the Old and New Testaments: A Bibliographical Survey." *Interpretation* 5 (1951): 134-52.

___ "The Unity between the Testaments." In *The Interpreter's One-Volume Commentary on the Bible,* ed. Charles M. Laymon, 989-93. Nashville: Abingdon, 1972.

___ *Which Books Belong in the Bible? A Study of the Canon.* Philadelphia: Westminster, 1957.

Fischer, John. *The Olive Tree Connection.* Downers Grove: InterVarsity, 1983.

Fohrer, Georg. "Das Alte Testament und das Thema 'Christologie'." *Evangelische Theologie* 30 (1970): 281-98.

Ford, D. W. Cleverly. *New Preaching from the Old Testament.* London: Mowbrays, 1976.

France, R. T. *Jesus and the Old Testament.* London: Tyndale, 1971.

Freedman, Benjamin. "Leviticus and DNA: A Very Old Look at a Very New Problem." *Journal of Religious Ethics* 8 (1980): 105-13.

Freeman, Hobart E. "The Problem of Efficacy of the Old Sacrifices." *Bulletin of the Evangelical Theological Society* 5 (1962): 73-79.

Fretheim, Terence. "The Old Testament in Christian Proclamation." *Word and World* 3 (1983): 223-30.

Fruchtenbaum, Arnold G. "Messianism." In *Hebrew Christianity: Its Theology, History, and Philosophy*, 52-58. Washington, DC: Canon, n.d.

Funderburk, G. B. "Promise." In *The Zondervan Pictorial Encyclopedia of the Bible*, ed. Merrill C. Tenney, 5 vols., 4:872-74. Grand Rapids: Zondervan, 1975.

Gaussen, L. *The Canon of the Holy Scriptures*. Boston: American Tract Society, 1862.

Gilkey, L. B. "Cosmology, Ontology and the Travail of Biblical Language." *Journal of Religion* 41 (1961): 194-205.

Goldingay, John. "'That You May Know that Yahweh Is God': A Study in the Relationship between Theology and Historical Truth in the Old Testament." *Tyndale Bulletin* 23 (1972): 58-93.

___ "The Old Testament and Christian Faith: Jesus and the Old Testament in Matthew 1–5." *Themelios* 8 (1982): 4-10; 9 (1983): 5-12.

___ "Diversity and Unity in Old Testament Theology." *Vetus Testamentum* 34 (1984): 153-68.

Gorgulho, Luiz Bertrando. "Ruth et la 'Fille de Sion,' mère du Messie." *Revue Thomiste* 63 (1963): 501-14.

Gowan, Donald E. *Reclaiming the Old Testament for the Christian Pulpit*. Atlanta: Knox, 1980.

Graesser, Carl, Jr. "Preaching from the Old Testament." *Concordia Theological Monthly* 38 (1967): 525-34.

Grant, Robert. "The Place of the Old Testament in Early Christianity." *Interpretation* 5 (1951): 194-97.

Gray, G. B. "The References to the 'King' in the Psalter in their Bearing on the Questions of Date and Messianic Belief." *Jewish Quarterly Review* 7 (1895): 658-86.

Grech, Prosper. "The Old Testament as a Christological Source in the Apostolic Age." *Biblical Theology Bulletin* 5 (1975): 127-45.

Greidanus, Sidney. *Sola Scriptura: Problems and Principles in Preaching Historical Texts*. Toronto: Wedge, 1970.

Grelot, Pierre. "Le Messie dans les apocryphes de l'Ancien Testament." In *La venue du Messie*, ed. É. Massaux et al. *Recherches bibliques* 6 (1962): 19-50.

___ *Sens crétien de l'Ancien Testament: Esquisse d'un traite dogmatique*. Tournai: Deschlée and Cie, 1962.

Grogan, Geoffrey W. "The Experience of Salvation in the Old and New Testaments." *Vox Evangelica* 5 (1967): 4-26.

Gunneweg, A. H. J. *Understanding the Old Testament*. Trans. John Bowden. Philadelphia: Westminster, 1978.

Hagner, Donald A. *The Jewish Proclamation of Jesus*. Grand Rapids: Zondervan, 1984.

Hall, Basil. "The Old Testament in the History of the Church." *The London Quarterly and Holborn Review* 190 (1965): 30-36.

Hansen, Paul D. *The Diversity of Scripture*. Philadelphia: Westminster, 1982.

Harris, R. Laird. *Inspiration and Canonicity of the Bible*. Grand Rapids: Zondervan, 1957.

___ "The Meaning of Sheol as Shown by Parallels in Poetic Texts." *Bulletin of the Evangelical Theological Society* 4 (1961): 129-35.

___ "Theonomy in Christian Ethics: A Review of Greg L. Bahnsen's Book." *Covenant Seminary Review* 5 (1979): 1 ff.

Hasel, Gerhard. "The Relationship between the Testaments." In *Old Testament Theology: Basic Issues in the Current Debate.* 3d ed., ed. Gerhard Hasel, 145-67. Grand Rapids: Eerdmans, 1984.

Hayes, John H. "Restitution, Forgiveness and the Victim in Old Testament Law." *Trinity University Studies in Religion* 11 (1982): 1-21.

Hebert, A. G. *The Authority of the Old Testament.* London: Faber and Faber, 1947.

___ "The Completion of the Canon and the Old Testament in the New." In *The Authority of the Old Testament,* 165-225. London: Faber and Faber, 1978.

___ *The Throne of David.* London: Faber and Faber, 1941.

Heick, Otto W. "If a Man Die, Will He Live Again?" *Lutheran Quarterly* 17 (1965): 99-110.

Hengstenberg, E. W. *Christology of the Old Testament.* Abr. T. K. Arnold. 1847. Reprint. Grand Rapids: Kregel, 1970.

Heras, Henry. "Standard of Job's Immortality." *Catholic Biblical Quarterly* 11 (1949): 263-79.

Higgins, A. J. B. *The Christian Significance of the Old Testament.* London: 1949.

Hoffman, E. "Promise." In *The New International Dictionary of New Testament Theology,* ed. Colin Brown, 3 vols., 3:68-74. Grand Rapids: Zondervan, 1979.

Honsey, Rudolph E. "An Exegetical Paper on Job 19:23-27." *Wisconsin Lutheran Quarterly* 67 (1970): 172-84.

Hultgren, Arland J. "The Old Testament and the New." *Word and World* 3 (1983): 215-83.

Hummel, Horace D. "Christological Interpretation of the Old Testament." *Dialog* 2 (1963): 108-17.

___ "Justification in the Old Testament." *Concordia Journal* 9 (1983): 9-17.

Irwin, William A. "Job's Redeemer." *Journal of Biblical Literature* 81 (1962): 217-29.

Jasper, F. N. "Relation of the Old Testament to the New." *Expository Times* 78 (1967-68): 228-32; 267-70.

John, E. C. "The Old Testament Understanding of Death." *Indian Journal of Theology* 23 (1974): 123-28.

Johnson, Alan F. "The Historical-Critical Method: Egyptian Gold or Pagan Precipice?" *Journal of the Evangelical Theological Society* 26 (1983): 3-15.

Johnson, Elliott E. "Dual Authorship and the Single Intended Meaning of Scripture." *Bibliotheca Sacra* 143 (1986): 218-27.

Juel, Donald H. "The Old Testament in Christian Proclamation—A New Testament Perspective." *Word and World* 3 (1983): 231-37.

Kac, Arthur W. *The Messianic Hope: Divine Solution for the Human Problem.* Grand Rapids: Baker, 1975.

Kaiser, Walter C., Jr. *Back toward the Future: Hints for Interpreting Biblical Prophecy.* Grand Rapids: Baker, 1989.

___ "The Book of Leviticus: Introduction, Commentary and Reflections." In *The New Interpreter's Bible,* Vol. 1, ed. Leander E. Keck, 983-1191. Nashville: Abingdon Press, 1994.

___ *The Communicator's Commentary: Micah–Malachi* (The Communicator's Commentary Series: Old Testament, Vol 21). Dallas: Word, 1992.

___ *A History of Israel: From the Bronze Age through the Jewish Wars.* Nashville: Broadman and Holman, 1998.

___ *The Journey Isn't Over: The Pilgrim Psalms for Life's Challenges and Joys.* Grand Rapids: Baker, 1993.

___ *The Messiah in the Old Testament.* Grand Rapids: Zondervan, 1995.

___ "Messianic Prophecies in the Old Testament." In *Dreams, Visions and Oracles: The Layman's Guide to Biblical Prophecy,* ed. Carl Armerding and W. Ward Gasque, 75-88. Grand Rapids: Baker, 1977.

___ *More Hard Sayings of the Old Testament.* Downers Grove: InterVarsity, 1992.

___ *Proverbs: Wisdom for Everyday Life.* Grand Rapids: Zondervan, 1995.

___ *Psalms: Heart to Heart with God.* Grand Rapids: Zondervan, 1995.

___ *Toward Old Testament Ethics.* Grand Rapids: Zondervan, 1983.

___ *Toward an Old Testament Theology.* Grand Rapids: Zondervan, 1978.

___ *An Urgent Call for Revival and Renewal in Our Day.* Nashville: Broadman and Holman, 1999.

Kaiser, Walter C., Jr., and Moises Silva. *An Introduction to Biblical Hermeneutics: The Search for Meaning.* Grand Rapids: Zondervan, 1994.

Katz, P. "The Old Testament Canon in Palestine and Alexandria." *Zeitschrift für die neutestamentliche Wissenschaft* 47 (1956): 191-217.

Kaufman, Stephen A. "The Temple Scroll and Higher Criticism." *Hebrew Union College Annual* 53 (1982): 24-43.

Kellermann, Ulrich. *Messias and Gesetz. Biblische Studien.* Neukirchen: Neukerken Verlag, 1971.

Kelly, George A. *The New Biblical Theorists: Raymond E. Brown and Beyond.* Ann Arbor: Servant, 1983.

Kikawada, Isaac M., and Arthur Quinn. *Before Abraham Was: The Unity of Genesis 1-11.* Nashville: Abingdon, 1985.

King, Nicholas. "Expectation: Jesus in the Old Testament." *Way* 21 (1981): 14-21.

Kirkpatrick, A. F. "The Use of the Old Testament in the Christian Church." In *The Divine Library of the Old Testament,* 112-43. London: Macmillan, 1906.

Klaaren, Eugene M. "A Critical Appreciation of Hans Fref's *Eclipse of Biblical Narrative.*" *Union Theological Seminary* 37 (1983): 283-97.

Kline, Meredith G. "Canon and Covenant: Part I." *Westminster Theological Journal* 32 (1969–70): 49-67.

___ "Canon and Covenant: Part II." *Westminster Theological Journal* 32 (1969–70): 179-200.

___ "Comments on an Old-New Error." *Westminster Theological Journal* 41 (1978): 172-89.

Knierim, Rolf. "Die Messianologie des ersten Buchen Samuel." *Evangelische Theologie* 30 (1970): 113-33.

Kraeling, Emil. *The Old Testament Since the Reformation.* New York: Harper, 1955.

Kromminga, Carl G. "Remember Lot's Wife: Preaching Old Testament Narrative Texts." *Calvin Theological Journal* 18 (1983): 32-46.

Kugel, James. "On the Bible and Literary Criticism." *Proof Texts: A Journal of Jewish Life and History* 1 (1981): 217-36.

Kuyper, Lester J. "Righteousness and Salvation." *Scottish Journal of Theology* 30 (1977): 233-52.

Kuzhivelil, Matthew V. "Reconciliation in the Old Testament." *Biblebhashyan* 9 (1983): 168-78.

Lapide, Pinchas. *The Resurrection of Jesus: A Jewish Perspective.* Minneapolis: Augsberg, 1983.

Larcher, A. D. *L'Actualité chrétienne de l'Ancien Testament.* Paris: Éditions du Cerf, 1962.

LaSor, William S. "The Messiah: An Evangelical Christian View." In *Evangelicals and Jews in Conversation: On Scripture, Theology and History,* ed. Marc H. Tanenbaum, Marvin R. Wilson, and A. James Rudin, 76-97. Grand Rapids: Baker, 1978.

Leiman, Sid Z. *The Canonization of the Hebrew Scriptures: The Talmudic and Midrashic Evidence*. Hamden, CT: Archon, 1976.

Levey, Samson H. *The Messiah: An Aramaic Interpretation: The Messianic Exegesis of the Targum*. Cincinnati: Hebrew Union College, 1974.

Lewis, Arthur H. "The New Birth under the Old Covenant." *Evangelical Quarterly* 56 (1984): 35-44.

Lewis, Jack P. "What Do We Mean by Jabneh?" *Journal of Bible and Religion* 32 (1964): 125-32.

Lightner, Robert P. "A Dispensational Response to Theonomy." *Bibliotheca Sacra* 143 (1986): 228-45.

___ "Nondispensational Responses to Theonomy." *Bibliotheca Sacra* 143 (1986): 134-45.

___ "Theonomy and Dispensationalism." *Bibliotheca Sacra* 143 (1986): 26-36.

Lightstone, Jack N. "The Formation of the Biblical Canon in Judaism of Late Antiquity: Prolegomena to a General Reassessment." *Studies in Religion* 8 (1979): 135-42.

Lofthouse, W. F. "The Old Testament and Christianity." In *Record and Revelation*, ed. H. Wheeler Robinson, 458-80. Oxford: Clarendon, 1938.

Logan, Norman A. "The Old Testament and a Future Life." *Scottish Journal of Theology* 6 (1953): 164-72.

Lohfink, N. *The Christian Meaning of the Old Testament*. London: Burns and Oates, 1969.

Long, Valentine. "Higher Criticism Has Gone Bankrupt." *Homiletical and Pastoral Review* 83 (1982–1983): 50-57.

Lys, Daniel. *The Meaning of the Old Testament: An Essay in Hermeneutics*. Nashville: Abingdon, 1967.

MacKay, W. M. "Messiah in the Psalms." *Evangelical Quarterly* 11 (1939): 153-64.

Mackenzie, Roderick A. F. "The Messianism of Deuteronomy." *Catholic Biblical Quarterly* 19 (1957): 299-305.

Maier, Gerhard. *The End of the Historical-Critical Method*. Trans. Edwin W. Leverenz and Rudolph F. Norden. St. Louis: Concordia, 1977.

Mandel, Hugo. "The Nature of the Great Synagogue." *Harvard Theological Review* 60 (1967): 69-91.

Manson, T. W. "The Old Testament in the Teaching of Jesus." *Bulletin of the John Rylands Library* 34 (1952): 312-32.

Marcus, R. A. "Presuppositions of the Typological Approach to Scripture." *Church Quarterly Review* 158 (1957): 4212-50.

Martin, Ralph A. "The Earliest Messianic Interpretation of Genesis 3:15." *Journal of Biblical Literature* 84 (1965): 425-27.

Mayer, H. T. "The Old Testament in the Pulpit." *Concordia Theological Monthly* 35 (1964): 603-608.

McCausland, S. Vernon. "The Unity of the Scriptures." *Journal of Biblical Literature* 73 (1954): 1-10.

McCurley, Foster, R., Jr. "The Christian and the Old Testament Promise." *Lutheran Quarterly* 22 (1970): 401-10.

___ *Proclaiming the Promise: Christian Preaching from the Old Testament*. Nashville: Abingdon, 1967.

McDermet, William W., III. "The 'Old' Testament as Revelation for Contemporary People." *Encounter* 44 (1983): 291-99.

McKeating, H. "Sanctions Against Adultery in Ancient Israelite Society with Some Reflections on Methodology in the Study of Old Testament Ethics." *Journal for the Study of Old Testament* 11 (1979): 57-72.

McKenzie, John L. "The Significance of the Old Testament for Christian Faith in Roman Catholicism." In *The Old Testament and Christian Faith*, ed. Bernhard W. Anderson, 102-14. New York: Harper and Row, 1963.

___ "The Values of the Old Testament." In *How Does the Christian Confront the Old Testament? Concilium* 30, ed. Pierre Benoit, Roland E. Murphy, and Bastiaan van Iersel, 5-32. New York: Paulist, 1967.

Meek, Theophile J. "Job XIX. 25-27." *Vetus Testamentum* 6 (1956): 100-103.

Meitzen, Manfred O. "Some Reflections on the Resurrection and Eternal Life." Lutheran Quarterly 24 (1972): 254-60.

Mellor, E. B. "The Old Testament for Jews and Christians Today." In *The Making of the Old Testament*, ed. E. B. Mellor, 167-201. Cambridge: Cambridge University Press, 1972

Mercer, J. E. "Is the Old Testament a Suitable Basis for Moral Instruction?" *Hibbert Journal* 7 (1909): 333-45.

Michaeli, F. *How to Understand the Old Testament*. London, 1961.

Mirtow, P. *Jesus and the Religion of the Old Testament*. London, 1957.

Mowinckel, Sigmund. *He that Cometh*. Trans. G. W. Anderson. Oxford: Blackwell, 1956.

___ *The Old Testament as Word of God*. Nashville: Abingdon, 1959.

Mozley, J. B. *Ruling Ideas in Early Ages and Their Relation to Old Testament Faith*. London, 1889.

Murphy, J. Roland E. "The Relationship between the Testaments." *Catholic Biblical Quarterly* 26 (1964): 349-59.

___ "Christian Understanding of the Old Testament." *Theology Digest* 18 (1970): 321-32.

Murray, John. "Christ and the Scriptures." *Christianity Today* (May 13, 1957): 15-17.

Nations, Archie L. "Historical Criticism and the Current Methodological Crisis." *Scottish Journal of Theology* 36 (1983): 59-71.

Neusner, Jacob. *Messiah in Context: Israel's History and Destiny in Formative Judaism*. Philadelphia: Fortress, 1984.

Newman, R. C. "The Council of Jamnia and the Old Testament Canon." *Westminster Theological Journal* 38 (1975–1976): 319-49.

Nichols, Aidan. "Imagination and Revelation: The Face of Christ in the Old Testament." *Way* 21 (1981): 270-71.

Nineham, S. E. (ed). *The Church's Use of the Bible*. London, 1963.

O'Doherty, E. "The Unity of the Bible." *The Bible Today* 1 (1962): 53-57.

Orr, James. "Immortality in the Old Testament." In *Classical Evangelical Essays in Old Testament Interpretation*, ed. Walter C. Kaiser, Jr., 253-65. Grand Rapids: Baker, 1972.

___ "The Old Testament Question in the Early Church." *The Expositor*. Fifth Series. (1895): 346-61.

Otwell, John. "Immortality in the Old Testament." *Encounter* 22 (1961): 15-27.

Patai, Raphael. *The Messiah Texts*. New York: Avon, 1979.

Peake, A. S. "The Permanent Value of the Old Testament." In *The Nature of Scripture*, 137-98. London, 1922.

Peters, Ted. "The Use of Analogy in the Historical Method." *Catholic Biblical Quarterly* 35 (1973): 475-82.

Porteous, N. W. "The Limits of Old Testament Interpretation." In *Proclamation and Presence: Old Testament Essays in Honor of G. Henton Davies*, ed. J. I. Durham and J. R. Porter, 3-17. London, 1950.

Premsager, P. V. "Theology of Promise in the Patriarchal Narratives." *Indian Journal of Theology* 23 (1974): 112-22.

Preus, James S. "Old Testament *Promissio* and Luther's New Hermeneutic." *Harvard Theological Review* 60 (1967): 145-61.

Purunak, H. van Dyke. "Some Axioms for Literary Architecture." *Semitics* 8 (1982): 1-16.

Ramlot, Marie-Léon, and Jean Giblet. "Promises." In *Dictionary of Biblical Theology,* ed. Xavier Leon-Dufour, trans. P. Joseph Cahill, 411-13. New York: Desclée, 1967.

Ramsey, George W. *The Quest for the Historical Israel.* Atlanta: Knox, 1981.

Read, D. H. C. "The Old Testament and Modern Preaching." *Union Seminary Quarterly Review* 12 (1957): 11-15.

Reid, W. Stanford. "The New Testament Belief in an Old Testament Church." *Evangelical Quarterly* 24-25 (1952–1953): 194-205.

Reist, Irwin. "Old Testament Basis for Resurrection Faith." *Evangelical Quarterly* 43 (1971): 6-24.

Richardson, Alan. "Is the Old Testament Propaedeutic to Christian Faith?" In *The Old Testament and Christian Faith,* ed. Bernhard W. Anderson, 36-48. New York: Harper and Row, 1963.

Ridderbos, N. H. "Canon of the Old Testament." In *The New Bible Dictionary,* ed. J. D. Douglas, 186-94. Grand Rapids: Eerdmans, 1962.

Ridenhour, Thomas E. "Immortality and Resurrection in the Old Testament." *Dialogue* 15 (1976): 104-109.

Ringgren, Helmer. *The Messiah in the Old Testament.* Chicago: Allenson, 1956.

Rivkin, Ellis. "The Meaning of Messiah in Jewish Thought." In *Evangelicals and Jews in Conversation: On Scripture, Theology, and History,* ed. H. Tanenbaum, Marvin R. Wilson, and A. James Rudin, 54-75. Grand Rapids: Baker, 1978.

Roberts, B. J. "The Old Testament Canon: A Suggestion." *Bulletin of John Rylands Library* 46 (1963): 164-78.

Robinson, T. H. "Epilogue: The Old Testament and the Modern World." In *The Old Testament and Modern Study,* ed. H. H. Rowley, 345-71. London: Oxford University Press, 1967.

Rowley, Harold H. "Future Life in the Thought of the Old Testament." *Congregational Quarterly* 33 (1955): 116-32.

___ "The Gospel in the Old Testament." In *The Enduring Gospel,* ed. R. Gregor Smith, 19-35. London, 1950.

___ *The Unity of the Bible.* London, 1953.

Ruler, A. A. van. *The Christian Church and the Old Testament.* Trans. Geoffrey W. Bromiley. Grand Rapids: Eerdmans, 1966.

Runia, Klaus. "The Interpretation of the Old Testament by the New Testament." *Theological Students' Fellowship Bulletin* 49 (1967): 9-18.

Rylaarsdam, J. C. "Jewish-Christian Relationships: The Two Covenants and the Dilemma of Christology." *Journal of Ecumenical Studies* 9 (1972): 249-68.

Ryle, Herbert E. *The Canon of the Old Testament.* 2d ed. London: Macmillan, 1885.

Saphir, Adolph. *Christ and the Scriptures.* London: Hodder and Stroughton, 1867.

Sawyer, John F. A. "Hebrew Words for the Resurrection of the Dead." *Vetus Testamentum* 23 (1973): 218-34.

Schep, J. A. *The Nature of the Resurrection Body,* 17-63. Grand Rapids: Eerdmans, 1964.

Schneiders, Sandra M. "From Exegesis to Hermeneutics: The Problem of the Contemporary Meaning of Scripture." *Horizons* 8 (1981): 23-39.

Schniewind, Julius, and Gerhard Friedrich. "Epangellō, epangelia." In *Theological Dictionary of the New Testament,* ed. Gerhard Kittel and Gerhard Friedrich, 2:576-86. Grand Rapids: Eerdmans, 1964.

Schoenfield, Hugh J. *The History of Jewish Christianity: From the First to the Twentieth Century.* London: Duckworth, 1936.

Schoors, Antoon. "Koheleth: A Perspective on Life After Death?" *Ephemrides Theologicae Louvanienses* 61 (1985): 295-303.

Seerveld, C. G. *Balaam's Apocalyptic Prophecies: A Study in Reading Scripture.* Toronto: Wedge, 1980.

Sheppard, Gerald T. "Canonization: Hearing the Voice of the Same God through Historically Dissimilar Traditions." *Interpretation* 36 (1982): 21-33.

Siebeneck, Robert T. "The Messianism of Aggeus and Proto-Zacharias." *Catholic Biblical Quarterly* 19 (1957): 312-18.

Smart, James D. *The Interpretation of Scripture*, 65-92. Philadelphia: Westminster, 1962.

Smick, Elmer. "Bearing of New Philological Data on the Subjects of Resurrection and Immortality in the Old Testament." *Westminster Theological Journal* 31 (1968): 12-21.

Smith, George Adam. "Modern Criticism and the Preaching of the Old Testament." *Expository Times* 90 (1979): 100-104.

Smith, W. R. "The Attitude of Christians to the Old Testament." *The Expositor,* 2d ser., 7 (1884): 241-51.

Smith, Wilbur M. "Promise." In *Evangelical Dictionary of Theology,* ed. Walter A. Elwell, 885-86. Grand Rapids: Baker, 1984.

Sparks, H. F. D. *The Old Testament in the Christian Church.* London, 1944.

Stamm, J. J. "Jesus Christ and the Old Testament: A Review of A. A. van Ruler's Book." In *Essays on Old Testament Hermeneutics,* ed. Claus Westermann, 200-10. Richmond: Knox, 1960.

Steinmetz, David C. "The Superiority of Pre-Critical Exegesis." *Theology Today* 37 (1980): 27-28.

Stevenson, Dwight E. "How a Writing Becomes Scripture." *Lexington Theological Quarterly* 17 (1982): 59-66.

Stuhlmacher, Peter. *Historical Criticism and Theological Interpretation of Scripture.* Trans. Roy A. Harrisville. Philadelphia: Fortress, 1977.

Sundberg, A. C. *The Old Testament of the Early Church.* Cambridge: Harvard University Press, 1964.

___ "The Old Testament of the Early Church." *Harvard Theological Review* 51 (1958): 205-26.

___ "The 'Old Testament': A Christian Canon?" *Catholic Biblical Quarterly* 30 (1968): 143-55.

Swanson, Theodore N. *The Closing of the Collection of Holy Scripture: A Study of the History of the Canonization of the Old Testament.* Ann Arbor: University Microfilms, 1970.

Talmon, Shmarjahu. "Typen der Messiaserwartung um die Zeitenwende." In *Probleme biblischer Theologie,* 571-88. Germany: Chr. Kaiser Verlag München, 1971.

Thieme, R. B. *Canonicity.* Houston: The Author, 1973.

Thomson, J. G. S. S. "Christ and the Old Testament." *Expository Times* 67 (1955): 18-20.

Tison, Everett. "Homiletical Resources: Interpretation of Old Testament Readings for Easter." *Quarterly Review* 4 (1984): 55-90.

Tollinton, R. B. "The Two Elements in Marcion's Dualism." *Journal of Theological Studies* 17 (1916): 263-70.

Toombs, L. E. *The Old Testament in Christian Preaching.* Philadelphia: Westminster, 1961.

___ "The Old Testament in the Christian Pulpit." *Hartford Quarterly* 8 (1968): 7-14.

___ "The Problematic Preaching from the Old Testament." *Interpretation* 23 (1969): 302-14.

Tournay, Raymond. "Les affinités du Ps XLV avec le Cantique des Cantiques et leurs interprétation messianique." In Congress Volume, *Supplements to Vetus Testamentum* 9 (1962): 168-212.

Vellanickal, Matthew. "Norm of Morality according to the Scripture." *Biblebhashyam* 7 (1981): 121-46.

Verhoef, Peter A. "The Relationship between the Old and New Testament." In *New Perspectives on the Old Testament,* ed. J. Barton Payne, 280-303. Waco: Word, 1970.

Vicary, D. K. "Liberalism, Biblical Criticism, and Biblical Theology."*Anglican Theological Review* 34 (1950): 114-21.

Vischer, Wilhelm. "The Significance of the Old Testament for the Christian Life." *Proceedings of the Fourth Calvinistic Congress Held in Edinburgh 6th to 11th July 1938,* 237-60. Edinburgh: T. & T. Clark, 1938.

___ "Everywhere the Scripture Is about Christ Alone." In *The Old Testament and Christian Faith,* ed. Bernhard W. Anderson, 90-101. New York: Harper and Row, 1963.

Waltke, Bruce K. "Is It Right to Read the New Testament into the Old?" *Christianity Today* 27 (1983): 77.

Welch, A. C. *The Preparation for Christ in the Old Testament.* Edinburgh, 1933.

Wenham, Gordon. "History and the Old Testament." In *History, Criticism and Faith,* ed. Colin Brown, 13-78. Downers Grove: InterVarsity, 1977.

West, Cornel. "On Frei's Eclipse of Biblical Narrative." *Union Seminary Quarterly Review* 37 (1983): 299-302.

Westall, M. R. "The Scope of the Term 'Spirit of God' in the Old Testament." *Indian Journal of Theology* 26 (1977): 29-43.

Westermann, Claus. "The Way of Promise through the Old Testament." In *The Old Testament and Christian Faith,* ed. Bernhard W. Anderson, 200-224. New York: Harper and Row, 1963.

White, Leland J. "Historical and Literary Criticism: A Theological Response." *Biblical Theology Bulletin* 13 (1983): 32-34.

Wiles, M. F. "The Old Testament in Controversy with the Jews." *Scottish Journal of Theology* 8 (1955): 113-26.

Wink, Walter. *The Bible in Human Transformation: Toward a New Paradigm for Biblical Study.* Philadelphia: Fortress, 1973.

Wolf, Hans Walter. *The Old Testament and Christian Preaching.* Philadelphia: Fortress, 1986.

___ "The Old Testament in Controversy: Interpretive Principles and Illustrations." *Interpretation* 12 (1956): 281-91.

Wood, Leon J. *The Holy Spirit in the Old Testament.* Grand Rapids: Zondervan, 1976.

Woods, J. *The Old Testament in the Church.* London, 1949.

Wright, David. "The Ethical Use of the Old Testament in Luther and Calvin: A Compari son." *Scottish Journal of Theology* 36 (1983): 463-85.

Wright, George Ernest. "Interpreting the Old Testament." *Theology Today* 3 (1946): 176-91.

___ "The Problem of Archaizing Ourselves." *Interpretation* 3 (1949): 450-56.

Zerafa, O. P. "Christological Interpretation of the Old Testament." *Angelicum* 41 (1964): 51-62.

___ "Priestly Messianism in the Old Testament." *Angelicum* 42 (1965): 315-45

Zink, James K. "Salvation in the Old Testament: A Central Theme." *Encounter* 25 (1964): 405-14.

Zyl, A. H. van. "The Relation between the Old Testament and the New Testament." *Hermeneutica* (1970): 9-22.

# Index of Hebrew Words

For the convenience of the general reader, this index is arranged by the English alphabet. Accents and most diacritical marks are not used, except for ḥ to indicate a sound like the *ch* in *Bach*. The apostrophe (') indicates the silent letter *aleph*, and the reverse apostrophe (') indicates the silent letter *ayin*; these have been ignored for alphabetization. No difference is shown between Hebrew letters having the same basic English pronounciation (*s, t*), and *b, d, k, t* are used instead of *bh, dh, kh, th*. Some words are listed as found in the text rather than by their roots: for example, *ba-ri'shon* is under *b* rather than under *ri'shon*. Hebrew scholars also will easily find words in this short index for a popularized book.

# Index of Scripture References

# Index of Subjects and Names